The Middle Ages

A POPULAR HISTORY

The Middle Ages

A POPULAR HISTORY

BY JOSEPH DAHMUS

Doubleday & Company, Inc.
Garden City, New York
1968

Text maps by Stephen Kraft

Library of Congress Catalog Card Number 68–22623
Copyright © 1968 by Joseph Dahmus
All Rights Reserved
Printed in the United States of America
First Edition

Contents

LIST OF MAPS

1. Roman Empire about 400 A.D. and Germanic Kingdoms about 485 A.D.
2. Europe and the Mediterranean World in the early ninth century.
3. Europe and the Mediterranean World about 1100 A.D.
4. Europe in the middle of the 14th century.

Foreword

By the Middle Ages scholars generally understand the centuries which intervened between the decline of Rome and the year 1500 A.D. Because Rome's decline was a slow process that covered several centuries, it is impossible to assign that development any specific date. For the peace of mind of those readers who insist upon a sharp periodization of the world's events, another development accompanied that of Rome's decline which assists the historian in fixing a reasonably precise beginning to the Middle Ages. That was the rise of Christianity. While the Christian church had been growing since its foundation in the first century, it had not become a force with which Rome had to reckon until the early fourth century, when Constantine extended it toleration. Since Rome was well advanced in her decline by that time, and since, too, the influence of the Christian church was destined to permeate the civilization of the Middle Ages, we can do worse than date the beginning of that new age from the early fourth century.

In his effort to justify 1500 A.D. as the terminal date of the Middle Ages, the historian has an easier task. Few epochs ended and fewer new ones got under way with as much commotion. Among a number of significant events to which the historian can point, there is the fall of the Byzantine capital Constantinople to the Ottoman Turks in 1453. It might be difficult to find an institution more typically medieval than the Byzantine empire which finally expired at that time. As Constantinople declined, so had Venice, the city which had been the leading maritime state of the Middle Ages. The future on the sea lay with the newer states along the Atlantic which were in a better position to exploit Vasco da Gama's epoch-making voyage around Africa to the Indies. Columbus' discovery of America had come a few years earlier, although its full impact would only be felt later. There was, finally, the Protestant Reformation, which destroyed the peculiarly medieval fabric of the Christian church.

As years pass by and generations pile upon generations, the pressure grows to revise the periodization of history which has become traditional in the West. The Middle Ages, as a separate epoch in world history, enjoys less validity today than it did a century ago, so many and so great in their consequences have been the events and developments of recent years. Still it is possible that the Middle Ages will be able to hold on to its identity, much as have ancient Greece and Rome, despite the passage of centuries of time. Certain institutions and characters, so peculiar to the period, such as the universal Christian church, feudalism, the Crusades, the burgher, monk, serf, and knight, will continue to conjure up the image of the Middle Ages long after that epoch might otherwise have faded into oblivion. In whatever manner future scholars divide history, these institutions and people will insist upon investing the centuries between Rome's decline and Columbus' discovery of America, that is, the Middle Ages, with a unique character all their own.

Of a rich variety of cultures that contributed to the formation of the civilization of medieval Europe, three merit special attention. They are the classical, the Christian, and the barbarian. Evidences of these three ingredients meet the reader of medieval history at every turn. Medieval scholars employed Latin, many people spoke a Romance tongue, while the law and arts of the period reflect heavy classical influence. To the Christian church medieval man owed the mold within which he developed his rules of moral conduct. Christianity implanted in him the conviction that this life on earth was but a testing period which would determine whether he would be happy or miserable throughout eternity. The barbarians contributed their vigor and ingenuity, the jury, principles of parliamentary government, and the seeds from which have sprung modern capitalism. What provides European culture its unusual richness is the varying proportions with which these and other ingredients have mixed, from Scandinavia to Sicily, and from Spain to the Urals. The oldest ingredient and the most persuasive during the first centuries was the classical. We begin our study of medieval history with Rome.

CHAPTER 1

Rome and Its Decline

"If a man were called to fix the period in the history of the world," wrote Edward Gibbon in his monumental *History of the Decline and Fall of the Roman Empire*, "during which the condition of the human race was most happy and prosperous, he would without hesitation name that which elapsed from the death of Domitian to the accession of Commodus." The period that Gibbon referred to extended from 96 A.D. to 180 A.D., an era known in Roman history as the age of the Good Emperors. This last term, Good Emperors, suggests a reason for Gibbon's affirmation, namely, the continuous rule for almost a century of able and responsible emperors who directed the powers of government "under the guidance of virtue and wisdom." So sensitive in times past was the well-being of a people to the character of its autocratic rulers, that an unbroken series of five emperors, all distinguished for their sense of duty and for their statesmanship, almost guaranteed a period of unparalleled tranquillity. To mankind nowhere, either before or since, has so great a blessing been vouchsafed.

It was the peace enjoyed by the sixty or more millions of people who lived within the confines of the far-flung Roman empire during the era of the Good Emperors that most appealed to Gibbon, but not only peace. He might otherwise have selected the first century as a period just as blessed as the second since the famous *Pax Romana* (Roman peace) spanned both the first and second centuries. The victory of Octavian at Actium over Antony and Cleopatra in 31 B.C. had ushered in this long period of peace, its peacefulness all the more serene for the turbulency of the generations preceding, when strong, brutal men like Pompey, Caesar, Antony, and, of course, Octavian, struggled over control of a dying Republic. Still there ruled occasional emperors in this first century of the empire, the madman Caligula, for example, and the tyrants Nero and Domitian, when life was insecure for men whom these autocrats disliked or whose wealth they might covet. For this reason Gibbon selected the second as the happiest of all centuries.

The second century found the empire at its height, both in terms of population and extent—some scholars will say of prosperity as well. It presents to view a Roman civilization which had reached maturity, one, in fact, which was about to enter the transitional period that would mark the beginning of its decline. Since so much of Roman civilization continued on after the collapse of the empire, we should take a long look at that empire before considering its decay.

Truly impressive were the area over which the *Pax Romana* of the second century prevailed and the large number of different peoples who enjoyed it. There never had been so extensive an empire in the Western world. All around the Mediterranean which the Romans referred to familiarly as *mare nostrum* (our sea) waved the eagles of the imperial army—from Egypt westward to the Atlantic, from Gibraltar to Scotland, from France and southwest Germany to the Balkans and Roumania, to Asia Minor, Syria, and, for intervals, to Mesopotamia. And all these territories and the peoples who inhabited them were at peace, not by accident, so many Christians insisted, but by God's design. "It is that God wills the unity of mankind," wrote Prudentius, "since the religion of Christ demands a social foundation of peace and international amity. Hitherto the whole earth from east to west had been rent asunder by continual strife. To curb this madness God has taught the nations to be obedient to the same laws and all to become Romans. Now we see mankind living as citizens of one city and members of a common household. Men come from distant lands across the seas to one common forum, and the peoples are united by commerce and culture and intermarriage. From the intermingling of peoples a single race is born. This is the meaning of all the victories and triumphs of the Roman Empire: the Roman peace has prepared the road for the coming of Christ."

Because the peace and prosperity of the empire in the second century depended in large measure upon the policies of its emperors, it will be necessary to introduce these men. The first of the Good Emperors, and the least important, was Nerva. He ruled for but two years. Almost a century and a half had passed since the senate had last asserted its claim to be the highest authority in the state, so that in the selection of emperors, it had never done more than formally approve what others had decided. Now the army, by way of exception, permitted the senate to voice its choice, and that body chose Nerva, one of its members, in 96 A.D., following the assassination of Domitian. Nerva's selection did not please the army. While he had had a distinguished public career, he was sixty years of age and in poor health, and, worst of all, was possessed of no military experience. Trouble was averted when Nerva adopted Trajan, who was probably the most popular general of the day, as his colleague and successor. So Nerva lived out the few last months of his brief reign in peace; and when he died, a grateful senate accorded him deification. There were many others, too, within the empire who were grateful for what he had done: the political exiles and philosophers to whom he had granted amnesty upon his accession; all citizens for his repeal of the laws of treason which his predecessor Domitian had abused; the poor farmers of Italy for the low-interest loans he had provided them; and the needy children of the area who drew for sustenance upon the interest these favored farmers paid on their loans.

Nerva's successor Trajan (97–117) ranks with the ablest rulers of history. Even Christian writers of the Middle Ages honored his name, a truly remarkable phenomenon since Trajan, like the other Good Emperors, persecuted Christianity. Dante assigned him a select place in heaven, the only pagan whom the poet permitted to rise to that hallowed place. Among the stories about Trajan that gained him the affection of medieval writers was one that told of a widow who grasped the bridle of his horse as he was riding out of Rome with his army, how upon her anguished appeal, he delayed embarking upon his campaign against the Dacians for an entire day in order to secure for her the justice she had warned him would never be hers if he left the matter to his agents.

Trajan has the distinction of being the first Roman emperor to come from the provinces. Still, Spanish Baetica, whence he hailed, was one of the most thoroughly Romanized areas of the empire, and Trajan was as Roman as any of his predecessors. That he showed a concern for the entire empire above that of most of the emperors who had come from Italy may have been the result of his provincial origin. In any event, the entire Roman world, army, senate, and people, all acclaimed him for the firm, prudent, and humane manner in which he administered his autocratic powers. His was the benevolent despotism that historians associate with the reigns of all the Good Emperors. He maintained a sharp lookout for corruption among the empire's officials on the one hand, while on the other expanding Nerva's alimentary system for the benefit of the poor boys and girls of Italy. He also allocated funds for the relief of those municipalities throughout the empire whose improvident or overly ambitious councils had brought to the point of bankruptcy. Trajan's motives in providing funds were laudable and the imperial assistance probably necessary; nevertheless, scholars interested in ferreting out early signs of Rome's decline discover one in the growing inability or unwillingness of the city-state to maintain itself. Through this institution pulsed the lifeblood of the empire. The efficiency of the imperial administration, even the imperial economy, depended in large measure on the prosperity of its cities and on their ability to manage their own affairs.

In the judgment of history, Trajan's efficient and just administration is thrown into shadow by his aggressive foreign policy along the Danube and in the east. His expansionist policy represented a fundamental departure from the defensive imperialism of Augustus which he and his successors (except Claudius, who added Britain) considered prudent in view of the tremendous size of the empire. Trajan's provocation came from the aggressiveness of the Dacians on the Danube, which had long been a source of concern, as well as the gold mines in the Carpathians that they controlled. Two campaigns accomplished the destruction of the tribe, and into the plains above the lower Danube, now largely swept of population, Trajan transported thousands of colonists from other parts of the empire. So thoroughly did these immigrants Romanize the country that although subsequent waves of invaders, Asiatic and Slav, swept over the country and submerged its Roman element, the people in that part of Europe (Roumania) still speak a Romance tongue. Good emperor though he was, Trajan brought back some fifty thousand Dacians as slaves, ten thousand of them to fight to the death in the Colosseum for the gratification of the Roman populace.

Against the powerful Parthians to the east of Syria Trajan won even more impressive victories, though their permanent consequences were minimal. No other Roman general had ever defeated this formidable foe, although several great men had tried. The Parthians killed Crassus in 53 B.C. A few years later Mark Antony was lucky to extricate himself and what remained of his shattered army after two serious defeats at their hands. The greater part of Trajan's territorial gains which he took from the Parthians did not outlive him, although at one point in his campaigns he held Armenia and the whole of Mesopotamia including the Parthian capital of Ctesiphon on the lower Tigris. More enduring and a greater boon to civilization was the extensive construction he left throughout the empire, which included bridges, aqueducts, canals, harbor works, and roads. The people of Alcántara, Spain, still use the bridge his engineers constructed across the Tagus.

Most historians honor Trajan's successor Hadrian (117–138) as without peer among Roman emperors in the field of administration. The new emperor was related to Trajan and hailed from the same Spanish province of Baetica. Trajan had adopted him on his deathbed as son and successor. From Trajan's aggressive foreign policy Hadrian reverted to the defensive imperialism of Augustus, for which the troops might have thanked him had he not set them to work instead strengthening the fortifications along the northern frontier. In Britain they erected a formidable wall, twenty feet high and eight feet thick, that ran the eighty miles across England from the mouth of the Tyne to Solway Firth with major fortresses every fourteen miles and smaller forts at mile intervals. This barrier Hadrian hoped would effectually block further raids by the fierce Picts and Scots to the north. In the east with the Parthians Hadrian chose to effect a settlement. He relinquished claims to almost the whole of Mesopotamia and Assyria, and retained merely a kind of lordship over Armenia.

The only major fighting to disrupt the peace of Hadrian's long reign was not along the frontier but in Judaea. Trouble had broken out there during the closing years of Trajan's reign, but it was Hadrian's decision to rebuild Jerusalem as a Roman city and to erect an altar to Jupiter on the site of Solomon's temple that sparked a bloody rebellion. Fighting only ceased with the virtual exile or extermination of the Jewish population. Not until the twentieth century did the area again become a center of Jewish culture.

No emperor paid more attention to the provinces than Hadrian. Half his reign he spent outside Italy in tours which twice took him about the empire. His purpose was a good one, not to receive the plaudits of admiring crowds, but to learn firsthand of the conditions that prevailed in their provinces. So great was his admiration for Greece and its culture that he aroused the indignation of critics back in Rome. They also objected to the liberality with which he extended citizenship to provincials. Hadrian's most important administrative reform was his reorganization of the imperial bureaucracy. This had seen little change since Claudius established it on a more or less permanent basis a century before. In order to raise its prestige and to improve its efficiency, he replaced freemen, who had dominated the service, with equestrians, raised salaries, and made provision for promotion and advancement in the service.

Hadrian continued the alimentary system of his predecessors and also Trajan's building program. Among his most impressive structures are the Pantheon, his tomb which since the sixth century has borne the name of the Castle of St. Angelo, the completion of the Temple of Zeus Olympios which Peisistratus had started, a magnificent villa at Tivoli, and the city of Adrianople. Though these and other undertakings cost much money, his careful use of imperial funds enabled the empire to sustain the financial burden without difficulty.

Hadrian treated the senate with deference—he even consulted the body on occasion—but depended principally for advice on a group of eminent jurists. One of these, Julian, he set to codifying the edicts that praetors had been issuing annually for many centuries and which embodied in substance the principles and procedures of Roman civil law. Hadrian's imperial edicts also tended to replace senatorial legislation, although what particularly embittered the senate was his suppression of their judicial and administrative powers in Italy. So strained did relations between emperor and senate become, that only the prompt intervention of Antoninus Pius, whom Hadrian selected as his successor, prevented that body from formally execrating his memory.

Antoninus (138–161), given the title Pius, the loyal, for his devotion to his adoptive father, enjoyed a long though uneventful career. He continued Hadrian's policy of defensive imperialism except in England where he added another barrier some eighty miles north of Hadrian's Wall, to provide a deeper buffer against Scottish raids. There were rumblings of trouble here and there in other parts of the empire, but no serious rupture of the Roman peace, even on the part of the army, which might have objected to the emperor's complete lack of military experience. To a grateful senate Antoninus restored some of its former judicial prerogatives in Italy. So prudently did he husband the imperial revenues, that, without raising taxes, he was able to continue the alimentary program, carry on considerable construction, and still leave a large balance in the treasury when he died.

Marcus Aurelius (161–180), whom Hadrian had ordered Antoninus to adopt, succeeded him without opposition. What has made his name most famous among the Good Emperors are not reform measures or conquests, but rather the reflections he left posterity in his *Meditations*. Their source was principally the teachings of Epictetus, the leading exponent of Roman Stoicism, their setting usually a rough camp along the upper Danube. His thoughts are neither original nor profound, yet their practical wisdom has recommended them to the attention of many readers. Men must live together in mutual love and respect, "for we are made for cooperation, like hands, like eyelids, like the rows of the upper and lower teeth. To act against one another then is contrary to nature."

It was the misfortune of Marcus Aurelius that not works of peace but the cruel business of war absorbed most of his energies. For years heavy and continuous fighting kept him along the upper Danube. Against the Parthians his generals conducted generally successful campaigns. Had it not been for the outbreak of a disease, probably smallpox, Roman armies might have permanently crippled Parthian power. The plague struck during the winter of 165 and was carried through the empire by soldiers returning from the east. In both east and west the plague caused a sharp decline in population. Marcus Aurelius' own efforts in containing several powerful German tribes on the upper Danube, including the Marcomanni and Quadi, were at first unsuccessful. They penetrated all the way to the Adriatic, and so serious was the crisis that the emperor was obliged to sell the treasures of the palace and to draft slaves and gladiators in order to save Rome. In time he defeated these Germans, and those he did not force back across the frontier, he permitted to settle on lands left depopulated by war and disease. They accepted the dual obligation of cultivating the soil and maintaining the frontier. His own objectives of pacifying and annexing the territories of Bohemia and Moravia he was on the point of attaining when he died in his camp at Vindobona (Vienna). To the people of the empire he left an empty treasury, a country weakened financially and suffering here and there from depopulation, and a reprobate of a son who succeeded him.

These five emperors, Nerva through Marcus Aurelius, ruled the empire during the last great century of its existence. Few people questioned their exercise of autocratic powers. By 96 A.D. when Nerva assumed the purple, the use of such powers had already become traditional. Imperial autocracy dated from Octavian's victory at Actium, although prudence recommended to the new emperor the wisdom of obscuring the fact of his dictatorship in order to placate what republican sentiments lingered on. So he nurtured the notion of a diarchy, himself as the *princeps* or first citizen, the senate as his imperial partner in the administration of the empire. But he carefully screened the senate that was to share his rule. Only his friends and supporters passed muster. They accordingly accepted the new order without demur and thereby helped establish the new tradition of senatorial subserviency. This posture, under an Augustus, was easy to accept; less so, under the tyrannical Nero and Domitian. Yet very few senators cared to risk position, wealth, or neck by open criticism. Nothing was done to halt the inevitable and almost progressive decline of senatorial authority even during the reign of the just Vespasian. Against Hadrian's reforms that deprived that body of most of its remaining powers, the members could only grumble among themselves. Even the privilege of execrating or blessing the memory of the newly deceased emperor they exercised only in accordance with the wishes of the new ruler. Nevertheless, position and wealth assured the senators of great prestige, while individuals might exert considerable influence in the capacity of imperial advisers. This was, of course, to be expected since the emperor raised men to the senate who had proved themselves loyal and efficient officials.

The emperor might honor the senate and even consult with its members, but he drew principally from the equestrian class for men to fill the most responsible posts in the imperial bureaucracy. Their lower rank and their dependence upon him for political advancement made them more dependable than senators. During the late Republic, this class had been known for their aggressiveness in making fortunes. Augustus hoped to satisfy their ambitions within the ranks of an expanding imperial service. There they could prove their worth as procurators (prefects) in charge of a variety of important services—the census, taxes, imperial post—and in the direction of imperial estates, the grain supply, the praetorian (imperial) guard, and even the country of Egypt. During the reign of the Good Emperors, an ambitious equestrian who was loyal and efficient could hope in time to receive appointment to one of these important prefectures and eventually to enrollment in the senate. Freedmen normally filled the lower offices in the imperial service.

A large share in their success in governing the empire during the second century the Good Emperors owed the city-state or municipality. Because the modern state, by contrast to the ancient, is usually a highly centralized political organism, the modern reader generally envisages the Roman empire as guided by an extensive bureaucracy, controlled from Rome, which exercised effective bureaucratic supervision down to the very last subject. Quite the reverse was the case. When Rome added a new province to the empire, she wisely left the conquered cities to continue their administration of local affairs, partly because she was not interested, partly because she was not equipped to assume those responsibilities herself. Therefore, from point of view of administration, the empire consisted of a collection of autonomous communities in whose hands rested the administration of all local matters, including the collection of taxes. The governing body in such a municipality was generally a council (*curia*) composed of local magistrates and ex-magistrates together with other leading citizens whose wealth and influence assured them a voice. They constituted the backbone of imperial rule in the provinces. They also provided the emperor a supply of responsible provincials from whom he recruited for the imperial service and for the senate.

Under this system of government lived in peace and relative prosperity some sixty million people at the beginning of the second century (A.D.). At one time, during Rome's final expansion of the second and first centuries B.C., these blessings had been limited for the most part to Italy, and even there were enjoyed principally by its more fortunate citizens. When these wars ended, however, so did the physical destruction suffered by the provinces, and, once Octavian had assumed authority, so did likewise the financial exploitation of their peoples. For if instances of corrupt rule still came to light under the emperors, such instances were exceptions to what had been the rule during the period of the Republic. Peace soon brought recovery, then often a measure of prosperity greater than that the province had ever enjoyed. Many provinces accepted not only the Roman peace but Roman culture as well. Where an older culture did not interpose itself, as in Greece and the eastern Mediterranean, and where Romans moved to in appreciable numbers, Roman arts, manners, and institutions gradually penetrated and took root. In certain areas the culture became thoroughly Roman in fact, as in the provinces of Africa (Tunisia), Baetica (southern Spain), Narbonese Gaul (southern France), and to a lesser degree in Upper Germany (upper Rhine) and Lower Moesia (lower Danube).

The most effective agency in Romanizing the outer reaches of the empire was the Roman army even though this was, of course, incidental to its primary role of guarding the frontier. For this critical task of maintaining the frontiers, the emperors employed one of the largest standing armies in the history of military annals. They divided the army into two major branches: the legionaries, who were recruited from the citizenry; and the auxiliaries, who were noncitizens. From the time of Hadrian the provinces along the frontiers furnished the majority of the troops in both services. That this had become a virtual necessity tells a disturbing story about the public-spiritedness of the Roman citizenry. It also represented the first major step that would lead in time to the estrangement of the army from Roman traditions and loyalties. Actually Hadrian has the distinction of introducing the first wholly foreign element into the Roman army. He took into the imperial service non-Romanized peoples from across the frontiers and permitted them to fight with their own weapons and after their own customs, but under Roman officers. This again was a disturbing development, since it marked the beginning of what was to become a progressively greater dependence upon non-Romans for the defense of the empire.

The greater part of Rome's huge army lay strung out along its vast frontier. The legions usually held themselves in fortified camps some miles behind the frontier, the auxiliaries up nearer the line. There they were expected to hold back the barbarian attack long enough to enable the legions to come up. Already during the reign of Marcus Aurelius, it had become clear that this kind of deployment of troops could not prevent serious breakthroughs. Historians have discovered the presence of another dangerous weakness, namely, the tendency of the Roman army to assume the character of a permanent border militia, with progressively fewer links with Rome, with Italy, and with civil authority. The Roman army gradually and inevitably became an institution to itself, its objectives the ambitions of its members, its generals the men who could satisfy their demands for privileges and bonuses. Still, only prophets could have foreseen the evil consequences of these developments. For the moment the vast army along the frontiers brought assurance that all was well, while the thousands of miles of military highways that stretched from Gibraltar to the Black Sea linked all parts of this tremendous empire, in the words of Aristides, "as one great family."

The huge Roman army and extensive defense system, which devoured enormous funds, required a large and separate treasury (*aerarium militare*) to maintain them. Into this poured the greater portion of the empire's revenues: a 5 per cent tax on inheritances (paid only by citizens), a 1 per cent sales tax, a 5 per cent tax on the value of emancipated slaves, and custom duties. Provincials were responsible for personal and poll taxes, for the provision of food, fodder, and services for the armies that were stationed there or might be passing through, and for the imperial post. The principal tax from which the government derived the bulk of its revenue was the land tax. In general the tax burden until the third century was not excessive, while the methods of collection were reasonably efficient, even though all tax collectors, by common consent, were dishonest. Even the Apostle Matthew admitted to earlier irregularities.

Because agriculture was in a moderately healthy condition during the second century, the land tax returned a good amount. It is imprudent to speak confidently, however, on the subject of imperial agriculture since a dearth of information constantly complicates the task of the historian. Still one may assume that the inertia of custom, so much a fact of life in antiquity, was particularly powerful in agriculture. Ways and conditions altered little and slowly in rural areas. Here changes in supply and demand remained small while the majority of farmers remained content to draw little more than a livelihood from their acres. Even these small farmers must, however, have had some produce to sell, for it was to alleviate their condition in the second century that the Good Emperors made available low-interest loans. Concerning the larger farms, or latifundia, our information is more substantial. Both their number and the size of individual estates tended to grow. Where large areas were given over to the raising of grapes, olives, or stock, an approach to commercial farming was not uncommon. On the latifundia, too, a trend of some significance had become evident in the second century; that was the shift from slave labor, which was growing expensive as peace cut off the principal source, to the use of tenant farmers.

During the second century trade generally prospered, thanks to the *Pax Romana*, a sound currency, and an expanding empire. Traders brought goods and wares from all parts of the known world: from China, India, and the Indies, from Russia and the Baltic area, and from the Sudan. Yet the volume of such trade was generally small. High was the cost of transportation, low the purchasing power of the masses. Only the wealthy person could afford spices from the East, for example, or to clothe himself in anything but homespun woolen garments. Even the small fee the trader paid to use the empire's system of military roads could not offset the expensiveness of land transportation. The cheapest transportation was provided by the Mediterranean, although shippers used its broad waters only during the summer months. Though trading fleets, especially in the shipment of grain, were not unknown, the ordinary carrier was the privately owned vessel which moved from port to port on its slow and irregular way within sight of the reassuring shoreline. With the exception of the shipment of grain upon which the city of Rome depended, and the establishment of friendly relations with its neighbors, the imperial government took no direct interest in trade. Nor for that matter did the individual Roman. The usual merchant was a Syrian or a Greek or a Hebrew, whose fore-fathers had had an ancient history of trade behind them when Rome was still nothing more than a village.

Several of the same circumstances, notably the high cost of transportation and the low purchasing power of the masses, which hampered the expansion of trade in the second century, exercised the same depressing effects upon industry. The wealthy classes, for their part, particularly those who had country estates, did less than one might expect to stimulate industry since it was fashionable to satisfy all but the most exotic needs from their own physical and human resources. Although no century in Roman history witnessed a higher degree of industrial activity than the second, even this never attained the level our modern standards would consider necessary for so powerful an empire. Except for industries engaged in the production of bronze and iron work, pottery, bricks, and tile, whose products were needed to meet military demands or the extensive construction programs of occasional emperors, manufacturing remained geared to local needs. Again, except for these industries where large numbers of laborers might be employed, the typical shop was that of the individual proprietor assisted by a hired laborer or a slave. What might have altered this situation would have been greater purchasing power on the part of the masses and a willingness on the part of the wealthy to invest in industry. Yet the abundance of cheap labor and the absence of patent laws discouraged the flow of capital to industry. It went instead into the exploitation of land, which was both more rewarding and dignified.

The impression a satirist such as Juvenal leaves the reader concerning the character of the population of the empire during the second century is of an aristocracy on the one hand whose affluence few civilizations have ever matched, and on the other a mass of poor who could not have maintained themselves without public assistance. The im-

pression is not entirely accurate. Between these two contrasting groups
there existed a small middle class, its members most conspicuous in
the provinces, where they included landowners, merchants, and financiers. The wealthy lived in luxurious villas, the more pretentious of
these staffed by several thousand slaves and domestics. The poor in
the larger cities huddled together in huge apartment houses, called
insulae. The more substantial of these were of brick and perhaps more
than a half-dozen stories high. All encroached on dark, narrow streets
which in Rome and in the larger cities approached in appearance the
lamentable condition of our worst modern slums. Except for "bread
and circuses," possibly one-half the population of these cities would
have starved or rebelled.

No one aspect of Roman life of the second century presents so sharp
a contrast to modern practice as does that of slavery. True, the terrifying slave wars of the Republic were far in the past together with the
barbarous treatment that had precipitated them. Slavery of the second century was a more humane institution, even on the latifundia,
where the rising cost of slaves had led inevitably to their better treatment. Yet the presence of hundreds of slaves in the villas of the
wealthy, where they served the personal demands of their masters, is
one foreign to modern notions of what is socially healthy. Pliny the
Younger, who from his letters appears to have been a man of ordinary
tastes, kept some five hundred slaves. Had he been asked whether he
actually needed to keep so many, he would have answered that convention insisted that he did. In fact the number of slaves (and clients)
who attended the Roman aristocrat when he went about his business
and pleasure proclaimed his social importance. They constituted a status symbol of the times. It must be said to the credit of Romans of
Pliny's character that they were generous in their treatment of slaves
and frequently extended them manumission. Still, as ex-slaves they
carried the stigma of their former condition to their graves; furthermore, even when free, economic necessity often forced them to assume
the demeaning role of attending their former master as clients.

Also inconsistent with modern notions of what is proper were certain
types of recreation in which the Roman indulged outside his home. The
practice of daily visiting the baths, which might consume as much as
three or four hours, was that of a society which had more time than
we do for leisure and a more luxurious idea of how to spend it. This is
not to suggest that the tradition of the baths was essentially pagan.
Romans continued to patronize them long after the city had become

Christian, although the popes never saw fit to restore the aqueducts once these had been destroyed in the sixth century. Without aqueducts the operation of the baths became impossible.

Baths took up only part of the Roman's leisure time. More exciting recreation awaited him at the theater, the amphitheater, and the circus, and usually at no greater cost. For the government, whether Republican or imperial, considered it prudent to provide shows for the populace in order to gain its good will or to allay possible discontent. Though such shows were a source of heavy expense to the state as well as to those members of the senatorial order who chose or were directed to finance them, their number and splendor tended to increase even under the Good Emperors. The calendar in the reign of Marcus Aurelius provided for 135 holidays when the Roman populace could expect free entertainment. Even the sober Trajan set aside 123 consecutive days to celebrate his Dacian victory.

As equally disturbing to modern sensibilities as the number of these shows was their barbarous and frequently degrading character. Most barbarous, and popular, were the gladiatorial combats, the public execution of criminals (and Christians) by means of wild animals, and shows where criminals would be forced to kill one another. Bloody encounters between fierce beasts were common. On a single day as many as five thousand beasts might be killed to sate the Roman's demand for excitement. Nor is it pleasant to remember how the Good Emperor Trajan allocated ten thousand of his captive Dacians for the Colosseum where they were to kill each other for the amusement of the Romans. The theater, though less brutalizing, was hardly a constructive force. Unlike his classical brother the Greek, the Roman had no taste for great drama. His taste seldom ventured above low comedy and gross pantomime. And where the Greek kept scenes of violence off the stage, the Roman might substitute a criminal, as he did in the mime *Laureolus*, who would be actually tortured to death as the script demanded. To the popularity of the chariot races in the Circus Maximus, modern censors might only object on the score of the widespread betting they encouraged and the rioting that often followed in their wake.

Roman pagan religion did little to combat the degenerating influences of the theater and arena. Vestiges of the old Roman deities lingered on in the rural areas, but no one has thought to credit their worship with exerting a constructive influence even in the early Republic when this thrived. The cult of Augustus, which had spread throughout the empire during the second century, was less a religion than a vehicle for expressing loyalty to the state. What the majority of Romans had adopted for the purpose of satisfying their need for security in this life and hope of immortality in the hereafter were such mystery cults from the eastern Mediterranean as that of Cybele (Great Mother), Isis and Serapis, and Mithraism. These cults possessed such general features as a ritual that exemplified legendary incidents in the lives of their gods, frequently built around their suffering, death, and rebirth, and a membership limited to those who had been duly initiated into the mysteries of the cult deities. It is not easy to gauge the popularity and influence of these cults. Christian writers hastened to denounce them as universally immoral and degrading, although the cult of Mithras, with its appeal to such manly virtues as honor and courage, surely did not fall into that category. Yet none of these mystery cults demanded the exclusive loyalty of its members, nor did any of them, when faced with persecution, leave a martyrology.

For some Romans the ethical doctrines of Stoicism served to supplement, often to serve as a substitute for, a formal religion. Stoicism had come from Greece although not without undergoing some change. Through the influence of such later exponents as Epictetus it had shed its originally egocentric character. Its founder Zeno had preached man's duty to accept cheerfully whatever happened, secure in the knowledge that whatever transpired was best since Nature (Reason, God) wanted it so. Such a man was to live a serene existence, no more moved by the adversity that might strike a neighbor than by that which might afflict himself. From this essentially selfish philosophy and its metaphysical rationalization Roman Stoics turned to the gospel of humanitarianism. They preached the doctrine of man's responsibility for others. Their influence has been seen in the jurists of the second century who sought to apply principles of equity to Roman law in an effort to soften its rigidly legalistic mold. Certain scholars also speak of Stoicism's benign influence upon Christianity. Be that as it may, Stoics generally chose not Christianity in the third and fourth centuries when faced with a choice, but its opponent Neo-Platonism. Roman Epicureanism scarcely deserves mention. It had degenerated from its Greek origins, when it had proposed a respectable philosophy of life, into sheer hedonism. Its influence was insignificant.

It is to the credit of the humanist Gibbon that he reckoned the second century the happiest age in the history of mankind despite its

undistinguished literary record. Although Domitian's death set the
Muses free again, writers found little to inspire them. In ideas and
ideals the second century was especially deficient. Even in an unin-
spired age men can write history, however, and Rome of the second
century gave posterity Tacitus, possibly its greatest historian. Had it
not been for the experience of his early career which he lived in the
stifling atmosphere of Domitian's tyranny, Tacitus might have written
with greater objectivity of the emperors who hold the center of his attention. For he wrote as a representative of the old Republican aristocracy to whom any kind of imperial rule was a misfortune. Historians
have spent a century seeking to correct the distortions his brilliant,
persuasive style saddled upon subsequent generations of admiring
writers. The same caveat applies to the satirist Juvenal. No evil escaped his myopic eyes.

With Tacitus damning the emperors and Juvenal the rest of society,
it is a relief to turn to the letters of Pliny the Younger. Pliny was less a
stylist than the other two, yet hopefully more authentic in the picture
he presents of the life of the times. Then there is Suetonius, at best a
biographer of twelve of the emperors (he begins with Julius Caesar),
at worst a gossip, but capable of writing in a clear, vivid style that appealed to both medieval and modern readers. A considerably superior
and even more popular biographer was the Greek Plutarch. His moral
essays and his moralizing *Parallel Lives* of illustrious Greeks and Romans continue to intrigue a host of readers.

Included among the most influential writers of the second century
were two other Greeks, Galen and Ptolemy by name, whose works,
counting pagan writers, ranked second only to Aristotle in their impact
upon medieval thought. Galen, who was a practicing physician to Commodus, gathered into twenty volumes most of the ancient world's
knowledge of medicine, together with his own discoveries concerning
the circulatory and nervous systems. Ptolemy, who was a mathematician, geographer, and astronomer, earned the gratitude of the Middle
Ages for his industry in assembling the astronomical knowledge of the
ancient world. In their reverence, the Arabs referred to his book as
Almagest, that is, "the greatest." No doubt, both Christian and Islamic
worlds profited enormously from his scholarship, even from one of his
errors. His treatise on geography convinced Columbus that he would
have no difficulty reaching Asia by sailing west. He might otherwise
have never started.

The most impressive achievement of the age of the Good Emperors in the field of scholarship came in law. Republican Rome had welcomed a number of great jurists, but no century exceeded the second in the brilliance and volume of legal literature produced. An important factor in inspiring this work was the encouragement of the Good Emperors. They were anxious to formularize the legal structure and to temper Roman law with the humanitarian doctrines of the Stoics. As seen above, Hadrian had Julian codify the edicts of the praetors. Gaius, who wrote under Antoninus Pius and Marcus Aurelius, was the author of the *Institutes*, a book that Justinian's lawyers incorporated almost unaltered into his monumental *Corpus Juris Civilis*. (See below, p. 121.) More renowned was Papinian, whom the monster Caracalla ordered killed when he refused to legalize the emperor's murder of his own brother. Together with Ulpian and Paulus, Papinian carried this, the brightest one hundred years in the history of Roman jurisprudence, into the third century, where it shortly came to an abrupt halt. Most noteworthy was the success of these men in applying general principles of equity, rather than custom or formal legislation in the solution of legal problems, and in appealing to a fundamental moral law in the study of human rights. Their work in humanizing Roman law was continued by the Christian jurists of the fourth and fifth centuries.

Such was the age of the Good Emperors. It was not a brilliant period except perhaps in jurisprudence, yet a century of peace and one that enjoyed many of the blessings peace makes possible. Before the miseries and tragedy of the third century, these blessings stood forth in all the sharper relief. As Dio, a historian of the following century, wrote: "Our history now descends from a kingdom of gold to one of iron and rust. . . ." There is no sorrier century in Roman history than the third.

The "iron and rust" of which Dio wrote dated from the moment of Marcus Aurelius' death in 180. For Aurelius unfortunately had a son, the reprobate Commodus, otherwise the system of adoption might have continued. If Marcus Aurelius suspected his son's weakness of character but hoped the responsibilities of the imperial office would mature him, he was mistaken. Instead of completing the destruction of the German tribes in the area of modern Czechoslovakia and annexing the territory as his father had planned, Commodus bought peace and hurried back to Rome in order to enjoy in riotous living the wealth and power his position afforded him. While he degraded the emperorship by displaying his physical talents in the arena as a reincarnate Hercules, he turned the government over to friends, as depraved as himself, who brought the state to the brink of ruin. Forced "benevolences" and the judicial murder of wealthy men kept him in funds until one day a wrestling companion joined a conspiracy and throttled him.

Though no one regretted Commodus' assassination, the violence of his passing bred more violence. The praetorian (imperial) guard whose commander had been partner to the conspiracy, seized the initiative in filling the imperial post. His choice was an admirable one, a senator by the name of Pertinax. Pertinax took his responsibilities seriously, insisted upon discipline in the guard and economies in the government, so the guard slew him. They then auctioned off the emperorship to the highest bidder. This outrage was too much for the provincial legions to stomach. Those in Syria put up their governor, those along the upper Danube, Septimius Severus. After several years of devastating civil war against other contenders, Septimius won out and established a harsh though essentially constructive rule over the entire empire. Most noteworthy among his achievements was the destruction of Parthian power; most surprising, in view of his cruel nature, was his restoration of the alimentary system; most bizarre, his repair of Hannibal's tomb and the introduction of Carthaginian gods; and most ominous, his generosity toward the troops. Tradition says his dying advice to his son, Caracalla, was to enrich the soldiers and to scorn all other men.

Several of Caracalla's acts force historians to note his infamous reign which they might otherwise prefer to pass over in silence. For the record of his monstrous conduct stains Roman history of the third century almost as deeply as that of Nero does the first. Nevertheless visitors to Rome continue to marvel at the ruins of his magnificent baths, while historians still puzzle over the motives behind his decree of 212 A.D. which extended citizenship to all free provincials of the empire. They can only wonder, too, how so debauched a man could have conducted so strong a frontier policy as he did, and that in person.

Macrinus, the praetorian prefect who ordered Caracalla's murder, succeeded him, but was himself murdered after a year. Then Bassianus, another debauchee like Caracalla, assumed the imperial power. He is better known as Elagabalus, after the sun god of that name, whose priest he was and whose depraved cult he sought to make supreme throughout the empire. His grandmother, who had first arranged his accession, now arranged his murder, then the accession of Alexander Severus, another of her grandsons. The development of most significance during the latter's reign was the emergence of a new and powerful Persian empire, the Sassanid, from out of the ashes of the old Parthian state. Alexander Severus' weak foreign policy along the Rhine led his troops, already disgruntled over his frugality, to murder him.

Now the story of violence grows still more violent. The emperors who occupied the throne during the next half-century go by the name of "barrack emperors." All but one or two were generals; all owed their accession to the army. More disturbing was the manner these men died. Of the eighteen emperors who ruled during this period before 285 A.D., sixteen died violent deaths. What a shattering end to the *Pax Romana!* Civil war among the scores of imperial rivals, the majority of them the candidates of their respective legions, carried destruction throughout the empire, while powerful barbarian tribes poured across the sagging frontiers and the Sassanid Persians set the east on fire. During this terrible period large sections of the empire declared their independence, and when the smoke cleared, Dacia and Britain were gone. Had it not been for tradition and other cohesive forces, and those fortuitous circumstances which pious people call miracles and puzzled unbelievers, chance, the empire would most certainly have disintegrated.

The first of the "barrack emperors" was Maximinus, once a peasant and "barbarian." The story that he was over eight feet tall and ate forty pounds of meat daily, even if exaggerated, probably suggests what qualities accounted for his rise from the ranks to the emperorship. For three years he maintained the frontier, for the same three years he conducted what amounted to a systematic extermination of the upper classes. His troops finally murdered him when opposition threatened, after which the teen-age Gordian III reigned for three years. When his father-in-law, the praetorian prefect, died, the new prefect Philip, who was of Arab origin, had him killed, then himself ruled for five years before being murdered by Decius, commander on the Dacian front. Though Decius was initially successful against a large body of invading Goths, he later stumbled into a trap they had prepared and both he and his army were destroyed (251 A.D.).

Gallus, the officer whose treachery had contributed to Decius' death, succeeded him but lasted only two years. Aemilianus had his troops kill him, but in less than a year they cut down Aemilianus as well. The army then called upon Valerian to save the empire from Germans who were crossing the northern frontier and from Persians who were menacing the east. Gallienus, Valerian's son, managed to drive back an

army of Franks which had penetrated to Milan, but in the east Valerian, while in conference with the Persians, was treacherously seized,
and ended his life serving the Persian king as his footstool. The story
is told that the king would have Valerian get down on hands and feet,
then step on his back to mount his horse! What prevented the Persians
from overrunning all the east was not a Roman army but Odenathus,
prince of Palmyra, whose country lay on the edge of the north Arabian
desert. Gallienus gratefully hailed Odenathus as commander of the
Roman armies in the east, a post he held successfully until his death
in 267. Odenathus' beautiful widow, Zenobia, had brighter ambitions
than serving a weakening empire. Instead she proceeded to establish
an independent state which in time included all of the east with the
exception of Asia Minor and the city of Alexandria. Gallienus out in
the west could do nothing more than protest. Not only did he have
more German tribes on his hands than he could handle, but some thirty
pretenders as well, one of whom set up his own empire in Gaul, Britain, and Spain. At the approach of still another pretender, Gallienus
was murdered by his own troops.

The next emperor, Claudius, one of the conspirators, fortunately
demonstrated an ability to do more than just plot. He inflicted so
bloody a defeat upon the Goths that for a hundred years they caused
no more trouble in Europe. Of all these barrack emperors, except for
the prisoner Valerian, Claudius was the only one not to be murdered.
The plague got him first! His successor was Aurelian, another con-
spirator in the death of Gallienus, but an emperor who would have
ranked with Rome's most illustrious had he been allowed a longer
career. His most pressing assignment was that of driving back the
Juthungi, a German tribe that had penetrated as far south as Ravenna.
Though he was first defeated by them, he managed to retrieve the
desperate situation when they broke up into small raiding groups,
which he then destroyed. Because of the real danger of the next German invaders being more successful, he proceeded with the construction of a wall about Rome which was completed soon after his death.
Not since the time of Hannibal, almost five hundred years before, had
Rome needed such defenses.

Next Aurelian dealt with Zenobia, defeated her famed cavalry, and
left a garrison in Palmyra. When Zenobia organized a revolt and massacred these troops, he returned and so razed the city that it disappeared beneath the desert's shifting sands. Its ruins only came to view
again in the eighteenth century. Then Aurelian hurried to the west,

restored imperial rule in Gaul and Britain, then returned to Rome where he celebrated a triumph. As he was about to lead an army eastward to dispose of the Persians, several of his officers murdered him.

Ten years of further turbulency followed Aurelian's tragic death. His successor Tacitus was cut down despite noteworthy victories over the Goths and Alans in Asia Minor. The troops then put up Probus, a man of the same Illyrian stock as Aurelian and possessing similar talents as general and administrator. During the six years of his reign Probus re-established the imperial frontiers on the Rhine and upper Danube. He also brought peace to the empire only to have his troops murder him. Next it was Carus' turn, another capable Illyrian general, who was so successful in his campaigning against the Persians that he might have destroyed them had not his troops murdered him. In 285 his son Carinus, who had ruled with him, suffered defeat at the hands of the pretender Diocletian, and was slain by his own officers.

With the accession of Diocletian in 285, the dreadful period of the barrack emperors came to an end. Although Diocletian was as much a general as the majority of his predecessors and, like them, owed his throne to his troops, fortune happened to be on his side. His troops did not cut him down; in fact, after twenty years of solid rule, he retired. Diocletian's origins were humble. His father had been a slave, probably a native of Illyricum, where Diocletian was born and reared. Like so many other young men of the area, Diocletian gravitated to the army for want of any better occupation. Had he nourished any ambition to rule, there was no better army to join than the one on the Danube. Because of geography and perhaps strength, that army had been most successful in forcing its choice of emperor upon the rest of the empire.

Diocletian's immediate task was military, to use the army to restore peace within the empire, then to employ that same army to preserve the peace. The first task was not so difficult as the second. The real problem was to make the army a force for peace, a role it had not filled for generations. The solution Diocletian hit upon was simple yet eminently successful. He placed Maximian, one of his trusted officers, in command of the troops in the western half of the empire with full powers to restore peace, then rule as co-Augustus. He himself moved his court to Nicomedia in Asia Minor, from which city he could effectively defend the Balkans, Egypt, and the East. When it became apparent a few years later (293 A.D.) that one military assistant was not enough, he appointed two additional generals, to whom he gave the title Caesar. One of these, Constantius, he placed in command of the troops along the Rhine; to the other, Galerius, he gave the command on the Danube. In order to ensure the loyalty of these men, Diocletian had Galerius marry his daughter, Constantius to marry the daughter of Maximian. As an added insurance in the case of Constantius, he ordered him to send his son, Constantine, to live with him in Nicomedia. Though heavy fighting was required to put down several revolts within the empire and to drive back the Germans and Persians, in time the four men were successful in re-establishing Roman rule throughout the empire and winning back Britain and the upper Tigris.

Though Diocletian's name was long held in execration because of his persecution of Christians, modern scholarship reveals him to have been a ruler of considerable courage, ability, and vision. Several of his reforms proved failures, such as his efforts to establish a stable currency and halt inflation. More enduring was his reorganization of the empire into four prefectures, fourteen dioceses, and some hundred provinces. What he hoped to accomplish by this reorganization was a separation of military and civil authority, a reduction of the administrative work handled by the central government, and, by reducing the size of the provinces, a reduction at the same time in the number of troops at the disposal of the individual provincial commanders. Included among the thousand edicts he issued are a number that reveal his concern with suppressing fraud and protecting the citizenry from corrupt administration. In order to raise the prestige of the imperial office and remove it from barrack intrigue, he assumed the title Jovius (Jupiter) and introduced ceremonials borrowed from the autocratic courts of semidivine Hellenistic monarchs. Rarely did he show himself in public, and only a few, carefully screened persons were permitted past hundreds of palace guards and functionaries into his august presence, where they prostrated themselves after the manner of suppliants and remained kneeling until bidden to rise. Finally in 303, probably upon the insistence of his son-in-law Galerius, who appears to have gained an ascendancy over the aging man, he ordered the persecution of Christians.

In 305 Diocletian retired to his splendid palace in Salona (Dalmatia) and forced the grumbling Maximian to do the same. The two Caesars, Galerius and Constantius, promptly moved up to the positions of Augusti, while Galerius appointed two of his friends, Severus and Maximinus Daia, to take their places as Caesars. For the moment, therefore,

Diocletian's plan of succession worked, but for no more than a moment. The next year when Constantius was killed fighting the Scots in northern England, his troops refused to leave the matter of succession to the senior emperor, but promptly hailed his son, Constantine, as Augustus. Within a few months the empire was again suffering the horrors of civil war. In 310 five Augusti ruled parts of the empire, one of them Maxentius, the son of Maximian. The following year Galerius died. Then in 312 Constantine won a decisive victory over Maxentius at Milvian Bridge, a victory he and his Christian contemporaries attributed to the intervention of heaven. For it was just prior to this battle that Constantine had his troops mark their shields with the Christian symbol *Chi Rho* (the first two letters of the word Christ). According to the story related by Eusebius, Constantine had seen a cross in the sky some time before the battle with the subscription, "By this sign, conquer," for which reason he adopted the *Chi Rho* monogram.* After ten years of uneasy rule with his co-Augustus Licinius, Constantine defeated and eliminated him. From 325 until his death in 337 Constantine ruled as sole emperor.

Constantine, whom contemporary Christian writers call "the Great" because of his pro-Christian policies, left an even deeper mark on his times than did Diocletian. His origins were as humble as those of any of the emperors. His father, the emperor Constantius, had been a peasant near modern Nish (in Yugoslavia) where Constantine was born. His mother Helena may have been a barmaid. When Constantius was obliged to dismiss her in order to marry Maximian's daughter, she dropped out of sight until the emergence of her son as emperor.

Constantine continued in the main the policies of Diocletian. His financial reforms proved more successful than had Diocletian's, and for the first time in more than a century the empire enjoyed a stable currency. Like many Roman emperors, he sponsored an extensive building program. This program included churches rather than temples, and of his churches he donated that of St. John Lateran in Rome to the city's bishop. Apart from several acts of brutality which were probably the result of a violent temper, he appears to have possessed a kindly nature. This might explain the relief measures he adopted in favor of the poor and his suppression of gladiatorial exhibitions. Two of his acts stand out for their extraordinary significance: first, the policy of toleration which he and Licinius agreed upon at Milan in 313 (traditionally

* See below, p. 50, for another description of this incident.

known as the Edict of Milan), and second, his decision to build a new capital on the site of the ancient Greek city of Byzantium.

The first of these acts, that of extending toleration to the persecuted sect of Christians, opened the way to the gradual transformation of the culture of the empire from pagan to Christian. Scholars may argue that this transformation had become inevitable. Some one emperor would have taken the steps Constantine did at this time, first to tolerate Christianity, then promote its growth, and finally become a Christian himself. Still, except for certain circumstances, that step might have been delayed for a century, and one such circumstance was Constantine's genius. It is difficult to exaggerate the importance of Constantine's act in gaining the cooperation of Christianity. Had it not been for the emergence of a strong, well-organized institution such as Christianity was, which found use for a large measure of Rome's culture and had a stake in its preservation, much more of classical civilization would have disappeared.

Constantine's other great deed, that of founding a new capital, also had far-reaching consequences. The site of the city, from point of view of military strength and commercial advantages, could not be matched in the whole of the Mediterranean. Because of the city's impregnability a long history remained to the eastern half of the empire after the western half had been lost. It was Constantine's aim to make the city the "New Rome," as much like the "Eternal City" on the Tiber as possible. So he brought in sculptures, gave it a senate of its own, a calendar similar to Rome's, even the bread and circuses that had aroused Juvenal's contempt. Constantinople remains yet today a great city.

Constantine left the empire to his sons Constantine, Constantius, and Constans, who promptly murdered other male relatives, including two nephews to whom their father had assigned provinces. Constantine II, the eldest, was the first to die. He was killed in a battle with his younger brother, Constans, who ten years later fell victim to a conspiracy of his officers. This left only Constantius, who ruled as sole emperor until his death in 360. Christian writers have no good to relate of Constantius, partly because he accomplished little despite considerable effort, principally because he encouraged Arianism, which had continued to flourish despite condemnation at the Council of Nicaea. (See below, p. 67.) Apart from religious controversies, the major concern of Constantius' reign was the critical situation along the frontier in the west. So dangerous did the situation become on the Rhine, that he finally sent his only remaining cousin, Julian, to Gaul to drive back the Franks. Constantius never quite trusted Julian, however, and became even more concerned when he learned of his success against the Germans and his popularity with the troops. When he directed Julian to send him many of his best troops in order to assist in the campaign against the Persians, Julian's troops mutinied, acclaimed him emperor, and marched eastward to settle accounts with Constantius. Before the two armies could meet Constantius died and Julian succeeded.

Julian's short reign of two years has attracted considerable attention chiefly because of his efforts to revive paganism and to cripple Christianity. Until recently he was known as "Julian the Apostate," a title that reflects the abhorrence contemporary Christian writers felt for him. Their testimony is partially neutralized by that of the pagan Ammianus Marcellinus, who greatly admired the man. "Julian," he affirmed, "was a man to be classed with heroic characters, and conspicuous for the brilliancy of his exploits and his innate majesty." Julian's interest in paganism was probably sincere, although his militancy may have been the result of harsh treatment he suffered at the hands of Constantine's sons. His study of Greek philosophy led him to accept much of Plato's idealism without, however, suppressing his obsession with superstition, the common failing of the age. "He was rather a superstitious than a legitimate observer of sacred rites," observed Marcellinus, "sacrificing countless numbers of victims, so that it was reckoned that if he had returned from the Persian wars victorious, there would have been a scarcity of cattle."

Immediately upon his accession, Julian announced his repudiation of his Christian faith, recalled heretical exiles—whether in the interest of tolerance or to cause harassment to the Christian community is not clear—and deprived the Christian church of the privileges and properties earlier emperors had granted it. His decree forbidding Christians to teach in the schools unless they apostasized, even his admirer Marcellinus classified as a "cruel one." What Julian appears to have had in mind as the future religion of the empire was an amalgam of Neo-Platonism, Stoicism, and paganism, over which the sun would shine as the supreme God, and with a liturgy, organization, even asceticism patterned after those of Christianity. It was these last features, Julian was convinced, that provided the Christian community its vigor. His concern with religion, together with the brevity of his reign, obscure his possession of real administrative ability and not inconsiderable military talent. In an effort to emulate the exploits of Alexander the Great and annex Persia, he undertook to conquer that empire and might have succeeded had he not been struck down by an arrow. The arrow came from an enemy, whether from a Persian or a Christian in his own ranks, is uncertain. With his death died Roman paganism and the dynasty of Constantine.

Upon Julian's death, his soldiers acclaimed Jovian, commander of the imperial bodyguard. The new emperor made peace with Persia by surrendering eastern Armenia and the territory east of the Tigris as well as the powerful Roman fortress at Nisibis, just west of the river. Of less questionable merit was the edict of toleration he issued and his repeal of Julian's anti-Christian legislation. When he died eight months later, the leading military and civil officials agreed on Valentinian, a general who had earned his reputation fighting the tribes along the upper Danube. Because the Persians could be expected to remain quiet, Valentinian left the east to his brother Valens, while he turned his attention to the Rhine frontier. There he gained impressive victories over the dangerous Alemans, Franks, and Saxons, and greatly improved the frontier defenses. Valentinian was an able, somewhat violent man, who ruled the empire with a strong hand for almost a dozen years. When he died, following a fit of anger, no emperor ever again ruled with such authority.

The first clear sign of the coming fall of the empire, as opposed to its decline, came under Valens. Though he was successful in meeting new Persian attacks in the east, he decided, unwisely as it proved, to permit a large body of Visigoths and other Germans to cross the Danube into the empire. When these began to pillage the area (more about this later), he foolishly attacked them at Adrianople (378 A.D.) without waiting for the assistance of Gratian, who was bringing up an army from the west. (Gratian was Valentinian's son who had been left in charge of the west.) The Germans were victorious, killed Valens, and destroyed his army. His successor Theodosius managed to pacify the Goths and, following the death of Gratian, to re-establish one-man rule over the entire empire. The large Visigothic nation remained, however, within the imperial frontiers and under its own leaders. When Theodosius died in 395, he passed this dangerous situation on to his two incompetent sons, Honorius and Arcadius, who divided the empire between them. Never again was the empire united and, what was worse, never again was the emperor who ruled in the west free in the exercise of his authority. There was usually a general at hand, ordinarily a German, who "advised" him. In a very real sense, Roman im-

perial rule ran its course in the west in 395 A.D. with the death of
Theodosius.

Long before 395, however, the fabric of the empire had suffered
fundamental change. Though one may continue to speak of Roman
civilization, its character had altered basically from what had prevailed
during the second century. Even in agriculture, the most stable of
civilization's bases, significant developments had taken place. The
trend toward large private domains had continued, as was to be expected, but now with the approval, if not insistence, of the government. For with the weakening of the imperial bureaucracy as a result
of the turbulency of the times, the government found it impossible to
administer its extensive imperial domains and had frequently directed
proprietors to assume the cultivation of the public lands that adjoined
their own. Land, too, had become increasingly attractive to capital
during this period as a safer investment than industry, whereupon ex-
soldiers and officials who had somehow become affluent, joined members of the old senatorial aristocracy in competing for large estates.

A more significant development in agriculture was the measure of
control these proprietors came to exercise over the tenant farmers and
slaves who lived on their estates. Again, because of the growing inability of the imperial bureaucracy to exercise its authority, especially in
the rural districts, these proprietors had assumed a paternalistic supervision which all but shut out the government's voice. For this development, incidentally, the poor farmer was generally grateful, since the
proprietor could often furnish him the protection against the tax collector and perhaps against marauders which the government had become powerless to provide. Scholars have given the name patrocinium
to this type of patronage in which the peasant population, even entire
village communities, passed under the direct control of the territorial
landlords in their vicinity.

The rise of patrocinium should be linked with developments that
affected the condition of the peasantry itself and which became visible
soon after the collapse of *Pax Romana*. The civil wars of the third century led to the impoverishment of the peasantry, directly through the
devastation they produced, indirectly through the heavier taxes and
increased services these wars entailed. It was inevitable, too, that as
imperial authority weakened, these burdens should fall more heavily
upon the small farmer who could not protect himself, less so upon the
influential owners of the latifundia. Furthermore, though population

declined during this period, the needs of the government mounted because of the wars and the demands of the soldiers, for which reason the burden of taxes weighed ever more heavily upon the farmers who remained. What most small farmers did as a consequence was to abandon their lands and join the tenants already working the estates of the large landowners in the vicinity. There many of them found little relief, for as tenants they discovered it was just as difficult to meet rental demands of the landlords as it had been impossible as free farmers to meet tax assessments. When they became involved in debt, they simply threw up their leases and departed, to try their fortune elsewhere. This development the government could not tolerate since it depended so heavily upon the land tax. It therefore intervened, and in order to protect the landlords and enable them to pay their taxes, it attached these tenants to their estates and deprived them of their freedom to move. Under Diocletian such a step had become imperative since the new tax that he introduced was based directly upon units of productive land, that is, land that was producing a return. Unless labor remained on hand to work this land, it could not produce. The result was a gradual rooting of the peasantry to the soil and the rise of the colonate, an institution which Constantine's decree of 332 A.D. made permanent and hereditary.

A similar lack of freedom to move or exchange occupations came to prevail among large sections of the industrially employed in the late third and fourth centuries, and for substantially the same reason. In order to secure the land tax which was paid in kind, the government depended principally upon the landed aristocracy. To secure services and equipment, it made use of professional colleges or gilds. These colleges had sprung up during the Republic. They were voluntary associations of persons whose trade, profession, or cult worship was similar and who for social reasons had organized such groups. As these colleges grew in size and number, the government which had first distrusted and suppressed them, began to make use of them. It first called upon those which were engaged in the procurement and distribution of such necessities as bread, wine, and oil for the huge population of Rome. By the early third century the government had assumed control of a majority of these associations (corporations). It was calling on them for services not only in the city of Rome but for the army as well, also in the collection of the land tax which, because it was being collected in kind, had created an enormous demand for transport and warehousing services and facilities. Inasmuch as these corporations could not provide such extensive services unless their membership remained stable, the government changed their voluntary membership into a hereditary obligation; in fact it might force men in less essential occupations to join them when the need arose.

A third group, the curials, was also caught up in the government's desperate efforts to cope with the crises of the third and following centuries. These were the same curials—merchants, industrialists, land-owners—who had once constituted the prosperous ruling element in the municipalities throughout the empire. As long as the empire prospered, their responsibilities, which included maintaining the public post and collecting the tax from landholders in their vicinity, were not heavy. But with the deterioration of economic life, these duties became increasingly burdensome. Because deficiencies must be made up by themselves, the curials now attempted to surrender their status. Again the government intervened. This time it froze the curials in their position. To these curials and to the many more numerous *coloni* and *corporati*, the state had become a harsh master.

The most serious consequence of the regimentation of so large a segment of the empire's population was its deleterious effect upon public-spiritedness. Equally serious, and more immediately so, was the decline of morale in the army. How selfish it and its officers had grown was evident from the many emperors they had made and unmade during the third century, not for the common weal but to advance their own fortunes. No doubt many soldiers had never had the opportunity to develop a sense of public responsibility since they had been recruited in the frontier provinces and had taken permanent service there. In many more soldiers, Germans and Celts for example, there had never existed much possibility of any such sense of responsibility even taking root. Actually the most ominous development in the army during the second and third centuries was the empire's increasing reliance upon non-Roman recruits. The dominance of this element reflects itself in the meaning of the word *barbarus* (barbarian), which by 400 A.D. had taken on the connotation of a soldier. During the fourth century, it was not uncommon for Germans to become officers; in the fifth, to rise to the position of commander-in-chief. The two final steps would shortly follow, as we shall see, when a barbarian general like Stilicho would make himself master of his emperor, then when another, Odovacar, would simply shove the emperor aside and rule in his stead (see below, pp. 86, 92). There were other people besides curials, *coloni*, *corporati*, and soldiers who were lacking in public spirit. These included the imperial bureaucracy and senatorial aristocracy whose ranks were permeated with corruption. If these last abused their positions of trust, why should soldiers not do the same? And under the circumstances, who should blame the common people for refusing to serve?

As the economic and social fiber of the empire decayed, so did the arts. Of great writers there were none after the second century, hardly even poor ones in the third. Ausonius' verses are typical of the best of the period, graceful and stylistically correct, yet devoid of substance and imagination. Even Ausonius recognized his limitations. "I know readers will find my poor verses wearisome," he wrote, "for such is indeed their merit." Somewhat superior was Prudentius' verse, not because he was a better poet, but simply because he was a Christian and had something to inspire him. One notable exception brightens the otherwise uninspiring history of the period's literature. That is the name of Ammianus Marcellinus. The ambition of this historian was to provide a respectable continuation to the superb historical writing of Tacitus. On the basis of what remains of his efforts, one would grant him possibly greater objectivity than Tacitus, but nothing approaching his literary style. Still, Ammianus Marcellinus had no illusions concerning his talents, for he confessed: "All this I, a Greek by birth and formerly a soldier, have related . . . to the best of my ability. . . . Let better men who are in the flower of their youth and possess greater talents, write of what I have left."

The last fine sculpture of any of the emperors is a bust of the wretch Caracalla. During the century that followed there is a blank, then a stylized portrait of Constantine. By presenting an idealized emperor, Constantine's sculptor hoped to hide the fact that he was no longer master of his chisel. The men who did the sculptures for Constantine's arch of triumph, however, proclaimed the fact of their inferiority. There next to the dull, shapeless figures that they carved are excellent reliefs Constantine ordered removed from older structures in order to add a beauty to his monument which none of his own artists was able to provide. The Romans continued, nevertheless, to throw up impressive structures well into the fourth century; witness the Basilica of Maxentius and the Church of St. John Lateran that Constantine had erected.

The only significant development in religion apart from the continued growth of Christianity was the rise of Neo-Platonism. The third-century philosopher Plotinus has been called its founder. He was the most important of a number of thinkers who sought to combine the idealism of Plato with the mysticism of the eastern Mediterranean.

Plotinus maintained that the body was corrupt and that the happiness of the pure spirit would come only with death. Before death, however, a person could free himself from the bonds of the body by means of mystical contemplation and thereby identify himself with the Mind of the universe. So substanceless a creed would have appealed to few, but under the influence of several of Plotinus' admirers, notably Porphyry, his corrupted mysticism became a religion and a popular one. It tended to absorb into itself most of Roman paganism, provide it a philosophical appeal, and make room within its complex of beliefs for all the pagan deities including the worship of the emperor. Only the Christians held aloof, for which reason the sole unifying element in the confusion of Neo-Platonism's superstitious beliefs was its fear and hatred of Christianity.

This was Rome in the centuries of its decline, an aging giant headed inexorably toward destruction. What were the causes of its decline? What had gone wrong? How was it possible for the most powerful and advanced of ancient civilizations to have so weakened as to succumb to folk who were not only less civilized, but even less numerous as well? Ever since the German Visigoths sacked the city of Rome in 410 A.D., thinkers have been pondering this question, from St. Augustine to Petrarch, to Montesquieu and Gibbon, down to modern thinkers like Spengler, Toynbee, and Dawson. No new generation of scholars appears entirely content with the explanations earlier writers have proposed. As each scholar takes up and turns this many-sided problem over in his mind, it reveals, like a diamond of many faces, new facets that seemingly escaped earlier investigation.

The first name to come to mind of those who contemplated Rome's decline is that of Edward Gibbon, and his thoughts are among the most provocative. He subscribes to the theory which was popular among ancient historians, that nations rise, mature, and decay in accordance with the pattern, if not law, of history. In the case of Rome, there were inordinate prosperity and bigness which aggravated that situation. "Prosperity ripened the principle of decay; the causes of destruction multiplied with the extent of conquest, and, as soon as time or accident had removed the artificial supports, the stupendous fabric yielded to the pressure of its own weight." To the reader who found that explanation unconvincing, Gibbon offered as a contributing factor the rise of Christianity, with whose otherworldly philosophy, its doctrine of "patience and pusillanimity, the sacred indolence of the monks," the Roman pagan genius simply refused to be reconciled.

Even those historians who do not accept the incompatibility that Gibbon painted between Christianity and Roman civilization agree with him in looking inside Rome for the sources of its decline. Few pay great attention to the vigor and number of the threatening tribes along the northern frontier; to the fact that as early as the second century B.C., when the state was still in good health, it seemed only a remarkable general such as Marius could save the Republic; to the fact that though these tribes were inferior in number, in terms of warriors they were not, since all able-bodied men fought; to the fact that they fought with the devotion of fathers and husbands anxious over the fate of their families, as contrasted to the many halfhearted, self-serving soldiers who joined the Roman army for a means of livelihood.

These scholars emphasize rather the decline in public spirit and morale as witness the growing unwillingness of the citizenry to serve in the army, and the general indifference non-Romans demonstrated as early as the third century to the acquisition of Roman citizenship. They regret the decline of the ancient republican virtues of sobriety, courage, and loyalty, even the bankruptcy of Roman religion, since there was no new source of idealism to replace these. Most Romans followed instead a variety of Oriental cults that tended to de-Romanize, if not demoralize, them. Instead of public-spiritedness, corruption became the mark of the senatorial aristocracy and imperial bureaucracy; instead of love of country, an apathy among the masses, who distrusted a regime that tolerated such corruption and at the same time froze them in their occupations or professions. Among more specific factors in the decline of Rome, certain scholars suggest the falling population of the empire and the manpower shortage this created. This in turn left the government no choice but to rely to an increasing degree upon non-Romans to protect the frontier. The shortage of manpower also caused the burden of taxation to grow ever heavier on a declining number of taxpayers who remained to pay it.

There are still other scholars, however, who refuse to accept as inevitable the gradual, inexorable deterioration of a people's spirit and condition which causes empires to decline and disappear. In their judgment, except for a series of fortuitous events, Rome might have continued on indefinitely. Had Valens been prudent and waited for Gratian, he would have defeated the Visigoths. These Goths would not have confronted Valens in the first place had the Huns not moved into

Europe in the late fourth century and have driven them to cross the Danube. (See below, p. 84.) Had the sons of Theodosius been young men when their father died and had they inherited his ability, the course of events would have been different. To the skeptic who dismisses these and other contingencies as purely temporary, there remains the solid fact that the eastern half of the empire continued on, even prospered, many centuries after Roman rule in the west had disappeared.

CHAPTER 2

The Rise and Triumph
of Christianity

"At that time Caesar Augustus issued a decree that a census of the whole world should be taken. So all the people went to be registered, each to his own city. And Joseph also went up from Galilee, out of the town of Nazareth, to David's town of Bethlehem in Judaea, since he was of the house and line of David. And he took with him Mary his wife, who was with child. While they were there her days were accomplished and she bore a son, her firstborn, whom she wrapped in swaddling-clothes and laid in a manger, because there was no room for them at the inn." So reads in brief the account which the Evangelist Luke gives of the birth of Jesus Christ, the child destined to become the most influential man in Western history. Though Luke was one of Christ's partisans, scholars do not question the essential accuracy of his account. No event in history has passed the test of more searching scrutiny than the existence of Christ.

The mighty Roman empire into which Christ was born remained ignorant of his existence until some years after his execution. Had ancient governments kept the records that modern states do, no doubt Pilate's scribe—Pilate was the procurator of Judaea—would have recorded how one Christ, troublemaker, had suffered crucifixion for causing the Jews of Jerusalem to riot. That, in any event, was probably the only notion Rome had of Christ, and no higher one of his followers. The historian Tacitus, who wrote about the year 100 A.D., spoke of the "notoriously depraved Christians" whom Nero charged with having deliberately fired the city of Rome in the year 64 A.D. "Their founder, Christ," Tacitus added, "was put to death as a criminal by Pontius Pilate, procurator of Judaea, in the reign of Tiberius." Suetonius, who wrote a short time after Tacitus, may have drawn upon the imperial archives, to which he had access, for his statement concerning disturbances in the city of Rome. He said these were instigated by the followers of the same "Chrestus," which disturbances led the Emperor Claudius in the year 49 A.D. to expel the Jewish community from the city. Though Christ was long dead before the year 49, his Jewish followers must have been causing dissension among the Hebrew population of Rome by claiming him to have been the Messiah, whence the rioting and their expulsion from the city.

There is little in pagan sources beyond these few references to Christ, so the reader must turn to the writings of the Christians, principally to the four Gospels, for an account of his career. These Gospels pass over with little or no mention the period of Christ's youth and early manhood, but provide a fairly full view of the man Christ: of the nature of the "good news" (gospel) he began to preach when he attained his late twenties, of the miracles he performed in order to convince his listeners of his divinity, and of the growing opposition to Christ on the part of the Scribes and Pharisees. These latter groups were teachers and experts in Jewish law whom Christ embittered by his claim to be the son of God and by his attacks on them as self-righteous hypocrites who had subverted the law of Moses and the prophets. Moses and the prophets, so Christ affirmed, had defined man's duty to his Creator as twofold: first, to love God; second, to love one's neighbor. These two laws Christ adopted as the foundation of his, the "new law," and to these he joined a strict insistence upon penance. "Unless you do penance," he warned his listeners, "you shall all perish."

The Pharisees were able in time to prevail upon Pilate to order the execution of Christ, but they could not extinguish his ideas. Those men who accepted his doctrines, the Christians, steadily increased in number—how rapidly and to what extent it is difficult to determine. By the early second century pagan Rome began to express concern. Tacitus noted that, despite the "temporary setback" occasioned by Christ's execution, the "pernicious superstition broke out afresh." If this disturbed him, so did it disturb his contemporary, Pliny the Younger, governor of the province of Bithynia. He wrote to the Emperor Trajan to warn him about the growth of the movement, since "this contagious superstition is not confined to the cities only, but has spread its infection among the neighboring villages and country. . . ." To the exultant Tertullian, Rome had already lost the battle. "We appeared only yesterday," he boasted in 200 A.D., "and already we have filled the earth." Everything that Rome held sacred—its cities, camps, councils, even forum—they had appropriated. "We have left you nothing but your temples." Even these would not long remain pagan, so the augur warned Alexander Severus, should the emperor persist in his plan to place an image of Christ in the Roman pantheon.

Few scholars have given the phenomenon of Christianity's growth deeper consideration than the historian Gibbon. The first cause to which he credits its growth was "the inflexible and . . . intolerant zeal of the Christians." Of such Christians, the most zealous was surely St. Paul. Paul's letters suggest a zealot who was forever on the move and usually in danger, if not from his ubiquitous persecutors, then from the perils that generally attended ancient travelers. Some may question the tradition of Paul's journeying as far west as Spain, although the tradition that attests to his death in Rome is fairly well substantiated. So much was St. Paul considered a partner with St. Peter in laying the foundation of the church, that it was only in the thirteenth century that the pope dropped his name from the formula upon which he officially based his claims to primacy. Paul, not Peter, persuaded the Christian community to separate itself from the Jewish and to develop its own distinctive theology, nor did any apostle contribute more than Paul to defining and applying the principles that molded early Christianity.

As a second factor in the spread of Christianity Gibbon lists the promise of immortality. To the ancient world of two thousand years ago when most men were convinced that supernatural powers controlled the forces of nature and guided the destinies of the world, and when death from illness and disease was so constant a companion, the gospel of immortality was a most appealing one. Upon these same people the miracles which Christ and his apostles were believed to have worked must have proved a powerful influence, so argues Gibbon, who lists miracles as a third factor. As a fourth factor he admits the high moral appeal of Christianity, which many people found attractive in an age such as ancient Rome's, whose moral decadence was so universal it was even pandered to by religious cults. A final, fifth factor to which Gibbon traced the growth of Christianity was the organization of the Christian church, more specifically the emergence of the episcopal form of government. This served to entrust authority into the hands of men whose prudence and general worthiness most frequently recommended for selection.

Had it not been for Gibbon's cynicism on the subject of religion, he might have included the persecution that Christianity suffered at the hands of the Roman state as a significant factor in its growth. But such an admission he could not bring himself to make. His own painful religious experience—raised a devout Anglican, converted to Roman Catholicism, only to be "reconverted" by a Calvinist minister with whom his horror-stricken father sent him to live when he learned of his "papism"—left him skeptical of the usefulness of faith and the sincerity of believers. He tended, therefore, to dismiss the traditional accounts from the early centuries that boasted of thousands upon thousands of martyrs as sheer propaganda. Even a sympathetic reader of these early accounts would have to admit that their Christian authors were less historians than preachers, their purpose more to edify the contemporary reader than to furnish factual statistics to the modern scholar. Yet since ancient methods of suppression were woefully inefficient by modern standards, and a poorly enforced persecution worse than none, one may ascribe a good bit of truth to Tertullian's defiant boast to the Roman authorities: "We grow the more numerous, the more frequently you cut us down. For the blood of Christian martyrs is seed." Such persecution must surely have spurred the zeal of the persecuted, have driven them to greater proselytizing efforts, have served to close their ranks against dissension from within and attacks from without, while bringing knowledge of the movement to non-Christians and arousing their admiration.

Once Rome discovered the nature of the Christian creed, its hostile reaction was inevitable even though few ancient states showed themselves more tolerant of alien religions and institutions. On two issues even tolerant Rome was insistent: first, that all men, whatever their creed, recognize the divine nature of the Roman state and pay it homage; second, that no association be permitted to exist which might conceivably pursue goals inconsistent with those of the state. The sole exception Rome allowed on this score was that of the Jews. Once the Roman state had concluded, after several attempts, that Jews, despite the harshest measures, would not pay homage to the cult of Augustus, it extended that nation toleration. That people was too small to pose any threat. Christians, on the other hand, constituted a sect, and a most aggressive one, with a missionary zeal suggestive of modern Communism. Its numbers were bound to increase. Before such a threat there could be no tolerance.

That the Roman emperors might actually have been convinced Christianity was a threat to the state few Christian apologists were ready to believe. They emphasized rather the barbarousness of the

Roman government, an argument the more plausible since it was the infamous Nero who initiated their persecution. The fact remains, nevertheless, that Christians suffered martyrdom not only under Nero, but during the reigns of the Good Emperors as well. The octogenarian Polycarp was executed during the reign of Antoninus Pius; Justin Martyr, during that of Marcus Aurelius. These persecutions have another facet that Christians are apt to find disturbing, namely, the general approval accorded them by the Roman populace. When Nero placed the onus for firing Rome on the Christians, he shrewdly selected as scapegoats a group that already suffered the opprobrium of the masses. Though the modern Christian reader may allow something for Tacitus' rhetoric, that historian's denunciation of Christians is apt to make him squirm. Tacitus writes how after Christ's execution the movement had reappeared, "not only in Judea where the mischief had originated, but even in Rome, whither all things horrible and disgraceful flow, from all quarters, as to a common sewer, and where they are encouraged."

That virtuous emperors persecuted Christians requires little explanation. The Roman state had long feared any kind of associations, and had suppressed such groups as the colleges of artisans, for example (see above, p. 36), until it had discovered a use for them. A more fundamental reason for Rome's fear of Christianity stemmed from the refusal of Christians to recognize the unquestioned supremacy of the Roman state in all matters, specifically matters dealing with religion. While Christians were willing to acknowledge and respect Rome's authority in civil and political affairs, they could not accept her claims to being a deified state nor, of course, her insistence that all subjects show her the reverence of a divinity. This refusal Rome felt she could not tolerate inasmuch as her very existence, her right to exercise authority, rested upon the principle of her divine character. When Christians, therefore, refused to worship an image of the deified Augustus as symbolic of the divine Roma, they were simply announcing their disloyalty.

What accounted for popular hostility toward Christians is less easy to determine. They suffered, to be sure, the ill will which has traditionally been the lot of minority groups. They refused to participate in popular religious exercises and to attend civic festivals because of their semireligious or immoral character. In not mingling with others on such occasions, they practiced the clannishness common to groups that suffer persecution. Although it was common for a cult to restrict attendance at its liturgies to the initiated, the secrecy of Christian rites led to the most preposterous charges since membership in the Christian Church was so difficult to achieve. Pliny in his letter to the Emperor Trajan appears most surprised to have nothing more horrible to report, after torturing two Christian deaconesses in order to ascertain precisely what monstrous things such Christians might be doing in secret, than that they partook of food at their rites, but "food of an ordinary kind." All he "could discover was evidence of an absurd and extravagant superstition."

The bloodiest persecution was that which Diocletian ordered in 303 A.D., just two years before his retirement. That Christian writers such as Eusebius lived through its horrors, may explain their tendency to attribute comparable severity to earlier persecutions. In this they probably erred. That Diocletian's order resulted in the destruction of some forty places of Christian worship in the city of Rome alone, suggests that Christians previously had been enjoying a large measure of safety, even openly practicing their religion. Still, from Tacitus' account it would appear likely that the profession of Christianity was already viewed as a crime in Nero's day. It surely was in Trajan's, as evident from the testimony provided by his correspondence with Pliny. This correspondence also throws light on the intensity and thoroughness of such persecution. Pliny had written to Trajan for a clarification of imperial policy concerning the punishment of Christians: whether they were to be punished for the mere profession of Christianity or only for the crimes customarily attributed to that sect. From the nature of Trajan's reply—"Do not go out of your way to look for them. If indeed they should be brought before you and the crime [of being a Christian] is proved, they must be punished"— scholars have concluded that it was ordinarily only bishops and presbyters who stood in any great danger of prosecution. Yet there must have been occasional governors and city officials who did "go out of their way." How else account for the question that constantly arose in Christian communities during the second and third centuries, over what to do with those Christians who had foresworn their faith when threatened with execution and who wished subsequently to be reinstated? And in any age which still accepted the existence of supernatural powers who might grow irritable over the presence of such nonconformists as Christians, these latter stood in fairly constant danger of being sacrificed to appease them. "If the Tiber overflows," complained Tertullian, "if the Nile does not overflow, if there is a drought,

48 THE MIDDLE AGES

an earthquake, a scarcity, a pestilence, straightway the people cry:
'The Christians to the lions.'"

That the policy concerning persecution of Christians reflected the
will of the individual emperor is graphically revealed by the experience of Origen. He preached before the mother of the Emperor Alexander Severus upon her request, but died as a result of injuries
suffered during the persecution of Decius. Gallienus reversed the
persecution policy of his father Valerian and even permitted Christian
communities to recover properties the state had confiscated.

The first official decree of toleration was that issued by Galerius in
311. Eight years after he had induced his father-in-law Diocletian to
introduce persecution, he had finally been obliged to admit that re-
pression had proved a failure, for which reason he was rescinding
the decree. "Christians might again exist and have their meetings,"
he announced, for which indulgence they "should pray to their God
for our welfare, for that of the commonwealth, and for their own."
Two years later, in 313, appeared the more famous decree of toleration,
the so-called Edict of Milan, according to tradition issued under the
names of the Emperors Constantine and Licinius. The circumstances
that attended the issuance of this decree are not entirely clear. It appears that Constantine, after his victory over Maxentius in 312, granted
Christians toleration, then shortly after at Milan in 313 persuaded
Licinius to do the same for the people of his Asian provinces, which
Licinius did by letter from Nicomedia. Since Licinius subsequently
reintroduced persecution in his provinces, it was only with his defeat in
324 that persecution finally ceased. (As noted above, the Emperor
Julian revived persecution during his brief reign.)

To refer to Constantine's initial and subsequent decrees as granting toleration to Christians leaves a faulty impression. The decrees
went considerably beyond extending toleration. Even Galerius' decree
had already represented a revolutionary reversal of policy. Instead
of hostility and persecution, the Roman state now engaged to accept
Christians as entitled to the same rights as other subjects. They might
worship in their own churches, for instance, and instead of doing
homage to the deified Augustus, the government would now be satisfied with a simple prayer for the well-being of the emperor and that
of the state. Constantine went still further. Hardly had he extended
Christians toleration in 313, than he followed this up with other decrees
that gradually established the Christian church as a semiofficial organ

of the state. He granted Christian priests the same privileges that pagan ministers enjoyed, such as exemption from heavy municipal burdens, and he indemnified Christian communities for property they had lost during the recent persecutions. A little later he had the state assume the cost of maintaining the clergy on the principle that the Christian church was an institution of public usefulness. So he announced: "the clergy provide a service which benefits the State and must, therefore, be rewarded with privileges." To bishops he granted the same juridical authority that magistrates possessed, permitted them to emancipate slaves and to decide private litigation, and ordered the adoption of the Christian calendar including the recognition of Sunday as a holyday. "All judges and city people and all craftsmen shall rest on the venerated day of the sun." The bishops who attended the Council of Nicaea (see below, p. 67) came by imperial post and were entertained in the imperial palace.

With these measures Constantine showed his favor to Christians; with others he revealed a growing hostility toward paganism. The old gods, with the exception of the *Sol Invictus* (the invincible sun), soon disappeared from imperial coins. Next Constantine forbade officials to preside at pagan rites, then halted the worship of the emperor which was perhaps the principal justification for paganism. He also banned gladiatorial combats, rewarded cities that had suppressed cult worship, and himself undertook the destruction of some pagan temples while plundering others of their bronze and marble in order to build his new Constantinople. The most eloquent step he took to proclaim a completely new order was the erection of a great church in Rome dedicated to the very Christian men and women his pagan predecessors had martyred.

Though Constantine's contemporaries were convinced that he was a Christian at heart, a measure of ambivalence in the emperor's attitude toward paganism has led some modern scholars to question his motives. Chief among those who attributed his act of toleration not to religious conviction but mere opportunism was Jakob Burckhardt. He maintained that Constantine simply recognized in the militant Christian minority a powerful source of strength for the state, and for that reason adopted policies that won him its adherence. The opposing view is more popular today, namely, that Constantine's pro-Christian policy arose from honest religious conviction. Point is made of the fact that Constantine's father, Constantius, had already been attracted to Christianity and had only adopted half-measures to suppress it when ordered to do so by Diocletian. When Constantine succeeded, he put an immediate stop to these measures and even selected Christian bishops to travel with him openly in order to serve him as advisors and to instruct him in the faith. The crucial moment in Constantine's life came during a dream when he beheld a vision containing the Christian monogram *Chi Rho,* accompanied by words of light reading *Hoc signo victor eris* (In this sign thou shalt conquer).* It was immediately after this incident that he ordered his soldiers to paint the Christian monogram on their shields so that he might gain the assistance of the Christian god in the coming battle with Maxentius. His subsequent victory over Maxentius and his much larger army at Milvian Bridge, left him fully convinced of the omnipotence of the god of the Christians.

That Constantine continued to use the symbol of the *Sol Invictus* carries no significance. The figure had become nothing more than the symbol of the supreme being, which explains why Christians selected the birthday of the *Sol Invictus,* the winter solstice, to mark the birth of Christ. Though Constantine also retained the title *pontifex maximus,* he did this probably only as a sop to pagan sentiment that remained strong among the Roman aristocracy. He never presided in that role. And if he put off baptism until his death, so did many other convinced Christians. There appears little doubt that had Constantine lived some years longer, he would have ordered the suppression of paganism.

When Constantine extended his favor to the Christian church it had already evolved a relatively stable government, although the outlines of that evolution are indistinct. The periodic destruction of records during the centuries of persecution permitted little written evidence to survive which might have dealt with the subject of the organization and administration of the early Christian church. From the Acts of the Apostles the picture emerges of St. Peter and other apostles managing the affairs of the struggling Christian community, sending out missionaries, and resolving differences over faith and practice. The reader also meets such officers as overseers (episcopi), elders (presbyters or priests), disciples, and deacons, all assisting the apostles

* This account is based on Lactantius. For another description based on Eusebius, see above, p. 31. András Alföldi in his *The Conversion of Constantine and Pagan Rome* (Oxford, 1948, p. 18) makes a strong case for the reading *Hoc signo victor eris.*

with their responsibilities. Doubtless both the titles of these officials and their responsibilities were shared somewhat indiscriminately. The only real power which appears to have set a certain group apart from the others was the laying on of hands, a rite which the apostles derived from Christ. By means of this rite, they conferred upon respective candidates the right or faculty to carry out the duties and assume the prerogatives of their particular office. Yet it is not clear whether all bishops, and only bishops, exercised this authority. That the small province of Africa boasted some ninety bishops in the third century suggests a church organization that had still not precisely determined the separate roles of bishop and priest.

What contributed powerfully toward the evolution of a hierarchy, that is, of a system of officials ranked according to authority, was the gradual localization of the bishop. Once he ceased being itinerant and instead became identified with a particular city or diocese (as the area under the jurisdiction of the bishop was called), the fluidity of the early missionary church came to an end. The first sees, that is, the seats of the first bishops, quite naturally appeared in the larger cities of the east, in Jerusalem, Antioch, and Alexandria, and then in Rome. Because of the antiquity of these sees and the importance of the cities, their bishops enjoyed from the beginning a position of precedence over other bishops. In time this precedence gained recognition in the title of patriarch which was reserved to them. In the fifth century, upon the insistence of the emperor, the bishop of Constantinople was admitted to this select company. Somewhat later the position of archbishop emerged as the large number of bishops made this development advisable. He was a bishop who ordinarily occupied the see in the largest city in the area, and who, because of that fact, frequently gained or was given a measure of administrative (never spiritual) authority over the other bishops in the province. The archbishop might bear the name metropolitan, his subject bishops being designated suffragans. But all bishops shared in ruling the church, and in this capacity would occasionally convene in provincial synods to discuss doctrinal and disciplinary problems. In the early centuries the decisions of such councils were generally regarded as binding. In matters of smaller moment, the word of the local patriarch might be decisive.

No facet concerning the organization of the early church remains more obscure or controversial than the position of the bishop of Rome. Was he designated from apostolic times as the first bishop of Christendom with authority over all other bishops, a position he apparently enjoyed in the sixth century, or were accident and circumstance principally, if not solely, responsible for that development? What renders this a difficult question is, first, the paucity of ancient evidence, and second, the mass of conflicting literature contributed by ancient and medieval polemicists who had a thesis to uphold. Those men who championed the primacy of the bishop of Rome as one investing him with highest authority in the hierarchy quite naturally emphasized scattered bits of evidence that served to enhance those claims. The opponents of primacy just as staunchly concentrated their attention on those bits that appeared to deny this. What the historian does in similar situations is let the evidence speak, only here there remains little evidence to listen to.

One clear point in the controversy is the basis of the pope's claim to primacy. This is set forth in the Petrine doctrine. According to this doctrine, Christ appointed Peter to a position of leadership among the apostles. For substantiation of this claim, among other biblical texts to which proponents of Roman primacy appeal, is that in Matthew (16:18): "Thou art Peter, and upon this rock I will build my church." The next step in the doctrine is the strong tradition that Peter was the first bishop of Rome, whence follows the conclusion that he passed on to his successor and subsequent bishops of Rome his position of primacy over all the bishops of Christendom.

A second fact that protrudes above the sea of uncertainties pertaining to this issue over the primacy of the bishop of Rome is the absence of any such institution as the papacy in the early centuries. For many centuries bishops generally were honored with the title "papa," and it may not have been reserved to the bishop of Rome before the eleventh. Then there is a third fact which tends to balance this last, namely, the persistence with which the bishops of Rome pressed their right to primacy. The first clear expression of this appears in the letter that Clement, bishop of Rome, directed to the church at Corinth in 95 A.D. in which he chided them for their factiousness and warned them to heed his instructions since these carried divine approval. After Clement's letter there is only silence until Victor (189–199) excommunicated the bishops of Asia Minor for refusing to celebrate Easter on Sunday after the Roman fashion, but instead following traditional Jewish usage.

The circumstances that attended Victor's excommunication justify a closer look at this incident. First of all, Victor took the initiative in regularizing this matter, a right or prerogative that was presumably his to exercise. He requested the different metropolitans to convene synods and discuss the matter, and upon their near-unanimous agreement to accept Roman usage, sent out instructions accordingly to all of Christendom. But opponents of Roman primacy quickly point out that Victor's excommunication of these bishops drew sharp criticism from other bishops as being not only too harsh but as exceeding his authority. Even Irenaeus, bishop of Lyons, a loyal champion of primacy, remonstrated with Victor on the score of disturbing customs of such antiquity. It should also be noted that the Asian bishops ignored Victor's sentence. They waited until the Council of Nicaea had passed on the matter in 325 before conforming. A modern scholar comments: "The real significance of the incident is its value as a precedent for subsequent imperialism by the Roman bishop."*

The bishop of Rome's greatest opportunity for implementing his claims to primatial authority came with the accession of Constantine —but he failed to exploit it. Given Constantine's willingness to defer to Christian bishops and his own absorption with imperial problems, there is no reason to believe that he had any desire initially to interfere in ecclesiastical affairs. There is every reason to believe that he would have thrown his full authority behind papal leadership had this been a fact. He seems actually to have been irritated when the Donatists appealed to him, rather than to the bishop of Rome or to a synod, in a dispute over the see of Carthage. Unfortunately Sylvester (314– 335), who was bishop of Rome during the greater part of Constantine's reign, lacked either the necessary authority to assert his leadership or the aggressiveness to assume it. Little authentic information survives concerning Sylvester, much that is legend, notably the Donation of Constantine by which act the emperor supposedly gave the pope control of the west and the entire church. (See below, p. 390.) One may safely state that Sylvester's failure to solve doctrinal and disciplinary disputes led Constantine to bypass him and to seek solutions to such problems from imperial councils such as that at Nicaea. In addition to delaying the establishment of primacy, Sylvester's quiescence opened the door to imperial interference which continued to plague the church for many centuries to come.

In one respect Sylvester's lack of aggressiveness may have paid dividends. Whether by design or accident, he failed to join the hundreds of other bishops who met at Nicaea in 325 to resolve the problem of Arianism. (See below, p. 67.) His absenting himself established a use-

* Edward G. Weltin, *The Ancient Popes*. Westminster, Md. (1964), p. 95.

ful precedent. The bishop of Rome should not participate personally
in such gatherings lest he find himself being classified simply as another bishop. Many of these councils proved, furthermore, to be affairs
as boisterous as they were fruitless. That the bishop of Rome held aloof,
therefore, did him no harm; quite the reverse. For as opposed to wrangling Eastern bishops disputing bitterly over theological subtleties, the
absent bishop of Rome presented by contrast an image of dignity and
moderation, if somewhat anti-intellectual stolidity. He became the logical person to whom Eastern bishops might appeal in their disputes
with one another.

One might even submit that the bishop of Rome and his advisors
inherited those same statesmanlike qualities which enabled the ancient
Romans to acquire and rule so large an empire. The bishop of Rome
was concerned above all with order and institutional growth, not with
dogmatic niceties. It is perhaps no exaggeration to say that were it
not for the grave heresies of Arianism, Nestorianism, and Monophysitism, which Eastern bishops hatched and fought over during the fourth,
fifth, and sixth centuries, the practice of appealing to the arbitrament
of the bishop of Rome would never have been established. As it was,
the most striking progress toward the goal of primacy was achieved
during these very centuries and quite probably as the direct result of
such wrangling in the East with subsequent appeals to Rome. The
Council of Sardica (343) recognized the right of bishops to appeal to
Rome, and the Second Council of Constantinople (381) accorded him
primacy throughout Christendom. All that remained to complete the
development of primatial authority was accomplished during the strong
episcopates of Innocent I (401-417) and Leo I (440-461). Still the
bishop of Rome could never be sure when some Eastern bishop or
bishops might question his authority, and the permanent schism of
1054 proved simply the last in a series between Eastern Church and
Rome. It should further be noted that the authority of the bishop of
Rome, even over Western bishops, was never so compulsive in the
Middle Ages as it came to be after the Protestant Reformation.

The most influential churchmen in terms of writings during the first
four centuries of the church's existence were not bishops of Rome. Of
the 135 authors St. Jerome listed in his *De Viris Illustribus,* only five
were popes and these appear among the minor writers. There were no
great scholars among the early popes. The term "father of the church"
applies, therefore, to few popes, but rather to other men, many of them

bishops, who by their writings on faith and morals contributed to the clarification, defense, or development of Christian theology during the early centuries of the church's existence. The term "father" is an apt one, for it was the efforts of men like Origen, Tertullian, Basil, Augustine, and Gregory the Great which gave the Christian church the character and form it was to carry during the medieval centuries to come.

What eventually swelled into a veritable flood of patristic literature remained little more than a trickle during the first century and a half of the Christian era, the age of the Apostolic Fathers. (These writers lived close to the time of the apostles.) What discouraged greater productivity during those years were the unsophisticated needs of the early Christian community, together with the strong expectation that the end of the world was imminent. What writings remain from this period include letters, gospels, acts, and apocalypses, among these the ones that eventually made their way into the New Testament. From this early period also date the first martyrologies.

Apologetic writings dominate patristic literature of the latter second century. The aim of such writings was the defense of Christianity against attacks from without, from Hebrews and pagans who accused Christians of disloyalty to the state, cannibalism, gross immorality, and atheism. Prominent among these apologists was Justin Martyr, martyred in Rome about 165. He addressed his *Apology* to the emperor, Antoninus Pius, in the hope of convincing him that Christians were virtuous and law-abiding subjects, and though not idolators, still not atheists. Justin's *Dialogue* takes the form of a discussion with a Jew named Trypho whom he seeks, unsuccessfully as it proves, to convince that Christ simply fulfilled the words spoken by the Hebrew prophets. Justin's knowledge of Greek philosophy led him to emphasize the high degree of compatibility between that philosophy and Christianity.

Patristic writing of the late second and third centuries devoted itself to the task of combating heresies. Among the more influential writers was Irenaeus, a Greek from Asia Minor, later bishop of Lyons, whose principal work, *Against All Heresies,* affirmed the apostolic succession of the Roman church and the unbroken tradition of orthodoxy that the Roman see had preserved. Irenaeus appears to have been the first scholar to make references to the New Testament in his writings. Apologetics was but one of several major concerns to which Origen, the foremost and most prolific of Christian scholars, devoted his extraordinary talents. His monumental study of the text of the Old Testament alone ran to nine thousand pages. So extraordinary was his reputation for learning that he was provided a staff of secretaries to take down his dictation. Almost nothing remains of his voluminous writings excepting some of his works that were translated into Latin. With complete justice has he been styled the father of Christian theology and the founder of biblical science.

The first distinguished church father of the Latin west was Tertullian (ca. 160–230). As a pagan, Tertullian taught rhetoric and practiced law, then became a convert and a priest. What Tertullian undertook, he attacked with a vigor that bordered on immoderation. In his first major work he directed a vehement attack on the Roman government for executing Christians and daring to justify that policy on the slanderous charges of cannibalism and gross immorality. Because as a youth he had himself been a dissolute pagan, he could counter charges of immorality against Christians with telling attacks on the viciousness of many pagan practices. Though he spent much effort in combating heresy and in explaining Christian doctrine, his most influential works were on the subject of Christian living. Tertullian was a rigorist. When the pope took a stand on the side of charity in extending the privilege of confession and reinstatement to persons guilty of grave moral lapses, he broke with Rome, joined the puritanical Montanist sect, then eventually organized a sect of his own. Despite his later heterodoxy, Tertullian's influence among Western church fathers in theology is surpassed only by that of St. Augustine.

The fourth and early fifth century produced a galaxy of eminent church fathers, including a number from the West which up to then had been largely silent. Among the most influential of Eastern fathers was Athanasius (295–373), who came into prominence during the course of the First Ecumenical Council at Nicaea (325). He attended this council as the principal advisor of Bishop Alexander of Alexandria, and so identified himself as the champion of Catholic Christianity that for the rest of his life he remained the prime target of Arian attacks. During the forty years that he occupied the see of Alexandria, no less than five times did they force him into exile. No Christian fought more courageously in defense of the divinity of Christ. "How could Christ make us divine," he demanded, "if He Himself was not God?" Of his works, which included a stream of polemical writings against Arianism in addition to scattered doctrinal and exegetical pieces, his *Life of St. Anthony* proved most important because of its influence upon the rise of Western monasticism.

Another church father who was caught in the bitter cross fire between orthodoxy and Arianism was Basil (330–379). His title "the Great" reveals the high regard the early church set upon his achievement. Basil's excellent education, which he completed at Athens where he met the future emperor Julian, served him well in his extended and bitter controversies with the Arians. Included among his writings are homilies, letters, dogmatic treatises, and, above all, ascetical and liturgical works which profoundly influenced the evolution of monasticism and liturgy in the East. Basil was also a man of action and an able administrator as well as a scholar. He abandoned a life of ascetic solitude, which he preferred, in order to wage a more direct war against Arianism and he also induced his close friend, Gregory of Nazianzen, to do the same. These two, together with Basil's brother, Gregory of Nyssa, also a bishop, were called the "Great Cappadocians," perhaps the most eminent triad of theologians in the history of the church.

Gregory of Nazianzen (329–389) was also involved in the long struggle with Arianism, more so in his writings than in personal controversy, which he shunned. In all, he occupied and resigned three sees including Constantinople. Although he was an eloquent preacher, his oversensitive nature left him ill-equipped to handle administrative responsibilities. For a few years he lived as a hermit, which was not unusual among Eastern Church fathers. What ranks him with the leading patristic writers are his writings on the subject of Arianism, his sermons, exegetical works, and several hundred letters. The literary quality of his Greek is high; less impressive, the poetic excellence of his verse even though one of his poems, that entitled "Soul and Body," Elizabeth Barrett Browning honored with an English translation.

The most influential name among Eastern Church fathers in the field of moral theology was that of John Chrysostom (345–407). John was born in Antioch and provided an excellent education by his widowed mother, with whom he lived until her death. For a few years he took up the life of a hermit, then returned to Antioch when his health gave way, became a priest, and in time gained such a reputation for oratory that people referred to him as the "golden-mouthed" (chrysostos). His attack as archbishop of Constantinople upon the low morals of the city touched too closely the person of the empress, so she ordered him into exile. Popular protests managed to block this first exile, although a second one a few years later sent him off to the Caucasus. He died from the rigors of the march. His best-known essay is entitled "On the Priesthood"; his greatest influence he exerted through his sermons and homilies. Though he was a learned theologian, he was first and foremost a moralist, forever reminding the faithful in his sermons that to live as Christians they must lead chaste lives and must share their means with the poor. "Never forget," he warned his listeners, "God has made you His friend."

While John Chrysostom was suffering persecution at the hands of the imperial court in Constantinople, Ambrose, one of the Latin church's leading fathers, was more than holding his own with the emperor in the West. Ambrose was a man of great stature. His integrity and dedication to truth gained the respect of all men. He was particularly popular with the people of the city of Milan, where the western emperor generally made his capital. And he stood high in the esteem of the Roman aristocracy. His father had been praetorian prefect of Gaul and he himself had risen to the position of governor of Liguria and Aemilia (northern Italy), when the people of Milan forced him to become their bishop.

As bishop, Ambrose strove through persistent study to remedy his lack of theological learning. Possibly because of those early deficiencies as a theologian, he appears from the beginning to have preferred the role of preacher discoursing upon Christian living to that of a writer of speculative erudition. This preference helps explain his unusual eloquence. So persuasively did he extol the virtues of virginity, for example, that ambitious mothers hesitated to allow their daughters to hear him preach. Augustine writes in his *Confessions* that he first came to hear Ambrose simply "in order to learn whether his eloquence matched his reputation." It was through his sermons and his personal influence in church and imperial circles that Ambrose left his mark. His best-known writing was "On the Duties of Priests." In this study he attempted to establish a system of Christian ethics with Cicero's moral essays and Christian theology to provide him a base. What gained him the affection of the Milanese was his humble, open manner and his accessibility. To the people his door was always open, so wrote Augustine, and he comments on the "multitudes of busy people whose weaknesses he served."

An incident took place in the spring of 386 which tells something of Ambrose's determination and resourcefulness. Justina, the mother of Valentinian II, was demanding that a church in Milan be turned over to the Arians of the city, and the emperor had issued the necessary orders. To block the seizure of the church, Ambrose organized the first recorded sit-down strike in history. He had the faithful of Milan occupy the church continuously day and night, in order to prevent the soldiers from entering and taking possession. After two weeks the emperor, who had hesitated to take a firm stand, canceled the order. What helped Ambrose gain the victory was a scheme he hit upon which he hoped would prevent the people from becoming bored during their long hours in the church. To lighten their burden, he introduced what might be called congregational singing and even composed hymns for the people to sing. This kind of singing became so identified with Ambrose that when songs were later introduced into the liturgy, they long went by the name of Ambrosians.

Ambrose's aristocratic origins and friends, his previous experience as an imperial governor, and his own courage and personality enabled him to deal with the imperial state more successfully than had any previous Christian bishop. He was the friend, even confidant, of several emperors, and on occasion used his good offices to ease political crises. His principal concern was that of defending what he considered to be the rights of the church vis-à-vis the state. He blocked the senate's attempt to restore the Altar of Victory in their chamber whence it had been removed, on the argument that since the empire was a Christian state, such an act would constitute an insult to the God of the Christians. Again, he prevailed upon the Emperor Theodosius to rescind his order that Christians rebuild a synagogue they had destroyed on the plea, among others, that it was not proper for Christians to erect non-Christian places of worship. On a later occasion he publicly denounced this same Theodosius for having ordered the brutal punishment of the seditious people of Thessalonica (Salonika) who had slain their military governor. On his orders the imperial troops slew seven thousand people, we are told, and Ambrose, in order to dramatize his disapproval, refused to hold services in the cathedral in Milan until the emperor had done public penance, which he did. "In matters of faith," Ambrose announced, "it is the bishops who are the judges of Christian emperors, and not the emperors who are the judges of the bishop." Though Ambrose appears to have treated the pope with respect, he dealt with church matters in northern Italy, Gaul, and the Balkans as though it was he, not the bishop of Rome, who was in charge. Both pope and emperor stood in awe of the great bishop of Milan.

Among contemporaries who stood in no awe of Ambrose was Jerome, the finest classical scholar among the church fathers of the west. Jerome excused himself for having omitted Ambrose's name from his *De Viris Illustribus* because Ambrose was still living. If Jerome simply employed this excuse to save himself from recording something uncomplimentary of Ambrose, as is suspected, it would probably have been one of the rare instances in his life when he was being diplomatic. For he seldom demonstrated any reserve in castigating the faults of contemporaries, whatever their importance and influence. Many high-placed ecclesiastics felt the sting of his tongue for their pride and laxity. Jerome "was of a restless, inquisitive, reforming temperament, and something of a trouble-breeder; he liked to go around doing good to those who did not like to be done good to."* What Jerome may have resented in Ambrose was the latter's eminence and the independent manner he assumed toward the papacy. Jerome was the secretary and principal adviser of Pope Damasus.

Jerome's fame among church fathers rests squarely upon his translation of the Bible which the Roman Catholic Church has used since the Middle Ages. Jerome undertook the immense task of preparing a new Latin translation only upon the insistence of Pope Damasus that there was nothing of which the church stood in greater need. As long as a multitude of variant versions and corrupt translations continued in use, there would be no end to theological controversy. Understandably Jerome hesitated to undertake the job. The project would be not only staggering in the amount and difficulty of the work demanded; it would also be a thankless task. "Is there a man," Jerome asked, "learned or unlearned, who will not, when he takes the volume into his hands and sees what he reads differs from what he had read time after time, break out immediately into violent language and call me a forger and a sacrilegious person, for having dared add anything to the ancient books, or to make any changes or corrections therein?" For twenty years Jerome labored at this endless job. The greater portion of the work of seeking out and collating the most ancient Greek, Hebrew, and Chaldaic manuscripts he performed himself. Only for the Chaldaic did he require an interpreter. The particular Latin style he chose to use deserves comment. Had he wished, he could have employed a highly literary Latin for his translation. Instead he selected a relatively simple Latin which ordinary people would find more comprehensible. This simpler Latin, together with the scholarly qualities of the translation, assured the popularity of Jerome's work. By the thirteenth century, it had become the common or vulgar version, whence the term Vulgate.

Jerome also produced treatises on a great many subjects. Among his most influential writings are those he composed on the subject of monasticism. His many letters reveal a wide variety of people with whom

* E. K. Rand, *Founders of the Middle Ages*. New York (1928), p. 105.

he corresponded. Included in these letters is one he wrote to a troubled mother who wished to know how to teach her little daughter her ABC's. For all his harshness, Jerome was a humble and kindly soul.

Among Jerome's younger contemporaries was one for whom he shared the universal respect of his age. This man was St. Augustine (354–430). We have a relatively clear view of Augustine from his *Confessions*, a sort of spiritual autobiography which he may have composed in order to proclaim the omnipotence of God's grace in his conversion and to disabuse admirers who had too high an opinion of him. Augustine leaves the reader convinced that it was God's grace, gratuitously bestowed, that brought him faith—unless this came by virtue of his mother Monica's unceasing prayers. Augustine tells how he stumbled from one error into another in his search for truth, from pagan philosophy to Manichaeism, to skepticism, the only constant theme in his life meantime being its dissoluteness. He had prepared himself to teach rhetoric, and it was his taking a position in Milan that led him to Ambrose. Upon Ambrose's advice, he turned back to the Bible, which he had earlier rejected as beneath study, was later converted, ordained a priest, then consecrated bishop of Hippo. For thirty-five years he zealously served the spiritual needs of his see. He died as the city was about to fall to the Vandals. (See below, p. 87.)

Augustine's influence runs deep through the Middle Ages. Even as late as the sixteenth century several Protestant Reformers adopted him as their inspiration. Everywhere in medieval thought scholars discover his ideas. Only Aristotle can compete with him in terms of influence upon Western thought, but that philosopher's impact came after the twelfth century. Students of philosophy have traced some of Augustine's ideas to Plato through Platonic philosophers of whom Augustine affirmed that "none came closer to us than they do." Yet the thoughts of none of these ancient writers, singly or in aggregate, dominates Augustine's genius. Augustine was one of the great seminal thinkers of all time. "In the history of Western thought few men have attained the profundity, the originality, and the intellectual stature of Augustine."[*] Yet whether he ponders his own thoughts, whether he draws upon others, upon philosophy, psychology, or history, Augustine's concern is always fixed: the rationalizing of the Christian faith in order to make it more intelligible to the believer. All knowledge must be made to serve

[*] J. A. Mourant, *Introduction to the Philosophy of Saint Augustine*. University Park, Pa. (1964), p. 3.

the one living God. The greater man's knowledge, the more capable
will he be, and the more willing, of serving that God.

After Augustine's conversion, his life assumed the even tenor which
he insisted should mark the life of every believer. It is with this thought
that he opens his *Confessions*. "You made us for Yourself, O Lord," he
wrote, "and we are restless until we rest in You." While his soul enjoyed this peace, his pen did not. He kept this busy throughout his life.
A great part of his writing gushed forth to refute the heretical views of
the Pelagians, Manichaeans, Arians, and Donatists. Here Augustine
revealed himself the fiery polemicist; he wrote with the urgency of a
man who felt the matter deeply. Other writings found him in a quieter
mood, when he composed treatises, for example, on different aspects
of Christian doctrine: on the Trinity, the church, on God, on the Psalms,
the Gospel of St. John whose mysticism intrigued him. For Augustine
was also a great mystic. In addition, he found time for treatises on the
liberal arts, on metaphysical problems, on cosmology, and epistemol-
ogy. His 300 letters and more than 360 sermons help swell the volume
of his writings to sixteen entire volumes in Migne (*Patrologia Latina*).

The secular reader will consider *The City of God* Augustine's most
notable work. As was the case with so much of his writing, something
had provoked Augustine into taking up his pen. In this instance it was
the charge certain pagans were making that Rome would not have
fallen to the Goths (see below, p. 87) had the city not abandoned its
pagan gods. The charge was, of course, ridiculous, so affirmed Augustine, who then proceeded to reach back into Roman history for earlier
calamities which that city had suffered. Where were Rome's gods
when those disasters befell her? A despicable lot of gods they were at
best! In any event, what had brought Rome to her knees was her vices.
Still the matter of her fall was actually of little consequence. Rome was
only a material city. Like all matter, she was bound someday to disappear. The only city of true importance was the City of God. Here those
men dwell who love God, whether they be toiling in this life or have
already passed over to heaven. Material evil will come to all, yet
"though good and bad men suffer alike, we must not suppose that there
is no difference between the men themselves, because there is no difference in what they both suffer. For even in the likeness of the suffer-
ings, there remains an unlikeness in the sufferers; and though exposed
to the same anguish, virtue and vice are not the same thing. For as the
same fire causes gold to glow brightly and chaff to smoke, and under
the same flail the straw is beaten small while the grain is cleansed

. . . so the same violence of affliction proves, purges, clarifies the good, but damns, ruins, exterminates the wicked." Such is the end for which God created man, that he grow strong and pure midst the trials and temptations of this earthly city in order to merit for himself the reward which awaits him in the eternal City of God.

The patristic age would have terminated with Augustine, so consummate was his theological learning and so extensive his writing, were it not for the appearance a century and a half later of Gregory the Great. Gregory's genius, that of organizer and administrator, complements the work of earlier fathers. They wrote of faith and morals. He sought the means of bringing their message to the semicivilized Germans who had taken over the west. Gregory's background was similar to that of Ambrose. He was born of a wealthy patrician family, entered the imperial service, and by the age of thirty had risen to the position of prefect of the city of Rome. A year later when his father died, he abruptly turned his back on a civil career and became a monk. The family palace in Rome he changed over to a monastery, the family fortune he used to found six other monasteries in Sicily.

Had Gregory consulted only his own wishes, he would have remained in his monastery, unknown and forgotten. Fortunately Pope Pelagius II thought otherwise. The church could ill afford the retirement of so dedicated and distinguished a young man. Upon the urging of the pope, Gregory set off for Constantinople to block, if possible, imperial interference in ecclesiastical matters, and to seek Byzantine aid against the Lombards. This assignment was distasteful enough for the would-be recluse, but worse followed in 590 when Gregory reluctantly allowed himself to be raised to the papacy. Too well did he realize how unmonastic his duties would be from now on. "Whoever is Pastor here," he complained, "is so overwhelmed with secular responsibilities that it is often hard to tell whether he is a pastor or a secular lord."

A less conscientious pontiff could have ignored some of the many responsibilities Gregory assumed. In his case, he might have pleaded ill health if nothing better. Not so Gregory. So tirelessly did he drive himself during the fourteen years of his pontificate, that it almost tires the reader to review the scope and variety of his activities. While he was pope, Roman senate and prefect disappear from view, so Gregory assumed their duties. This meant that it now became his responsibility to organize the defenses of the city against the Lombards, to raise troops, and to negotiate with potential allies. He also accepted as his obligation the care of the sick and needy of the city and of refugees who sought his protection. The letters which he sent regularly to the stewards who administered the papal estates upon which he depended for revenues reveal the born administrator, conversant with agricultural problems, and concerned about the efficient albeit honest exploitation of those estates. The low state of the church in Gaul disturbed him no end, but he could gain no concessions from the dissolute, ambitious Brunhild. (See below, p. 109.) Partly to offset his failure in Gaul, he sent St. Augustine and a band of forty monks to Britain to convert the pagan Angles and Saxons, a move that profoundly affected the cultural life of Britain and western Europe. He succeeded momentarily in thwarting caesaropapist policies of Byzantium, as well as the pretensions to equality put forth by Constantinople's patriarch. He set his hand to reforming the liturgy, so encouraged plain chant that it still bears his name, suppressed enclaves of Arians and Donatists where they still existed, and extended significantly papal rule in the west. This last he accomplished through a wide correspondence and by means of legates. He also received the loyal assistance of the Benedictine monks whom he freed from episcopal control in order to secure more faithful lieutenants of his own.

Gregory even found time to write. His writings were of a practical nature or intended to edify. He addressed them to priests and bishops whose duty it was to preach to the faithful, to convert the pagan, to live such lives of their own as would reflect their high mission. Because of the inadequate training of the clergy, they stood in great need of instruction on how best to discharge their responsibilities, how to admonish the many kinds of people they would meet, and they also needed spiritual literature to inspire them. In his most important book, *On Pastoral Rule*, Gregory considered all these matters. Of the character of the one to be chosen to guide others, he wrote: "It is necessary that in thought he should be pure, in action exemplary, discreet in keeping silence, helpful in speech, a brother to every one in need of sympathy, exalted above all in his love of contemplation; a humble and constant friend of the just, unyielding in his zeal for righteousness against the vices of evil-doers; never relaxing his concern lest his interior life suffer from concern with external matters, yet not permitting his solicitude for the interior life to lead him to neglect his responsibilities for external matters."

In Gregory's lengthy commentary on the Book of Job, popularly known as *Moralia*, he sought to construct a system of Christian ethics.

In his *Dialogues* he supplied the reader a wealth of edifying material built around the lives of saints, whose heroic virtues and the miracles they performed moved the faithful and confounded the unbeliever. He tells of the occasion when St. Benedict's monks were finding it impossible to move a stone at Monte Cassino. Though the stone was a large one, to be sure, under normal circumstances they should have been able to move it. So they appealed to Benedict, who simply made the sign of the cross over the stone, whereupon his monks moved it with ease. Gregory was not a historian, only a teacher and a most perceptive one. He instructed his missionaries in England to retain what pagan observances they could harmonize with Christianity. "For it is certainly impossible to root out all errors from stubborn minds at one stroke, and whoever wishes to ascend to the highest place, rises by degrees, step by step, and not by leaps."

A great deal of patristic writing arose out of the efforts of the church fathers to defend what they believed to be orthodox from opposing beliefs called heresies. Such heresies appeared almost as soon as Christians left the shelter of their Jerusalem community and came into contact with other beliefs outside. For several generations the letters that the apostles and their successors sent out to the scattering Christian communities helped counteract doctrinal divergencies, as did the New Testament when it appeared late in the second century. Yet the New Testament offered variant texts from the beginning, while a number of its passages invited conflicting interpretations. There were several fundamental Christian doctrines, the Trinity, for instance, and the nature of Christ, which were frankly mysteries. Until Christian leaders had reached substantial agreement on how the gospels should be understood and how several mysteries should be clarified, the door stood open to wide disagreement. Beyond conflicting texts and puzzling mysteries there existed other sources of doctrinal diversity. Some Christians, like Tertullian, demanded a more rigorous moral code; others wished it liberalized. Occasionally the emperor might insist upon his personal preference in the interpretation of Christian theology. Frequently political considerations affected the life of a heresy since these often followed national and territorial lines.

Scores of heresies come into view in patristic literature. Some pass by with scarcely more than mention, others receive extended consideration such as Irenaeus provides Gnosticism in his *Refutation*. Their study poses for the historian a major difficulty. For some heresies scarcely anything remains except their names. What literature he finds about other heresies is from the pens of their opponents who felt they had God's blessing in painting heretical doctrines and their authors in the darkest colors possible. The virulence of their attacks serves to obscure the fact that many Christians, even bishops, accepted on occasion a position that lay somewhere between the starkly orthodox and the clearly heretical. Pope Liberius (352–366) welcomed a delegation of semi-Arians to Rome, at a time when Athanasius was presiding over a synod in Alexandria which accepted as virtually synonymous *homoousios* and *homoiousios*, terms which at the Council of Nicaea had marked the two bitterly opposed positions regarding the nature of Christ.

Among the earliest heresies to vex the Christian church were Gnosticism, Docetism, and Montanism. All three represented attacks on Christ's human nature. Gnosticism attacked all matter as evil, which would rule out Christ's having had an ordinary human body. It held salvation attainable by means of mystical knowledge and contemplation. Docetism maintained that the body of Christ had been an illusion. He was only God, not man. Montanism preached a rigorous denial of the pleasures of this world and the necessity of unrelenting dedication of self to the task of sanctifying one's corrupt nature. Its founder Montanus claimed to have received a special inspiration from the Holy Spirit. Mani, who gave his name to Manichaeism, a far more dangerous heresy, claimed to be the Paraclete himself. This remarkable man had traveled all the way to China in search of religious creeds and philosophies. From Buddhism he borrowed the transmigration of souls, from Zoroaster the doctrine of two fundamental and eternal forces, one good, the other evil, the first identified with the spirit, the second with matter, who were joined in mortal and eternal conflict. The fact of man's dual nature, part flesh, part spirit, projected him inextricably into this conflict. From these religions and from Christianity Mani wove an appealing syncretism to which even the astute Augustine subscribed for nine years.

The most formidable heresy that threatened the early church appeared with Arianism in the fourth century. Its founder was Arius, a learned priest of Alexandria who had attacked the doctrine of Christ's divinity. His eloquence and the hymns he composed gained him considerable fame and followers, but the adverse judgment of a local synod in Egypt forced him to flee to Syria. Arius' views were not original, although no one before him had urged them with greater persuasiveness. Arius maintained that from all eternity there had been but one God, known theologically as the Father, who in the course of time had created all things that existed, including Christ, whom he had endowed with divine attributes. Such attributes made Christ an extraordinary person, in fact similar (*homoiousios*) to the Father, but nothing more. Arius' views, generally presented in more moderate form, gained wide acceptance in the East where there had always lurked some uneasiness over the doctrine of a dual-natured Christ composed of God and man.

In order to resolve the fierce controversy that threatened to disrupt the Christian church, Constantine summoned the bishops of Christendom to meet at Nicaea in 325 for the First Ecumenical Council. There at Nicaea Athanasius led a successful battle in defense of the view that Christ was of one and the same substance (*homoousios*) with the Father. Constantine ordered all those attending the council to accept the majority decision and exiled the two bishops who refused. Arianism proved unusually tough. When Constantine died a dozen years later, he had himself baptized by Eusebius, the Arian bishop of Nicomedia. His son, Constantius II, almost succeeded in establishing Arian Christianity throughout the empire. In 381 the Second Ecumenical Council at Constantinople confirmed and supplemented the decisions of Nicaea, which views were incorporated in the so-called Nicene Creed. Shortly after, Arianism disappeared in the East, although it lived on among the Germans in the West until the seventh century.

While Arianism was dividing the Christians in the eastern Mediterranean, the heresy of Donatism was harassing the West. This heresy had its name from Donatus, a schismatic bishop of Carthage, although his views were no more original than Arius'. It was his aggressiveness and theological acumen in pressing objections raised as early as the second century, against permitting disloyal Christians to return to the church and declaring invalid sacraments administered by unworthy priests, that brought him into prominence. Augustine's powerful defense of orthodoxy broke the back of Donatism, after which he turned his attention to Pelagianism, another heresy that had found a following in the West. Pelagius, a monk from Britain, questioned the doctrine of original sin and the need for baptism. According to Pelagius, man had never been so corrupted by sin as to lose the ability to attain a state of virtue that would gain him admittance to heaven without the grace of God.

The East meantime refused to settle down with the pronouncements of the Councils of Nicaea and Constantinople. For centuries it kept proposing new solutions to the problem of Christ's nature. One such solution bears the name of Nestorianism, from Nestorius, bishop of Constantinople. He proposed two natures in Christ, a divine and a human, each sharply distinguished from the other and associated only in a moral union. Christ in his divine nature did not suffer; in fact, Mary was not the mother of God (*theotokos*). She should properly be addressed simply as the mother of Christ.

Hardly had the Third Ecumenical Council of Ephesus (431) condemned Nestorianism than bishops and theologians began gathering at Chalcedon to judge the acceptability of Monophysitism. The irony of it was that many of the same men who had been stalwart defenders of Christ's uniquely divine and human nature against Nestorianism now found that they had stumbled into a heresy of their own. They preached that Christ had but one nature, his divine, a conclusion that the Fourth Ecumenical Council at Chalcedon (451) judged an oversimplification and condemned. Both Nestorians and Monophysites (Copts) have lived on into the present world, whose ecumenism experiences some difficulty in appreciating both the intensity and the point of these ancient theological controversies.

While orthodox theologians were contending with other theologians over what Christians should believe and do, there was emerging an institution of men and women in the eastern Mediterranean which dedicated itself exclusively to the practice of Christianity. That institution was monasticism. In challenging the statements of heretics and proving them false, the church fathers helped preserve orthodoxy. Yet had it not been for the example and achievement of the monks, that orthodox gospel of itself might not have endured. It is not easy to judge who made the greater contribution to Christianity, St. Augustine, the leading theologian of the Christian church, or St. Benedict, the father of Western monasticism.

Almost two centuries of monasticism had already elapsed when Benedict was born. Its origins dip back as far as the third century, probably earlier, when the first monks—they were called hermits or anchorites—drew away from society in order to serve God in the desert. Were our sources less scanty, historians might perhaps discover a fairly constant stream of ascetics, from John the Baptist, who was considered the forerunner of Christian monks, to Basil and Jerome, who spent some years in the wilderness in order to get away from men and closer to God. Still, there was nothing particularly unique about the origins of Christian monasticism. Fairly constant and ancient has been man's urge to withdraw from society in order to lead a more spiritual life. Other religions have produced analogous movements, although few of these have approached the proportions of Christian monasticism or the measure of its material and spiritual accomplishments.

Christian monasticism grew directly from Christian origins. (If the Essenes, a Hebrew monastic community at the time of Christ, exercised any direct influence, this still remains to be established.) Of the factors which inspired it none was surely more immediate than Christ's own example and words. He himself spent time in the desert, and he repeatedly urged those who wished to attain perfection to turn away from material goods and devote themselves to spiritual. "If you would be perfect," he admonished the rich young man, "sell all you have and follow me." The first monks of whom there remains any record were men who fled to the Egyptian and Syrian deserts during the third century in order to escape persecution. In the fourth and fifth centuries other Christians took to the desert, these to flee the corrupting influences of semipagan city life. There were others who joined them there: men, even women (organized communities of women probably antedated those of men in Egypt), who took up the harsh existence of the desert in order to do penance, to meditate without distractions, or by mortification to gain mastery over their sensual natures. "I crucify my flesh," wrote St. Paul, "in order to bring it into subjection."

The first clear step toward the establishment of organized monachism was taken at roughly the turn of the third century when Anthony introduced a measure of order into eremitical (hermit) monasticism. In his life of Anthony, Athanasius tells that as a young man of twenty Anthony had been so moved by the gospel story of Christ and the rich young man that he gave up his wealth and retired to an uninhabited oasis in the desert, where he lived out the last forty years of his life in the company of two other hermits. There he died in 356 at the advanced age of 105. Anthony was the father of eremitical monasticism. The hermits whom he counseled lived as recluses in separate cells. They only gathered on Saturdays and Sundays for services.

With Pachomius, who was Anthony's contemporary, monasticism took a major stride toward the development of cenobitism or communal monachism. Pachomius first lived as an anchorite, then assumed leadership of a community of hermits who had occupied a deserted village near Tabennisi in upper Egypt. Each of these monks lived as a hermit in a hut of his own and practiced what austerities he chose, only gathering with the others for communal prayers and instruction. In order to furnish guidance to similar communities which he established, Pachomius drew up the first formal monastic rule. The most revolutionary feature of Pachomius' rule was its aim at establishing an economically independent social unit. His monks engaged in such activities as tailoring, basketmaking, blacksmithing, even calligraphy, in order to maintain themselves.

The most important name in the history of Eastern monasticism was that of the church father Basil. He took an institution which many churchmen viewed with suspicion, even hostility, subordinated it to the church, and made it a part of the ecclesiastical order. What had aroused the anger of many bishops was the presence of charlatans among the monks, a measure of anticlericalism shown by even the better element, their indifference to regulations governing Christian conformity, and the practice of austerities they considered more exhibitionism than asceticism. A group of hermits, Stylites they were called, spent years on the top of their pillars. One of them, Simeon Stylites, remained aloft for thirty-five years. Other hermits walked about with heavy stones strapped to their backs, some beat themselves bloody, others chained themselves to posts, while still others carried on "competition" in ascetical practices. The cure for these bizarre practices was regulation, and this is what Basil introduced. He was the first to bring the hermits out of their individual cells to eat, sleep, and worship under a common roof, a monastery. In addition to the basket- and mat-making and similar occupations that Pachomius had introduced to his monks, Basil had them engage in eleemosynary activities, caring for orphans, the poor, and the infirm. He supplemented these reforms with extensive writings on the subject of monasticism which proved so influential that much of Eastern monasticism still honors him as its founder.

The fourth century witnessed the introduction of monasticism in the West. There it came as a direct importation from the East, not an evolution from a native anchoritism as in Egypt. This helps explain its early difficulties. The less spiritually advanced West was simply not prepared to accept the austerities and lack of regulation that characterized Eastern monasticism. Among the first to acquaint the West with the institution was St. Athanasius. When he was exiled from Alexandria in 339, he came to Italy and brought with him two Egyptian monks as companions. His *Life of St. Anthony* also exerted some influence even though the eremitical form of monasticism it described never took root in the West. St. Jerome's name also appears among the founders of Western monasticism principally on the basis of treatises and letters he wrote on the subject. One of his earliest experiences with a monastic community, that in Aquileia, was hardly encouraging. He tells how this disorganized company of hermits and vagrants dissolved in "a sudden storm." Despite this experience he retained a high opinion of the vocation of the monk, which he considered superior to that of a priest.

Near Poitiers in Gaul, St. Martin of Tours established in 360 what might be called the first monastery in the West. Another early name is that of St. Augustine, who lived as a monk for a short time after his conversion, then as bishop laid down a series of monastic regulations for the clergy of his diocese. The most influential monastic center in the West prior to Monte Cassino was located at Lerins, an island off the southern coast of Gaul. Here Honoratus founded a monastery about the year 400. Lerins remained more an intellectual center and a training ground for bishops and priests, however, than a monastery. Another founder of Western monasticism was John Cassian, who appears to have sensed at least one of the weaknesses that hampered the growth of that institution. "We see almost as many types and rules set up for use," he lamented, "as we see monasteries and cells." Unfortunately he saddled the two houses he established near Marseilles with a harshly austere rule similar to those in the East where he had learned his monasticism. Somewhat apart from these monastic strugglings were the origins of Irish monasticism, but these are so obscure that they have been traced to St. Patrick for want of a more worthy founder. If St. Patrick studied at Lerins, as some tradition holds, that may have been the source of Irish monasticism, for it possessed an austerity similar to that of Egypt. The missionary zeal of Irish monasticism, however, was a native characteristic.

The historical founder of Western monasticism was St. Benedict. He was born in 480 in Nursia of well-born parents who sent him to Rome to complete his education. There the vices of the city, possibly of his own companions, so shocked the youth of eighteen, that he fled to Subiaco, some forty miles east of the city, where a sympathetic monk helped him find a cave. For the three years that he dwelt in this cave, his only contact with society was this monk who had befriended him. During this time he suffered his famous temptation of the flesh, which he overcame, so tradition has it, by flinging himself unclothed into a thornbush. If the story is not true, it at least provided

the wellspring from which many similar stories flowed during the
Middle Ages. As time passed, Benedict's charm and holiness brought
him considerable renown, and a monastic group nearby prevailed upon
him to become their abbot. When he attempted to bring order into
their unregulated lives, however, they tried to poison him. He returned
to his former cave, later set up twelve separate communities of monks
from those who had joined him, then abruptly left the area with some
companions to find a new home to the south. It appears he had been
given rights to the broad plateau above Monte Cassino along the road
to Naples, for that is where he and his group stopped. They demolished the pagan temple they found there which had been the scene
of sacrifices to Jupiter, Apollo, and Venus, and began erection of what
was to become the most influential monastic center in history.

About the year 540 St. Benedict drew up his rule for the monastic
community at Monte Cassino. He had long years of experience behind him, ten years at Monte Cassino and almost that many previous
ones among the vicissitudes of Subiaco and its environs. He had also
acquainted himself with what literature he could find on the subject,
the writings of Cassian, for instance, and, in particular, those of St.
Basil, from which he derived some of his ideas and principles. No doubt
he also consulted monks from other lands and communities. Several
conclusions appear to have impressed themselves upon St. Benedict
concerning monastic rules, none more forcibly than this, that a monastic rule must provide regulation and order. This love of order St.
Benedict may have inherited from his Roman ancestors, and from
this same heritage his preference for a moderate and practical rule,
one that many men might find acceptable. And as a positive inspiration from which the community would derive its spiritual vigor, he
prescribed the recitation of the Psalms (divine office).

St. Benedict assured his monastic community a regulated routine
by setting down in detail in his rule what the monks would do in the
way of prayer, work, and sleep during the twenty-four hours of the
day. He enjoined upon them strict observance of this rule, and swore
them to unquestioning obedience to their superior, the abbot. Nothing
quite like this abbot appeared in earlier monasticism. He was to serve,
not just as counselor and administrator, but as a father as well, and a
stern one should he choose. Still he was to be selected by the members of the community, while in all important matters he must first consult them before undertaking action, even the younger members, "for
the Lord often reveals to the younger what is best." Then only would

he be free to do what reason and conscience advised, although he must never forget, so the rule warned him, that one day "he will have to give the Lord an account of all these souls, as well as his own soul."

St. Benedict simplified the abbot's task by giving him a monastic rule to enforce which was moderate in its demands—moderate, that is, by monastic standards of the time. He seems, in fact, almost to have apologized for imposing a regimen so lacking in austerity. "In founding this school for the service of the Lord," he wrote, "we hope to introduce nothing harsh or burdensome. . . ." The monks were to receive an adequate amount of food, even some wine, sufficient sleep, and clothing. They were not to practice any private mortifications of a physical kind, even during Lent, without first securing the abbot's permission. Diligent observance of the rule would provide all the spiritual drill they required. Many men, indeed, would find the life of a monk distasteful, even intolerable, for which reason each candidate must remain on probation for an entire year before gaining acceptance into the community. This test would hopefully eliminate all those not suited to monastic life. The monks who joined following this year of probation must remain permanent members of the community. Benedict made sure of this by requiring a vow of stability from all members. He had sufficient experience with vagrant monks, "gyrovagues," he called them, who spent their whole lives tramping from province to province. "Of the miserable conduct of all such men it is better to be silent than to speak."

No formal vows beyond that of stability was required of the monk except the promise that he would live as a monk should. This implied what came in time to be the traditional triple vow of the religious, namely, to observe the rule of chastity, to obey his superiors, and to forswear all wealth. Upon these last two vows, obedience and poverty, Benedict placed special emphasis in his rule. His longest chapter he devoted to humility. The vow of chastity he passed over in silence; it was self-evident. Beyond the practice of traditional Christian virtues and the observance of the rule, the central source of the spiritual life of the community was to derive from the daily recitation of the Divine Office. Nothing must be permitted to interfere with this "Work of the Lord, (Opus Dei), so that each week the Psalter with its full number of 150 Psalms be chanted." The addition of the Compline may have been Benedict's own contribution.

Benedictine monasticism prospered from the beginning. What counted most toward its success was the superiority of the rule, later

the favor of Gregory the Great and subsequent popes, still later the
encouragement of Charlemagne and Louis the Pious. Lombard destruction of Monte Cassino in 589 proved a turning point in the history of
the order. Until then the Benedictines were not substantially different
from other monastic orders in their concentration upon personal sanctification within the confines of the monastery. Their appearance in
Rome after having been driven from Monte Cassino came at a most
opportune time, for what the indefatigable Gregory most needed was
men like these monks to assist him in reconstructing the West. When
he sent Augustine and his fellow monks, who were probably Benedictines, to England in 597, Gregory changed the history of the order,
of the papacy, and the church. And because successive waves of semicivilized Germans had sharply depressed the level of civilization, the
Benedictines were able to assume a role in the West which had never
been open to monasticism in the more highly developed world of the
eastern Mediterranean. They became the principal preservers and
teachers of classical and Christian culture. Benedictine monasticism,
in the judgment of Toynbee, was "the matrix of Western civilization."

SCOTS
PICTS

IRELAND

JUTES

ANGLES

BRITAIN
BRITONS
ANGLES
SAXONS
JUTES

FRISIANS

SAXONS
LOMBARDS

THURINGIANS

LOMBAR

BRITONS

KINGDOM OF THE FRANKS
Trier
Tours
Mainz
Strasbourg
ALEMANS

Poitiers
AUVERGNE
KINGDOM
OF
THE
BURGUND-
IANS
Milan
Pavia
Aquileia
OSTRO-
GOTHS
Sirmiun
ILLYRIA

GALICIA

SUEVES

ALANS

KINGDOM OF THE VISIGOTHS

Bobbio
Lerins

KINGDOM OF ODOVACAR

Ravenna
Nursia

Seville
BAETICA

Rome
Monte
Cassino

Hippo
NUMIDIA
Carthage

KINGDOM OF THE

VANDALS

MAP 1
*Roman Empire about 400 A.D.
& Germanic Kingdoms about 485 A.D.*

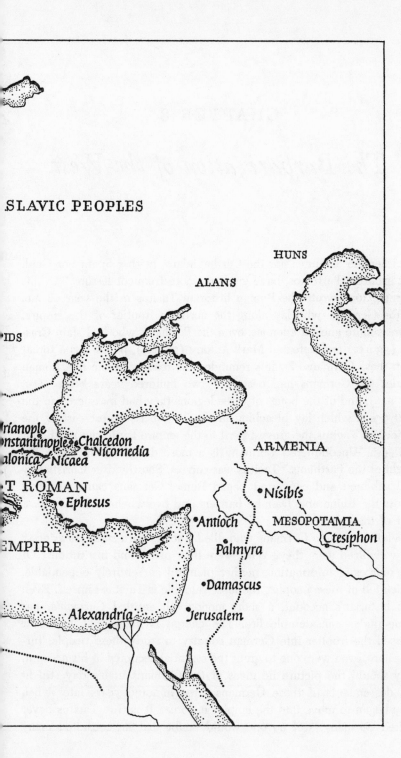

SLAVIC PEOPLES

HUNS

ALANS

IDS

ARMENIA

rianople
nstantinople Chalcedon
alonica Nicaea Nicomedia

T ROMAN
Ephesus

EMPIRE

Nisibis

Antioch MESOPOTAMIA
Ctesiphon
Palmyra

Damascus

Alexandria Jerusalem

CHAPTER 3

The Barbarization of the West

"Neither the Samnites nor the Carthaginians, neither Spain nor Gaul, nor even the Parthians, have given us more frequent lessons." In this warning tone wrote the Roman historian Tacitus in the year 98 A.D. of the Germans who lay along the northern frontier of the empire. Rome's more ancient enemies, even the Parthians who had slain Crassus (53 B.C.) and defeated Mark Antony (36 B.C.), posed less a threat than these Germans. Tacitus reminded his readers of the five Roman armies the Germans had destroyed two hundred years before (ca. 105 B.C.), and of the bones of three legions they had massacred in the year 9 A.D. which lay bleaching in the Teutoberg Forest east of the Rhine. To Tacitus the gravest peril to the empire lay to the north, not the east. "Unconquered Germany is a more dangerous foe than the might of the Parthians." Tacitus was correct. Shortly after Christianity had subdued and converted pagan Rome, Germans came plunging across the Rhine and Danube barriers and overwhelmed the western half of the empire.

Who were these Germans who filled Tacitus with such uneasiness? How civilized were they? What were their mores and institutions? Of the sources of information, neither plentiful nor entirely dependable, which tell of these peoples, the most valuable is Tacitus himself. Even this historian's account, a short monograph entitled *Germania*, has come under considerable fire. The charge is made that he never crossed the frontier into German country to study these people; furthermore, even were one to grant the essential accuracy of his account, why should the picture he gives of the Germans in his day still fit the descendants of these Germans three hundred years later when they began to move into the empire in force? It is true Tacitus never visited Germany; still no one would doubt that he consulted many people who had firsthand knowledge of these people. He was too careful a historian, a fact other contemporary evidence, including archaeological, tends to confirm. Concerning the suitableness of his description for Germans who lived several hundreds of years after he lived, there is the fact that primitive peoples alter their mores very reluctantly. The aborigines of Australia have clung to their ancestral ways in our own day, despite the presence of higher cultures about them.

Tacitus has also drawn the charge that he deliberately exaggerated the prowess and virtues of these Germans in order to give his country-men greater pause concerning the danger these peoples held for the empire. One may question the validity of this criticism. Tacitus makes mention of vices these Germans possessed along with their virtues, and one or the other of these vices would actually have provided comfort to Romans like himself who worried about the danger to the north. He points out that "During the intervals of war, they pass their time less in hunting than in sluggish repose, dividing their time between sleep and feasting. The bravest of the warriors do nothing and commit the management of the house, the home, and the lands to the women, the old men, and all the weakest members of the family. They themselves lie inert in their sloth." The Germans were also inveterate gamblers, but worst of all was their love of drinking. "Their drink is a liquor prepared from barley or wheat which is fermented and brought to a certain resemblance of wine." This, Tacitus wrote, the Germans drank in such quantity and with so much eagerness, that "If one ex-ploits their limitless craving for drink, he can overcome them by in-temperance as easily as by force of arms."

So much for the vices of these Germans; their virtues, in the judg-ment of Tacitus, more than offset these deficiencies. They were a strong people, with "fierce blue eyes, red hair, and large frames," wholly un-touched by the sophisticated vices that were enervating the Roman character. They were a nation of fighters, and this included the women who "bring food and encouragement to their men when they are fight-ing." Not only did the Germans like nothing better than to fight; they were not easily overcome. "When they go into battle, it is shameful for the chief to be outdone in bravery, and shameful as well for his followers not to match the bravery of their chief. To survive one's chief and to return from battle is a foul disgrace which endures as long as life itself. . . . After a defeat many survivors have been known to hang themselves to end their infamy." The German boy, too, looked eagerly to the time when he became eighteen, for that announced he had become a man, a warrior. On that birthday he would join a warrior band, called *comitatus*, membership in which group would demand as unquestioning a loyalty from him as the tribe itself. Indeed those tribes ran grave risk of losing their most aggressive warriors to some more warlike tribe if they remained at peace too long a time, "both because they hate peace and because fame is gained more readily in times of danger."

What may have prompted Tacitus to write so eloquently of the fierceness of the Germans was his contempt and concern over the reluctance of the Roman citizenry of his day to accept military service. Romans were rather leaving this responsibility to noncitizens and foreigners. Tacitus very surely had Roman women in mind, especially upper-class women with their easy morals, when he extolled the excellence of German women. These women worked hard, he wrote—because of the laziness of their husbands, of course, they had no choice! and accompanied their husbands to the battlefield to spur them on to greater efforts. Their virtue too was unassailable. "They are not corrupted by the allurements of the theater or the subtle temptations of banquets. Clandestine correspondence is equally unknown to men and women. For so numerous a people adultery is very rare, and the husband is allowed to take immediate reprisal. He cuts off his wife's hair, strips her naked in the presence of her family, and flogs her up the village street. For in Germany no one laughs at vice, nor calls mutual corruption 'the spirit of the age.'" Tacitus even had praise for the morals of German men, a tradition that had earlier drawn Julius Caesar's attention when he campaigned against them in Gaul.

The religious beliefs and practices of the Germans did not set them apart from other peoples of the same cultural level. Several of their principal gods had acquired such Roman identifications as Mercury and Mars by the time Caesar and Tacitus had heard of them. The majority of their deities remained nameless. "They do not deem it consistent with the majesty of heavenly beings to coop them within walls or to depict them in any human shape." They commonly associated gods and spirits with sacred groves, springs, lakes, and rivers. From Wotan (Odin or Woden), the highest god, their kings might claim descent, although equally powerful was Thor, the god of war and thunder. Tiw was another war god, Frigg was the wife of Wotan. These four deities have given their names to Wednesday, Thursday, Tuesday, and Friday. The Germans propitiated their gods with burnt offerings, on occasion by sacrificing warriors they had captured in battle. The most common sacrificial offering was the horse. They would burn what was not eatable and feast on what remained. So much was this a national custom that the eating of horseflesh long passed as a distinctly heathen practice. The Germans also practiced divination. They studied "the flights and cries of birds . . . and noted the neighing and whinnying" of the sacred white horses. Special respect did they also show the counsels of their women, nor did they "despise their advice or neglect their answer."

What Tacitus wrote about the political customs and institutions of the early Germans did not mark those people as substantially different from other folk living at their same cultural level. Families, presumably related by blood, formed clans, and these joined others to establish tribes. When war threatened, tribes would combine to form alliances, which would ordinarily dissolve again once peace returned. The head of the tribe, whether a king or chieftain, exercised the patriarchal authority anthropologists find common among most primitive folk. Like the early Greeks, the real authority with these Germans rested in the assembly, which was composed of those men in the tribe who were able to bear arms. This group met, "except in case of chance emergencies, on fixed days, either at new moon or full moon: such seasons they believe to be the most auspicious for beginning business. . . . Silence is demanded by the priests, to whom are granted special powers of coercion. Next, the king, or one of the chief men according to claims of age, lineage, or military glory, receives a hearing, which he obtains merely by power of persuasion than by any right of command. If the opinion expressed displeases them, their murmurs reject it; if they approve, they clash their spears."

The judicial practices of the early Germans, as described by Tacitus, suggest a people who had progressed sufficiently far beyond the most primitive level of tribal existence to appreciate the institution of the state. When the assembly acted as a court and levied a fine upon some defendant, "part of the fine is paid to the king or state," no doubt in recognition of the tribal peace that had been violated. The remainder of the fine, Tacitus writes, was ordered paid to the injured plaintiff or to his relatives. It appears the injured party or his relatives had no choice but accept such satisfaction despite their strong loyalties to family feuds. Such feuds "are not irreconcilable. Even homicide has its price in a fixed tale of cattle or sheep: the whole family receives the recompense." Crimes of a more public nature could not be expiated.

"They hang traitors and deserters on trees: cowards and cravens and those guilty of vicious crimes they drown in a muddy swamp and put a hurdle on the top. These different penalties imply the distinction that crimes in being punished ought to be made public, while shameful offenses ought to be concealed."

If one remembers that Romans and Germans had been neighbors for several hundreds of years when Tacitus drew up his *Germania*, the propriety of questioning his reliability itself comes under question. Why should not a sober historian have had access to as much knowledge of these folk as thousands of Romans who lived in the provinces south of the Rhine and Danube? From the close of the second century B.C. until the northern frontier collapsed in the fifth century A.D., Romans had been encountering these people, more often as warriors, it is true, but only less frequently as shepherds, farmers, peddlers, and, finally, as allies. For many generations the pressure of population and the lure of a warmer climate and higher culture to the south had been driving these Germans constantly against and across the frontier. During intervals between outbreaks of fighting, when the frontier was quiet, one can imagine many scattered German families crossing over, with the permission or connivance of Roman officials, to squat on unused lands or to join *coloni* on lands that were under cultivation.

There were other men, Romans and Germans, who passed back and forth across the frontier—Roman merchants from the south to dispose of textiles, wine, pottery, and trinkets of gold, silver, and glass among the Germans; peddlers from Germany to sell their furs, hides, gold, amber, wool, soap, cattle, and slaves. These merchants could be found in largest numbers around Roman army camps which were strung out along the frontier. A number of these camp sites, those at Cologne, Mainz, Trier, Vienna, and Budapest, for example, were destined to grow into large cities. In such towns or on lands nearby, veterans who had completed their service in the army settled down with their common-law wives, many of whose fathers had once roamed the forests of Germany.

The largest number of Germans moved into the empire in the wake of border warfare. Several of the emperors of the second century, including Hadrian and Marcus Aurelius, settled many thousands whom they had defeated within the empire, where they gave them the status of *laeti*. For the Germans this status meant that when called upon they must furnish military service along the frontier and at the same time cultivate the lands they occupied, from which they paid a rental in kind to the state. During the civil wars of the third century when many emperors and pretenders fought over the throne and the demand for recruits skyrocketed, the number of Germans in the army swelled to alarming proportions. Beyond these Germans who served in or with the regular army, there were many more who assumed the status of allies (*foederati*). In return for a kind of tribute, which Rome granted willingly or only after having inflicted defeat upon them, they agreed to use their manpower to bolster Roman authority along the frontier.

Meantime marriage, that great social leveler, was breaking down barriers between Germans and Romans throughout the frontier provinces. Such unions had come easily between Roman *coloni* and Germans, since economically and socially they were equally depressed, and no color or strong religious barrier existed to keep them apart. The Romans admired the physique of the German men; Roman women envied the blonde and reddish hair of their wives and daughters. As Germans grew in number and importance, they entered the officer class, then in the late third and fourth centuries compelled emperors to open to them the highest positions in the army. Such rank in turn led to marriages between German generals and members of the Roman aristocracy. The emperor Honorius married the daughter of Stilicho, his Vandal commander-in-chief, while Valentinian II married the daughter of his Frankish general, Bauto.

This peaceful movement of Germans from the north continued uninterruptedly from generation to generation despite the flaring of intermittent warfare along the frontier. Had the empire continued as strong as it had been in the second century, had it been able to produce a sequence of emperors as capable as Constantine and Valentinian I, the slow progress of Germans into the empire might have gone on without major incident until the pressure north of the Rhine and Danube had abated. For Germany was in ferment, the frontier bending under weight of their numbers. New tribes kept moving in from the north and east to contend with older tribes over hunting grounds and cattle. Some of the older tribes which Tacitus had described, the Goths, Sueves, and Lombards, still remained powerful nations in the fourth century and threatened the frontier on the north. Other tribes had disappeared, some without trace, others absorbed by their conquerors, some occasionally forming new groups as those that produced the Alemans (all men).

Until the late fourth century, Rome had somehow managed to muddle through. On occasion, when it appeared that the dire prophecies of men who had predicted the dissolution of the empire were about to be fulfilled, an Aurelian would come forward, or a Diocletian or Julian, who would retrieve the situation. Though the Goths had annihilated the Emperor Decius and his army back in 251, Gallienus had in turn annihilated them, after which pressure along the Danube had subsided and that front had grown reasonably quiet. The situation on the Rhine, on the other hand, continued critical. During the third and fourth centuries the gravest danger came from the powerful Alemans and Franks. Groups of Franks had swarmed across Gaul in the middle of the third century and had carried their forays all the way through Spain into Africa. Then Julian and Valentinian I had succeeded in re-establishing imperial authority throughout the west, and when Valentinian died in 375, the frontier appeared as solid as ever.

That same year a new factor appeared which permanently altered the system of imperial defense and announced the coming of the end. In the year 375 emissaries of the formidable Visigoths, a tribe that lay just east of the Danube, appeared before the emperor Valens with the urgent request that he permit their people to cross the river. Their nation was in grave peril, they warned the emperor. The terrible Huns had already overwhelmed the Ostrogoths, their cousins to the east, and only flight had preserved them from the same fate.

What had happened was that the Huns, a Mongolian people from Asia, had crossed into eastern Europe above the Black Sea and had defeated and enslaved the Alans and Ostrogoths. The Visigoths to the west had not dared face them. Some took refuge in the highlands of Transylvania; the bulk had fled westward and were now seeking sanctuary within the Roman empire. Valens was in a quandary. If he allowed them to enter, they would constitute a potential threat within the empire; if he denied so powerful a tribe admittance, they might force their way in. Prudence recommended that he make allies of these Visigoths against the day when the empire might face these same Huns. So he permitted them to come in, and they came in such numbers that a contemporary likened their coming to "the rain of ashes from the eruption of Etna."

What kind of people were these Huns who had frightened the powerful Visigothic nation to flee before them? They were different from the Germans, very much different according to contemporary reports. Jordanes called them "a stunted, foul and puny tribe, scarcely human and having no language save one which bore but slight resemblance to human speech. By the terror of their features they inspired great fear in those whom they perhaps did not really surpass in war. They made their foes flee in horror because their swarthy aspect was fearful, and they had, if I may call it so, a sort of shapeless lump, not a head, with pinholes rather than eyes. . . . They are short in stature, quick in bodily movement, alert horsemen, broadshouldered, ready in the use of bow and arrow, and have firm-set necks which are ever erect in pride. Though they live in the form of men, they have the cruelty of wild beasts."

Ammianus Marcellinus offers a more reasoned description of them. He was willing to admit that, despite their fearsome appearance, "They are certainly in the shape of men, however uncouth. . . ." Undoubtedly it was their appearance that aroused most fear, since this was so different from what the Romans and Germans were accustomed. Their race was Mongolian, as revealed by their squat figures, the wheat-color of their skins, their slit eyes, and the short black hair that covered the heads of the males. Because they lived almost continuously on the backs of their horses, the men were inclined to be bowlegged, their calves undeveloped, and their walk undignified. Their homeland, if one can speak of a home for a people as restless as the Huns, was the vast, unproductive expanse that lay between the Ural and Altai Mountains to the west and east and to the north of the Caspian. Here they were ever on the move, seeking out food for their flocks and horses. They lived off the milk of their mares and sheep, and what millet a short growing season could produce. Their organization was similar to that of nomadic peoples. Several families formed a camp, a number of these a clan, these in turn a tribe, several of these a people, which a popular, aggressive leader might combine with others into a horde. Because they had no fixed abode, they remained "homeless and lawless," and never developed a high civilization. Their mobility gave their foes the impression that they were more numerous than they were, while the distorted reports of their ferocity and barbarousness completed the consternation of the more highly civilized peoples to the west. Both Romans and Germans regarded them with horror.

The Visigoths had meantime crossed over the Danube where they were promised provisions and assigned lands. Such at least were the orders that Valens had given his officials. What actually happened is not clear. For some reason the arrangement broke down, but by whose doing is not apparent. The Visigoths blamed the Romans for letting them starve, for extorting money, even for seizing their children as hostages, then selling them into slavery. The Romans blamed the Visigoths, specifically bands of their warriors who refused to respect the terms of their treaty and instead joined other groups, Ostrogoths and even Huns, to plunder the countryside. When Valens learned that the situation had deteriorated, he hurried over from Asia Minor, then unwisely attacked the Goths without awaiting the arrival of his nephew Gratian from the west. At Adrianople on August 9, 378, the heavy-armed cavalry of the Goths and their Sarmatian allies cut the Roman army to pieces and Valens himself was killed, either by an arrow during the battle, or burned to death in a cottage where he had been carried.

The battle of Adrianople marked a major break in the history of Rome. Roman armies had suffered defeat before, but Rome had always recovered and eventually driven back or destroyed the enemy. In the case of the Visigoths, Gratian and the more capable Theodosius, whom he appointed as Augustus in the East to replace Valens, appeared either unwilling or incapable of avenging the defeat. Gratian returned to the west, where the situation continued threatening; Theodosius decided that diplomacy was preferable to staking the empire's future on the dubious fortunes of war. The Visigoths, for their part, following their failure to take Adrianople and their repulse before Constantinople, proved reasonable and accepted the lands Theodosius offered them in Moesia just south of the Danube and settled down. Still the situation was not good. The powerful Visigothic people remained within the imperial frontiers, where they retained their Germanic ways and made no effort to accept Romanization. Except for the sagacity of Theodosius and his ability to gain the confidence of their chieftains, the Visigoths might never have quieted down.

This became evident a few months after the death of Theodosius in 395 when Gothic bands rose in revolt under their new leader, Alaric. Now there was no longer the sober Theodosius to meet this threat, only his two young sons, the incompetent Arcadius in Constantinople and the younger but equally incompetent Honorius in Milan. Had it not been for the Vandal chieftain Stilicho whom Theodosius had appointed guardian for his two boys, the empire might have collapsed at this time. Stilicho had married Serena, the niece of Theodosius, which alliance had facilitated his rise to the high position of master of the troops. At first Stilicho appears to have entertained ambitions of becoming actual ruler of both East and West. Then, when thwarted in this, he moved to Italy, married his daughter to Honorius, and as father-in-law of the emperor and commander-in-chief of the Roman armies became virtual ruler of the West.

Meantime Alaric and his Visigoths were plundering their way down into Greece with Arcadius and his advisers looking on helplessly from behind the defenses of Constantinople. But Alaric had little taste for mere plunder. What he and his Visigoths wanted were lands, and these Arcadius finally convinced him to seek in the west, in Italy. So Alaric began moving his people up through Dalmatia, now fighting Stilicho who blocked his way, now conspiring with him. Stilicho's actions must have puzzled Honorius. Though never willing or able to destroy Alaric, he never permitted himself to be defeated. On two occasions, once at Pollentia and again at Verona in northern Italy, he administered solid setbacks to his Gothic opponent. Then suddenly Honorius ordered Stilicho seized and executed. It seems that Stilicho's enemies, and he had many among the aristocracy, had aroused the emperor's suspicions. They looked upon him as the center of German power and as a threat to their own position, and they could not stomach his Arianism.

The tragedy of Stilicho's execution took place in 408. For two years Alaric dallied with Honorius and Rome as a cat plays with a mouse. Lands would have satisfied him, but these the unstable Honorius refused to surrender. Twice Alaric accepted gold and pepper from Rome for sparing the city. Finally on August 24 in the year 410, he lost all patience and seized the city. For three days he let his Goths plunder the city, then led them southward toward Sicily. Across from the island he gathered a fleet which was to take him and his people to the grain fields of Africa. When a storm scattered and destroyed his ships, he turned northward but died before the end of the year. His devoted followers had slaves divert the river Busento, buried him in its bed, had the river returned to its course, then slew the slaves to keep his burial place a secret. So it remains today. The Visigoths then chose as their king Ataulf, Alaric's brother-in-law. Under his leadership they trekked to southern Gaul, then as *foederati* of the empire drove the Vandals and Alans out of Spain and extended their control over the greater part of that area. They could not dislodge the Sueves in northwestern Spain.

These peoples, the Vandals, Sueves, and Alans, had taken advantage of Stilicho's policy of denuding the northern frontier of troops with which to fight Alaric, by crossing over the Rhine on the last day

of the year 406, then plundering the cities and countryside of Gaul
on their way to Spain. The Sueves and Alans were small nations and
left no mark on Western history. The Vandals, on the other hand,
though not a large tribe, proved themselves one of the fiercest and,
under their talented leader, Gaiseric, one of the most successful. One
of their branches fell victim to the Visigoths in Spain. Gaiseric led the
other branch over to Africa to Numidia, where they were satisfied for
a time with the status of *foederati*. Then they revolted, seized Carthage, and despite desperate efforts by Constantinople, established a
powerful maritime empire that included all of Roman Africa, the Balearic Islands, Corsica, Sardinia, and part of Sicily. In 455 Gaiseric and
his Vandals had their turn sacking Rome. The charge of wanton destruction with which an eighteenth-century French historian saddled
them for this raid, whence the connotation of the word vandalism
today, is no longer accepted.

A less formidable Germanic tribe was the Burgundian, even though
its history far outlived that of the Vandals. The Burgundians crossed
the Rhine in 413 and occupied the area about Strasbourg. The status of
imperial *foederati* did not long satisfy them, but when they attempted
to move southward toward the Mediterranean, they suffered a crushing
defeat from the Roman army under Aetius and his Hunnish mercenaries. (In the old German epic, the *Nibelungenlied*, it is Attila, called
Etzel, who inflicts this defeat upon the Burgundians.) The remnants
of the Burgundian nation eventually settled in Savoy, whence they expanded to occupy the greater part of the Rhone Valley (to the Durance
River).

Those parts of Gaul which the Visigoths and Burgundians had left
unappropriated, the Franks now proceeded to occupy. The Salian
branch, which the emperor Julian had permitted to settle south of the
mouth of the Rhine, moved southward to the Somme, then under
Clovis seized all the territory to the Loire. The other great branch of
the Franks, the Ripuarian, crossed the Rhine farther up the river and
laid claim to the area about Trier. The Alemans, still farther up the
Rhine, crossed over to seize control of Switzerland and the country
about Strasbourg.

While these Germans were crossing the Rhine, other Germans who
lived along the North Sea east of the Rhine and on the Jutland Peninsula were crossing the North Sea to Britain. These were the Angles,
Saxons, and Jutes. For more than a century they had been plundering
British shores, and the Romans had assigned a special officer, called

the count of the Saxon Shore, the job of repelling their raids. Once the Roman legions had left the country (406 A.D.) these raids grew in intensity until about the middle of the century when the Germans began to establish footholds, first in the southeast, then in the east. They eventually overran all of what is known as England today with the exception of Cornwall and the area of the Cumbrian Mountains. Some of the Britons who could not escape to these mountainous areas and to Wales, fled across the channel to Brittany to which they gave their name.

While these German Visigoths, Vandals, Burgundians, Franks, and others were busily carving out parts of the Roman empire for themselves, the people who had precipitated all the trouble, that is, the Huns, were building an empire of their own in eastern Europe. Exactly how extensive this was no one will ever know, but it surely included what is present-day Hungary, Roumania, and southern Russia. No trace remains of what are supposed to have been their headquarters on the Theiss River in Hungary from which they ruled scores of German and Slavic tribes they had subjugated. The Danube presumably marked the southern limit of their power, although even a heavy tribute which Constantinople began paying them in 424 did not prevent occasional raiding parties from crossing into imperial territory. About 444 Attila, one of their chieftains, slew his brother Bleda and united the different Hunnic tribes under his authority.

In his day this man Attila was the most powerful man in Europe. According to Jordanes, "He was a man born to shake the races of the world, the scourge of all lands, who in some way or other terrified all mankind by the dreadful rumors noised abroad about him. He was haughty in his walk, rolling his eyes about him on all sides, so that the power of his proud spirit appeared in the movement of his body. He was indeed a lover of war, yet personally restrained in action, mighty in counsel, gracious to suppliants, and generous to those to whom he had once given his protection." Like many of his people, he "was short of stature with a broad chest and large head. His eyes were small, his beard thin and sprinkled with gray; and he had a flat nose and a swarthy complexion showing thus the signs of his origin."

For some years Attila had continued on friendly terms with Aetius, master of the troops under Valentinian III and the real ruler of the West. Aetius had earlier fled to the Huns in order to escape seizure and probable execution on orders of the mother of Valentinian. Later, with the help of the Huns, he had been restored to imperial favor, and still

later, with the assistance of Hunnish mercenaries, had crushed the
Burgundians. Aetius' personal ambitions remain a puzzle. Some writers
accuse him of having pursued wholly selfish aims, that he was concerned solely with preserving his powerful position and his own extensive properties. Other scholars insist he was loyal to Rome. Whatever
may have been the case, he represented the only bulwark of Roman
power in central and southwestern Gaul.

Early in 451 Attila moved westward with a half-million men, most
of them Germanic and Slavic mercenaries. The year previous, Constantinople had cut off tribute payments, which had steadily grown more
enormous. This action is what probably prompted Attila's attack. For
those readers who prefer a more romantic explanation there is the tale
of one chronicler who writes of the offer Attila received from Honoria,
the ambitious sister of Valentinian III, of her hand and half the western empire as dowry. Upon Valentinian's refusal to countenance such
a marriage settlement, Attila had attacked.

Attila moved directly west rather than toward the south, it is said,
in the hope of finding allies among the Ripuarian Franks. His first objective was Orléans. Before he could take the city, he found himself
attacked by a huge army composed of Salian Franks, Burgundians,
Celts, Visigoths, and "Romans" under command of his former friend
Aetius. The battle took place on June 14 on the Mauriac plain about
five miles from Châlons-sur-Marne. Each side suffered heavily, although
Attila had clearly had the worst of it when night put an end to the
fighting. Because Aetius secretly feared the rise of Visigothic power
should Attila be routed, he decided to retire and persuaded the reluctant Theodoric, king of the Visigoths, not to resume battle on the following morning. Attila withdrew unmolested to Hungary to lick his
wounds.

By the following spring he had sufficiently recuperated to attempt a
drive down into Italy. He had captured and destroyed the cities of
northern Italy with the exception of Ravenna when he was met by an
embassy from Rome headed by Pope Leo I. Leo and a group of senators
had come to plead with him not to move farther south. Whether it was
their persuasiveness, whether famine and disease were making Attila's
mercenaries restive, whether he feared the arrival of troops from Constantinople—these all remain unanswered questions. What is certain is
that he turned his back on Italy and returned to Hungary where he
died the following year (453). This happened on his wedding night,
according to one account, which has his new wife Ildico assuming the

role of murderess. A more likely account tells that he died of a hemor-
rhage and that his attendants found Ildico weeping beside his dead
body when they visited the bedchamber in the morning. The manner
of his death is unimportant; of critical importance, however, is the fact
that the feared Attila was dead. His sons could not maintain their father's position and Hunnish power melted away overnight.

There is a famous legend concerning Pope Leo and this embassy
to Attila, based on the account of Prosper, a contemporary, that bears
telling at this point. Leo, who was then "an old man of harmless simplicity, venerable in gray hair and his majestic garb," had determined
to go to meet this "scourge of God," as Attila was called. "He met Attila
in the neighborhood of the river Mincio, and he spoke to the grim
monarch, saying: 'The senate and the people of Rome, once conquerors
of the world, now indeed vanquished, come before thee as suppliants.
We pray for mercy and deliverance. O Attila, thou king of kings, thou
couldst have no greater glory than to see suppliant at thy feet this people before whom once all peoples and kings lay suppliant. Thou hast
subdued, O Attila, the whole circle of the lands which it was granted
to the Romans, victors over all peoples, to conquer. Now we pray that
thou, who has conquered others, shouldst conquer thyself. The people
have felt thy scourge; now as suppliants they would feel thy mercy.'

"As Leo said these things, Attila stood looking upon his venerable
garb and aspect, silent, as if thinking deeply. And lo, suddenly there
were seen the apostles Peter and Paul, clad like bishops, standing by
Leo, the one on the right hand, the other on the left. They held swords
stretched out over his head, and threatened Attila with death if he did
not obey the pope's command. Wherefore Attila was appeased by Leo's
intercession,—he who has raged as one mad. He straightway promised
a lasting peace and withdrew beyond the Danube."

Rome, at this juncture, proceeded to commit its second blunder of
the century. In 408 the Emperor Honorius had slain Stilicho, the only
man who could have saved Rome. Two years later the Visigoths sacked
the city. Now, three years after the battle of Châlons when Aetius had
saved Roman rule where it still existed in the West, Valentinian III
had him murdered. He may have feared Aetius' imperial ambitions.
Aetius' son was betrothed to his daughter and Valentinian had no son
of his own. He surely envied Aetius his fame. Whatever his motives,
to kill Aetius was a blunder of the first order. As one Roman told Valentinian when asked his opinion of the deed: "You have acted like a
man who cuts off his right hand with his left." Six months later several

of Aetius' officers avenged their general's death by murdering Valentinian (454 A.D.).

Upon the death of Valentinian III, the last and least worthy emperor of the dynasty of Theodosius, imperial authority to all intents and purposes disappeared in the West. Other emperors succeeded Valentinian, but one hardly less a puppet than the other. Actual power rested in the hands of the German commander who happened to be master of the troops. Ricimer made and unmade emperors from 456 A.D. until his death in 472. Leo, the emperor in the East, sent over Nepos in 474 to rule Italy; but Orestes, whom Nepos had appointed master of the troops, drove him out. For reasons unknown, Orestes, who was neither a German nor a Hun, preferred to rule through his young son, Romulus Augustulus. When Orestes refused to distribute lands among his German mercenaries, they found a new leader in the Scirian Odovacar and slew Orestes (28 August 476). Romulus was too young and harmless to kill, so they left him his life and granted him a pension. Odovacar, in fact, sent a group of senators off to Constantinople carrying with them the imperial insignia and a petition to Zeno, the emperor there, that he recognize him as his representative, which he did.

The deposition of Romulus Augustulus in the year 476 A.D. has evoked a spate of literature. Did that deposition mark the end of the Roman empire? Some scholars maintain it did. They point to the name of Romulus Augustulus, none more Roman in all of Roman history, and to the measure of Roman blood that probably coursed through his veins. As opposed to this "Roman," after 476 A.D. there was only Odovacar. Historians are still not entirely agreed as to what particular barbarian group Odovacar belonged. They only agree that he was no Roman, and that after his rise to power in 476 no Roman emperor ever again ruled from the Tiber. It is this fact, and its interpretation as symbolizing the ascendancy of the Germans, that has led eminent scholars to assign that awesome event, the fall of Rome, to that particular year. So Ferdinand Lot writes: "The year 476 really marks the end of the Roman Empire in the West," even though he admits that "it fell without a sound. . . ."*

Yet Romulus Augustulus had never received imperial recognition from the Eastern emperor, neither did he ever exercise the slightest measure of imperial authority. Those scholars who object to attaching any great significance to the year 476 also point to the two years during the period of Ricimer's control when he never even bothered having a

* The End of the Ancient World and the Beginnings of the Middle Ages, p. 215.

puppet on the throne. Western emperors since the death of Theodosius had been, in fact, a most unprepossessing and inactive lot. They scarcely ventured outside their fortified capitals and seemed to be content with hatching conspiracies against troublesome masters of the troops like Stilicho and Aetius. It is true they held the imperial title and that generally by some hereditary right. Therefore, even if saying that "476 marks the end of the Roman empire" is too strong a statement, it still possesses an element of truth. Perhaps Oman's position can be accepted as a compromise on the issue. "If we must select any year as the dividing line between ancient history and the Middle Ages," he declared, "it is impossible to choose a better date than 476."*

Other than that Odovacar extended his rule over Italy and also Sicily (by agreement with the dying Gaiseric), his reign of seventeen years has drawn little commendation, or criticism for that matter. He enjoyed the cooperation of the Roman senate, interfered in no way with the church despite his Arianism, and left imperial administrative machinery to function as before. His demand for lands to give to his troops did not entail any great adjustment since only the large proprietors suffered. His principal weaknesses arose from the absence of a strong compact tribe behind him and the dissatisfaction of the emperor Zeno in Constantinople. The latter induced Theodoric, king of the Ostrogoths, to lead his people to Italy, there to displace Odovacar and rule in his name.

When last seen, these Ostrogoths had been subjects of the Huns. When Hunnish power collapsed following the death of Attila, they settled along the middle Danube as imperial *foederati*. For about ten years the young Theodoric lived in Constantinople with other hostages in order to ensure his people's honoring their treaty with Zeno. Later the Ostrogoths elected him their king, followed his leadership in pillaging the Balkans, then upon Zeno's suggestion, moved westward with him into Italy. Three times Theodoric met Odovacar in battle and three times he defeated him, but still gained no complete victory. Finally after a siege of two and a half years of Ravenna where Odovacar had taken refuge, the two chieftains agreed on joint rule of the peninsula. Theodoric appears never to have had any intention of honoring the treaty. At the banquet celebrating their pact, he slew the old man with his own hand. That was in 493 A.D.

Although Theodoric was guilty of this and other barbarous acts, he proved himself the ablest and most enlightened of all the German

* Charles Oman, *The Dark Ages*. London (1914), p. 3.

conquerors. For thirty-three years he maintained a vigorous rule over an empire that stretched from the middle Danube to Sicily and included all of Italy and the Provence. For more than a decade he governed Spain in the name of his grandson, while through his sister who had married the king of the Vandals he enjoyed a powerful voice in African affairs. His own wife was the sister of Clovis. No one since Theodosius had exercised so extensive an authority in the Western empire. His greatest cross was the lack of a son, and his haunting fear as he grew older was that the emperor at Constantinople, with the assistance of the pope, would bring about the destruction of Ostrogothic rule as soon as his daughter Amalasuntha would succeed. Two years before his death in 526, he ordered the execution of Boethius, the first scholar of the age. The precise basis for Theodoric's unfortunate act is not entirely clear. He may have considered Boethius to be the leader of potential Catholic and senatorial resistance. (For Boethius, see below, p. 104.)

Theodoric's hostility toward Catholics and the senatorial aristocracy cast a pall over the closing years of his reign. Until then he ruled with a statesmanship that belied his barbarian origins. Since "religion is a thing which the king cannot command, because no man can be compelled to believe against his will," he was tolerant toward all religious communions and gave even Jews the favor of his protection. His purpose, so he told one of his officials, was "so to rule that our subjects will grieve that they did not earlier acquire the blessing of our dominion." Though the statement smacks of self-righteousness, few emperors since the Antonines of the second century furnished greater evidence of a concern for the common good.

Quite noteworthy, since he was a German, were the efforts Theodoric made to preserve Roman culture and institutions. He treated the senate with such deference that several of its members began to imagine that body possessed an importance it had lost many centuries before. As his first minister he selected the scholar Cassiodorus, upon whose correspondence historians depend for much of their knowledge of his reign. The administrative machinery of his kingdom he left to the Romans on the principle, "Yours the work of peace, ours of war." He only interfered to the extent of ensuring honest appointees and to force the aristocracy to pay their proper share of imperial taxation, something they had generally escaped doing since the close of the second century. As most tangible proof of his admiration for things Roman, one may cite his encouragement to the magistrates of Rome to restore their city's beauty. "If the people of Rome will beautify their city," he promised, "we will help them," and he did. Yet despite his considerable expenditures in the construction and repair of public buildings, ancient monuments, roads, and aqueducts, to say nothing of his enlightened rule, he never gained the good will of the Italo-Romans. He was an Arian; they, Catholic Christians. One suspects, furthermore, that the cultural gap between his people and the natives was too wide to bridge within the few generations fate allotted Theodoric and his short-lived successors.

A few years after the death of Theodoric, what the aged Ostrogothic chieftain feared came to pass. Roman armies from Constantinople invaded the Italian peninsula, and though long years of fighting were required to do the job, in the end Roman power triumphed and the Ostrogothic nation passed into oblivion. This was the work of Justinian, who ascended the imperial throne in Constantinople in 527 A.D. (see following chapter). Justinian had hoped to reconquer all the territory ancient Rome had once ruled, and with luck he might have accomplished this. After his death imperial rule again weakened, and another powerful German nation crossed the Alps to threaten Roman rule in Italy. This was the nation of the Lombards.

The Lombards were one of the fiercest and most barbarous of German peoples to invade the empire. They had little earlier contact with Roman culture and had instead to maintain themselves against neighbors such as the Heruls and Gepids who were even more savage than they. Toward the close of the fifth century they had migrated from the lower Elbe to the Danube where they were first subjugated by the Heruls, then revolted and almost destroyed their former masters. Next they accepted the status of Roman *foederati* and in that capacity aided Justinian's generals in breaking the back of Ostrogothic resistance in Italy. A few years after Justinian's death they marched back into the peninsula under Alboin, their king, and took possession of much of the north.

Contemporary sources depict this Alboin as having the prowess of a Beowulf and the ambition of Alexander the Great. War and violence were his constant companions and even love did not soften him. He married the beautiful Rosemond, daughter of the king of the Gepids, then later with the aid of the Avars, practically exterminated that people. According to a gruesome tradition recorded by Paul the Deacon, he had the skull of the slain Gepid king, Cunimund, his father-in-law, fashioned into a cup and mounted in gold, which he would use to toast visitors on high occasions. On one such occasion, Alboin "sat longer than was proper with his wine," too long as it proved. While still deep in his cups, he ordered the grisly goblet brought in, handed it to Rosemond, and "invited her to drink merrily with her father." Whereupon Rosemond, who had spirit of her own, "burned to revenge the death of her father by the murder of her husband." She first seduced Peredeo, a "very strong man" in the king's household, so he would do her will. Then one day when Alboin was taking his siesta, she "bound his sword tightly to the head of the bed so that it could not be taken away or unsheathed," after which she let her paramour into the room. Alboin defended himself as best he could with a footstool, but in the end "this most warlike and very brave man being helpless against his enemy, was slain as if he were one of no account, and he who was most famous in war through the overthrow of so many enemies, perished by the scheme of one little woman."

Before his death, Alboin had conquered a good portion of northern Italy and made Pavia his capital. The king who succeeded him was murdered after a year, whereupon the Lombard nation divided into more than a score of tribes, each with its own duke. Despite their lack of unity, the Lombards managed to conquer much of the Italian countryside and the smaller communities. The larger cities, particularly those that could draw upon the imperial navy from Constantinople for supplies, held out against them, as did the southernmost part of the peninsula (the toe and heel). Lombard lack of ships also prevented their conquering Sicily, Corsica, or Sardinia. Their failure to conquer the entire peninsula had several significant consequences: first, Italy remained disunited through the medieval period and proved a constant battleground for conflicting interests, both internal and foreign; second, this disunity, coupled with the weakness of the emperors in Constantinople, made possible the emergence of a papal state in Italy; third, imperial rule continued to exist in parts of Italy as late as the latter eleventh century.

It now comes time to examine the nature of the civilization which emerged in the land appropriated by the Visigoths, Vandals, Franks, and other Germanic peoples, from the mingling of their cultures with that of the native "Romans." Because of the paucity of contemporary evidence this is not an easy task. The lack of uniformity with which the German and Roman cultures fused also complicates the task. To present two examples, one the reverse of the other: in Britain, the

Romans left the island in such numbers or were so thoroughly submerged, that nothing Roman remained to fuse with the Anglo-Saxon; in Africa, on the other hand, the Vandals who came into the country either died or were assimilated, so there also one need not ponder the question of fusing. In the first country, only a wholly Germanic civilization survived; in the other, a purely Roman. The culture that emerged in the other parts of what was once the western half of the Roman empire, in Italy, Spain, and Gaul, for instance, must have presented a most uneven picture. In an area such as northern Italy where depopulation had enabled the Lombards to establish a preponderance, more of a Germanic culture prevailed than one would suppose possible in a land so steeped in classical traditions. In the Provence, where a contrary situation existed, a way of life survived which was probably not substantially different from that of late Roman times.

A study of the royal authority the new Germanic kings exercised yields the picture of confusion one should expect. Gaiseric, king of the Vandals, not only claimed to be independent of the empire, but with his fleet forced that acknowledgment from Constantinople. The other kings who ruled former Roman territory—that is, except for Britain where only confusion reigned—generally paid the emperor formal allegiance and only got around to repudiating imperial authority in the sixth century. Until then it was not uncommon for them to mint coins that bore the image of the emperor even though they would have ignored any imperial directive had an emperor been so naive as to issue one. The robes and regalia that the Emperor Zeno sent Theodoric probably denoted, in fact, an actual partnership with Constantinople in ruling the empire. The emperor was probably pleased that these Western kings accepted the largely meaningless titles of imperial patrician or consul. Their use of such offices suggested at least a willingness on their part to tolerate the continuance of Roman customs and institutions.

The kind of authority the Germanic king enjoyed among his own people, in particular his aristocratic followers, depended upon a number of factors. The critical factor was the monarch's own personality and talents. If the king could command the loyalty of his subjects and if he was aggressive, as was Alboin, his authority might approach that of an autocrat. If he was neither capable nor popular, his chiefs might leave him nothing but his title. Such was the fate of Alboin's successors. The position of the new Germanic ruler was generally stronger than that Tacitus describes. The old assembly that had ruled with, and had checked, him was now gone. Its only reminder was the occasional gathering of the leading warriors in the spring when the warming weather promised a reopening of warfare. There existed no group of crown officials or institutional body that could legally have limited his authority. If the king enjoyed and retained the confidence of his principal men, called counts or dukes in Gaul and eorls in Britain, he could hope to live out his reign in peace and pass his crown on to his son. If he antagonized his counts, they might assassinate him, which was not difficult, and put up his son or another near relative in his place. That his followers recognized his authority and that of his dynasty as legitimate provided the king his chief assurance concerning the permanency of his position. That they could assassinate him if they chose constituted their principal check upon his autocracy.

What effectively denied the Germanic king the means of exercising any kind of autocratic authority except in his immediate presence was the absence of administrative machinery. Even in Roman times the imperial bureaucracy had lacked the personnel, loyalty, and efficiency that, by modern standards, could have made possible an autocracy (as opposed to tyranny). The Germanic kings, after establishing their authority, made some effort to preserve the Roman administrative system, but without much success. They and their counts lacked the sophistication to manage it, while the number of Romans capable of doing so shrank progressively in number with the decay of law schools and the decline of jurisprudence. Even the precious fiscal machinery was permitted to collapse. The Germans were incapable of handling it, the Roman masses abominated it. It was the hope, indeed, that German conquest would entail the end of taxation that made it "the one wish of all the Romans . . . to escape from Roman domination." As one contemporary wrote: "So far are the Germans from tolerating the evil taxation of the Romans, that not even the Romans who live under German rule are compelled to endure it."

The collapse of the Roman fiscal system had two significant consequences. Its disappearance, as suggested, helped reconcile Romans to the advent of Germanic rule and by so doing contributed to the breaking down of social barriers. Its collapse also deprived the new governments of the means of maintaining little beyond their own elementary administrative systems, with the consequent deterioration and eventual disappearance of the ancient forms and modes of Roman civilization. This was especially lamentable in the realm of law. For a generation or longer, the conquerors ordinarily promulgated a series of laws by which their Roman subjects were to live, laws which they drew for the most part from the Theodosian Code. Their own natives continued to live under their own laws, the Salian Franks of Clovis, for example, under *Salic Law*. That this latter was now written down and recorded in Latin, since there existed no Germanic script, represents the chief influence which contact with the higher Roman civilization exercised upon barbarian law.

Apart from these minor influences, the presence of Roman law scarcely made itself felt. Germanic judicial procedures replaced those of the Romans since they were simpler and involved less legalism, time, and expense. In an effort to decide the validity of a charge or a claim, for instance, the Romans had employed a procedure not substantially different from our own. They protected the rights of both the plaintiff and defendant and they did not permit the rendering of a judgment until after a careful examination of the evidence. For this time-consuming and relatively elaborate procedure the Germans substituted a simple system of compurgation. They either had no interest in the evidence pertinent to the case or felt this unnecessary in view of the high esteem they had for the word of a man. What they demanded of the defendant was a solemn oath denying the charge, then a number of supporting oaths from "oath-helpers" who would vouch for the purity of the defendant's oath. Since the Germans attributed a greater worth to men of aristocratic birth, the oath of one noble "oath-helper" might equal in force those of six ordinary freemen.

Should the defendant be charged with a particularly heinous crime or be of such ill repute that he could not produce the required number of compurgators, he was subjected to a method of trial called the ordeal. This involved putting the defendant to a physical test in which he would triumph, it was believed, if he were innocent, since a formal appeal was made to the gods (or God) to see that justice was done. The ordeal might be one of several. That by cold water required binding the defendant hand and foot and throwing him into a pond. If he sank, he was judged innocent since water, being pure, would not accept anything defiled. In the ordeal of boiling water, the defendant picked an object out of a caldron of hot water. If after three days the injured arm appeared to be healing properly, he was adjudged innocent.

A crude method of ascertaining guilt such as the ordeal could only have served a simple folk who stood in awe of the supernatural. The conviction that spiritual powers did take a hand in such tests must have prompted many a guilty defendant to confess his guilt prior to having that guilt revealed by the ordeal. In small communities where crime had difficulty hiding, one may also assume that the men selected to judge the nature of the wound resulting from the ordeal varied their judgment to suit their convictions concerning the guilt or innocence of the defendant. At best, however, the judicial ordeal must have manifested its inadequacy many centuries before the thirteenth, when it fell into disuse. Henry II of England ordered defendants "of very bad reputation" whose "innocence" had been confirmed by the ordeal, but who were "publicly and disgracefully spoken ill of by the testimony of many and lawful men," to quit the kingdom within forty days.

The impact of the Germanic invasions upon the social structure of the Western empire was less severe than one might suppose. Why these invasions did not involve a general degradation of the Roman aristocracy similar to that suffered by the Saxons in 1066 at the hands of their Norman invaders might be attributed to several circumstances. One was surely the respect the German conquerors felt for the superior Roman culture. Another was the preference the Germans had for acres and for grazing lands. Once peace settled on an area, this preference permitted urban society to continue on largely unaffected. Even that in the rural areas did not suffer any great dislocation since there were usually sufficient lands, either unused or seized from some previous barbarian group, to accommodate the new German aristocracy without necessitating the expropriation of Roman estates. (Only in Africa did the Vandal invaders expel most of the Roman proprietors.) The *coloni* continued to work the Roman latifundia. Gradually intermarriage, common interests, and, among the *coloni* and lower-class Germans working the estates, a common condition produced a new society in which those characteristics which had earlier distinguished Roman and German grew progressively less distinct.

Until recent years scholars were generally agreed that nowhere except possibly in its impact on classical culture did the coming of the Germans work greater change than in the economy of the Western empire. These scholars wrote movingly of the destruction of urban life and the wide devastation of the countryside by semicivilized conquerors whose economic development had not progressed far beyond the pastoral level. They counted among the immediate consequences of these invasions an abrupt decline of industry and commerce and a sharp acceleration of agrarian tendencies that had appeared as early as the late second century. Because such developments furnished corroboration for the view, so popular a generation ago, that a sharp cultural break had also occurred when Rome declined between the ancient and medieval world, they served to confirm the validity of that analysis.

Then in the 1920s the distinguished Belgian historian, Henri Pirenne, introduced a wholly different interpretation, so revolutionary that it has since been identified as the Pirenne thesis. Pirenne declared it was a mistake to charge the German invaders with having precipitated a major break in the general flow of history during the centuries of Rome's decline. Their coming did not disrupt the unity of the Mediterranean world, he argued. So long as the economic unity of the ancient Roman world remained intact, the degree of decline could only have been small. To Pirenne the true break between the ancient and medieval worlds came much later, in the seventh and eighth centuries with the rise of Islam. Moslem conquest of Syria, Egypt, North Africa, and Spain destroyed for the first time the unity of the Mediterranean world and forced western Europe into precipitate decline.

So bold a reinterpretation as Pirenne's was bound to come under heavy attack. No scholar accepts it *in toto,* many do not accept its substantial validity. His thesis disturbed, nevertheless, long-held views concerning the decline of Rome and prompted scholars to give another and a more careful look at the evidence. From this restudy has emerged a disposition to reduce the extent of the impact which the coming of the Germans was traditionally assumed to have had upon the aging empire. It is no longer fashionable to paint the appearance of the Germans in the darkest possible colors. The pillaging of towns and villas that accompanied these invasions no doubt contributed to a further decline of the West's economy and an encouragement to agrarian self-sufficiency. The depredations of the Vandal fleet disturbed in particular traditional arteries of trade. Beyond this it is dangerous to go.

The principal stabilizing agency to preach peace and patience during these troubled centuries when Roman institutions and power were crumbling and semibarbarous Germans assuming control was the Christian church. It was her bishops, too, who ordinarily moved into the vacuum left when Roman officials dropped their responsibilities and fled. As Gregory the Great did in the case of Rome and the Lombards (see above, p. 63), so did these prelates frequently take charge, direct emergency measures among their own people, and deal with the enemy. Jerome in his doleful litany of the cities these barbarians had destroyed and populations enslaved breaks off long enough to commend the "merits of the holy Bishop Exuperius [which had] prevailed so far to save [Toulouse] from destruction." One may assume, too, that the message which bishops and clergy taught, of a just and almighty God who punished the wicked and violent, exerted a sobering influence upon the German invaders. They believed in the same Christian God even though they were Arians, and one may recall in this connection that both Orosius and Augustine stressed the moderation with which Alaric's Visigoths had "sacked" the city of Rome.

Another facet of the work of the church in the West during these turbulent centuries was its role in the preservation of learning. These were the Dark Ages, when schools, learning, and the arts in general seemed in danger of perishing. The more apprehensive among earlier observers had feared this would come to pass. As early as the fourth century Ammianus Marcellinus had made the disturbing statement that the "libraries, like tombs, are closed forever." His comment may be misleading. Apollinaris Sidonius, fifth-century bishop of Auvergne, writes of schools and the pursuit of learning in his section of southern France, and in the early sixth century Cassiodorus speaks of the schools in Rome "as swarming with students." Of course, Cassiodorus left Rome before a series of destructive sieges and captures during the long war between Justinian's armies and the Ostrogoths had left that city in ruins. A similar situation may have prevailed in Gaul where Gregory of Tours lamented: "Woe to us, for the study of letters has disappeared from amongst us." Fortunately Gregory was speaking only of Gaul, a country that had borne the brunt of Germanic invasions. Anglo-Saxon Britain had fared no better, but surely an appreciable measure of classical life lived on in parts of Spain and in North Africa, and even in several of the cities of Italy such as Ravenna which still remained under Constantinople's control.

There remains one disturbing statistic that proclaims how different from earlier centuries had become the bases of learning and the character of its exponents. After the year 500 A.D., among those men whose erudition and interest in learning set them well above the masses, appears the name of but one layman. That man was Boethius. What had happened to the group of humanists, to use the term generously, who had carried on the traditions of the Scipionic circle, through Cicero and his company, past the Augustan age and into the third century? By the middle of the fourth century their number had dwindled to such a degree that men whose mediocre talents would have passed unnoticed during preceding generations now enjoyed the adulation of the crowds and accepted appointment as provincial governors and consuls from emperors anxious to honor a disappearing breed. By the late fifth century these scholars and their empty, albeit literary eloquence was fast disappearing—no great loss, to be sure, except that their passing symbolized the passing too of the only formal group in Roman society that was conversant with classical literature, knew its language, and above all had directly and indirectly through their fame helped preserve the tradition of secular scholarship.

Two events took place in the year 529 which proclaimed in symbolic language the end of one era and the beginning of another. In 529 Benedict founded his monastery at Monte Cassino. That same year Justinian closed the doors of the Platonic Academy in Athens. Monte Cassino was to be an exclusively religious community; the Academy had been just as thoroughly secular, even pagan. From that time onward, at least in the West, the pursuit of learning would be the preserve of churchmen, more particularly of the monks of St. Benedict. And not before the closing centuries of the Middle Ages would the secular scholar and humanist reappear on the scene.

This fact explains the fundamentally Christian character of learning during the Middle Ages. If scholars did not concern themselves directly with the Bible and with the explanation of theological problems, their search aimed only less directly toward a better understanding of the world that God had made. From almost the first Christian scholar to the last, from Tertullian, through Jerome, Augustine, Bede, Anselm, Thomas Aquinas, and Roger Bacon, so overwhelming did these men judge the almighty power of God and the pervasiveness of the Divine Will, that they could not have pursued any serious study which ignored or was indifferent to that conviction. Roger Bacon, the most "modern" of medieval scientists, the man who foresaw the day when men would travel on power-propelled ships and on airplanes, proposed as further justification for the study of mathematics, the claim that it would "aid us in ascertaining the position of paradise and hell, and promote our knowledge of scriptural geography and sacred chronology. . . ."

So thoroughly Christian did medieval thought become after the sixth century that the possibility of engaging seriously in scholarly pursuits of a purely secular nature probably never entered the minds of the

learned. To the early church fathers, on the other hand, the choice
was a very real one. Their world was still largely pagan, as were
many schools and scholars. To a rigorist like Tertullian who usually
saw all things in black and white, there was no choice. The Christian
must shun secular learning, philosophy in particular. "What has Athens
to do with Jerusalem?" he asked. "What has the Academy to do with
the church? . . . What wisdom is there in this hankering after con-
jectural speculations? . . . It served Thales of Miletus right, that when
looking around at the stars as he walked about, he should have suffered the mortification of falling into a well."

No church father assumed so intolerant a position as did Tertullian,
although there were some who had reservations about the propriety of
classical studies for members of the clergy. Jerome, who had an excellent classical training and retained a continuing love for pagan literature, seems, on one occasion, almost to have apologized for that
fact. He tells of a vision he had in which he found himself before the
judgment seat of God where he was sharply charged with being a
Ciceronian. Still one cannot help but feel that the question of Christians' acquiring secular learning and reading pagan classics was one
of those theoretical issues that vexed only puritanical minds like
Tertullian's. Educated Christians received their education in the same
secular schools as did the pagans and read the same pagan Homer,
Vergil, and Horace. Basil, Gregory of Nazianzen, and John Chrysostom
not only received a classical education but praised its usefulness.
This explains the horrified protest Christian leaders raised against Emperor Julian's order that they be excluded from the secular schools.
Julian may have decided to call the bluff of the more vocal "Tertul-
lians." Without a liberal education, without a knowledge of philosophy,
how could Christians provide fellow-Christians the tools to study the
Bible or to answer the attacks of pagan rhetoricians? Augustine, a
very levelheaded man for all his erudition, recommended the approach
most men accepted as reasonable, namely, to study the "poets and
philosophers in order to sharpen the intellect and make it better able
to explain the mystery of the Divine Word. . . ."

To return now to the Dark Ages and to the most distinguished
scholars, who kept learning alive during those dreary centuries, there
appears in first place chronologically the name of Boethius. He has
been called the "last of the Romans," which may mean that he was
one of the last humanists of the classical period who still pursued
learning and truth for their own sake, whose cultural accomplishments,

therefore, were principally secular. This does not mean that Boethius was something of a pagan; quite the contrary. His religious convictions may, indeed, have had a direct bearing on his execution, and though he does not mention Christ in his most famous work, *The Consolation of Philosophy,* the argument he outlines there is not unlike that presented in the Scriptures.

He wrote his *Consolation of Philosophy* in prison while awaiting execution. Its theme was one his own career suggested: he who had achieved high honor, wealth, and position, now like a common criminal, was to die. Was there anything left but despair? No, Lady Philosophy assured him, for virtue is its own reward and its fame is eternal. Fortune is fickle, and man's unhappiness springs from his setting up material values, such as wealth, honor, and influence, as ultimate goals. "There is nothing Fortune has which is worth striving for; there is nothing in her nature which is good, for neither do good men always possess her gifts, nor do these gifts make those good who possess them." Only God who is the supreme and unchanging good can satisfy man's search for happiness and only good men can attain that good.

More valuable than Boethius' *Consolation* to the centuries immediately succeeding were his treatises on music, arithmetic, and astronomy, and, above all, his translation of several of the logical works of Aristotle and Porphyry's introduction to Aristotle's *Categories.* These last were just the beginning of the magnificent goal Boethius had set for himself, that of translating "every work of Aristotle . . . and all the dialogues of Plato, and to evoke a certain concord between them." Had Boethius been able to accomplish this work the Dark Ages in all probability would have been less dark, and the intellectual reawakening of the West would surely have come considerably earlier than the eleventh century.

Cassiodorus (d. 580), who was Boethius' contemporary, while not so great a scholar, made a more substantial contribution to the preservation of learning. His own individual writings are no more precious, although their more religious content better served the needs of scholarship for the next five hundred years. His career resembled that of Boethius up to a point: he was also of an aristocratic family, rose to the position of private secretary to Theodoric, then that of praetorian prefect, but contrary to Boethius, accepted the presence of Arian Goths in Catholic Italy and bent his efforts to further the coexistence of the two groups. Only after the death of Theodoric and the appearance of Justinian's armies, did he leave the court and retire to Calabria.

Cassiodorus founded two monasteries in Calabria, one for anchorites, the other for cenobites. That he elected to live in the latter was a blessing for Western learning. For it was he above any other monastic leader who introduced the monk to the critical role he was to assume in the task of preserving learning and teaching it to the unlearned. The traditional image of the monk tirelessly copying manuscripts in the dusky monastic scriptorium is largely a product of Cassiodorus' inspiration. He convinced monasticism that few occupations were more valuable or more suited to its monks. "The devil should be fought with pen and ink," he admonished, "for Satan receives as many wounds as the scribe copies words of the Lord." He also left his monks directions on how to copy manuscripts, how to emend texts, how to organize a library. For their own education and to facilitate their teaching others he composed treatises on the seven liberal arts, prepared instructions on reading the Bible and the Fathers, a commentary on the Psalms, and several theological works. These proved of greater value to the darkening Europe of his day than the official letters he drew up as Theodoric's secretary. But historians consider these most valuable, and their high quality increases the regret scholars feel over the loss of his history of the Goths. This remains in a compend by the unlettered Jordanes.

Cassiodorus in his concentration upon training the monk who was to preach and civilize represented a major step from Boethius, whose major concern was the intellectual value of learning. The position of a younger contemporary of Cassiodorus, Gregory of Tours (d. 594), represents still a further step removed from humanistic learning, if one may call Gregory learned. Pious he was, and a devoted and courageous bishop when few had the will to stand firm against the blandishments and threats of the brutal Merovingian (Frankish) court. What provides him immortality are not, however, learned manuals on the seven liberal arts or textual studies of the Bible, neither of which he could or did prepare, but a *History of the Franks*. Even this is not a scholarly history. Among other deficiencies the Latin is faulty, for which the humble Gregory apologizes. He prefaces his history by begging the indulgence of those who may read what he had to write "should I violate the laws of grammar to a serious or minor degree, since I have not been well schooled in that subject." Still someone had to do that task "since there has been found no grammarian sufficiently competent in the art of writing to relate, either in prose or verse, what had happened in our country."

Like his age, Gregory's history lacks organization, and the author likes to digress. Still this is not a serious defect. His history constitutes a gold mine out of which scholars have taken almost all they know of the Merovingian age. Gregory writes in a simple, easy-flowing, yet vivid style of an age when men appeared to have been either saints or devils, when "there have been done good things many, and evil many; the peoples savagely raged; the fury of kings grew sharp . . . the faithful enriched the churches while the unbelievers stripped them bare." Historians are grateful to Gregory for his history. The Middle Ages were more pleased with his hagiological writings, which led other men to write of saints and also furnished medieval breviaries many of their inspiring stories.

Gregory must have been acquainted with Fortunatus, who was the leading poet of the day. Although Fortunatus was born in Italy, he spent the greater part of his life in Gaul, in fact visited Tours, Gregory's home, to pray at the shrine of St. Martin, to whose intercession he attributed his escape from blindness. For several years he wasted his still immature talents as a court poet in the household of the Frankish kings, then moved to Poitiers where he became bishop. Among his many poems, panegyrics, epitaphs, even some secular verse, two of his hymns have gained immortality, the *Vexilla Regis* and *Pange Lingua Gloriosi*.

Brighter than the cultural atmosphere of Gaul was that in Spain. Classical influences had seeped deep in the southern part, in the province of Baetica, which had bred Seneca, Trajan, and Quintilian. That land too had not suffered such grievous destruction at the hands of the Germanic invaders. Its principal luminary during the period of the Dark Ages was the influential bishop of Seville, Isidore (d. 636). Few scholars have written more voluminously, yet with less originality or critical judgment. His most original idea was his belief that the etymology of a word (often quite ingenious) suggested its essence: *viz.*, medicine from *modo*, meaning moderation, "For nature is grieved by excess whereas she rejoices in moderation." From his fondness for using derivations to introduce the meaning of terms, his encyclopedic work derives its title of *Etymologies*. Its range of subjects is impressive: peoples, languages, education, science, anatomy, natural history, navigation, astronomy, geography, cities, stones, metals, trees, weapons, war, and what have you. Its all-embracing nature and its authoritative tone made it the *Britannica* of Western Europe for many centuries to come. Isidore also composed treatises on a variety of subjects including the mystical value of numbers, in addition to biographies of eminent people, some history, commentaries on the Bible, even a rule for monks. Little escaped his notice, but to the accuracy or truth of the information he unfortunately gave little attention. His preference for the unusual and his tendency to oversimplify bespeak both his own intellectual limitations and the lack of intellectual maturity he found among his readers.

The role of churchmen in preserving learning during these Dark Ages stood most clearly revealed in Ireland, Scotland, and Britain. The man who traditionally receives credit for having initiated the conversion of the peoples in these insular areas was Patrick (d. 461). He came to Ireland first as the slave of Irish raiders who had kidnaped him in Britain, later as a missionary. Between these two appearances he had managed to escape to Gaul and acquire monastic training at Lerins, a small island off the southern coast. Honoratus, the founder of the monastery at Lerins, had traveled to Egypt and Syria to learn of monasticism in its birthplace, then on his return selected Lerins for its isolation, drove out the snakes, and built a monastery. Patrick took with him to Ireland the same ability to drive out snakes, so pious Irish believe, and more importantly, the same austere, loosely organized monasticism that characterized that of the East. This austerity may have contributed to the vigor of Irish monks, surely to their relative freedom of spirit that sent them swarming all over the British Isles, Scotland, and the islands of the north Atlantic, in search of solitude and souls.

Fairly representative of these Irish monks was Columba (d. 597), son of a chieftain from the country about Donegal. From his father he may have had his autocratic, ambitious temperament, for "he was not a gentle hero," observed his Gaelic eulogist. About the age of forty-five he left Ireland and the thirty monasteries he had founded there, and moved to Scotland to the wild, desolate island of Iona, which he made the monastic and intellectual center for Scotland and northern England. From Iona he established another thirty monastic centers and converted the king of the Picts. His disciples later founded Lindisfarne on the North Sea. From Britain Irish monks crossed over the Atlantic to the land of the Franks, to Germany, and Italy. The most successful of these monks was Columbanus, who led his twelve companions across England to Gaul where a grandson of Clovis gave him an estate at

Luxeuil in Burgundy. Many Franks, including nobles, accepted baptism, but in Queen Brunhild he met his match. When he attempted to convert and reform her son, the king—Brunhild had encouraged her son to content himself with mistresses so there would be no queenly rival to dispute her influence—she ordered Columbanus sent back to Ireland. With the aid of sympathetic guards, however, he escaped to Germany, made his way to Switzerland, and finally to Bobbio in north Italy where death finally closed his tireless career.

The year that Columbanus died (597), Augustine and his band of Benedictine monks landed at Canterbury. (It is not entirely certain that they were Benedictines.) The coincidence of these two events may carry some significance. At least Columbanus was the last distinguished representative of Irish monasticism to carry religion and learning to the Continent. The future lay with Anglo-Saxon monks like Boniface who owed their education perhaps more to the "Romans" who followed in the wake of Augustine than to the Irish teachers who remained in the northern part of Britain. For zealous though the Irish were, men like Theodore of Tarsus and Hadrian who came from Italy were not only their equal as scholars, but had the authority of Rome behind them. In 664 at Whitby (see below, p. 213), the Irish agreed to recognize this authority, after which they gradually withdrew and left the field to the newcomers. Some of them remained, including the Irishman who shared with Hadrian in giving Aldhelm his education.

An even greater scholar than Aldhelm was his disciple, the Venerable Bede, the principal intellectual ornament of the monastery of Jarrow. Jarrow owed its establishment to Benedict Biscop, a Northumbrian nobleman, who also endowed it with precious volumes he brought back from a visit to Rome. These books and others he found at Jarrow provided Bede his tools and inspiration. "It has ever been my delight," the scholar reflected in later life, "to learn or teach or write." Few men have applied themselves to these tasks with greater devotion. He assimilated what learning the Irish and Romans had brought to England, then when he was not setting down this knowledge in countless treatises on a variety of useful subjects, he was teaching it to the younger men who had come to Jarrow to learn. Much of his time he devoted to the simple task of copying and compiling, so critical was the sheer need for materials to use in the schools.

Most original and valuable to posterity was Bede's charming *Ec-*

clesiastical History of the English People upon which rests his reputation as the "first modern historian." His piety reminds the reader of Gregory of Tours, but little else. Bede's Latin is excellent, the organization of his materials clear and balanced, and his whole purpose patently that of a historian. Few authors have offered their readers a preface more likely to win their confidence and good will. "Should the reader discover any inaccuracies in what I have written, I humbly beg that he will not impute them to me, because, as the laws of history require, I have labored honestly to transmit whatever I could ascertain from common report for the instruction of posterity. I earnestly request all who may hear or read this history of our nation to ask God's mercy on my many failings of mind and body. And in return for the diligent toil that I have bestowed on the recording of memorable events in the various provinces and places of greater note, I beg that their inhabitants may grant me the favor of frequent mention in their devout prayers."

A direct consequence of the agreement at Whitby was the gradual replacement of the Celtic missionaries on the Continent by the triumphant Anglo-Saxon monks. Of these the most active and successful was St. Boniface (d. 755). Boniface may not have labored any more zealously than Columbanus, but the positive support both pope and Frankish rulers gave him assured his work greater scope and permanence. It would be difficult to say in what capacity Boniface, "the Apostle of the Germans," made his principal contribution: in reforming the church, in establishing monasteries such as Fulda which remained Germany's leading center of learning for centuries to come, in founding new bishoprics, or in converting the Germans. One of his companions describes what these pagan Germans must have considered his greatest deed, that of cutting down the great oak of Thor: "The man of God was surrounded by the servants of God. When he would cut down the tree, behold a great throng of pagans who were there cursed him bitterly among themselves because he was the enemy of their gods. And when he had cut into the trunk a little way, a breeze sent by God stirred overhead, and suddenly the branching top of the tree was broken off, and the oak in all its huge bulk fell to the ground. And it was broken into four parts, as if by the divine will, so that the trunk was divided into four huge sections without any effort of the brethren who stood by. When the pagans who had cursed did see this, they left off cursing and, believing, blessed God. Then the most holy priest took counsel with the brethren and he built from the wood of the tree an oratory, and dedicated it to the holy apostle Peter."

At the age of seventy-four, Boniface and a band of fifty companions ventured among the pagan Frisians, who massacred them to the last man.

CHAPTER 4

The Byzantine Empire

"God has given us to subdue the Vandals, Alans, and Moors . . . and we have taken hope that the Lord will grant us the rest of the empire which the Romans of old extended to the bounds of the two oceans, and which they lost through indolence." With these bold words did Justinian, the man who ascended the imperial throne in 527 A.D., announce his determination to recover all the ancient Roman territories which the Germans and other barbarians had overrun. Justinian ruled from Constantinople, the city on the Bosporus which Constantine had chosen for his court and capital. Though little more than the eastern provinces remained of the ancient imperial territories, these emperors in Constantinople always insisted that the Roman empire still ruled the Mediterranean world. Had anyone dared, indeed, to ask Justinian whether the Roman empire had come to an end in 476, he might have had that person incarcerated. That is what happened to the papal envoys in 968 when the letters they presented to Nicephorus II addressed him simply as "Emperor of the Greeks." The patriarch of Constantinople continues even today to refer to himself as patriarch of the Romans.

The claim of Constantinople to wield the authority of the Caesars has generally not impressed those scholars who ponder the end of the Roman empire. Yet the eastern half of the empire, actually much more than half of it in terms of population, economic development, and resources, remained a strong institution after the western half had been lost. Zeno and his successors spoke only of the loss, hopefully temporary, of the western provinces, even though these included Italy and the ancient capital on the Tiber. In their judgment the Roman empire still continued to be the most formidable power in the world, and they were its rulers. They would, therefore, have approved as only proper that Edward Gibbon should in his *Decline and Fall* have carried the story of its fortunes, principally misfortunes as they proved, down to the Turkish capture of Constantinople in 1453.

Most modern historians prefer rather to identify this eastern half of what was once the Roman empire as the Byzantine empire. From the beginning this eastern half of the empire, they argue, had never been a truly Roman partner to the west. It had remained too Greek, and shortly after the loss of the western provinces its basically Hellenistic character had reasserted itself. Even Justinian, who had spoken so confidently of restoring the Roman empire, himself confessed that the people in his eastern half used Greek, not Latin. Actually Rome had established herself as the greatest power in the Mediterranean world long before she set out on her conquest of the east. She first added Pergamum, then Greece and Macedonia, next Asia Minor and Syria, and finally Egypt in 31 B.C. Almost five hundred years of Rome's history had elapsed before she added Egypt. To look at the empire at the time of Augustus when it filled the entire Mediterranean world, is to see a new empire, one that was "Roman" only in a political sense. Of all the provinces, these to the east were the least Roman of all. They had fiercely opposed Roman conquest, and as provinces they had steadfastly resisted Romanization. The cultures of the two halves of the empire were and remained different, their economies were not complementary, nor was travel between the two easy or frequent. Apart from a veneer of Roman officials and a physical façade created by Roman temples, civic buildings, roads, and aqueducts, the east had clung to the ways to which it had become accustomed centuries before Rome had turned its mind to conquering it.

Such considerations appear to justify the view that the loss of the western half of the empire represented the end of the Roman empire as history understands that empire. When the Roman west fell, the empire fell. It was only the non-Roman, the eastern half, that survived. Its emperors might call themselves Roman Caesars until 1453, and, of course, Roman legal traditions might remain strong there until the end. Yet it never was nor became the pagan state ancient Rome had been, rather the most thoroughly Christian state that has ever existed. So most scholars employ, without apology, the modern term "Byzantine empire" to designate this state, the term "Byzantine" being the adjectival form of the name of the old Greek town where Constantine had decided to build his new capital.*

Before taking a long look at the career of Justinian, it will be useful to glance briefly at the history of the emperors who ruled the Eastern Roman empire during the century preceding his accession. Such a glance, if nothing more, will reveal the different course that events there took as opposed to those in Italy and the west.

Arcadius, the son of Theodosius who ruled from Constantinople (his brother Honorius ruled the West; see above, p. 86), never amounted to much; so his death in 408 changed nothing. His infant son, Theodosius II (408–450), enjoyed an unusually long and not entirely innocuous reign even though his limited talents were those of a student rather than administrator. His sister Pulcheria, a remarkable woman, together with his wife Eudocia, and his advisers deserve principal credit for his reign's achievements. These included a thorough rebuilding of the wall to the west of Constantinople and the publication of the Theodosian Code. The latter constituted a codification of all the imperial constitutions which Constantine and his successors had issued. Both wall and code were of considerable significance. The influence of the Theodosian Code was reflected in the Germanic codes in the West, while the rebuilding of Constantinople's fortifications greatly strengthened that city's defenses on the only side where they were vulnerable. Except for the strength of this wall and other fortifications which time after time saved the city, the fate of the Eastern empire might not have been greatly different from that of the West.

After the death of Theodosius II followed Marcian (450–457), who cut off the ruinous tribute payments to the Huns. Though this move led Attila to make his swing around the west (see above, p. 90), thereby relieving pressure on Constantinople, little was gained in the end. No sooner had the Huns disappeared, than the equally dangerous Ostrogoths moved in to take their place. After Marcian's death the Alan chieftain Aspar, who was the imperial master of the troops, attempted to assume the role of emperor-maker similar to that played by Ricimer in the west. Leo I (457–474) refused to stoop to being a puppet, however, and brought in semicivilized Isaurian mountaineers from southern Anatolia with whom he defied Aspar and his Germans. One of the

* No doubt Diocletian and Constantine would have denied that their empires were any less Roman for their having chosen to rule them from the East. Julius Caesar may even have contemplated moving his capital to Alexandria.

Isaurian chieftains married his daughter, then succeeded to the throne under the Greek name of Zeno (474–491). Zeno's principal accomplishment, apart from maintaining his precarious throne in the face of bitter religious conflict, Gothic pressures, and the general abhorrence the Byzantine people had for his Isaurians, was his success in persuading Theodoric to take his semicivilized Ostrogoths to Italy. Zeno's successor, Anastasius I (491–518), devoted his major attention to the fierce theological controversies that threatened to erupt into civil war. It would be as futile to attempt a precise definition of the views of the three religious groups striving for supremacy as were the attempts Anastasius made to reconcile them. Of the three, the Orthodox (Roman), Monophysite, and what remained of the Nestorian, Anastasius favored the Monophysite. He enjoyed more success in improving the imperial tax structure and in breaking the power of the Isaurians. The court was most pleased with the immense reserve he left in the treasury when he died, the people of Constantinople with the new wall he had erected forty miles to the west of the city.

Out of the confusion over who should succeed when Anastasius died, a confusion which, incidentally, almost regularly attended the death of an emperor, there emerged this time an old soldier named Justin (518–527), commander of the imperial bodyguard. Some twenty years before—Justin was now in his late sixties—he had left his peasant home in Illyria to make his fortune in the metropolis on the Bosporus. His physique earned him admittance to the guard, and his long, loyal service eventually its command. Procopius, the principal historian of the period and an excellent one, was among those who disapproved Justin's rise to the imperial office. For Justin "was already an old man with one foot in the grave and so utterly ignorant of letters, that he did not know one letter from another. . . ." Justin did have the wit, however, to recognize his deficiencies, and for counsel and leadership leaned heavily on his young nephew and adopted son, Justinian. Justinian was his sister's boy, had the same peasant background, but had acquired an excellent education which his fond uncle made certain to provide him.

Historians date Justinian's actual, not official, reign from the time of his uncle's accession. They find no good reason to doubt Procopius' testimony that "Justin did not succeed in doing his subjects either good or harm; for he was so utterly simple, a very poor speaker, and a complete boor. His sister's son, Justinian, who was still young, practically governed the state." The most significant development of the uncle's reign was the re-establishment of friendly relations with the papacy, a move dictated perhaps less by Justinian's religious convictions than by political expediency. The evidence suggests that Justinian so early in his career may have been laying plans for the recovery of the western provinces. And prudence recommended as a necessary preliminary a *rapprochement* with Rome even though his own subjects, Monophysites for the most part, were not at all pleased.

In August 527 the old uncle died, and Justinian succeeded him without opposition. No Roman emperor since Augustus left a deeper imprint upon his times and those that followed than Justinian, so a description of the man's character is in order. Under ordinary circumstances this would not be easy. Only rarely, as in the case of Alexander the Great for instance, or Julius Caesar, do contemporary sources provide sufficient light to furnish more than a man's silhouette. That Justinian stands forth from the shadows of time in some substance is the work of Procopius, the last distinguished "Roman" historian. There will be more of Procopius later. Suffice it to say here that the modern reader must be wary when Procopius writes of Justinian or, for that matter, of most of the major characters who cross his pages. Though Procopius was an able historian, he lacked the virtue of detachment. In the case of Justinian, he wrote either to flatter the emperor or to calumniate him. In Procopius' *Buildings* Justinian appears as a superman and genius, in the *Secret History* as so consummate a scoundrel that "Nature appeared to have taken all baseness from the rest of mankind and to have planted it in the soul of this man."

Clearly Justinian's character lay somewhere in between, but exactly where remains a matter of doubt. He was of medium height, had a strong physique and constitution, and was moderate in his tastes. His marriage to Theodora, the leading actress of her day, was the only luxury he permitted himself. By nature he was most industrious—"he never sleeps"—strongly motivated, and a man of scholarly talents as well. Few rulers have possessed his grasp of statecraft and finance, even fewer his knowledge of architecture and theology. The well-known mosaic in the nave of San Vitale in Ravenna shows Justinian in a serious, thoughtful pose which surely fits the man's character if not his appearance. His shrewdness stands best revealed in the remarkable men (and Theodora) whom he selected to assist him, and, of course, in the fruition of most of his great projects. Justinian must have been a man of extraordinary faith and determination to have borne up so long and so successfully under weight of the overwhelming pressures that sprung from theological, fiscal, and military difficulties.

About the only weakness occasional writers fault Justinian for is a want of resolution. In view of the enormous accomplishments of the man, the charge strikes one as unjust, and that it might well be. The sole evidence, and not very convincing evidence at that, of this presumed lack of resolution is the emperor's behavior during the *Nika* riots. The setting for these riots was the Hippodrome, the huge stadium that Constantine had erected in order to provide the citizens of his new Rome the same opportunities for sports events as those available in the Circus Maximus in old Rome. The stadium may have accommodated as many as eighty thousand spectators and had a special "palace" reserved for use of the emperor and his court.

Of all the spectacles the public enjoyed in the Hippodrome, the most popular were the chariot races. Four chariots ordinarily took part, each carrying a different color: white, green, blue, and red. By the time of Justinian's accession, the Blues and Greens had absorbed the other two; and it was usual for the supporters of the Blues to occupy the west stands, those who cheered the Greens and wore their colors to sit to the east. This arrangement of itself served to intensify a rivalry already apt to be sharpened over disagreements concerning matters more serious than horses. For over the years the Hippodrome had acquired a secondary function, that of furnishing the populace a means of giving expression to their feeling on popular issues whether political, financial, or religious, which might be exciting them. Perhaps this tradition grew out of the practice of the new emperor's going to the Hippodrome to be acclaimed. The ebullience of the crowd may even be traced back to ancient Greece when the Athenian citizen had a deme and an assembly in which to voice his views. Now that autocracy had silenced those institutions, the only means of expression left to the populace was that of demonstrating in the Hippodrome in the presence of the emperor and his court. For this reason the races frequently became the occasion of riots; and Justinian, who had earlier been a Blue, since that group favored the Orthodox view concerning Christ's nature as opposed to the Monophysite Green, assumed a neutral position upon his accession and took steps to curb the turbulency of the crowds.

What caused the races on January 13, 532, to spawn the most dangerous riot in Byzantine history was first, the bitterness of many of the spectators over the fiscal policies of the government; and second, an accidental circumstance that had made allies of the ordinarily hostile

Greens and Blues. An earlier riot at the Hippodrome had resulted in the death of a number of spectators, and the government had ordered the execution of the ringleaders. In the case of two of those to be hanged, a Blue and a Green as it happened, the executioner had bungled his job; whereupon both factions demanded that the two men be reprieved. When Justinian refused to bend to their demands which they pressed during the games on January 13, the two groups closed ranks, raised the cry of *Nika* (conquer), and began to riot. To pacify the mob, which was pillaging and burning public buildings and churches (among the latter was the first Hagia Sophia which Constantine had built), the government dismissed several ministers including the hated John the Cappadocian, the financial minister; but the mob refused to be appeased. Powerful elements among the aristocracy, it appears, who resented the autocratic manner in which Justinian was excluding them from the government, had taken over direction of the tumulting. They wanted nothing short of the deposition of the emperor. They even induced a nephew of the late Anastasius I, Hypatius by name, to become their unwilling candidate.

Under the circumstances there was nothing other than force that Justinian could have employed to quiet the rioting. He could not appeal to the city police nor even to the palace guards, since neither could be trusted. His first attempt to use the troops which two of his generals, Belisarius and Mundus, happened to have in the city, barbarians for the most part, only roused the mob to greater fury. At great personal danger he had risked appearing at the Hippodrome to make a personal appeal to the rioters to settle down, with a promise upon the gospels of amnesty for all, but to no avail. Only when the palace itself came under attack and Belisarius, his most trusted general, along with his other advisers were urging him to flee, did Justinian finally decide upon flight.

It was at this juncture, so writes Procopius, that Theodora came forward to announce dramatically that she was not fleeing. They might all go if they wished, but not she. As an empress she had lived, and as an empress she would die. "Let me never come to be without this purple robe," she declared, "nor live that day when they that speak to me do not call me their Lady and Mistress. If sir, you have a mind to escape, this is not difficult. We have plenty of money, there is the sea, and yonder are ships. But consider whether, once you have saved yourself, you may not have cause most willingly to exchange your safety for death. But as for me, I like the old saying that royalty is a good burial-shroud."

According to Procopius, Theodora's firmness led Justinian and his advisers to reconsider the situation. It was decided that a combination of force and bribery might yet retrieve the situation. First Narses, a loyal court official, was sent off to the Hippodrome where the rioters had congregated to hail their new emperor, with gold to buy off the rebel leaders and with "stories" that might arouse their suspicions concerning Hypatius' qualifications and intentions. Next Belisarius and Mundus marched separate detachments to the stadium and forced entrance from opposite ends. The combination of money and force did the work and the revolt was put down, although some thirty thousand people were slain in the slaughter. The *Nika* riots took place just five years after Justinian's accession. While the destruction caused by the rioters was enormous and the blood bath that attended its suppression tragic, the harsh handling of dissenters surely simplified Justinian's tasks during the thirty-three years ahead. Never again during his reign would the Blues and Greens cause trouble, nor would a chastened aristocracy, after the execution of its leaders and the confiscation of much of its wealth, occasion the crown any further difficulties.

If Procopius' account of Justinian's escape in the *Nika* rioting is correct, Theodora comes in for at least accidental credit. She appears indeed to have been a remarkable woman. Procopius, who goes to psychopathic lengths to destroy her reputation, admits she "was fair of face and had a graceful figure, but was short and lacked color. . . ." Her eyes, which "were brilliant and piercing," must have attracted first attention. Of morals and principles she had none, if we are to do the impossible and believe Procopius. It is true that she grew up among people and circumstances which discouraged the practice of chastity. Her father was a bear-keeper at the Hippodrome, while during her adolescent years she appeared on the stage as a comic entertainer. That she followed the profession of a prostitute is possible, although when she caught Justinian's fancy she must have gained acceptance into the kind of social circle similar to that in which Pericles found Aspasia. After the death of Euphemia, Justin's strait-laced wife, Justinian persuaded the emperor to repeal the law that barred the marriage of members of the noble class to "actresses, freedwomen, and hostesses."

Theodora was about twenty when she married Justinian, who was that many years her senior. For twenty-one years they lived together in a wedlock that would have been considered remarkably harmonious even between commoners. Justinian treated his former mistress with great honor, was faithful to her, and did not remarry when she died of cancer in 548. He made her his co-Augustus, lavished upon her rich presents, and built for her, her own magnificent palace. And he regularly consulted her about matters of state. Procopius has Theodora affirming, in fact, that Justinian could "be counted upon not to do anything whatsoever without consulting me." The two did not always agree, particularly concerning the nature of Christ. Justinian shifted his position from time to time because of political circumstances. Throughout her life Theodora appears to have remained staunchly Monophysite in her sympathies and regularly gave refuge to Monophysite leaders in her palace.

Justinian's first major undertaking and, as it proved, his most important and enduring, was the codification of Roman law. During the reign of his uncle he had gained firsthand acquaintance with the manner legal confusion was hampering the administration of justice. Scarcely six months after his coronation he proceeded to carry through a thoroughgoing reform. While this act might be put down as not unusual for an ambitious new ruler bent on providing his state a more efficient and equitable administration, the fact remains that no emperor before Justinian had attempted this. All his predecessors, that is, the responsible ones, must have appreciated the grave need for introducing order into the accumulated mass of legislation; and two of them, Hadrian and Theodosius II, had carried out limited codifications. Hadrian had codified the edicts of praetors, Theodosius the imperial decrees promulgated by Constantine and his successors.

There were present other sources of law beyond praetors' edicts and recent imperial decrees which the judge might consider before issuing a decision. Among the most ancient were the enactments of the Roman popular assemblies and the senate; more recent, the decrees of emperors who had preceded Constantine. The dedicated Byzantine judge also felt some obligation to search through the enormous mass of decisions and opinions which a long series of eminent jurists had handed down from the past. Aside from the duplication, obsolescence, and inconsistency that the accumulation of almost a thousand years of lawmaking would inevitably have left in its wake, there existed for the judge the added problem of reconciling the jurisprudence of a pagan state with the demands of a militantly Christian government, which Justinian's had become.

Early in 528 Justinian appointed a commission of ten distinguished jurists under the chairmanship of the pagan scholar, Tribonian, with instructions to codify the laws. In their scrutiny of old legislation they were to limit themselves to imperial edicts and only to those promulgated by Hadrian and his successors. This was a prudent decision. Hadrian, above all the other Good Emperors, had made a special effort to liberalize the law. He had also introduced measures which he hoped would improve the efficiency of the government. For a year the commission busied itself with sorting through laws, eliminating those that were redundant, obsolete, or inconsistent with Christian morality. When their work was finished, Justinian promulgated it under the title of *Codex Constitutionum* (Book of Laws). As slightly revised a few years later, the *Codex* listed a total of 4562 enactments, all carefully arranged by subject matter and following roughly the twelvefold organization laid down in the ancient Twelve Tables (451 B.C.).

The *Codex* represented the first phase of Justinian's codification of Roman law. More important because of its greater influence upon the law codes of future European nations was the *Digest* (Greek *Pandects*). This was the work of a second commission, again under Tribonian's presidency, which Justinian appointed with instructions to sift through the mass of legal literature contributed by ancient jurists and to reduce this to workable proportions. As noted, the most eminent of Roman jurists were those of the second and early third centuries, and it was upon their writings that the commission concentrated. Late in 533 they completed this assignment and Justinian formally declared this summary, called the *Digest,* the law of the empire.

A few weeks before the appearance of the *Digest,* Tribonian and several of his assistants published a short work of some fifty pages under the title of *Institutes.* This was little more than a revised edition of Gaius' commentaries (see above, p. 25). It was intended to provide the student an introduction to the principles of Roman law. Some time after Justinian's death a compilation of 154 of his laws appeared under the name of *Novels* (New Laws). These four parts, the *Codex, Digest, Institutes,* and *Novels,* constitute what is known as the *Corpus Juris Civilis.* No collection of legal writings has enjoyed higher repute among students of law nor exerted greater influence upon systems of jurisprudence.

The *Digest* is particularly unique. It has been referred to as the most important lawbook ever written. Because it concerns itself with legal principles and with principles of equity which never grow old, because it represents, in the first place, the quintessence of the best legal minds of the most legally conscious people in the world, many Western nations have found its pronouncements quite as suitable and acceptable for themselves as they were for the ancient Romans. Conversely, of the four parts of the *Corpus Juris Civilis*, the *Novels* is least important since it lists merely laws and those of a single reign, Justinian's. The *Novels* do, however, reveal Justinian's earnest concern about governmental reform and his deep interest in the cause of Christianity. The entire *Corpus* serves to preserve the law of ancient Rome, which of Rome's contributions to Western civilization remains the most original and precious.

If the codification of Roman law represents Justinian's most enduring accomplishment, his least permanent, despite the enormous effort and resources he expended, was his military achievement. The *Corpus* continues to influence Western nations. The bulk of Justinian's conquests had melted away within a century of his death. Still Justinian could not see what the future had in store. He only saw how barbarous Germans, most of them Arian heretics, were swarming over the most ancient and sacred Roman provinces. As the imperial successor of Augustus and Trajan, as the spiritual leader of Christendom, his first responsibility was to rectify that intolerable situation. That is what God wanted, and with the help of God, he would correct it.

Had Justinian been free to concentrate on recovering these provinces in the west, he would, in all probability, have reconquered the whole of them, even including Britain had he chosen. From the interminable story of the battles and campaigns that burden the greater part of his reign, two facts emerge and especially impress the reader: first, the marked superiority of Byzantine armies over those of the Germans; second, the seemingly inexhaustible resources of men and money Justinian had at his disposal. What prevented full attainment of his objective in the West was not the lack of soldiers for that undertaking. It was the necessity of conducting heavy defensive operations against German, Slavic, and Hunnish tribes on the Danube, and against the Sassanian empire in Syria and the area of Armenia.

War that had broken out intermittently during Justin's reign against the Sassanids, broke out again shortly after Justinian's accession. A constant factor in all these wars that stretched centuries back to Trajan and beyond was the relative openness of the frontier between the two powers. This condition tempted now the Romans, more often the Persians, to attempt a "rectification." A more immediate cause for war was the bitterness which existed between Christians and Zoroastrians in the area of Lazica (northern Armenia), which both powers wanted. Its occupation would enable the Persians to establish a foothold on the Black Sea from which to attack Byzantine shipping and possibly even Constantinople itself. Byzantine possession of Lazica, on the other hand, would facilitate the establishment of direct trade relations with China, which the Sassanids were blocking. The pretext used by the Sassanid emperor for reopening hostilities was Byzantine strengthening of the fortifications about Daras in upper Mesopotamia. In June 530, Belisarius, the Byzantine governor in that area, won a crushing victory over a Persian army almost twice his in size. Two years later the two empires agreed to a "Perpetual Peace."

The Persian monarch who agreed to this peace was Chosroes I (531– 579). That he subsequently proved himself to be the ablest and most aggressive of the Sassanian kings explains why Justinian found little peace in the East. For about eight years Chosroes remained quiet. Then in 540, when an appeal from the Ostrogoths who were fighting Justinian's armies in Italy reminded Chosroes how Justinian was gaining territories while he did nothing, he invaded Syria. Byzantine defenses had been permitted to decay, so Chosroes plundered at will. When he captured Antioch, the largest city of western Asia, leveled the city, and enslaved its population, Justinian hurriedly recalled Belisarius from Italy. Two years of campaigning slowed the Persians, but then Belisarius had to hurry back to Italy where the situation had deteriorated. Heavy fighting continued for many years in the East, particularly in the area of Lazica, although much of it was waged by the respective Arab and Hunnish allies of Byzantium and Persia. Only exhaustion finally forced the two to agree to a fifty-year peace in 562. Justinian retained Lazica although he agreed to pay thirty thousand pieces of gold annually, in return for which Persia assumed defense of the Caucasus passes against the Huns to the north.

Back in 532, that is, many years before the establishment of this final peace with the Persians, Justinian embarked upon his great project, the recovery of the West. Even though he had the prudence to begin with the Vandal kingdom in North Africa, which was the smallest of the major Germanic states, he did so "against the advice of all men, who shrank in terror from the undertaking. . . ." Justinian may have

counted for support from the large Afro-Roman population which
hated the Vandals for their arrogance and their Arianism. He may, too,
have realized that any attempt to take Italy could never succeed so
long as the powerful Vandal fleet stood on the side, ready to intervene
when the time appeared opportune.

Against the Vandals Justinian had a *casus belli*. In 530 the Arian
Gelimer had deposed Hilderic, Justinian's ally who had become an
orthodox Christian. So it was a punitive expedition that Belisarius
landed without opposition in the late summer of 532. Had Gelimer
been waiting for him, that might have been the end of Justinian's
grand enterprise. His fleet was away in Sardinian waters instead and a
large part of his army was in Tripolitana. Belisarius defeated Gelimer's
hastily assembled army, took Carthage, then in a second engagement
destroyed the remainder of Vandal forces. The imperial armies encountered little difficulty in annexing Sardinia, Corsica, and the
Balearic Islands. It required some dozen years, however, before they
persuaded the fierce Berbers to accept Byzantine rule. No attempt was
made to add Mauretania, which lay to the west.

Before permitting the Vandals to pass into the oblivion which
awaited them, mention might be made of a magnificent triumph Justinian accorded Belisarius on his return to Constantinople. Gelimer and
other captured chieftains, plus an enormous store of loot which the
piratical Vandals had plundered over a period of a century from Mediterranean ships and countries, passed before the eyes of wondering
crowds. Among the most precious items were the seven-branched
candlesticks and golden vessels which the emperor Titus had carried
to Rome from the Jewish temple in Jerusalem and which were now to
be returned to Jerusalem. After the celebrations Gelimer and his family
retired to a rich estate which Justinian had promised him.

With the easy collapse of the Vandal kingdom Justinian's move to
reconquer the west had gotten off to an auspicious beginning. At first it
seemed that Italy, too, where the powerful Ostrogoths were entrenched, would fall with similar ease. One Byzantine army moved
into Dalmatia without much opposition. The other under Belisarius
landed in Sicily, seized the island, then went on to capture Naples
and Rome. The Goths made no attempt to hold the Eternal City since
they believed it could not be defended. Belisarius believed he could
hold it, and he succeeded despite a long siege of more than a year
against an army of approximately 100,000 Goths. When the Goths finally withdrew, he moved northward, won a series of engagements,

and might have completed the conquest of the peninsula in short order had not Justinian needed him on the Persian front. This gave the Goths another opportunity, and in their new chieftain, Totila, they finally found an extremely capable leader.

Within a short time Totila had re-established Ostrogothic rule over most of Italy, whereupon Justinian hurried Belisarius back to retrieve the situation. But even Belisarius could do little, as he complained, "without men, horses, arms, or money." Totila took Rome, then after demolishing the gates and sections of the walls, left the broken city to Belisarius. The latter managed to thwart Totila's attempts to retake the city, then asked to be recalled. Justinian replaced him with Narses, a eunuch, who was his grand chamberlain and an excellent general as well, and gave him a superb army to command. In a decisive battle in Umbria Narses defeated Totila who was left dead on the field, captured Rome for the fifth time, and destroyed the last Gothic army in Campania. Then he permitted the remnants of this once great nation to pass northward across the Alps where they disappeared forever from view.

Except for a large Frankish army that had plundered its way down into southern Italy and which Narses annihilated near Capua, this completed the long and tragic story of Byzantine conquest of Italy. That peninsula, broken and desolate to be sure but finally at peace, was back within the empire. Justinian had gained Italy, the most prized of the western kingdoms, had also destroyed the Vandal nation, and occupied the coastal regions of southern Spain, roughly from above Cadiz on the Atlantic to Cartagena on the east, which Byzantine forces had seized shortly after 554. No attack was made on Gaul nor one contemplated. The exhaustion of the empire and the continuing critical situation along the Danube left that out of the question.

For what was bleeding the empire of men and resources only less seriously than the fighting against Persia and that in Italy was the fighting along the Danube. That no one foe contested Byzantine control here, only a series of semibarbarous tribes, may have led Justinian to pay it less attention than it deserved. A variety of German, Slavic, and Hunnish tribes fought each other and Byzantium for the freedom to ravage the defenseless peoples who occupied the huge area extending from the Danube to the Adriatic and the Peloponnesus. Scattered here and there throughout the area were fortresses, and Justinian kept building more. Yet he lacked the manpower to make them real bastions of Byzantine power. They served little more than refuges for those of

the nearby peasants who were fortunate enough to escape the waves
of marauders that constantly swept down from the north. An occasional
Byzantine army might defeat this group or that, but like grasshoppers
in a grasshopper year, they kept coming. Some of them accepted imperial "subsidies" and withdrew after having collected all the loot they
could carry and enslaved all the men, women, and children they could
manage. A more effective tactic was that of paying one barbarous tribe
to attack another, a maneuver to which the empire probably owed its
escape from destruction as much as it did to the impregnability of
Constantinople. Yet it was a situation that remained as critical when
Justinian died as when he had begun to reign.

Herein stands revealed one clear weakness in Justinian's military
policy, namely, his failure to correct a dangerous situation so close to
Constantinople that it threatened the very existence of the empire. If
he caused eighty fortresses to be constructed along the Danube, as
Procopius affirmed, they proved insufficient. After his death, waves of
barbarians continued to sweep across the Danube into the Balkans
and down into Greece where they burned and plundered and all but
extinguished classical civilization in its very birthplace. Neither would
the Persian front long remain quiet, and shortly after Justinian's death
Sassanid armies were driving all the way to the Bosporus. In Italy
Lombards forced their way across the Alps three years after Justinian's
death and shortly after had the greater part of the peninsula under
their control. Within a century of Justinian's death, of the impressive
conquests made by Belisarius and his fellow generals, only Sicily and
a few cities in Italy remained under Byzantine rule.

It is this last fact that makes the price of Justinian's military efforts
appear so appallingly high in terms of lives, resources, and culture.
Even had Italy remained longer within the empire, the cost would
have been excessive. Twenty years of devastating warfare had proved
almost as fatal to classical civilization there as the ravages of barbarous
Slavs and Avars would shortly be in Greece. Rome, which five times
had been captured by hostile armies, remained for hundreds of years
to come a city of ruins. Scarcely twenty-five thousand scared souls ventured back within its shattered walls which at one time had sheltered a
half-million. The tragic irony of it was that a more classical culture
obtained in the Italy of Theodoric, the Ostrogoth, than did under Justinian, the Roman. In the east the most serious consequence of his vast
military undertaking was the heavy taxation these operations had necessitated. Never before was the imperial tax collector so hated as he

came to be in the sixth century. In those provinces where anger over Byzantine fiscal policies was combined with bitterness over its harsh religious policies, as in Monophysite Syria and Egypt, the door was open to revolt. It is no exaggeration to say that the immense cost of Justinian's military efforts made possible the rise of Islam.

Justinian also made history as a builder. In this role, as in his interest in restoring Roman law and the imperial frontiers, he was being true to Rome's past. Several of Rome's most eminent emperors had been builders. Yet not tradition only, but the critical need for more fortifications explained Justinian's construction, as well as his desire to please God with churches. Little remains of the fortifications, but a sufficient number of churches still stand to enable art historians to speak of a new and distinct art epoch, the Byzantine. Justinian must have kept a small army of masons busy during his reign, not only on fortresses and churches, but on aqueducts as well, and on roads, reservoirs, cisterns, hospitals, baths, harbor works, and public buildings. Even if one discounts much of Procopius' testimony in his *Buildings* as fulsome flattery, enough construction remains in Ravenna, Constantinople, and elsewhere to mark Justinian as possibly history's greatest builder. In Constantinople the destruction attendant upon the *Nika* riots provided him the opportunity for rebuilding that city on a scale more grand than any in the Western world. On the ruins of the early church, he caused a new and more magnificent Hagia Sophia to be born, the most impressive edifice of its day. The brilliance of its mosaics and marbles, the grandeur and harmony of its proportions, and its architectural daring evoked from Procopius the most extravagant praise. "Whoever enters there to worship," he wrote, "perceives at once that it is not by any human strength or skill, but by the favor of God that this work has been perfected; his mind rises sublime to commune with God, feeling that He cannot be far off, but must especially love to dwell in the place which He has chosen. . . ."

Justinian's construction of churches may have sprung less from monumentalism than from faith, for he appears to have been a deeply religious man. In this respect, he would not, of course, have been greatly different from many of his subjects. Few societies have displayed greater sensitivity over religious issues than that of Byzantium. What helped produce this sensitivity was the long history of persecution at the hands of pagan Rome. What kept it at fever pitch was the presence of dissident groups who quarreled bitterly among themselves over theological issues they considered fundamental. As in the Reformation of the sixteenth century, there was no such thing as tolerance, only the faithful and the reprobate, with one group clearly marked off from the other. For that reason, given the intimate association of church and state in Byzantium, doctrinal issues might and did convulse the state and on occasion threaten its overthrow. This was an age when bishops, not statesmen, led the people, when every man was a theologian, and when Justinian was only the most serious of them all. For while they might indulge in vigorous controversy and even riot, for him it was essential that he provide an orthodox creed to which all could subscribe. The stability of his throne depended upon that, and that, too, is what God demanded. So it became his wont "to sit without guards, far into the night, in the company of old priests, deep in the study of the holy books of the Christians."

What he hoped to discover in those books was a formula which would resolve the centuries-old problem of Christ's nature. Though everyone agreed that this was a mystery, they all nonetheless insisted upon having a solution, that is, all but the bishop of Rome. He would willingly have left the matter remain a mystery and to have avoided only the two extremes, the one of giving Christ a single divine nature, the other of making His human and divine natures so distinct as to produce two separate personalities. This latter view, that of the Nestorians or what their opponents accused them of maintaining, had been discredited and its adherents were in exile. Still the opposing Monophysites were not satisfied. They would have nothing less than their single nature, and they accused Rome of nurturing in its somewhat middle-of-the-road position the substance of Nestorianism.

For a solution, Justinian knew not where to turn. As noted above, he and his uncle Justin had broken with the pro-Monophysite policy of Anastasius partly in order to advance political aims in Italy where the assistance of a sympathetic pope would be of considerable help. Justinian's wife Theodora, on the other hand, was strongly inclined toward Monophysitism, as were the patriarchs of Antioch and Alexandria, not to mention the majority of the people under their jurisdiction. For this reason the enforcement of harsh anti-Monophysite legislation would mean revolt. About all Justinian could be sure of was that he must take the lead in seeking a solution. Precedent and tradition made this his prerogative; and prudence, too, demanded that he take the initiative. The very existence of his empire was at stake while popes, patriarchs, and bishops were manifestly incapable of coming up with a solution. The tragedy was his inability to announce what was orthodox doctrine since he was not quite sure himself.

So while he began his reign with decrees against Monophysitism, he almost immediately suspended their enforcement and in 535 approved the selection of the Monophysite Anthimus as patriarch. Then a year later to please the pope, imperial policy was reversed and Anthimus went into hiding in Theodora's palace along with other Monophysite leaders. Later Theodora had her revenge by securing the deposition of Pope Silverius and having him exiled to the island of Palmaria where he died. The new pope, Vigilius, the man Theodora wanted, proved less accommodating than expected, so Justinian summoned him to Constantinople. There he argued, fought, and compromised, then finally persuaded Justinian to summon the Fifth Ecumenical Council (553). Vigilius' death on his return to Rome saved him from facing his irate bishops there who were not pleased with the concessions Justinian had wrung from him to placate the Monophysites. Yet these Monophysites for their part were no more pleased than the Western bishops. The distraught emperor appears to have been adopting a frankly Monophysite position himself when death solved his problems.

Toward groups whose doctrines had received formal condemnation, Justinian's position was unbending. He tolerated none, and active heretics and extremists such as the Manichaeans he had executed. Pagans on the other hand, like Tribonian and John the Cappadocian who made no nuisance of themselves, remained unmolested. He did close the school of Platonic studies in Athens which had developed into a center of pagan Neo-Platonism. The scholars who fled Athens found a haven in Persia. In keeping with his claim to legislate in the internal matters of the church, Justinian enacted laws against simony and other clerical irregularities, regulated the election of abbots, and issued orders dealing with monastic discipline. He also showed himself generous in his gifts to monastic establishments, and his legislation in their behalf "became in the Byzantine Empire the true foundation of monastic institutions."* The monastery of St. Catherine at the foot of Mt. Sinai which he founded continues to this day to serve God in the manner it did when Justinian lived.

Religious controversy continued to torment Byzantine history during the long centuries that followed Justinian's death. Since the circum-

* J. B. Bury, *History of the Later Roman Empire*. New York (1958), II, p. 362.

stances that had produced conflict during his reign persisted after his death, this was to be expected. The people of Constantinople, Syria, and Egypt continued to press their particular theological preferences quite as intolerantly as before while Justinian's successors, either from doctrinal conviction or to preserve the state, took the same direct hand he had taken in establishing "orthodoxy." The situation under Justinian's successors, as it affected relations between Constantinople and the papacy, did, however, undergo an ominous change which augured poorly for that relationship. Because occasional emperors after Justinian supported doctrinal views which the papacy refused to stomach while the papacy began to adopt a more intransigent position as Byzantine authority in Italy weakened and that of the Franks increased, the centuries after the sixth witnessed a slow but fairly progressive estrangement between Constantinople and Rome which helped prepare the way for the schism of 1054.

There were present other factors which sowed friction between Constantinople and the West. The language of the East was Greek, that of the Western Church Latin. Greek and Latin theologians had difficulty communicating, a serious consideration in view of the grave theological controversies that frequently divided the two. During the centuries preceding Eastern acceptance of papal claims to primacy certain differences in liturgy and ecclesiastical discipline had crept in to create an impression that sharper contrasts existed between the two Christian worlds than was actually the case. Westerners ate eggs during Lent, fasted on Saturdays, and used unleavened bread in the Eucharistic service. The East permitted the laity wine at communion, celebrated Easter on a different date, and allowed its lower clergy to marry. Of more critical importance than these differences in deepening the chasm between the two was a mutual lack of charity that impeded efforts at closer cooperation. The East generally looked down upon the West as its cultural and intellectual inferior, the West in turn covered its inferiority with the charge that the East was corrupt and decadent.

Yet because schism eventually divided Christendom into two worlds, there is danger in stressing unduly the cultural and liturgical differences between East and West. Once schism had become an accomplished fact and had endured several generations, these differences did, it is true, loom large and make reunion difficult. They can scarcely be reckoned of basic importance in precipitating that break. Several popes of the seventh and eighth centuries hailed from the eastern Mediterranean, while during the bitter iconoclastic controversy that broke in the eighth century, the leading theologians of the East, John of Damascus and Theodore the Studite, together with the great majority of clergy and religious, were on the side of Rome. Illustrative of efforts by responsible churchmen in both east and west to maintain good relations was the pope's delay in ordering insertion of the Filioque clause in the Nicene Creed—that the Holy Spirit proceeded from both Father and Son and not just the Father as the East insisted. Charlemagne had demanded that Rome do this.

The most disturbing of the factors which strained relations between Western and Eastern Christendom was the authoritarian position assumed by the emperor. Like his ancient imperial predecessors he ruled as an autocrat, and this extended to matters touching doctrine. We have seen how Justinian exiled Pope Silverius when he refused to accept the imperial will and later ordered Pope Vigilius to come to Constantinople in order to break down his resistance. In 653, agents of Constans II brought Martin I to Constantinople, whence he was exiled to the Crimea where he died of privation. Only the local militia prevented Justinian II from dragging off Pope Sergius I from Rome when he refused to endorse the decisions of a church council the emperor had summoned. And had a storm not destroyed the Byzantine fleet, the emperor Leo III might have succeeded in carrying off Pope Gregory II.

It was this same Leo III who precipitated the controversy over images known as iconoclasm (from the two Greek roots meaning to break images). In 726 he issued a decree which forbade the worship (veneration) of images and ordered the icon of Christ removed from above the bronze doors of the imperial palace. That an angry crowd pushed the man off the ladder who attempted to do this and then killed the imperial agents who sought to remove a statue of Christ from a public place in the city, reveals the fierce emotions this issue engendered. Already for several years the attacks of iconoclasts had aroused fear and indignation among the iconodules. Their objective was to suppress the worship (veneration) of images which, particularly in the European parts of the Byzantine empire, had become the most popular form of pious expression among both laity and clergy. In the judgment of the iconoclasts this devotion approximated, if it did not constitute, idolatry. In many instances, among the unsophisticated at any rate, the charge was undoubtedly correct. Still it was not only the abuses associated with images that offended many people who lived in the Asiatic provinces of the empire. Their opposition went much deeper. It reflected the same abhorrence the Hebrews had felt for

graven images, the same attitude which led Mohammed to proscribe
their use to his followers. Because of his iconoclastic policies the enemies of Leo III nicknamed him the "Saracen-minded," and it was no
doubt contact with the Islamic world that had intensified his antago-
nism and the hostility of eastern Christians toward images. There also
existed an ancient Christian tradition against images that carried back
to the early centuries. This had found strongest endorsement among
groups such as the Gnostics and Monophysites who preached the spir-
tual Christ to the exclusion of his body. (Some scholars view iconoclasm as a revival of Monophysitism.)

Leo's iconoclastic policy may have had another objective, that of
reducing the powerful influence of monasticism. Conversely, among
those who supported the iconodules were reformers who hoped to deprive the emperor of his dominant voice in church affairs. The persecution of the iconodules reached its height under Leo's son Constantine
V who attempted to suppress, not just the use of images, but even
the veneration of Mary and the saints. In the course of the iconoclastic
persecution, thousands of monks, some say fifty thousand, fled to Italy
in order to escape mutilation or death. Many monasteries closed, much
church property was confiscated, and thousands of images and other
physical representations of Christ and the saints were destroyed.

Most eloquent in their defense of the use of images were John of
Damascus and Theodore of the Studite house in Constantinople. Constantine's widow Irene, who acted as regent for their young son, summoned the Seventh Ecumenical Council (787) to resolve the issue. It
formally condemned iconoclasm and threatened with anathema all
"who called the holy images idols, and who asserted that Christians
resort to idols as if the latter were gods, and that the Catholic Church
had ever accepted idols." The council went on to announce that veneration was not of the icon itself but of the person it represented, and
that such veneration was to be sharply distinguished from worship
which was only due God. (Iconoclasm reappeared under Leo V, but
was permanently proscribed by a synod summoned by the regent Theodora in 843.)

Though Rome and the majority of Eastern churchmen were on the
same side during the controversy over images, the hostility of successive emperors on this issue served to alienate the pope and lead him
to seek a new protector in the Frankish king. While this political step
did not contribute directly to ultimate schism, a closer cooperation between pope and emperor might have prevented this. Also instrumental

in weakening ties between Rome and Byzantium were the Slavic and Bulgar invaders of the Balkans and Dalmatian regions who destroyed Christianity there and in so doing broke the principal bridge between East and West. That these were two distinct worlds was further emphasized when German pressure forced the expulsion of the disciples of Cyril (Constantine) and Methodius from the area of modern Czechoslovakia in favor of Latin missionaries. Leo III had already deprived the pope of jurisdiction over the Greek dioceses in Sicily, southern Italy, and Illyria, and had given these to the patriarch in Constantinople. Gradually the area administered by the patriarch became as extensive as that of the popes and extended over all Byzantium and the entire Slavic world to the Urals. Men, including the patriarch, began to ask why the latter should not have equal authority with the pope, one to rule the West, the other the East. From the tenth century on it was indeed the patriarch who moved with greatest aggressiveness, not the emperor who wished to retain ties with Rome. The particular patriarch who forced the issue was Michael Cerularius, "the most strong-willed and ambitious prelate of Byzantine history. . . ."* Since Cardinal Humbert whom Pope Leo IX sent to Constantinople to investigate charges brought against the patriarch was an equally violent and reckless man, a clash and break became inevitable. One excommunicated the other, and ever since eastern and western Christendoms have remained apart. To contemporaries this schism of 1054 promised to be no more long-lived than earlier ones (*e.g.*, Photian), and pilgrims on their way to Jerusalem continued to find welcome in Constantinople; so were even Crusaders, although with less cordiality.

The motive which frequently impelled Byzantine emperors to take an active hand in religious matters was the hope of composing theological controversies which might otherwise have collapsed their unstable thrones. For instability characterized the thrones of Justinian's successors. Other factors in addition to theological issues contributed to this lack of stability: the falling prestige of the government due to its exhaustion following the prodigious exertions of Justinian; the loss of territories in Spain, Italy, and the Balkans; the outbreak of new wars with the Persians. Shortly after Justinian's death the Lombards overran the greater part of Italy. In Spain the Visigoths snuffed out Byzantine rule early in the sixth century. Closer home, in the moun-

* Georgije Ostrogorsky, *History of the Byzantine State*. Oxford (1956), p. 297.

tainous regions and valleys south of the Danube, ravaging Slavs and Avars spread destruction, then after slaying or driving off the population, appropriated these lands for themselves.

Two short-lived emperors had ended their inconsequential reigns by 582 when the able Maurice assumed control. His most enduring work consisted in organizing Byzantine North Africa and the lands remaining in central Italy into two strong administrative units called exarchates. He even gained peace with the Persians by restoring Chosroes II to the throne which some rebel princes had taken from him. He failed in his efforts to drive the Avars and Slavs back, nor could he restore discipline in the army. So in 602 rebellious troops murdered him and placed their brutish officer Phocas on the throne. For eight years this monster terrorized the people and decimated the ranks of the upper classes. Then as Avars and Slavs closed in on Constantinople from the west and Persians from Asia Minor, a revolt headed by Heraclius, son of the exarch of Carthage, overthrew the tyrant and restored order.

Heraclius' achievements rival those of more famous rulers even though Islamic victories during the closing years of his reign undid much of his military achievement. Upon his accession Byzantium appeared on the point of succumbing. Only a few scattered cities in the Balkans held themselves above the Slavic and Avar flood, while across the Bosporus were the threatening Persians, fresh from their capture of Jerusalem and the greater part of Asia Minor. So desperate was the situation that Heraclius pondered moving the capital to Carthage. He stayed, however, reorganized the remaining portions of Asia Minor into military districts called themes, and promised lands to the sturdy peasantry he settled there in return for military service. As more territories were recovered, the same military administration was extended to them. Though one might regret the passing of the civil rule of the praetorian prefects, the new system, which was extended to other areas by his successors, served to provide a steady supply of hardy recruits for the empire for centuries to come. Heraclius left Constantinople to its own defenses and with his new troops campaigned successfully in Armenia, then in 628 destroyed Persian power at Nineveh. So after seven centuries of warfare, Rome's ancient enemy lay prostrate at her feet. Thirteen years later Heraclius died in deep despondency. Islamic armies had swept up from the south, shattered his army in the Yarmuk River valley (634), and subjugated the greater part of Syria to Allah.

Heraclius' tremendous victories over the Persians had been wasted; they may even have made Islamic expansion possible.

What deepened Heraclius' despondency was the fear of what would happen to his wife Martina and the succession when he died. She had been his niece, and the people and clergy condemned their marriage as incestuous. When Constantine III, his son by his first wife, succeeded, then died almost immediately of consumption, the opposition accused Martina of poisoning him, cut off her tongue and the nose of her son in order to render him incapable of ever reigning, and hailed Constantine's son Constans II as emperor. Constans had a long and full reign (641-668), but filled for the most part with troubles and tragedy. The Arabs took Alexandria partly because the Monophysites there preferred their rule to Byzantine, then swept over North Africa, Asia Minor, and Armenia, in addition to destroying the Byzantine fleet in 655. Only civil war in Islam prevented Arab exploitation of this victory. Within the empire bitter theological controversy raged, still over the nature of Christ. Now it was the doctrine of Monotheletism, that Christ had a single will although two natures, which was offered as a compromise and rejected. Constans finally left hostile Constantinople and moved his capital to Syracuse where he was murdered in his bath. (His assailants first blinded him with soapsuds.)

The most important development during the reign of his son Constantine IV (668-685) was the dangerous and prolonged siege of Constantinople (674-678) by the Arab fleet. What saved the city was the first recorded use of Greek fire which was employed with deadly effect upon the Arab ships. So many of these were later destroyed by storms during their retreat that worried Islam agreed to pay Byzantium three thousand gold pieces each year to keep the peace. Among contemporary nations whom this tremendous victory impressed was the Avars who now offered Constantinople its homage.

Constantine's son Justinian II (685-695, 705-711) was a man of considerable vision, but he permitted the prestige of his name to tempt him to undertake more than his talents warranted. The excesses of his last years earned him the name Nero. He did manage to recover territory in central Greece and moved some of the Slavic tribes from there to Bithynia. These and other groups whom he recolonized in depopulated areas of Asia Minor assured the empire a valuable source of man power, now of critical importance following the loss of Syria, Egypt, and Armenia to Islam. Meantime his increasingly heavy financial demands were arousing opposition, and in 695 he was deposed, his nose

cut off, and he was exiled to the Crimea. Three years later the new
emperor, Leontius (695–698), after suffering loss of the exarchate of
Carthage to the Arabs, also lost his throne and his nose as well, and
was placed in a monastery. His successor Tiberius II (698–705) was
not so fortunate. The exiled Justinian II managed by a series of in-
credible adventures to make his way into Constantinople—he crawled
through an aqueduct when his Bulgar allies failed to take the city—
seized control and executed Tiberius. In fact he executed everyone,
even entire communities which had opposed him. He in turn was murdered and his son as well, thereby ending the dynasty of the great
Heraclius.

After brief reigns by three emperors, two of whom ended their lives
in monasteries, Leo III, an Isaurian peasant who owed his rise to his
having befriended the exiled Justinian II, seized the throne. For more
than twenty years (717–741), he ruled with a strong hand. His first
accomplishment was to throw back another fierce Arab attack on Constantinople (717–718), again with the help of Greek fire and with the
help of Bulgars as well. The Khazars, who occupied a huge area north
of the Caucasus and east of the Caspian, helped him drive the Arabs
out of Asia Minor. There he created new themes and divided several
of the old ones whose size had tempted their military governors to revolt. He also introduced a new legal manual called *Ecloga* which consisted of the principal rulings of private and criminal law considered
most pertinent to his age. This made it more practical than the older
manuals based on Justinian's *Corpus*. While the *Ecloga* expressed a
generally more liberal philosophy than Justinian's, it introduced a system of penalties involving mutilation—cutting off the nose, hands, feet,
blinding, and similar corporal punishments—brought in from the Orient.
Leo's most controversial policy and one that had most serious consequences was his support of iconoclasm. As noted above, the hostility
of Rome led him to detach dioceses in southern Italy and place these
and others under the jurisdiction of the patriarch of Constantinople.
Beyond punishing Rome, he hoped by means of this reorganization to
secure greater control of the empire through the office of the patriarch.
This may have been a prudent step from his point of view. But since
it resulted in making the empire and patriarchate practically cotermi-
nous, for Christendom it meant yet another major step toward division.

Constantine V (741–775) enjoyed an even longer reign than his
father, whose policies he continued. His marriage to a Khazar princess
brought him the assistance of that people in winning several brilliant

victories over the Bulgars and Arabs. In Italy, however, he permitted the Lombards to take over Ravenna and the exarchate. The expulsion of Byzantine power from central Italy, coming as it did on the heels of Constantine's iconoclastic policy, which was harsher than that of his father, removed the pope's last reluctance against establishing an alliance with the Franks. Constantine's son Leo IV (775-780) is less well known than his ambitious and energetic wife Irene. As regent for their young son Constantine VI she repealed the iconoclastic decrees, an act which pleased most of her subjects. Many of them may even have approved her ordering the blinding of her son so she might establish sole rule for herself. Constantine had earlier blinded his uncle, cut the tongues off four other uncles, and, what was worse, had put away his wife and married his mistress. Irene's autocracy eventually aroused much opposition, which coupled with reverses at the hands of the Bulgars and Arabs led to her deposition in 802.

Troubles continued to harass the empire despite a change of rulers and the real ability of the new emperor Nicephorus I (802-811). Territory was lost to the Franks in Italy, but more serious was Nicephorus' defeat and death in a battle with the Bulgars. Their great leader Krum had Nicephorus' skull encased in gold, then used it when toasting his boyars and visiting envoys. (Nicephorus was the first Roman emperor since Valens to fall in battle against a foreign foe.) Leo V (813-820) was able to drive the Bulgars back, then as fighting died down with them and the Arabs, stirred trouble at home by reviving the iconoclastic decrees. The reign of the illiterate Michael II (820-829) witnessed the loss of Crete and Arab landings on Sicily. It was his daughter-in-law Theodora, following the death of his son Theophilius (d. 842), who finally terminated the era of iconoclasm.

Some years later Theodora's brother Bardas seized control and for over twenty years ruled in the name of her son Michael III (843-867). While Michael idled away his time in frivolous living, Bardas ruled with a strong and able hand. Though he could not prevent new Arab conquests in Sicily and southern Italy, he won a devastating victory over them in Asia Minor which forced Islam on the defensive. It was during his reign in 860 that the Russians made their first appearance with an unsuccessful attack on Constantinople. Toward the papacy Bardas assumed an independent position and supported Photius, his patriarch, in his defiance of papal authority during a short schism. The intellectual circle which he patronized in Constantinople counted among its savants Photius and Leo the Mathematician, two of the most distinguished scholars of the age. Meantime Michael was making dubious friends, the most dangerous being an illiterate groom by the name of Basil. Basil first persuaded Michael to agree to the murder of his uncle Bardas, then a year later he had Michael killed. The new Macedonian dynasty which this murderous groom ushered in furnished Byzantium its last period of greatness.

From the deft manner Basil I (867–886) handled the reins of state, it was evident that he had done more than groom horses during Bardas' rule. Few emperors revealed so sound a knowledge of statecraft. His first act was to terminate the schism with Rome. While this pleased the papacy, Rome objected to his placing the territories south of the Danube under the jurisdiction of the patriarch and sending eastern (Greek) missionaries among the Bulgars and Slavs. His military efforts against the Arabs in upper Mesopotamia and southern Italy were generally successful, although his most enduring contribution was his legal reforms which were incorporated in the extensive revisions promulgated by his son Leo VI (886–912). These revisions, known as *Basilica*, gradually replaced the *Corpus* of Justinian in the courts of Byzantium because they were more modern and systematically organized. While not substantially different from the *Corpus*, they reflected the growing omnipotence of the emperor, the extreme centralization of the administration, and the dominant position enjoyed by the military. An interesting incident of Leo's reign was his appeal to Pope Sergius III for a dispensation to marry a fourth wife. The Eastern Church frowned even on a second wife, and the patriarch of Constantinople barred Leo from Hagia Sophia until the pope granted him a dispensation.

Leo's widow Zoe engineered the rise of the peasant Romanus, then a successful commander of the fleet, to the position of co-emperor to rule with her son Constantine VII. Romanus proved himself an able general and thwarted the attempt of Simeon, khan of the Bulgars, to establish an independent empire south of the Danube. He also appreciated the vital importance of a free peasantry to the nation and enacted legislation aimed at preventing the absorption of its small holdings by the landed aristocracy. His own sons foolishly exiled the old man, but Constantine VII (913–959), now forty years old, blocked their attempt to seize control and took over in his own right. Constantine's interests had been exclusively those of a scholar and such they continued to be. (See below, p. 144.)

Constantine's son Romanus II (959–963) was a weak man. His lowborn courtesan wife Theophano dominated him, then had him mur-

dered to clear the way for her marriage to Nicephorus Phocas, the
ablest general of his day. His victories over the Arabs were indeed
impressive—he was called "the white death of the Saracens"—for he
drove them out of a large part of Syria and the strategic islands of
Crete and Cyprus. Unfortunately, while his zeal was winning him victories, it was losing him Theophano. She transferred her favors to
another able general, John Tzimisces by name, shortly after which Nicephorus followed Romanus to a sudden grave. Now church and public
opinion interposed and forced Tzimisces to banish Theophano. Before John died of typhoid, he had extended Byzantine power to all of
Syria including Damascus and had won major victories over the Russians and Bulgars.

Upon John's death, Basil II (976–1025), son of Romanus II and now
eighteen, inaugurated what proved the most impressive reign in Byzantine history since Justinian. His stern, ruthless manner won him no
popularity, and so committed was he to pursuing his goal of establishing a powerful empire that he did not even take time to marry. The
most serious threat to his position came from the landed aristocracy,
whose dangerous revolt he put down with the assistance of the Russian prince Vladimir. Vladimir then became his ally, married his sister
Anna, and accepted Christianity for himself and his people. Basil's most
spectacular military achievement was his destruction of the Bulgars.
After his final victory over them he blinded fourteen thousand Bulgar
captives, then sent them back to their czar in groups of one hundred,
each group led by a Bulgar who was left one eye to do the job. After
his conquest of Greece he knelt in the Parthenon, now a Christian
church dedicated to the Virgin, and paid his homage to the Mother
of God. He died midst preparations for a major campaign against the
Arabs in Sicily.

When Basil died, Byzantium was again a mighty empire. Her dominion extended from Palestine (not Jerusalem) to southern Italy, encompassed all the territories from the Adriatic and Peloponnesus to
the Danube, upper Mesopotamia and Armenia, and the strategic islands of Crete and Cyprus. So great was Byzantine prestige and so
solid had been Basil's victories, that for a generation the outside world
was not tempted, nor did it dare, to test the strength of that empire. It
would have learned much earlier what an incompetent lot were the
men and women who succeeded Basil. Byzantium had suffered in-
competence before but never over such a long period of time. The
consequences were tragic. Most serious was the victory of the landed

aristocracy in its efforts to submerge the free peasantry. Basil had been able to prevent this, but his successors were either indifferent in the matter or incapable of doing anything. The extinction of the small farmer removed not only the major source of loyal native troops, but it also cut off a critical source of revenue upon which the system of imperial defense depended. Within a few years Byzantium was on the verge of bankruptcy, and being without troops of its own, was obliged to fall back on the dubious loyalties of barbarian mercenaries.

The ineptitude and moral obloquy of the rulers who followed Basil make interesting reading in the colorful pages of Psellus, and one can only marvel at the loyalty of their long-suffering subjects for tolerating them so patiently. Basil's weak brother, Constantine VIII (1025–1028), waited until he lay dying before ordering his daughter Zoe, already fifty although wonderfully preserved, to marry a high city official by name Romanus (III, 1028–1034). Romanus was little better than a fop, though this hardly excused Zoe for having him murdered in his bath when she tired of him and that same evening marrying a former peasant's son who had become attached to the court. This husband, Michael IV (1034–1041), proved more capable than expected although his health was bad and he retired to a monastery where he died. Whereupon Zoe adopted Michael's nephew, also a Michael (V, 1041–1042), but he sent Zoe off to a nunnery. She was back in a year midst the plaudits of her subjects, had Michael blinded, then married Constantine IX (1042–1055). Two tragedies which a capable emperor might have prevented mar his frivolous reign, namely, the invasions of barbarous Petzinaks and other tribes from across the Danube and the schism with the Latin church. After the deaths of Zoe, Constantine, and Zoe's aged sister Theodora, the quality of rulers improved somewhat, but this was more than offset by the appearance of several new foes. Wild Magyars and Cumans began sweeping across the Danube, and in the year 1071 Robert Guiscard and his Normans captured Bari, the last outpost of Byzantine power in Italy. That same year the Seljuk Turks destroyed the Byzantine army at Manzikert in Armenia. Among the generals who fought over control of the reeling empire was Alexius Comnenus, whose story will be told later in connection with the First Crusade.

The ruler of Byzantium was an autocrat: his title often included the very word *autocrator*. He based his imperial authority on his position as heir of the Roman Augusti of which he claimed to be as much one as Trajan or Constantine. To enhance the imperial office Diocletian had introduced ceremonials from the east which included the diadem, expressive of the semidivine character of the Hellenistic god-king. These ceremonials had remained on a modest scale during Diocletian's rule, as befitted an old soldier. As the years passed, so did this moderation, and in time no court west of India or China, unless it was that of the Abbasid caliphs in Baghdad, could approach the Byzantine in magnificence and splendor. Hundreds of household officials moved about the sumptuous palace, all in their special robes and splendid titles, while thousands of regimented guards policed the sacred precincts outside. So august was the atmosphere that surrounded the emperor that should any creature make his way through the mass of courtiers and officialdom to the imperial presence, even if protocol had not required, he might almost automatically have fallen on his face and remained there in humble prostration until bidden to rise.

Of all men in the empire, lay and cleric, the emperor stood closest to God. He was God's sole representative. Since he ruled by divine right, no man might question his authority. Not only did he demand submission from those who lived under his direct rule but from those who occupied territories once enclosed within the ancient imperial frontiers, even from those peoples outside those frontiers who had accepted Christianity. For as there was no God but the Christian God, there was no temporal ruler whom Christians should recognize as emperor save the Byzantine ruler himself. A mosaic of the eleventh century shows the seated Christ, the Empress Zoe on his left, her husband the Emperor Constantine on his right, the two of them ruling Christendom with Christ's blessing and in His name. No one might presume to appropriate the title "emperor," which was theirs alone. If the weak Michael I, in order to recover Venice, might accord Charlemagne momentary recognition as a sort of western Roman emperor, the equally weak Isaac II would still stubbornly refer to Frederick Barbarossa three centuries later as simply king of Germany.

The Byzantine emperor recognized no limitation upon his imperial authority among Christians outside the empire, neither did he accept any from within. No constitutional body existed that might question him in the exercise of his absolutism. The advice of his counselors he could seek if he chose and ignore when he would. He appointed all important officials, replaced them when he saw fit, and decided what powers they should exercise. He commanded the army, made war and

peace, his will was law, his judgment the final court of appeal, and
he might, and did, carry out periodic revisions of the laws.

Such was the position of the emperor in theory; it was a great deal
less Olympian in fact. The sobering reminder that emperors could be
deposed—half of those who succeeded Justinian were either deposed
or died violent deaths—served to discourage most emperors from ruling
tyrannically. Byzantine subjects were a remarkably loyal lot; the loyalty they showed such incompetent females as Zoe and Theodora was
quite typical. On the other hand, once a dynasty had been overthrown,
the people readily accorded the new ruler their allegiance, evidently
on the principle that God must have approved the change. As for the
imperial succession itself, that was in theory decided by the people,
the army, and senate. In practice it was hereditary. The emperor usually chose his successor, either a son or close relative in most instances,
and frequently crowned him in a preliminary service with his own
hands. When the patriarch formally crowned the new emperor, as he
customarily did, he performed that office as the representative of the
people, never of God, as the popes claimed in the west when they presided at royal coronations.

The Byzantine emperor derived a large measure of his authority
from the powerful position he enjoyed in the Christian church. There
was seldom any question who took precedence, emperor or pope. The
emperor was Christ's viceregent. This office, together with that of emperor, assured him the pope's obedience. As the defender of the faith,
the emperor signed a profession of faith before his coronation. So Leo
III announced: "I am emperor and priest whom God has ordered to
feed his flock like Peter, prince of the Apostles." Like Constantine, he
was, indeed, a thirteenth apostle, and church councils referred to him
as priest-king. The liturgy hailed him as God's representative, and religious and secular art customarily portrayed him with the nimbus.
Though he did not presume to dictate in doctrinal questions, he did
not leave these wholly to the pope but summoned church councils,
signed their decrees, and enforced their regulations. He might even
pack such gatherings as Justinian did the Fifth Ecumenical Council
that met at Constantinople. (Not until after the schism of 1054 did
the pope summon an ecumenical council of his own.) As emperor he
might appoint bishops, including the patriarch, institute them in their
offices, and replace those who defied him. Like Charlemagne, he assumed the right to issue decrees concerning ecclesiastical administration and religious discipline. Given the unquestioned faith of many of

its emperors, it is safe to say that the Byzantine state came closer to approximating a theocracy than any in the history of Christendom.

In no respect was the Byzantine empire more the heir of the ancient classical world than in education and learning. No other state preserved in so undiluted a form the heritage of ancient Greece. Contrary to the west, where successive waves of barbarian invaders had swept away so much of the old order that Gregory of Tours could find no one to teach him grammar (see above, p. 106), behind its impregnable walls Constantinople preserved academic and intellectual traditions that reached back almost undisturbed into the ancient past. At one time Alexandria, Antioch, and the cities of the eastern Mediterranean had maintained strong links with the past, but the triumph of Islam had gradually severed these. Moslem civilization, which shortly prevailed there, proved so pervasive that, except for the actual schools and scholars themselves, only scattered memorials of the past remained in what were once the most thoroughly Hellenized countries outside of Greece. It was in Constantinople and the larger cities of the Byzantine empire where an intense love, even fierce pride, for the antique kept this alive, that a visitor from ancient Athens would have felt most at home.

This visitor would also encounter in Byzantium an intellectual atmosphere infinitely superior to that in the West. In Italy, Gaul, and beyond, because of the low level to which civilization had fallen following the Germanic invasions, secular learning was considered almost a luxury, and Sulpicius Severus could ask: "Will Latin grammar save an immortal soul?" Yet his saintly contemporary Gregory of Nazianzen in the east could affirm without fear of contradiction: "I think that all those who have sense will acknowledge that education is the first of the goods we possess." In Byzantium secular education and scholastic traditions had never disappeared. Learning and its teachers remained in high regard. Because of these traditions, because, too, an education would provide access to the imperial bureaucracy, to the courts, and to the teaching profession, most boys of the middle and upper classes attended the schools, many of them into their twenties.

Constantinople boasted the best schools in Byzantium, even what some scholars like to designate as a university. During the reign of the scholarly Constantine VII this university offered four chairs—astronomy, rhetoric, philosophy, and geometry—while also providing instruction in all the traditional liberal arts including music and medicine.

From time to time cities such as Alexandria, Athens, Caesarea, Antioch, Berytus (Beirut), Thessalonica (Salonika), and Edessa could also boast of the eminence of their schools. For the high level of Byzantine learning the amazing erudition of such scholars as Photius and Psellus furnishes eloquent proof. That Psellus offered instruction in philosophy, astronomy, and music, besides eight other subjects, suggests, on the other hand, that the school of higher studies in Constantinople did not attain the specialization one associates with a modern university.

Byzantium presents no galaxy of philosophers, scientists, and mathematicians to match those of Islam even though research in the neglected area of Byzantine scholarship and literature may someday bring more to view. A number of circumstances hampered greater productivity. There was the lack of closer contacts with the cultures of Persia and India, also the curse of near-constant warfare which on a number of occasions carried to the very walls of Constantinople. A century of tragic controversy over iconoclasm absorbed the efforts of the best minds in Byzantium, then destroyed the records of their controversies and, more important, their other scholarly writings in its violence. Beyond these factors there existed an unreasoningly deep reverence for the past which discouraged originality. So what arouses the curiosity of the modern student who works his way through the voluminous writings of Photius, Byzantine's most famous scholar, reputed to be the most learned man since Aristotle, is not so much what Photius himself had to say, but what he gleaned from the hundreds of books from the past, many of which are no longer extant.

Of the erudition of Leo the Mathematician who headed the "university" of Constantinople in the ninth century and that of his contemporary John the Grammarian, nothing remains but their reputations. The preceding century produced John of Damascus, Byzantium's leading theologian. His *Fountain of Knowledge* anticipated by five centuries the *Summa Theologiae* of Thomas Aquinas in providing Christian theology a philosophical basis. The polymath Psellus (see below, p. 146) revealed something of the same broad erudition of Photius in his writings, while Constantine VII's *Ceremonies* and *Administration of the Empire* furnish the modern student an invaluable introduction to the study of the Byzantine court and government.

The oldest and most popular class of Byzantine literature was hagiography, as one would expect in a country whose people were so religiously minded and where monasticism was so deeply entrenched. While the aim of hagiography was principally to edify, with greater consideration given to miracles than to the prosaic, social historians find this literature of considerable value since it dealt with men and women in all walks of life and in all manner of experiences. And, of course, the saint might himself have been a man of prominence or, on his journey to sainthood, have come in contact with men who were. Under such circumstances the writing would acquire significant historical value. The model for hagiographical writing remained Athanasius' *Life of St. Anthony*, which happens to be the main source of our knowledge of the father of monasticism.

Just a short step divides hagiographical literature from monastic chronicles since some of these also hoped to edify, even if need be by the deliberate inclusion of the palpably miraculous. Since the chroniclers assumed that everything in the past happened in accordance with God's plan, they ordinarily began their accounts with the Creation, although the only interest the modern reader has for what "history" antedated the writer's own era concerned the source of the writer's information. Among the more valuable chronicles is that of Theophanes the Confessor, upon which scholars depend for the events of the seventh and eighth centuries. Less dependable is the writing of the iconodule George the Monk whose pen breathes the fierce passions aroused over the efforts of the emperor Leo III to suppress the worship of images. Though the chronicle of John Zonaras, which covers the tenth and eleventh centuries, emanated from a monastery, its author did not retire there until after a long secular career. He was, therefore, better educated, more conversant with the political events of the times than the ordinary monastic chronicler, and more objective.

Of a higher order than chronicles, in fact qualifying as formal historical writing, were the products of a series of nonmonastic writers. The first of these was Procopius, our chief authority for the reign of Justinian. Though trained in law and perhaps intended for the civil service, Procopius became Belisarius' secretary and followed him on his campaigns, a fact which renders his *Wars* the most valuable of his writings. Procopius was a careful observer, more successful in recording events than in analyzing motives, and, like Herodotus whom he admired, willing to introduce interesting information about the customs of foreign peoples with whom he came into contact. Yet he wrote without depth and often without objectivity, his lack of detachment being particularly marked in his *Secret History* and *On the Buildings of Justinian*. In the first he slanders the emperor, in the second he panegyrizes him.

The historian, Leo the Deacon, describes in dull detail but with reasonable accuracy the events of the years 959–975. The most learned scholar to try his hand at historical writing was Michael Psellus (d. 1018). His *Chronographia* presents a firsthand and generally accurate description of the events that transpired during his turbulent years in Constantinople. What adds interest to his account is the evident perceptivity with which he wrote, the author's vanity, which is just as manifest, together with his amazing fortune in always emerging from all palace upheavals on the side of the winner. Anna Comnena, daughter of Alexius I, who had "read thoroughly the works of Aristotle and the dialogues of Plato," composed her long epic of the First Crusade, the *Alexiad,* from the shelter of a convent to which the failure of her political ambitions had driven her. The modern reader will excuse Anna's tendency to embellish her father's achievement and will even commend her feminine failing in noting details about the rough Crusaders from the West which the more professional male historians would have passed by. Special interest attaches to the writings of Nicetas Choniates, who described the fall of Constantinople in the course of the Fourth Crusade and also told of the destruction sometime previous of what might have been Phidias' statue of Athena Promachos by a drunken mob. Among several excellent accounts of Constantinople's last days is that of Georgios Phrantzes, who described the city's final capture by the Turks.

Very little secular poetry remains from Byzantine times although we have a considerable amount of what must have been an enormous quantity of religious verse. The accentual meter which Gregory of Nazianzen had employed, was brought to perfection by Romanus the Melodus, the greatest of Byzantine hymn composers. Romanus was a prolific poet—a thousand hymns are said to have flowed from his pen —and in terms of poetical forms, an inventive one. He drew his themes from the Bible, from the lives of the saints, and from legends. He introduced them as hymns, dramatic episodes, and dialogues: *viz.,* the Magi tell Mary about the paganism of the East, while she counters with a sketch of Jewish history. In the long list of hymn writers appear the names of John of Damascus and Theodore of the Studite monastery in Constantinople.

One epic deserves mention, the eleventh-century poem which extols the valiant exploits of Digenes Akritas, a half-Greek, half-Arab prince who defended the eastern frontiers of the Byzantine empire from his palace on the Euphrates. Hundreds of Akritic poems attest to the enormous popularity of this hero. Probably no tale in literature prior to modern times enjoyed such popularity as that of Barlaam and Josephat. A Byzantine monk of the seventh century took this story, which must have originated in Buddhist India, and adapted it to Christianity, whence it moved westward into European literature. Little else did the West owe Byzantium in the realm of literature. In view of the generally modest character of the Byzantine literary achievement, this is not surprising. Though one hesitates to explain the reasons for the presence or absence of literary genius, among circumstances which might explain its absence in the case of Byzantium were the steady pattern of political and economic decline after the eleventh century and the preference most writers showed for classical rather than popular Greek. Classical Greek robbed the composition of poets of that flexibility which imagination demands if it is to flow.

Byzantine literature lived a quiet life of its own. Apart from its hagiography, which aided in the conversion of the Slavic peoples, it lived in a world apart. Greek remained a strange language to western Europe until the late Middle Ages. And when the humanists began to study that language in the late fourteenth and fifteenth centuries, what interested them were not the products of Byzantine thought and poetry but the works of the ancient Greeks. Considerably more Greek was spoken throughout the Slavic world to the east and southeast, but here the use of a native tongue in the liturgy discouraged the reading of Byzantine literature except among the better educated. Byzantine art forms, by contrast, followed the Byzantine missionary wherever he preached, and in his wake came Byzantine architects, mosaicists, and painters to build and adorn his churches in the Balkans and Russia, in Italy and Sicily, in Georgia, Armenia, and in Asia Minor and Syria. For these lands Byzantium constituted the main source of inspiration from the tenth to the twelfth centuries.

The most distinctive features of Byzantine architecture were the dome and cupola. Because of the lack of wood in Syria and Asia Minor, these structural forms had evolved before the construction of Hagia Sophia, but the impact of that church's magnificent dome upon the imagination of the unsophisticated Slavic world was overwhelming. History furnishes no more persuasive evidence of the influence Byzantium exerted upon those peoples than the white cupolas and onion-shaped domes that glisten in the sunlight from the Bosporus to the Adriatic and northward to Moscow and Novgorod. The churches of

Ravenna and Venice, of southern Italy and Sicily, also reveal extensive Byzantine influence, an influence which carried even to Charlemagne's chapel in Aachen. Yet the same indifference which Justinian's architects showed the exterior of his Hagia Sophia reveals itself, too, in the generally monotonous brickwork and stuccowork which characterize the churches erected in those lands into which Byzantine architectural forms emigrated.

The interiors of these churches were brilliant with light and color. There the painter and mason spared no effort in unfolding for the gaze of the faithful, in rich mosaics and frescoes, dramatic and instructional themes from the Bible. Though little remains of secular buildings, of secular rulers and their consorts, a number of striking portraits, such as those of Justinian and Theodora in San Vitale in Ravenna, can still be seen gracing the interior walls of church naves. The presence of these rulers in such holy surroundings served two purposes: one, to proclaim the reverence that heads of state, too, had for their God; second, to suggest to the faithful that their rulers were closest to Christ and His saints and shared with heaven the reverence and obedience owed by their subjects. During the iconoclastic period when the depiction of the divine in human form was viewed as abhorrent, landscapes of trees and flowers came to predominate in wall coverings. When images returned, they remained flat although often appearing in even more brilliant colors than before and being depicted with greater realism. For the art of Byzantium, because it reflected the living faith of the people, never became static and frozen as did other facets of her culture. By reason of its creativity, versatility, and craftsmanship it continued to be the inspiration of the European world. Even Islamic artists and artisans had difficulty matching the illuminated manuscripts, tapestries, silks, mosaics, frescoes, ivory carving, metalwork, draperies, and enamel-work of Byzantium. The art of Byzantium "for this reason must always remain one of the most remarkable aspects of Byzantine civilization and one of its lasting glories."*

Except when Byzantium constituted little more than Constantinople itself, agriculture remained the principal occupation of the majority of its people. The trend toward latifundia which marked the last centuries of the Roman empire continued unabated until the eighth when a number of circumstances reversed the trend and increased signifi-

* Baynes and Moss (eds.), *Byzantium: An Introduction to East Roman Civilization.* Oxford (1961), p. 199.

cantly the number of small holdings. These circumstances included barbarian invasions across the Danube and into Asia Minor which broke up large estates; the tyranny of emperors like Phocas and Justinian II which fell heaviest on the aristocracy; the colonization, principally in Anatolia and Thrace, of refugees from Moslem-conquered lands, religious dissidents, and of conquered Slavs and other peoples. Then in the tenth century, and especially after the death of Basil II, large estates again began to engulf the small farmer as they had done in late Roman times and generally for the same reasons, namely, the unwillingness or inability of the government to prevent the aristocracy from investing their capital in land. No doubt there were many peasants who were willing to exchange their free status for the protection the aristocracy could afford them against the tax collector. Because of the demands of commerce and the proximity of a number of large cities, Byzantine agriculture never assumed the closed-economy character of the manor in western Europe. A market always waited for its cereals, wine, fruit (dried), cotton, sugar, and flax. The hills and mountains of Thrace, Macedonia, and Greece produced timber, while in the Peloponnesus in the south so extensive were the mulberry groves that that area came to be known as Morea. Withal, the ravages of war, high taxes, and occasional short harvests kept the lot of the peasantry a generally hard one.

Until the thirteenth century the industrial development of the Byzantine empire exceeded that of any country to the west and possibly even that of Islam to the east and south. The factors which contributed to that development included the distinctly commercial character of its economy, the heavy demands made by the army, the church, and the wealthy classes for its products, and the high level of craftsmanship displayed by her artisans. Throughout the Christian world Byzantium enjoyed the reputation of producing the finest silks, brocades, glassware, metalwork, luxury commodities, and liturgical goods. The sound character of the Byzantine coin, the bezant, which continued unimpaired until the difficulties of the twelfth century, attracted trade, while the Byzantine fleet, except for short intervals of Moslem ascendancy, could assure safe passage to ships going into the Black Sea or westward to Venice. The government made the stranger feel welcome, and it negotiated commercial treaties with any people willing to do business. In order to stimulate the growth of industry the government organized the principal industries into craft gilds and maintained a close supervision over their activities. Since custom duties brought in more revenue than any other source, the interest of the government in these matters was understandable.

The heart of Byzantium's industrial life was Constantinople. Its location was ideal. For most of its existence it lay at the geographical center of the empire and on what remained until the close of the Middle Ages the main trade route between Europe and Asia. Because of its location at the point between the Black Sea and Mediterranean where the channel was narrowest, it could easily bar those strategic waters to ships of unfriendly states. The Golden Horn to the north of the city provided the finest harbor, particularly when enemy shipping might be in the vicinity. When the winds from the north or the current were too strong, ships could find excellent wharves on the south side of the city. A Jewish traveler, Benjamin of Tudela, who visited the city in 1161 after having seen Baghdad and other great metropolises wrote that the city's "riches and buildings are equaled nowhere in the world." Strangers from every quarter of the world helped swell its population well over the half-million mark, a truly huge figure for the Middle Ages. No wonder Crusaders marveled as they entered the great city through the Golden Gate to the west, proceeded eastward along the Triumphal Way through a series of imposing public squares (the Fora of Arcadius, Bovi, Tauri, Constantine), until they reached the most awesome forum of all, with the Hippodrome on one side, Hagia Sophia on the other, while below, beyond a series of terraces and galleries, stood the great Sacred Palace of the emperor.

Now that Slavic blood colors two-thirds the population of Europe, the substantial contribution that Byzantium made to European culture by way of the peoples of eastern and southeastern Europe whom she civilized during the Middle Ages is less difficult to urge than some centuries ago. Part of Byzantium's achievement has long been accepted, that of guarding the eastern approaches of Europe against hostile Moslems and Turks. Actually her role as "savior" of Western civilization may indeed have been overstated. One may wonder how the armies of Islam, so well suited to the semiarid reaches of North Africa and western Asia, would have fared midst the wooded highlands and forests of western Europe. (It may be significant that they never overran the Asturias nor Montenegro.) There may be some who will even question Professor Ostrogorsky's dictum that "Byzantium stood for a thousand years as the most important stronghold of culture and learning," surely the implication that without Byzantium these would inexorably have been lost. Western Europe owed considerably more to Islam than to Constantinople. Be that as it may, the culture of the Slavic world clearly hailed from Constantinople, and the modern Serb and Russian among others owe as much to the city on the Bosporus as the descendants of the medieval Franks and Saxons do to Rome.

Among the barbarous peoples who came into contact with Byzantium but accepted none of its civilizing influences, were the savage Avars. They were of Hunnic origin and had once ruled a large empire from central Asia. Like the nomadic peoples of Asia, they were a nation of horsemen who lived off raids and tribute and acquired no culture. When their Turkish vassals revolted early in the sixth century and their empire crumbled, they moved westward and established a new home west of the Caspian Sea. There they conducted negotiations with Justinian who persuaded them with gifts to do their raiding north and west of his empire. In alliance with the Lombards, they destroyed the Gepids, then occupied their former territory in Hungary. From there they extended their tyranny over various Slavic groups and shortly after Justinian's death crossed the Danube into the empire. During the course of their third attack on Constantinople which they made in conjunction with the Persian siege in 626, they suffered a serious setback at the hands of the Byzantine fleet. This marked the beginning of their decline. Shortly after the Bulgars threw off their power, but it remained for Charlemagne to complete their destruction (see below, p. 204).

The most important people to live in subjection to the Avars were the Slavs. Seldom are the origins of so great a nation so obscure. Herodotus speaks of a people who may have been Slavs, as does Pliny the Elder. Tacitus located them east of the Germans, and it is believed that when the Germans moved across the Rhine and toward the Black Sea, the Slavs followed in their wake. This would make their most probable homesite the forests of western Russia, whence they spread, following the destruction of the Huns, to the Elbe and Danube. A branch of the family, the Antes, may have served Justinian as allies, although the fact that he added *Anticus* to his name suggests that he must also have defeated them. In 540 they joined other barbarous groups in an attack on Constantinople and ten years later repeated that attack. Their raids into Byzantine territories became more regular after Justinian's death when they ravaged the Balkans either as allies of the Avars or their subjects. When Avar power waned they became Byzantium's principal threat. By the year 700, they had, in fact, Slavonized almost the whole of Thrace and Greece. They unfortunately made no attempt, as had the more civilized Germans to the west, to assimilate classical culture. They simply replaced it with their own.

Exactly what this civilization was remains as much a puzzle as their origins. A wild polytheism which included river gods and sprites of all kinds suggests contact with many different peoples. One of their deities bore the curious name Trojan, the name no doubt deriving from reports of Trajan's great victories over the Dacians back in the second century. The Slavs appear to have been an unusually prolific people, a characteristic which might account for their adherence to agricultural pursuits and their indifference to trade. An agricultural economy also provided them a measure of immunity from such powerful enemies as the Goths, Gepids, Avars, and Bulgars, who were more interested in the kind of wealth and possessions they could carry off. Probably because of their preference for a stable to a nomadic existence, the mores of the Slavs appear closer to those of the Germans than to those of Asiatic tribes. Like the Germans they practiced monogamy, were organized into clans, and held their lands in common. Although the Slavs were not unwarlike, their agricultural ways created no demand for great technological advances, and their inferior weapons and lack of military experience usually left them the slaves of more powerful neighbors.

So numerous were the Slavs that they generally Slavonized the peoples with whom they came in contact. Among these were the Bulgars, a Turkish people, who were once part of a huge empire that covered the steppes of central Asia. When this empire disintegrated in the sixth century, a branch moved westward and allied itself with Heraclius against the Avars. These Bulgars later settled along the Black Sea both north and south of the Danube, whence they extended their control over the greater part of the Balkans. From the decline of the Avars until the early eleventh century, they constituted Byzantium's principal threat in Europe. As noted above, their khan Krum destroyed Nicephorus and his army in 811. Boris I (852–889) accepted Christianity and, after some diplomatic sparring between Rome and Constantinople, decided that Byzantine, rather than Latin, missionaries should convert his people. This assured the eventual Slavonization of the Bulgars, but they remained a threat to Constantinople until their ruthless destruction by Basil II. Their name, language, and some of their blood continue to live in the Balkans.

Of a dozen other tribes whose movements carried within the sweep of Byzantine history, mention might be made of the Khazars. When the Turkish empire of west-central Asia, of which they had been part, broke up, they moved westward and established a state of their own that centered about the Caucasus. From here they ruled a sprawling empire which included Armenia to the south and a large part of southern Russia. For almost three centuries they assisted Byzantium as allies, now against the Persians and Bulgars, more often against the Arabs whose penetration northward into Russia they probably prevented. Their civilization, the highest of any of the peoples moving out of Asia, led them to develop wide trade connections from their great center Itil on the Volga. In the course of the ninth century the Arabs conquered their lands east of the Caspian, while rising Russia destroyed their power in Europe during the following century.

These Russians were destined to have the longest history of all the peoples who owed so much of their culture to Constantinople. They represented in the main an eastern branch of the Slavic nation which occupied the plains above the Black Sea and northward toward Scandinavia. It was only when the Swedes had begun to bring them into subjection that the Byzantine chroniclers notice these Slavs. These Swedes or Varangians, as they were called, began to move southward about the middle of the eighth century along the Dnieper and the middle Volga in search of trade. It appears the native Slavs called these newcomers who subjected them Rus (the name might have meant oarsmen originally), a classification which Byzantine writers then applied to the mingling of these two peoples. By the end of the eighth century they had moved into the Crimea, then in 860 joined in an attack on Constantinople. Though the attack failed, the experience helped transform them from pirates to traders. They negotiated a trade treaty with Byzantium, took back missionaries with them to Kiev, which was their headquarters on the Dnieper, and left the first of the famous Varangian Guard at the imperial court in Constantinople.

These first missionaries had no great success, neither did the Russians halt their efforts to capture Constantinople, even though there were few years when their furs, wax, tar, hemp, and slaves were not sold in the marts of the great metropolis. In 989 Vladimir, the prince of Kiev, negotiated a new treaty with Byzantium and accepted baptism. (By this time the Slavs had pretty well assimilated the Swedes, a fact suggested by Vladimir's name.) One story has it that Vladimir decided against the religion of Islam because of the Koran's prohibition of alcohol. Without alcohol, Vladimir believed no one could be happy in Russia. A more likely story tells how the beauty of Hagia

Sophia and other Greek churches led him to choose Christianity. For his agents had reported to him on their return from Constantinople: "We knew not whether we were in heaven or on earth. For on earth there is no such splendor or such beauty and we are at a loss how to describe it."* So after being himself baptized, he ordered the mass baptism of his people in the Dnieper. Kiev went on to become the leading commercial city, after Constantinople, in all of Europe. Under Yaroslav "the Wise" (1019–1054) it attained an importance never again enjoyed by a Russian state before the close of the Middle Ages. When Yaroslav unwisely divided his empire among his sons, he opened the door to civil war and decline. In 1169 a rival Russian prince destroyed the great city of Kiev, in 1203 the barbarous Cumans (Polovtzy) sacked the city a second time, and in 1240 the Mongols ended its existence as an independent state. (See below, p. 368.)

* *The Russian Primary Chronicle.* Translated by S. H. Cross and O. P. Sherbowitz-Wetzor. Cambridge, Mass. (1953), p. 111.

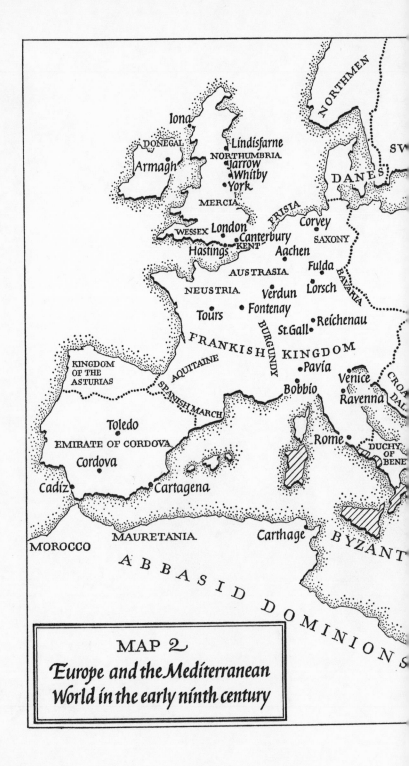

NORTHMEN

Iona

DONEGAL

Lindisfarne

NORTHUMBRIA

Armagh

Jarrow

Whitby

York

MERCIA

SW

DANES

FRISIA

Corvey

SAXONY

WESSEX London

Canterbury

Hastings KENT

Aachen

AUSTRASIA

Fulda

BAVARIA

NEUSTRIA

Verdun

Lorsch

Tours

Fontenay

St.Gall

Reichenau

BURGUNDY

FRANKISH KINGDOM

KINGDOM OF THE ASTURIAS

AQUITAINE

Pavia

Bobbio

Venice

CROA

Ravenna

DAL.

SPANISH MARCH

Toledo

EMIRATE OF CORDOVA

Rome

DUCHY OF BENE

Cordova

Cadiz

Cartagena

MAURETANIA

Carthage

BYZANT

MOROCCO

A B B A S I D   D O M I N I O N S

MAP 2
Europe and the Mediterranean World in the early ninth century

Novgorod

SLAVIC PEOPLES

Kiev

KHAZARS

MAGYARS

AVARS

CRIMEA

LAZICA

BULGARIANS

ARMENIA

THRACE

Constantinople

BITHYNIA

Thessalonica

Caesarea

Edessa

Daras · Nineveh

MESOPOTAMIA

Athens

Baghdad

Antioch

Ctesiphon

MPIRE

Berytus

· Damascus

Kadesiya

YARMUK R.

Alexandria

· Jerusalem

ABBASID DOMINIONS

Cairo

CHAPTER 5

Islam

The thoughtful student who reads of Christ and Mohammed, the Prophet of Islam, will note interesting parallels between their origins and the circumstances which attended their births. Both of their families belonged to the lower classes. Because of this circumstance the particulars of their births are unknown, except as their devoted followers have filled these in with what the secular historian may dismiss as pious legend. The mothers of the two boys had strange experiences, and about both boys there were predictions telling of what great men they would be and of the marvelous deeds they would perform. Once they were born, even legend ceases. Blank pages cover the passage of their youthful years until they reached manhood except, curiously enough, an incident that happened to both of them when they were twelve. That was the year the Evangelist tells of Christ's being lost for three days to his anguished parents. When Mohammed was twelve, so the story goes, he accompanied his uncle Abu Talib on a journey to Syria. On the way they passed the hermitage of a Christian monk, by name Bahira, who had had visions telling him about a boy that would someday pass his way who would be a great prophet. When Abu Talib's caravan stopped to eat the repast the monk had prepared for them, he insisted upon examining Mohammed, "saw the seal of prophethood between his shoulders," and warned the uncle to hurry back to his country and guard the boy with care, "for great importance is in store for this your nephew."*

There are, of course, more points of difference between the origins of Christ and Mohammed and the circumstances of their births than there are parallels. In the case of Mohammed, none are of greater

* *The Life of Muhammad*, tr. A. Guillaume. Oxford (1955), pp. 80–81.

significance than the geographical and cultural surroundings into which he was born. Of the two homelands, Arabia and Judaea, the land of Christ's birth was the less distinctive. Its culture had witnessed (suffered) the passage of many civilizations. When Christ was born, Judaea was in fact but another province in the far-flung Roman empire. Of such casual importance do many scholars who write of Christ's birth view his homeland that they do not bother to describe Palestine, and so little attention do they give the fact of Christ's Jewish ancestry, apart from his religion, that many of Christ's modern followers seem scarcely aware of his having been a Jew. To an understanding of Mohammed, an acquaintance with Arabia and the mores of its people are of fundamental importance. For Mohammed and his views were almost as much the products of his land as were the date palm and camel. Give Christ his Hebrew religion, and it might not have greatly affected the course of Christianity had he been born in Spain or in Italy or in Greece. Only Arabia and, more immediately, only Mecca could have produced a Mohammed. For this reason one must take a look at both the country of Arabia and of Mecca, the city of his birth and upbringing, before going on to consider the man himself.

Arabia is a huge peninsula, almost one-third the size of the continental United States. The principal physical features of this land mass are its lack of rainfall and the intense heat which are so overwhelming in their influence that they force the life of the inhabitants of the area into the mold which has prevailed there through the millennia of its history. Were it not for the high mountain range along the west coast (that is, east of the Red Sea), which prevents the moisture-laden clouds from continuing on to the east, almost the whole of Arabia would simply constitute an extension eastward of the trackless Sahara of North Africa. Such is the condition of the southeastern part of the peninsula, the so-called Empty Quarter. Fortunately along the west coast rain does fall, enough in the Yemen in the southwest to permit the cultivation of grain crops. The Hejaz to the north enjoys less precipitation, yet sufficient to enable the Bedouins to pursue here and there a pastoral economy based upon stockbreeding (mostly camels). During the summer months the tribes will remain among their wells where their camels, goats, and sheep nibble on the scrub that manages to grow, then in the fall trek to the grazing lands which the rains have turned green, only to return again in the late spring to the hot dusty existence of the previous summer. Beyond these areas in Arabia where life is possible, the traveler will encounter scattered oases, some quite extensive as that at Medina, where he will find water and palm trees and perhaps some productive soil. The palm tree provides the Arabs the date, one of their staples. Their other staple is milk, camel milk for the most part, produced by the same beast that provides them their means of transportation. A wonder from the Lord is the camel, says the Koran. "Lo! this is the camel of Allah, a gift to you. . . ." (Sur. 7:73).

So uninviting was the land of Arabia in ancient times that few, other than the native Arabs, came to make their home there. Only in such larger communities as Mecca and Medina did non-Arabs stop to live —Jews for the most part, some Christians from Syria, and emigrants from Abyssinia with which the Yemen was closely linked. If the word Arab derives from the root meaning "nomad," as has been suggested, that term would fit the great majority of the people who lived in the Arabian peninsula in the day of Mohammed's birth. They bore the name Bedouins, that is, "desert-dwellers," although because the desert is so unproductive, they never remained long in one place. The customary reference to them in the Koran is to the "wandering Arabs." Such a life made the Arab lean and tough. He was ever on the go, seldom did he have more to eat than what sheer existence demanded. Because of the poverty of the land he must be ready to fight to keep what he had from those as poor as himself who might covet it, while at the same time holding himself ever alert to take from members of unfriendly clans and from strangers anything he might need. As the poet sang: "Our business is to make raids on the enemy, on our neighbor, and on our brother, in case we find none to raid but a brother!"* Life was a constant struggle. Such conditions bred bravery and self-reliance, and since hardship and want were his constant companions, patience and a measure of fatalism. So little of his life could the Arab control! Yet because he was himself so frequently in need, to the stranger who sought assistance, he could show himself a most generous host.

The harsh conditions which molded the Bedouin bred in him still another virtue, that of loyalty. If the Bedouin wished to survive, he must be loyal to his clan (or tribe), since without its protection he was completely helpless. There existed no law in Arabia save that of the clan, no supreme law or national state to whose sanctions he might

* Quoted in Philip Hitti, *History of the Arabs*. New York (1956), p. 25.

have recourse as an individual, no abstract notion of right and wrong to which he could appeal. The weight of physical pressures made survival the sole consideration. So raiding one another's villages or caravans was entirely legitimate, and it was only a regrettable necessity to bury girl infants where there was not enough food to go around. Outside the clan the individual stood alone and helpless, although the clan quite willingly proffered him its protection since it in turn needed his cooperation. Only by loyalty to one another, individual to clan and clan to individual, could either survive. If a member of a clan suffered injury or was slain, the clan for its own protection took revenge on the guilty party or on his clan. If one of its members was guilty of injuring a person from another clan, his fellow clansmen stood prepared to protect him, whence the interminable blood feuds against which Mohammed inveighed. Fortunately most of the clashes between Arab clans over injuries stirred more dust than they shed blood, nor was it uncommon for the aggrieved party or his clan to accept satisfaction in terms of a number of camels, a hundred for a slain man, for example, or fifty for a lesser injury.

The hard circumstances of his nomadic life left the Arab little opportunity to develop his culture. Apart from crude images of his gods which he carried with him, and the weapons he fashioned, there was only his poetry which revealed his inner genius, although this was quite beautiful. It was the product of desert bards who lived the life of other members of their clans, but who lightened with their songs the dreadful monotony and harshness of desert life. They sang of gods and jinn, of the wonderful things these spirits did, of the stirring accomplishments of their tribes and their great forebears. They sang, too, of love and beautiful women, and all the fascinating pleasures most Arabs could only dream about: shady groves, bubbling fountains, luscious fruit, cool breezes, and precious stones. While they entertained their fellow Bedouins with their songs, these native bards also bred into Arabic the qualities of an elegant and graceful language and in their listeners the ability to appreciate literary beauty. Mohammed was himself something of a poet, and there are those who find the secret of the Koran's popularity in the beauty of its rhythmic prose and its attraction to people who possess a sense of the beautiful.

Like most primitive peoples the Arabs accepted a universe inhabited by a myriad of spirits. Some of these were powerful and beneficent, others equally powerful but wicked, vicious, or merely mischievous. These spirits made their abode in rocks, trees, wells, or oases where the natives paid them worship, or even in sticks and stones that a tribe might gather and use as an altar. Probably because of the influence of higher cultures about them, the Arabs began in time to give names to the most important of these spirits. And it was surely contact with Jews and Christians that contributed to the evolution of the concept of Allah, a highest god, who ruled supreme over all other deities. The Arabs' view of the afterlife was not greatly different from that of the very ancient Hebrews and the peoples of Mesopotamia, namely, a shadowy and generally unpleasant existence.

The most sacred shrine in all of Arabia, and one of the most ancient, was at Mecca. There stood the Kaaba (shaped as a cube), in which were placed several hundred of the deities the Arabs worshiped; and, it is said, a picture of the Virgin and her child painted on the wall. So holy and popular had this sanctuary become that it was traditional for thousands of Arabs to make a pilgrimage to Mecca during the sacred period of truce in the spring. The entire area about Mecca for a distance of twenty miles in all directions was, in fact, holy ground. Once inside this, any refugee enjoyed sanctuary. Among the holy objects in the Kaaba none was more precious than a black stone that had been built into the eastern wall. This stone, it was believed, Abraham had placed there "when Abraham and Ishmael were raising the foundations of the house" (Sur. 2:127), as the Koran said. Nearby was the well Zamzam, whose salty unpalatable water Arabs regarded as holy.

Mecca's most valuable asset, next to the Kaaba, was its location. Without these two assets to attract Bedouins and traders, it would have remained nothing more than a dusty village situated among bare hills and dependent upon Taif, about fifty miles to the southeast, for much of its food. It lay directly on the caravan routes that linked the Yemen and Abyssinia to the south with Syria and Iraq to the north and east. These connections enabled its fairs to boast many of the commodities with which Egypt and the Fertile Crescent were familiar: silks and spices from China and India, slaves and ivory from Africa, together with such native products as frankincense and myrrh. By the sixth century the Kuraish tribe had risen to a dominant position in Mecca and governed the city by means of a council (mala) composed of the chiefs of the different clans. Because the council lacked an effective executive, only measures that were agreeable to all the clans could expect adoption; nevertheless, the interests of the wealthier members of these clans were sufficiently similar to assure a high

degree of cooperation among them. The Kuraish had also extended
its influence throughout west-central Arabia by means of a system of
alliances with outlying tribes which its control of trade enabled it to
exploit. But modern scholars have detected beneath the surface of
what appeared to be a flourishing economy and a relatively satisfied
society a large measure of tension and discontent. These were the
products of dislocations that might appear during a period of transition
from a nomadic civilization to one approaching capitalism.

Though Mecca was an important community in Arabia, neither the
city nor the country itself counted for much when weighed against
the great cities of Egypt and the Near East. The land was so much on
the corner of the ancient world and its desert face so uninviting, that
would-be conquerors passed it by. Contacts were largely limited to
trade. One of the few biblical references to the country tells of Joseph's brothers who sold him to Arabs on their way to Egypt. Beyond
trade and the caravans that moved up and down the west coast, there
were Arab tribes who conducted raiding expeditions along the edge
of the desert into Syria and Mesopotamia. On occasion large groups of
Arabs such as the Phoenicians, Hebrews, and Chaldeans would detach themselves from their ancestral home and establish new ones in
Babylonia or Syria. The first great power to contemplate the conquest of Arabia (the Yemen) was ancient Rome, but the desert and
heat turned back the army Augustus had sent into the Hejaz. Trajan
destroyed the flourishing city of Petra and made Nabatea in northern
Arabia a Roman province. In the third century, as we have seen, the
emperor Aurelian crushed Zenobia's Arab empire and destroyed its
capital city of Palmyra. These two, Petra and Palmyra, were promising cities along the northern frontiers of Arabia. The most powerful
state to the south was in the Yemen, in Saba, the land of the queen
of Sheba (Saba). There Abyssinian interests had grown strong as
Roman influence declined. In the sixth century Abyssinia had actually
conquered the area and had done so with the encouragement of Justinian as a way of forcing out Persian influences. Some years later the
viceroy of the Yemen drove northward in an unsuccessful attempt to
conquer Hejaz and Mecca. To dramatize his effort and to awe the
Bedouins, he brought with him the largest and strongest elephant in
all of Abyssinia. That was in 570 A.D., the Year of the Elephant as
Arab annalists date the event, the year in which Mohammed was
born.

Only a very few facts protrude above the legendary lore that surrounds Mohammed's birth. As suggested, he was probably born about 570. His father Abdallah, a member of the Hashim clan, died before his birth. This Hashim clan, incidentally, had seen better days and no longer counted among the more important that made up the Kuraish tribe. Mohammed's mother gave him into the care of a Bedouin family for two years of his infancy, either because of real want on her part or the tradition that nothing was better for "city" babies than desert air and Bedouin nursing. When Mohammed was six, his mother died, so he became the charge of his grandfather. Two years later when his grandfather died, he moved into the household of his uncle Abu Talib, the leader of the Hashim clan. For the next twenty years his life remains a blank. Since he was a bright boy, one may suppose that he learned to read and write, also that he must have accompanied his uncle on an occasional caravan trip to the north. At any rate, a wealthy widow by name Khadija was attracted by the young man's bearing and trustworthiness, gave him employment, then when he proved successful on a small commercial mission, proposed marriage. He accepted and their marriage, despite the disparity of their ages, he twenty-five and she presumably forty, proved most successful. Throughout his life Mohammed retained a high regard for his wife. While she lived he married no other women, either out of attachment to her or from prudence. She bore him seven children, although only the daughter Fatima outlived him.

Mohammed had the features and physique characteristic of his people. He was of middle stature and broad-shouldered, had dark eyes, hair, and beard, spare cheeks, and a large forehead. From the manner in which he conducted himself during his years of discouragement and persecution, one must conclude that he was a man of courage and determination, and that he was wholly sincere in his claim to being the messenger of God. His disposition was kindly and amiable, and his personal charm probably won as many to his cause as his persuasiveness. Still he could be harsh, even vengeful. His apologists insist, however, that when he ordered the execution of opponents and enemies, this had become necessary lest his mission be compromised. Even the execution of several poets, including two women, who had attacked him in verse, could not be avoided. Among primitive folk who had such admiration for poetry, the recitation of satirical verse could have been fatal to his cause.

Mohammed appears to have been a man of simple tastes—he

mended his own clothes and cobbled his shoes—except in his sexual life. Here the nine or more wives he married and the few concubines he kept has given rise to the charge of sensuality. Again his apologists protest that political considerations led Mohammed to marry most of his wives, or sympathy, since several were widows and would have suffered want had he not taken them in. In any event, given the polygamous world in which Mohammed lived, his conduct in this regard must be accepted as proper. There is, however, the case of his wife Zaynab which poses a real problem. She was first the wife of Mohammed's adopted son Zayd. When the young man learned of Mohammed's interest in his wife, he promptly divorced her in order to enable his foster father to marry her. This Mohammed did after first receiving in a revelation assurance from Allah that he could marry the woman since her husband had only been his adopted son. Mohammed's principal motive in marrying Zaynab, his apologists declare, was not love; only his wish to announce the abrogation of the ancient Arab condemnation of such marriages. Aishah, Mohammed's youngest wife, must have demurred, for it was probably on this occasion, when the Prophet had asked for a revelation to facilitate his marriage, that she commented drily on the speed with which Allah did his pleasure. There is even a suggestion in the Koran that Allah wished him to curb his marriages, for it reads: "It shall not be lawful for thee to take other women to wife hereafter, nor to exchange any of thy wives for them, even though their beauty please thee. . . ." (Sur. 33:52).

Several of Mohammed's critics question the genuineness of his revelations. These he began to experience at about the age of forty, that is, after some fifteen years of married life with Khadija. By then it had become his wont to go off to a cave outside the city where he would spend several days in prayer and contemplation. God himself may have addressed Mohammed in his first visions. Later the angel Gabriel became the usual intermediary through whom Allah made known his wishes to Mohammed. At times God seems to have placed "words in his heart" without any visible or imagined intermediary. Allah even recommended that he search the Bible for information. On one occasion Mohammed appears to have accepted as divine revelation instructions which later proved to have come from the devil. At the time he happened to be under pressure from the Kuraish leaders to permit the worship of three goddesses who were popular with the Meccans. When Gabriel shortly after upbraided Mohammed for having mistaken Satan's voice for God's, the Prophet promptly denounced the goddesses as idols. At first Mohammed's revelations appear to have come freely, later only in response to some specific problem that was perplexing the Prophet. That Mohammed grew greatly excited when receiving these revelations and sweat would pour from his body has led some critics to suggest that he suffered attacks of epilepsy.

For a year or so after the revelations started coming, Mohammed may himself have wondered about their authenticity and the genuineness of his mission. There is talk of despair, even contemplated suicide which an angel prevented. Who finally convinced Mohammed that he was indeed the messenger of God with a divine mission to carry out was his sympathetic wife Khadija. So he began to preach, at first only secretly to close friends, then after three years openly in Mecca. The ideas he emphasized in these early years stressed the almighty power of God and his beneficence; man's duty, therefore, to worship and obey him; his duty, too, because of God's goodness, to be generous to the poor; and, finally, man's obligation to avoid sin because of the day of judgment that would inexorably come to every person. His mission, like that of a prophet of the Old Testament, was to "rise and warn" the people of God. For "When the trumpet shall sound, verily that day will be a day of anguish and of uneasiness for the unbelievers."

For some years Mecca took little notice of Mohammed and his proselytizing. Converts were few and came hard. Khadija, who was his first convert, encouraged her impatient husband. The adherence of Abu Bakr, a wealthy merchant, was most gratifying. And even though Abu Talib, his uncle and head of the Hashim clan, refused to forswear his pagan beliefs, he assured his nephew the protection to which he was entitled as member of the clan. The majority of Mohammed's first converts were men below the age of forty whose motives for accepting his gospel ranged from sincere religious conviction to the hope of material and political gain. There was Bibal, the Negro slave, for instance, later Islam's first muezzin, who was being tortured to death by his persecutors when Abu Bakr intervened and purchased him. The motives of other of Mohammed's adherents were more opportunistic. They hoped to achieve through the Prophet and the triumph of his revolution a larger voice in the affairs of Mecca.

What first aroused the hostility of the Kuraish leaders was Mohammed's attack on the idols that Arabs worshiped in shrines like the Kaaba. Should he press this attack successfully and idol worship be suppressed, Mecca might cease being a holy city. Would the thousands of pilgrims still come to the city to buy when no deities remained there to be worshiped? Other cities would also suffer, notably Taif with its shrine dedicated to the goddess Al-Lat. Several important Meccan merchants had establishments at Taif. Mohammed's charge that all dead pagans were in hell, including the souls of their ancestors, infuriated the leaders of the clans. They also feared Mohammed's emergence as virtual ruler of the city once a majority of the people accepted his claims to being Allah's messenger. They interpreted, too, his attack on selfish material ethics with its indifference to the poor as aimed directly at themselves and as a gospel likely to stir unrest among the depressed classes in Mecca.

The hostility of the leaders of the Kuraish gradually assumed the form of actual persecution and some of Mohammed's poorer followers were subjected to mistreatment and torture. It may have been this situation that prompted Mohammed to persuade the humbler of his adherents to flee to Abyssinia. An emigration of about a hundred Moslems did take place about 615 A.D., although scholars have advanced reasons other than persecution to account for it. These Moslems may have gone to Abyssinia to secure military assistance, or it may have been dissension among the ranks of the faithful in Mecca that impelled them to leave. Be that as it may, as long as Abu Talib lived Mohammed's life was in no danger. When the Hashim clan refused to repudiate him upon demands of the Kuraish leaders, these organized a boycott and refused to engage in business with the clan or permit intermarriage. But the Hashim clan held firm.

Then in 619 A.D. both Khadija and Abu Talib died and Mohammed's security suddenly disappeared. The new leader of the Hashim clan, although Abu Talib's brother, was unsympathetic and withdrew the clan's protection. Since Mohammed could now be mistreated and even slain with impunity, he set out anxiously in search of another protector. At Taif he was pelted out of the community with stones, and the tribesmen to whom he appealed at various fairs turned him a deaf ear. He was fortunate, finally, to secure a qualified promise of protection from one of the Meccan clans. Still he must have considered it a direct intervention by Allah when a group of pilgrims from Medina, a city 250 miles to the north, approached him with the proposal that he remove to their city. They promised him a haven and the position of arbiter and judge in their community.

Medina (the city of the Prophet) was less a city than a collection of hamlets and farms scattered over an area of some twenty square miles, all dependent upon a single large oasis for their existence. Unlike Mecca, whose barren hills left it no choice but to develop trade, the economy of Medina was based upon the production of cereals and dates. Until the early seventh century it seemed to have been content to remain a seminomadic, agricultural community. Then friction began to appear, even violence and bloodshed. Some of the trouble may have come from the presence of three Jewish clans—whether native Jews or Arabs who had accepted the Hebrew religion is not clear. At one time they had dominated the area. Now the more numerous Arab clans had gained the ascendancy. The community's growing population may have occasioned some tension as well as the shift from a nomadic economy to one based upon agriculture.

These then were the circumstances that had led some of the clan leaders of Medina to seek Mohammed's presence. One need not ignore another possible motive, that of developing caravan trade of their own at the expense of Mecca, using the advice of a refugee from that city who had once himself been engaged in commerce. It appears that Mohammed did not long hesitate over the invitation. It was agreed that his Moslems would flee as soon as possible but in small groups so as not to arouse the suspicions of the Kuraish. When word reached the Kuraish of what was afoot, they sought to block Mohammed's escape, even to kill him. Finally after most of his followers had gone, Mohammed and Abu Bakr fled to a cave outside the city, hid out there for three days until the Kuraish had abandoned its search, then proceeded on to Medina. This, the Hejira (migration) of the Prophet, took place in July 622. So holy and momentous have Moslems considered this event that it has always served them as the base year in their calendar.

Though Mohammed had come to Medina upon that community's invitation, he did not assume leadership for several years. His position was not at all secure, in fact, and had he ventured to exert pressure on the Medinans, his cause would probably have collapsed. To most Medinans he and his Moslems were in Medina on sufferance, while many of the Jews were positively unfriendly. At no time did Mohammed demonstrate greater tact and prudence than during these first years at Medina. One small mistake, and his career would have ended before it had fairly gotten started. To strengthen his position he contracted several political marriages, and to ingratiate himself with the Jews he directed his followers to turn to Jerusalem when they prayed.

What Mohammed did do almost immediately' after arriving in

Medina was to organize raiding parties which harassed Meccan caravans that crossed to the west of Medina on their way to and from
Syria. At first his raiders fired a few harmless arrows as if the Prophet
was not entirely sure of himself. The first real attack on a caravan
came, oddly enough, during the sacred month when fighting was prohibited. Though the act aroused considerable criticism, Mohammed
was able to convince his followers and the Medinans that Allah had
approved the deed. While it was a serious matter to violate the sacred
truce, it was a greater crime to permit pagans to remain undisturbed
in their idolatry. A bloody skirmish at Badr (624 A.D.) which left seventy Meccans dead and Mohammed's companions in possession of
much booty convinced the wavering Medinans that he was indeed the
messenger of Allah. And Mohammed quite wisely gave Allah credit
for the victory. "And ye did not slay those who were slain at Badr, but
God slew them" (Sur. 8:17).

There were reverses as well, notably one at Uhud (625 A.D.) which
did his cause no good. This setback was also Allah's doing, so Mohammed explained. Allah was displeased when the Medinans had gone
off to loot when they should have remained to fight. Two years later
Mecca organized a huge force of ten thousand men with which they
hoped finally to put an end to Mohammed and to the raids that were
ruining their trade. To meet such a force Mohammed took the advice of a Persian convert and had his followers dig a deep trench on
the only side where Medina was vulnerable. After several weeks of
futile effort, the Meccan army ran out of food and water and was
forced to withdraw. This proved a heavy blow to Mecca. Now many
tribes that had been in alliance with that city joined Mohammed instead.

In a final bid to the Meccans to accept him as one of their own
and his religion as that of their ancient forefathers, Mohammed organized a large pilgrimage in 628 and set out for the holy city. He
managed to reach the sacred precincts of the city before he could be
turned back, whereupon an agreement was reached which would permit him and his followers to return in a year for a three-day visit to
the Kaaba, during which interval the Meccans would vacate their city.
Two years later, in January 630, Mohammed marched on Mecca with
an army of ten thousand and after only slight resistance occupied the
city. He ordered the execution of several of his enemies, including
three poets, forced loans from wealthy Meccans, and destroyed the

idols in the Kaaba. After eight years the refugee who had fled Mecca
was back to stay, master of the city.

Some years before Mohammed had also become master of Medina.
His ascendancy there had been slow but steady. Each victory over
Mecca and its caravans brought his followers more booty and with
each victory the number of unconvinced Medinans dwindled. His victories also facilitated the negotiation of alliances with tribes in the
Hejaz and to the north, particularly since Medina had replaced
Mecca as the principal commercial center of the area. The only group
to hold out were the Jews. Only a few accepted him despite his sincere efforts to win them over. He had directed his Moslems to turn to
Jerusalem when they prayed, he had introduced a fast to correspond
with the Hebrew Day of Atonement, and he had designated Friday
when the Jews were preparing for the Sabbath as the holiest day of
the week. Still they grew no friendlier; instead their rabbis ridiculed
him for his ignorance of the Bible and derided his claims to being a
prophet. Such open opposition he could not afford. He had his
Moslems turn to Mecca when they prayed, replaced the Day of Atonement with Ramadan (see below, p. 175), and announced that it was
to Abraham, who he said was not a Jew, not to Moses, to whom God
had given the true religion. First he expelled one Jewish clan from
Medina, then a second, and when the third failed to cooperate against
the siege of the Meccans in 627, he ordered the execution of the men,
some eight hundred of them, and the enslavement of the women and
children. The few Jews who remained and recognized him as a
prophet, he left unmolested.

Mohammed had but two years to live following his occupation of
Mecca. He defeated a last coalition of enemies in a major battle at
Hunayn, then led a large army of thirty thousand men northward toward Syria. What he had in mind by this march is not clear since he
did not penetrate Byzantine territory. Several tribes along the way accepted alliances. How much of Arabia was under his control at the
time of his death is not clear although the Yemen and most of the western tribes must have accepted his leadership. If he had plans for
further expansion, these were cut short with his death. Soon after returning from a "farewell" pilgrimage to Mecca, he contracted a fever
and died in early June 632.

That Mohammed's death caused no rupture in the advance of his
work reveals the greatness of the man and the immensity of the impact

he made on Arabia. Except for a brief interval of readjustment, the spread of the gospel he had preached and the movement he had initiated continued on unchecked until they had encompassed more than two-thirds the Western world. Within a hundred years of his death Moslems prayed to Allah in Gaul and worshiped him in western India. Part of the secret of Mohammed's success is found in the revelations he gave his people, revelations which he insisted came from Allah, revelations whose matchless eloquence convinced his followers that they were divine. These revelations are incorporated in the deathless pages of the Koran.

The Koran, the word of Allah as revealed to Mohammed, is divided into 114 chapters or surahs. The word Koran takes its name from Allah's command to Mohammed to "recite in the name of thy Lord that which man knew not." Mohammed maintained, and so did his followers, that the Koran was the spoken word of God. Most of it appears in the first person, that is, God speaking to Mohammed or to man. God had given the Jews the Torah, to the Christians the New Testament. Now through his prophet Mohammed he was revealing his religion to the Arabs. For some twenty years God kept on revealing to Mohammed what he should "recite." When Mohammed died, these revelations had not all been properly assembled, although the greater number had surely been recorded by his secretary. It was the latter, under instructions of Othman, the third caliph, who supervised the selection and setting down of these revelations in the form they appear in the Koran today.

Once their work was completed, these compilers wisely destroyed all variant versions, thereby saving future Islamic scholars the interminable labor Western experts have expended in an effort to establish an authentic version of the Bible. They did leave one problem, however, although not a very serious one. This concerns the particular sequence they gave the 114 surahs. Modern scholars can detect no pattern beyond the purely mechanical one of listing them by length, the longest surahs coming first, the shortest last. And this may have been the only rationale these Moslem compilers had in mind. Because of the historical character of the Old Testament and the chronological setting of the New, Western scholars may be demanding a schematization that Mohammed never contemplated. For him and his followers they remained revelations, meditations.

The Koran instructed the Moslem in what he must believe and in what he must do to be saved. For the Shiites (see below, p. 183), nothing beyond the Koran is required. For the Sunnites, who make up the majority of Allah's followers, there is also the Hadith, or tradition, which must be given consideration. This consists of words (beyond those expressed in the Koran) and actions of the Prophet, which his devoted followers considered almost as sacred as the Koran itself. While the Sunnites accept the inspired character of the Hadith, they could not agree on its precise contents, which disagreement has produced many of the Sunnite sects in existence today. Be that as it may, the Koran remains the most widely read and quoted book in the world. (It even serves as the most popular textbook in the teaching of Arabic.) No book has exerted anything approaching its influence upon the development of the language and literature of a great people. No book is more honored and reverenced. Among Moslems, the injunction which the Koran expresses on this point, has never lost its early force: "Let none touch it but those who are clean" (Sur. 56:78).

While the Moslem is convinced that the Koran is the word of God, the non-Moslem seeks in less lofty places the origin of the thoughts expressed there. Much of the matter clearly derives from the Bible, from both the canonical and Apocryphal books. Since Mohammed could read neither Greek nor Hebrew, if he could read at all, his biblical information was at best secondhand. From the inaccuracy of what he presents as supposedly Christian theology, one must conclude that the Christians to whom he spoke, among them Khadija's cousin, were less than well informed on the subject. Some of his ideas came from Nestorian Christians, such as the view that man remains in an unconscious state after death until angel trumpets call him forth from the grave to give answer on the Last Day. Who told Mohammed that Solomon knew the language of birds and that the baby Jesus spoke from the cradle remains a mystery. Though the Koran presents the stories of the Annunciation and birth of Christ as they appear in the Gospels, he somehow confuses Mary with Miriam, the sister of Aaron. And the twist which the Koran gives the story of Joseph, the son of Jacob, is almost modern. The Koran tells how Putiphar's wife admitted to her husband her infatuation and her unsuccessful attempt to seduce Joseph, then demonstrated by means of a trick that other women would have been just as helpless before the young man's physical charms. Whereupon the levelheaded Putiphar agreed with Joseph that the safest place for him under the circumstances was in jail! The Koran reveals, of course, considerable influence of Arabic mores and thought, as well as acquaintance with the sacred books of the Persians.

Of the fundamental truths expressed in the Koran, none stands forth with greater clarity than that proclaiming the existence of one God and man's utter subjection to that one God. This thought is expressed in the opening prayer of the Koran, sometimes referred to as the Lord's Prayer of the Moslem: "Praise be to God, the Lord of all creatures; the most merciful, the king of the day of judgment. Thee do we worship and of thee do we beg assistance. Direct us in the right way, in the way of these to whom thou hast been gracious, not of those against whom thou art incensed, nor of those who go astray" (Sur. 1:1–7).

Mohammed called his religion Islam, meaning submission. A more apt term he could not have proposed. Nothing so marked the faithful Moslem as his humble submission to the will of God. It approximated the deep faith that in the Christian world was found only in the genuinely pious. So strong was the Moslem's faith in the almighty power of Allah that anything short of an unreasoning submission to the divine will was scarcely possible. "Whatever is in heaven and earth singeth praise unto God, and he is mighty and wise. His is the kingdom of heaven and earth; he giveth life and he putteth to death; and he is almighty. He is the first and the last, the manifest and the hidden, and he knoweth all things" (Sur. 57:1–3). Islamic liturgy fairly exhausts the Arabic language of adjectives in extolling the wonderful qualities of God. Each of the ninety-nine beads of the Islamic rosary expresses in still a different way one of his many virtues. He is the incomparable, the absolute, highest, magnificent, and almighty. Yet while his transcendent position above men is immeasurable, he remains none the less immanent in men, "nearer to you than your jugular vein." So he is also just, gentle, and compassionate, forgiving, merciful, gracious, and loving.

So powerful is Allah's will that puny man of himself cannot even believe. Allah saves those he wills and allows those to err whom he wishes to destroy. This suggests that Allah had foreordained everything that would happen, although the Moslem stopped short of absolute predestination. Man still retains a choice, as it were, of cooperating with or ignoring Allah's grace, and for the faithful Moslem who does his duty to God, "we will cleanse you from your evil deeds and will introduce you into paradise with an honorable entry" (Sur. 4:31). The Moslem's position regarding Allah's power and grace and man's responsibility to cooperate with that grace is illustrated by the story of the Bedouin who asked Mohammed if it were necessary for him to secure his camel. The Prophet replied: "Secure thy camel, and trust in Allah."

For those who believed in Allah and did his will, an eternity of bliss awaited, "reposing on couches adorned with gold and precious stones . . . youths shall go about to attend to them with goblets and beakers and cup of flowing wine—their heads shall not ache by drinking the same, neither shall their reason be disturbed—and with fruits of the sorts which they shall choose, and the flesh of birds of the kind which they shall desire. And there shall accompany them fair damsels having large black eyes, resembling pearls hidden in their shells. . . . And they shall have their abode among lote-trees free from thorns, and plantains loaded with produce, and deep shade, near a flowing stream and midst fruit in abundance . . ." (Sur. 56:11–32). For those who did not believe in Allah or who transgressed his commands, there awaited an eternity of misery "amidst burning winds and scalding water, under the shade of a black smoke, neither cool nor agreeable" (Sur. 56:41–44).

The profession of faith which was the first of the "five pillars of Islam" expresses first and foremost the Moslem's belief in one God. It also contains a second part, that telling of Mohammed's role. He is Allah's messenger, the intermediary who brought man God's final message. God had used other prophets, among them Abraham, Isaac, Jacob, Elijah, John the Baptist, and Christ. Because the Jews and Christians had permitted Allah's words, as delivered by these prophets, to become corrupted or had simply neglected to listen to them, it had become necessary that God send still another messenger. This messenger was Mohammed, his final and greatest prophet. So the formula of faith affirmed: "There is no God but Allah and Mohammed is his prophet." With this statement a man became a Moslem.

The second pillar of Islam (*salat*) was prayer, which the Moslem will recite five times a day. Of the five pillars this may be counted the most important. Through these five prayers the Moslem worships his God, while at the same time giving public profession to his faith.*
Koranic expressions of praise and worship provide the substance of these prayers, all of which open with that introducing the Koran (quoted above).

---

* "It is true that Mohammad did not place such great importance upon any other religious duty as he did upon prayer. Even today the hour of prayer, called out from the gallery of the slender minaret by the muezzin, the melancholy modulation of his voice reminding us of the old Gregorian chant, lends to the Muhammadan city its unique character, and for a long time . . . the readiness with which the call to prayer was heeded in the streets, markets, and bazaars attracted the humble admiration of Christian observers." Tor Andrae, *Mohammed, the Man and His Faith*. New York (1960), p. 80.

Before the Moslem began his prayers, he was to cleanse himself, with water if this was available, otherwise with sand. "O true believers, when ye prepare yourselves to pray, wash your faces and your hands unto the elbows, and rub your heads and your feet unto the ankles" (Sur. 5:6). Essential to the proper performance of the prayer requirement were physical expressions of piety and worship, namely, kneeling, bowing, and prostration. "The signs," says the Koran, "are on their foreheads from the marks of frequent prostration" (Sur. 8:29). While prostration was a gesture of subjection traditional to eastern courts, it is probable that Mohammed borrowed the idea from Christian monks who had adopted it to give expression to their humble subservience to God. Only on Friday at noon was the Moslem required to join other faithful in public worship under the guidance of a leader (*imam*). But Friday was no day of rest.

A third pillar was almsgiving (*zakat*), which because of its binding character might be considered more a tax than alms. It was intended for the poor, for the purchase of slaves, the ransoming of captives (Moslems), and for the work of proselytizing. "Alms are to be distributed only unto the poor, and the needy, and those who are employed in collecting and distributing the same, and unto those whose hearts are reconciled, and for the redemption of captives, and unto those who are in debt and insolvent, and for the advancement of God's religion, and unto the traveler. This is an ordinance from God" (Sur. 9:60). So much was it a duty, indeed, that officials saw to its collection. It amounted to one-fifth the Jewish and Christian tithe.

A fourth pillar was a strict fast which Moslems were to observe during the month of Ramadan. That was the month in which God had revealed the greater part of the Koran. The principle of a fast Mohammed drew from the ascetic practices of the Hebrews and Christians although what he ordained went considerably beyond theirs in severity. During the daylight hours for an entire month, as soon as "the white thread becometh distinct to you from the black thread," the faithful must abstain from food and drink, from sexual gratification, and from anything else as well that might please the senses. Nor was such fasting sufficient. During that month "be constantly present in the mosques" (Sur. 2:187).

The fifth and final pillar of Islam was a pilgrimage to Mecca. This duty Mohammed placed as a strict charge upon all Moslems, men and women alike, except those too ill or too poor to make the journey. "And it is a duty towards God, incumbent on those who are able to go thither, to visit this house [Kaaba]" (Sur. 3:97). This was the house that Abraham had built, so Mohammed believed, and he it was, too, who had introduced the practice of the pilgrimage. At least the rites that attended the pilgrimage date from pre-Islamic days, even to the kissing of the black stone which Mohammed retained. Perhaps as much as the religion of Islam itself does this annual trek of tens of thousands of Moslems from all over the world to Mecca, the "Holy City," weld the powerful bond that unites the faithful who worship Allah.

These five requirements, in particular the five prayers, the long fast during Ramadan, and the pilgrimage to Mecca, gave Islam a religious character quite distinct from that of the Christian West. Other practices, the results of the Prophet's injunctions, also heightened the distinctiveness of Islam. One was the prohibition to Moslems from eating pork and drinking wine. Mohammed also forbade the charging of usury. To the credit of Islam, this prohibition enjoyed greater observance there than the similar one in the West. The calendar that Mohammed decreed also set its stamp on Islam. Although this was a lunar calendar, Mohammed abolished the intercalary period that pre-Islamic society had interpolated to bring it in conformity with the solar year. As a consequence Islam accepts a year in which the four seasons keep constantly shifting. There are no summer or winter months in the land of Allah.

Mohammed denounced waste, pride, and boastfulness. He reminded the Moslem to "show kindness unto parents, to near of kin, and orphans, and the poor, and to your neighbor who is of kin to you, and also your neighbor who is not, and to your fellow-traveler and to the stranger, and the slaves whom your right hands shall possess" (Sur. 4:36). Though he accepted slavery, he promised Allah's blessing to those who manumitted their slaves. Gambling was outlawed as well as the practice of infanticide. "Kill not your children because of poverty. . . . We will provide for them and for you" (Sur. 17:31), assured the Koran. Mohammed would have abolished the blood feud had this practice not been so deeply entrenched in Arabic life. He did, however, mitigate the practice. "If ye punish," he admonished, "then punish with the like of that wherewith ye were afflicted. But if ye endure patiently verily it is better for the patient."

Mohammed legislated on no subject more extensively than upon women and their status. While he urged men to treat their wives with consideration, of the husband's absolute authority there was no question. "Men shall have authority over women because Allah has made the one superior to the other. . . . Good women are obedient." As for those who disobeyed, "rebuke them, send them from your beds, and chastise them" (Sur. 4:31). Such an attitude might follow reasonably from the institution of polygamy which Mohammed endorsed. His apologists attribute his failure to adopt the Western practice of monogamy although attracted by other Christian traditions to his desire to provide for widows and the unmarried daughters of fathers who had been slain in fighting. So "Marry of women who seem good to you, two or three or four." Of concubines there was scarcely any limit, nor any restriction on the number of wives a man might divorce. Mohammed's grandson married and divorced one hundred during his lifetime of forty-one years. For the Prophet, a dispensation enabled him to wed more than four, "a privilege granted thee alone, not for the rest of the true believers" (Sur. 33:50).

It is doubtful whether Mohammed could have suppressed polygamy had he wished; like feuding, the institution was so much a part of Arabic life. Of the hard lot of widows and orphaned daughters he was quite aware, as noted above. In replacing the practice of matrilineal descent with one derived through the father, he removed a major form of sexual promiscuity. He also enjoined other forms of immorality. As a matter of fact, the censures expressed in the Koran against those who violated Allah's moral laws gave Islam mores a more puritanical character than that which obtained in the monogamous Christian world.

Mohammed's death in 632 precipitated a crisis in Islam. Though no one could presume to aspire to his role of Prophet, it was imperative that his position as spiritual and political leader be filled immediately, otherwise the centrifugal forces of ancient Bedouin tribalism would surely bring about the rapid dissolution of the young state. So promptly on the morrow of Mohammed's death, a group of Moslem leaders proclaimed Abu Bakr the Prophet's caliph (successor or deputy). The choice was a prudent and popular one, though a few protested the rights of the young Ali, Mohammed's cousin and son-in-law, on the basis of hereditary succession. Abu Bakr had been one of Mohammed's very first and most loyal followers. He was also the father of the Prophet's favorite wife, Aishah, and, when Mohammed was ill, had led the Moslem community in prayer.

Abu Bakr's rule was short (632–634), although it proved a momentous one in Islam's history. The new Moslem state did not disintegrate as some of the faithful had feared. Instead it embarked on a program of expansion that would change the history of the world. Against those tribes that seized upon Mohammed's death to repudiate their ties with Islam, the new caliph took immediate measures. Several tribes objected to payment of the *zakat*, others simply assumed that in keeping with Arab traditions the treaties they had agreed to with Mohammed had lapsed with his death. In a few quick campaigns in the so-called *riddah* wars (secession or apostasy), Abu Bakr's generals re-established Moslem authority over those tribes which had attempted to secede, next extended Islam's rule to the other tribes inside Arabia which had not accepted the faith of the Prophet. Then, with an uneasy peace proclaimed throughout the peninsula and a large army readied for more campaigning, Abu Bakr announced the moment had come to drive outside Arabia. When he died, Moslem Arabs were on the march northward.

Scholars are not entirely sure what these first expeditions aimed to achieve, whether they were any different from the lightning attacks upon vulnerable caravans and outlying towns which Arabs had been carrying out for millennia. Surely only a prophet or fool could have dreamed that these semicivilized Arabs could humble the mighty Byzantine and Persian empires which had dominated that part of the world for so many centuries. That these raids quickly assumed the character of major campaigns may have surprised the Arabs as much as it did their enemies. Some scholars take a longer view of these raids, or rather conquests, as they shortly came to be. They point to other Semitic peoples—Hebrews, Phoenicians, and Chaldeans, for example— who had left Arabia in ancient times and later established states of their own. Why should not the same factors of overpopulation and the desiccation of the peninsula which may have impelled these earlier tribes to leave Arabia also have been operative here in the seventh century A.D.?

Whatever the ambitions of Abu Bakr and his advisers in taking the step of sending an army northward, never before the rise of Islam had Arabia been so united nor more ready to undertake conquests outside the peninsula. Within a few years Arabs on their horses and camels had gained smashing victories over the famed armies of Byzantium and Persia. Of the various explanations offered for their spectacular success, the most popular is the exhaustion of these Byzantine and Persian empires. Few scholars will question the ability of either empire to have thrown back an attack from Arabia had this come at the beginning rather than at the end of Heraclius' reign, that is, before his wars with the Persians had worn out his own empire and brought that of Persia to the brink of collapse (see above, p. 134). Few historians will also hesitate to classify as a tragic mistake Heraclius' decision to cut off subsidies to the Arab tribes that lay between Syria and Medina and which had traditionally served Byzantine interests. The emperor's policy, too, of persecuting the Copts of Egypt, the Jacobites of Syria, and the Jews of Palestine left Byzantium without friends in those countries when the Arabs appeared on the frontiers. The religious policy of the Zoroastrian Persian state proved equally intolerable to many of its subjects, while in both the Byzantine and Persian empires many people nourished the hope that a change of government would lighten their heavy tax burden.

In an analysis of Moslem success over Byzantine and Persian armies, something must be credited the prowess of Arabs as fighters and to the kind of warfare they waged. As warriors they were not superior to their foes, nor even more numerous. Their newly born faith and their native fighting instincts did furnish them an enthusiasm which was usually lacking in Byzantine and Persian armies. They also managed to fight the kind of warfare against their enemies, that of the desert, at which they had no match. The ability of their camels to cover huge distances through arid country enabled them to map strategy their foes could not anticipate, while their faster horses made possible tactics on the field of battle that the slower chargers of their enemies could not contain. At Yarmuk and Kadesiya where they gained their most spectacular victories, they fought under conditions that approached those of a desert sandstorm. And when they found themselves without these advantages as in storming a city, they could count on embittered citizenry within helping them gain entry. At Alexandria "heretical" Christians opened the city to them; in Spain Jews betrayed Toledo.

Under Omar (634–644), Abu Bakr's successor, Islam gained its most glorious victories. Though the new caliph left the fighting to other leaders, their victories—above all, the successful assimilation of the newly conquered territories—were largely the fruit of his firm, statesmanlike leadership. He broke with the Prophet's policy of confiscating the lands and property of a defeated enemy, left landowners and peasants in control of their acres, and assured them the free practice of their religion. To placate his Arabs for being deprived of the booty they had come to expect, he arranged to pay them pensions. The money for these pensions came principally from the land and poll taxes which the subject populations paid, neither of which were as burdensome as the imposts which the Byzantine and Persian governments had levied. Because any mass conversion would endanger this fiscal arrangement, Christians and Jews, the "people of the Book [Bible]," suffered no pressure to convert. Omar also retained as far as possible the administrative systems that existed in the lands the Islamic armies overran, even to the use of the Greek language and coinage in the former possessions of the Byzantine empire.

Khalid, one of Islam's ablest generals, had led an army into Iran even before Omar's accession. When he learned that Arab forces in Syria needed assistance, he doubled back in that direction, laid siege to Damascus, and after six months took the city. Upon the arrival of a powerful Byzantine army he withdrew to the Yarmuk, a tributary of the Jordan, where he destroyed the imperial host in August 636. Within a few months almost the whole of Syria had fallen to Islam. Jerusalem held out for some months, then announced its willingness to surrender provided Omar, whom it trusted, would come to receive its submission. Some years later Moslems erected a great mosque (mistakenly known as the Mosque of Omar, better as the Dome of the Rock) on the site of Solomon's temple whence Mohammed, they believed, had ascended to heaven on a winged horse. To Moslems Jerusalem has always remained "The Holy [City]."

After Syria had been conquered, Omar sent an army to Iraq where the Arabs were encountering serious resistance. Among other circumstances that were occasioning them difficulty were the elephants that the Persians had imported from India. Arab arrows simply could not penetrate their tough hide. But at Kadesiya the Arabs trained their arrows on the eyes and trunks of the huge beasts and, with the help of a windstorm, annihilated their foe (June 637). Ctesiphon, the Persian capital, fell shortly after, although progress from then on came slowly against the proud, warlike Persians. Finally about 652 the last Sassanid ruler was killed and the whole of Persia to the Oxus was annexed. Conquest of Persia proved less difficult than did absorption. Some scholars maintain, in fact, that the Persians forced their own civilization upon their rude conquerors and under the Abbasids (see below, p. 184) even assumed control of the empire. That lay in the future. What had already occurred in 644 was the death of Omar by a Persian slave's dagger.

In the meantime Egypt had fallen to Islam. In 630 Omar had given Amr, another of Islam's superb generals, his reluctant permission to invade the country. Amr had no difficulty routing the main Byzantine army and overrunning the country. Babylon held out for a few months, and Alexandria, the second city in size and strength in the empire next to Constantinople, only a short while longer. Under normal circumstances, its garrison of fifty thousand could have held off the Arabs indefinitely since the enemy lacked siege equipment while the Byzantine navy could provision the city from the sea. Inept rule in Constantinople, however, and treachery in Alexandria handed the city over to the Arabs without fighting. Three years later the city revolted, Amr returned, defeated the Byzantine army, and leveled the massive walls that protected the city. Then from the shipyards of Syria and Alexandria Islam sent out ships, manned by Christian seamen, to contest Byzantine control of the eastern Mediterranean.

By this time internal difficulties were causing the Arab drive to falter. When Omar died in 644 and Othman succeeded, trouble appeared. Othman was easygoing, was even charged with cowardice. Worst of all, he belonged to the Meccan oligarchy which had once opposed the Prophet. A few military successes did brighten the otherwise clouded twelve years of his caliphate. The Moslem navy defeated the Byzantine in the "Battle of the Masts" when Arab "seamen" covered their inferiority by lashing their ships to the Byzantine vessels and fighting "on land." Crete fell to Islam and so did Rhodes, where the Arab conquerors sold the fallen Colossus to a Jewish junk dealer. (An earthquake back in 224 B.C. had caused this "Wonder of the World" to collapse.) During these years the Arabs had also pushed to the Oxus. Still these victories had been slow and costly, while at home discontent grew over the manner Othman was promoting his Umayyad relatives. In 656 mutineers broke into his home in Medina and murdered him, "one of the most fateful events in Islamic history."* The act proved that caliphs were only human, that they could be slain, and that dissident groups could take control of the caliphate.

The new caliph was Ali (656–661), Mohammed's son-in-law. Modern scholars may exonerate him from any direct guilt in the assassination of Othman; the dead caliph's followers thought differently. They and their leader, the distinguished general Muawiyah, then governor of Syria, refused to recognize Ali. Despite several bloody victories Ali won over his enemies, fortune appeared to have cursed him. He died by an assassin's dagger. Then when his son Hasan, the Prophet's grandson of the one hundred divorced wives, accepted a royal pension which would enable him to continue his sensuous living, Muawiyah went on

---

* J. J. Saunders, *A History of Medieval Islam*. New York (1965), p. 62.

to establish the new Umayyad caliphate with Damascus as his capital.

The Umayyad caliphate (661–750) brought the empire of Islam to the peak of its might and extent. To the northeast Moslem armies overran Transoxiana with its fabled cities of Bukhara and Samarkand, clashed with Chinese still farther to the east, and crossed the Indus into Punjab (713). Pakistan still retains in unbroken reverence the message of the Prophet which its ancestors received back at this time. Meantime other troops were carrying Moslem power and religion westward along the North African coast. The Byzantine bastion at Carthage held up their march until its capture in 698. To punish the city for its heroic defense, the Arabs left it a ruin, which it remains to this day. In the Berbers of Tripoli, Tunis, and Morocco, the Arabs encountered some of the toughest warriors in history. Ancient Carthage and Rome had never wholly succeeded in conquering their ancestors, nor have the Spanish and French experienced greater success with their modern descendants. The land and mores of these Berbers were similar to those of the Bedouins, and so poor were they that they had little to treasure but their freedom, which they carried with them as they eluded their pursuers midst the crags and shifting sands of the desert. In time they agreed to accept the religion of the Prophet and a measure of Moslem control, together with the promise of participating in raiding expeditions to the west.

Such a raiding party of several hundred Berbers crossed over to Spain in 710, followed a year later by an army under the Berber chieftain Tarik who gave his name to Gibraltar (Jabal Tarik or mountain of Tarik). With the aid of re-enforcements and treachery he then attacked and annihilated a much larger Visigothic army, after which resistance melted away except in the cities. Several of these, including Cordova and Toledo, were betrayed, others were stormed. Tarik's success had meantime aroused the envy of Musa, governor of Morocco, who disciplined him for his "independence," and himself completed the conquest of Spain (with the exception of the Asturias in the northwest). Then in 715 he led his triumphant army back to Damascus with an enormous store of booty and thousands of slaves and beautiful girls in tow, only to have the jealous caliph discipline him in turn for exceeding orders. Musa spent his last years roaming the streets of Damascus as a beggar.

Back in Spain the Moslem drive carried across the Pyrenees in 718, overran a large part of southwestern France, then suffered defeat at the hands of Charles Martel and his Franks at Tours in 732. (See below, p. 201.) Islamic armies also ran into resistance in their attempt to press northward beyond the Caucasus into the steppes of Russia. There the Khazars, allies of the Byzantine empire, held firm and blocked their way. Almost completely successful, however, were Islamic efforts in sweeping Christian shipping from the Mediterranean. Still the ultimate goal of Islam's ambitions eluded her. This was the city of Constantinople. Moslem navies made several stupendous efforts during the years 674–678, then tried again in 717–718. Storms and Greek fire (see above, pp. 135–36) defeated both attempts. According to Theophanes, the Byzantine chronicler, only five of the eighteen hundred ships that had sailed against Constantinople in 717, returned safely to their base. Islam had to wait until 1453, when Constantinople had itself decayed to the point of collapse, before taking the city.

Meantime Muawiyah, who proved himself the ablest of the Umayyad caliphs, was busy laying the foundations of a stable, centralized state from his headquarters at Damascus. What recommended Damascus rather than the holy cities of Mecca and Medina was its superiority as the capital of a new secular state which was to replace the old theocracy. While an Arab aristocracy continued to fill the higher posts in the government, Muawiyah retained the Byzantine administrative structure and the services of many Copts, Syrians, and Persians. In the course of time regular administrative departments emerged, and in time, too, the men who filled the offices in the public service became predominantly Moslem. Their parents had been Christian. For them the promise of lower taxes and higher social status proved more persuasive than their faith. So many Christians accepted Islam, in fact, that to avert a fiscal crisis the government was obliged to hold the landowner responsible for the land tax whether he became a convert or not.

Moslem armies would have been even more invincible during the period of the Umayyad caliphate had not serious internal unrest, even civil war, interrupted their march. Of a number of groups who came to oppose the government, the oldest and most intransigent were the Shiites, the followers of the murdered Ali. They had never accepted Muawiyah nor his dynasty, and in 680 their hostility became even more implacable when Muawiyah's supporters slew Ali's son Husain which gave them another martyr to revere. To the Shiites the Umayyads were traitors who had subverted the sacred mission of Islam and were maintaining a thoroughly secular and sinful regime at Damascus. An even larger group who were hostile to the government were the *mawali* (clients), that is, non-Arab converts to Islam, mostly Persians, who by 700 A.D. actually outnumbered the Arab faithful. They included shopkeepers, merchants, and artisans rather than peasants, and constituted, consequently, an important element in the population. Despite their acceptance of Islam and their importance, the *mawali* were kept in an inferior position socially and economically. They were not permitted to marry Arabs, they paid taxes from which Arab Moslems were exempt, they could not serve as cavalry in the army, while as foot soldiers they drew less pay and received less booty than Arab infantrymen. Understandably they made easy targets for Shiite propaganda.

A third group, smaller than the other two but better organized, spearheaded the assault on the Umayyad caliphate. These were the Abbasids, so-called because they pressed the claim to the caliphate of a descendant of Mohammed's uncle Abbas. Shortly after the Alid faction had joined hands with the Abbasids, black flags of revolt appeared in Khurasan in northwestern Persia. From here the revolt spread to Iraq and westward, and almost before the last of the Umayyad caliphs appreciated the seriousness of the situation, his army was defeated, he himself captured and executed. The new caliph, Abu al-Abbas, called himself *saffah*, the Bloodshedder, and well did he deserve the name. Anyone who had been a member of the Umayyad aristocracy or could be counted a potential foe was hunted down and slain. Even the graves of all the Umayyad caliphs but one were broken open, their bodies desecrated and destroyed. One group of eighty princes of the blood who had gathered to eat a banquet with the uncle of the new caliph, upon the most sacred assurances of good will and safety, were clubbed to death by executioners. Their assassins then spread leather cloths over their still writhing bodies and proceeded on with the banquet. Only one member of the Umayyad dynasty, Abd al-Rahman, grandson of an earlier caliph, managed to escape his grim pursuers to make his way to Spain where he set up an independent state. (See below, p. 220.)

With such slaughter and treachery was ushered in the Abbasid caliphate, traditionally the most glorious in medieval Islamic history. That the upheaval represented more than a palace revolution became clear with the removal of the capital to Iraq where al-Mansur, the brother of Abu al-Abbas, erected a new capital at Baghdad. Near here a navigable canal linked the Tigris and Euphrates, although the particular site for the new capital was chosen, so the story goes, because scouts sent out by the caliph to find a location, reported that in that mosquito-

infested land the only place they could sleep was in the village where
Baghdad was eventually built. Here in Baghdad Persian influence became supreme, the rule of the Abbasids representing, in fact, the triumph of the non-Arab, Persian element in Islam. Persian costumes,
festivals, ceremonials, and officials replaced those of Arabia. Though
the caliphs pretended to restore the principles of pristine Moslem piety,
theirs was a monarchical despotism almost as far removed from that
of the Prophet's as was the Byzantine court. Their highest official was
the *wazir* or vizier, a Persian official, who served as vice-caliph and
often directed the work of the government. The caliph was himself lost
to view behind a vast assembly of officials, ministers, eunuchs, wives,
and concubines who shared his brilliant court. No trace remained of
the Arab tribalism which had witnessed Islam's birth. Only in the matter of religion did Arabia retain its primacy.

The caliph who best illustrates the altered character assumed by the
Abbasid caliphate was Harun al-Rashid, grandson of al-Mansur. His
reign covered the years 786 to 809, but for a full seventeen years of his
caliphate he handed the business of state over into the hands of Yahya
Barmakid, the vizier he had inherited from his father. The industry and
loyalty of Yahya and his elder son al-Fadl left Harun free to devote
himself to pleasure and to prayer, to conducting several military campaigns, and to presiding over the most brilliant court west of the Orient.
To his subjects he always appeared the devout Moslem. Five times
daily he prayed and one hundred times a day did he prostrate himself. He dispensed alms with a generous hand and he led no less than
ten pilgrimages to the holy city of Mecca. In his serious moments he
moved midst a circle of eminent scientists, philosophers, and other
scholars whom he encouraged to reside in his palace.

Of the other side of Harun his subjects had only rumors: that he had
seven wives and perhaps a thousand concubines, that he permitted
artists to paint figures of men and animals; that wine flowed freely
during the revelries at the palace when musicians and poets in the caliph's pay regaled him with irreverent and lascivious songs. Djafar, the
younger and libertine son of Yahya, joined Harun regularly in these
revelries, that is, until one day in 803, when seemingly out of a blue
sky, the caliph ordered him executed and his father and brother imprisoned. For three years Djafar's head blackened on one of Baghdad's
bridges, the two halves of his dismembered body darkening the other
two. Of this side of Harun, his cruelty and rapaciousness, the court
poets never sang.

Harun's military record was unimpressive, as was true of most of the Abbasids. Only al-Mansur distinguished himself as a warrior, and even he found it impossible to extend Baghdad's authority over Moslem Spain. Upon his death a slow but progressive loosening of the bonds of empire set in which neither Harun nor succeeding caliphs could stay. The probable cause, the "most obvious cause" in the judgment of Gibbon, for the decline of the empire "was the weight and magnitude of the empire itself." Given the simple administrative structure of the day, only a young and aggressive empire possessing the ambitions of a powerfully dedicated group to urge it forward, could have maintained such an immense jurisdiction. Already by 750 A.D. Islam had the marks of an aging state. The religious zeal and tribal fanaticism which had supplied it vigor since the death of the Prophet had themselves died. When they disappeared Islam had reached the limits set by nature to its "desert" empire. Rarely did it move beyond arid plains and sand dunes across highlands or into fertile lands that sustained a numerous peasantry.

The appearance of internal frictions, similar to those which had harassed the Umayyads, sapped the lifeblood of the Abbasid empire. There were three principal sources of trouble: the desire of certain provinces, non-Arab for the most part, for autonomy or independence; dynastic struggles over succession to the caliphate; schismatic movements of a religious character. Harun al-Rashid was obliged to recognize the autonomy of the lands west of Egypt. By 900 A.D. Abbasid authority to the east of Iraq had become equally nominal. The man generally classified as the last able caliph, Muktafi (902–908), demonstrated his ability by reconquering Egypt from a Turkish chieftain who had seized the province. Then there were dangerous disputes over the succession which a polygamous ruler and the absence of a strict system of hereditary succession made fairly persistent. The caliph, instead of designating his eldest son, might nominate a younger one for the succession or even a brother. Harun's sons al-Mamun and al-Amin fought over the empire, and only ten years after the death of Harun did al-Mamun fight his way into what was left of ruined Baghdad. Then he almost precipitated a new civil war when he announced that a brother, not his son, would succeed.

The most common and critical source of peril for the caliphate rose from religious dissension. Religious dissent was, of course, not new, although it only acquired a dangerous character in the late ninth century when widespread social and economic grievances gained it nu-

merous adherents. In a society so spiritually oriented as Islam, it was
only natural that many people should look to religious reform and to
Allah for a cure of their ills. Such "reform" movements are also apt to
be violent. The Karmathians, for example, who were a quasi-religious
sect of Arabian origin, ambushed a pilgrim caravan of twenty thousand
souls one day in 906 A.D. as it was leaving Mecca and butchered them
to the last man. They then desecrated the Kaaba and made off with
the sacred black stone. Scholars find a link between these Karmathians
and the resurgence of the Shiite, more properly Fatimid, movement
that emerged as a power among the Berbers of Tunis toward the close
of the ninth century. From there the Fatimids moved eastward, extended their rule over Egypt, Syria, and Arabia, and would have overwhelmed Baghdad as well had not the Buyids, a Persian clan, already
taken over that city and reduced the caliph to a puppet. On the eve
of the Crusades, therefore, Islam was no longer a vigorous nor a united
empire.

Despite civil war and secession which disrupted the world of Islam
from time to time, its scholars and men of letters went about their
business seemingly undisturbed by the turmoil about them. For this
great blessing posterity is most grateful. The products of medieval Islamic scholarship furnished a significant contribution to the advance
of Western learning. Without the work of Islamic scientists, mathematicians, and philosophers, the marked advance that the Western
world began making in scholarship as early as the middle twelfth century would not have come until appreciably later.

The importance of this contribution poses the ready question: How
could an Islamic world, particularly one based upon a culturally backward Arabic civilization, have supplied anything a Christian society
could have used? The question is not entirely accurate in its assump-
tions. The culture of the Islamic world had not sprung from Arabia.
What the Arabs had done was to conquer that world, give it their
language and their religion. They had not forced their seminomadic
mores upon the millions of peoples who lived within the frontiers of
their immense empire. As a people the Arabs had little to offer. But
their armies had conquered lands which possessed high cultures, principally the Hellenistic (Jewish and Christian) and Persian, and had
obliged these to live together within the confines of one empire. They
next provided the scholars of these conquered lands a favorable climate in which to work and a common language in which to communi-

cate. Islamic culture represents substantially an amalgam of these two cultures, the Hellenistic and Persian, together with significant contributions from Byzantium and India.

That many of the scholars whose learning graced these different cultures remained Christian, Zoroastrian, or Jewish, reveals the generally tolerant attitude Islam assumed toward non-Moslems. During the reigns of a number of caliphs, the government in fact undertook to support scholarship and the arts. Al-Mansur, for example, had Euclid's geometry and other Greek and Syrian manuscripts brought from Constantinople and paid for their translation. In addition to scientists and philosophers, Harun al-Rashid also patronized singers and poets. To one poet who composed a sonnet in his honor he gave five thousand gold pieces, a robe of honor, ten Greek slave girls, and one of his best horses. His son al-Mamun established a "house of wisdom" in Baghdad, a kind of institute of advanced studies, where scholars from all over the Islamic world pursued their studies, with libraries, laboratories, and paid assistants furnished from the munificence of the caliph. A story has it that al-Mamun offered the Byzantine emperor two thousand pounds of gold and perpetual peace if he would induce Leo the Mathematician to come to live in Damascus. In this concern over scholarship and the arts, the caliphs were continuing a tradition their Sassanian predecessors had inaugurated before them. Even after the rise of Islam the Persian city of Jundishapur continued to flourish as a center of scientific study. It owed its prominence to refugee Nestorian and Neo-Platonist scholars who had been expelled from Byzantium in the fifth and sixth centuries and who brought many manuscripts with them.

Of all cultures to which Islam was indebted, none was owed a greater debt than the Hellenistic. This was especially true in the field of medicine. To the medical theories of Hippocrates and Galen, Islamic scholars added little, although they supplemented their findings with a store of solid information learned through careful observation and experience. For Islamic scholars revealed a thoroughly modern appreciation of what might be called the scientific method. Before deciding where to erect a hospital in Baghdad, al-Razi (d. 923) hung up pieces of meat in different parts of the city, then located the structure where these showed least evidence of putrefaction. This al-Razi, who was a Persian, has been called "the greatest and most original of all the Moslem physicians."[*] His encyclopedic writings on the subject

* Hitti, History of the Arabs, p. 366.

of medicine included a particularly famous treatise on the subject of smallpox. This disease was a scourge in that part of the world.

Second only to al-Razi, among a score of eminent Islamic physicians, was ibn-Sina, or Avicenna (d. 1037), of Bukhara. So extraordinary were his talents that experienced physicians sought him out when he was still only a youth of sixteen. His renowned medical encyclopedia known as *The Canon* was recognized as authoritative by Western physicians as late as the seventeenth century. The ninety-nine treatises that make up this monumental study consider almost every phase of medical learning and practice. Of drugs alone it identified 760. When the sultan of Bukhara invited ibn-Sina to treat his malady, he gained access to the royal library where he found "a mansion with many chambers, each chamber having chests of books piled one upon another. In one apartment were books on language and poetry, in another law, and so on; each apartment was set aside for books on a single science. I glanced through the catalog of the works of the ancient Greeks, and asked for those which I required; and I saw books whose very names are as yet unknown to many and works which I had never seen before and have not seen since." In general the Islamic medical profession made its most valuable contribution in the field of ophthalmology (eye diseases were common in Iraq) and in the development of pharmaceutical science. The Christian West considered Islamic physicians the best in the world, which they were.

In astronomy the nature of the Islamic contribution was similar to that in medicine. They added few principles to those upon which Ptolemy and other Greeks had based their astronomical system, although their study and application of these principles enabled them to make improvements in the observing instruments they used and, consequently, to draw up more accurate tables for the use of astrologers and mariners. Astronomers such as al-Battani contributed some original research and introduced minor corrections to Ptolemy. Al-Biruni (d. 1048), the most distinguished Islamic astronomer, contributed studies dealing with the rotation of the earth and with latitudes and longitudes. Better known as a poet (to the West) though pre-eminently an astronomer was Omar Khayyam (d. 1123). His calendar is said to have been more accurate than the Gregorian. While these scholars accepted the principle that the earth was round, they did not rise above their less sophisticated fellows and deny the claims of astrologers.

Not surprising in view of the enormous size of the Islamic world and the contact this brought them with many peoples and climes was the advance its scholars made in the field of geography. The pilgrimages that faithful Moslems were under obligation to make to Mecca, from whatever country in which they might be living, must also have brought in additional information. Interest in travel and geography was quite general, indeed, and many scholars who were not strictly geographers, men like al-Kindi, al-Khwarizmi, and al-Masudi, for instance, contributed valuable information. Some of this geographical knowledge they acquired firsthand, a good amount they owed to merchants who had visited or who hailed from strange lands. It was the stories of these merchants that gave birth to the tales of Sindbad the Sailor. In their study of geography Islamic scholars started with Ptolemy, the ancient Greek authority on the subject, but shortly advanced far beyond him. Particularly valuable are their descriptions of the topography, products, and mores of the peoples of many different lands, and the maps they produced. Of a large number of geographers who deserve mention, note should be made of the encyclopedic writings of Yaqut (d. 1229) and of al-Idrisi (d. 1166). The latter, who is the most renowned of all Islamic geographers, dedicated his monumental work to Roger II of Sicily at whose court he lived.

In chemistry, better known as alchemy (*al chemie*) in the Middle Ages, Islamic scholars contributed worthwhile knowledge concerning such processes as distillation, crystallization, calcination, solution, sublimation, and reduction. Though this information proved useful to staid scientists, Islamic scholars came by it in their search for a talisman, a philosopher's stone or similarly magical catalyst, which would enable them to transmute base metals into gold. While such research helped give alchemy its dubious name, the principle by which the alchemist justified his search was Aristotle's view that one substance could be changed into another by changing its primary qualities. Among the by-products of the alchemist's investigations was the preparation of steel, dyes, varnishes, and hair dyes. The names of al-Razi and ibn-Sina appear among the more prominent scholars in the field of Islamic chemistry.

The Islamic contribution in the field of mathematics was more modest than generally believed. What may have given it exaggerated importance are the Arabic numerals which were not Arabic at all. They were introduced from India. In all probability merchants brought knowledge of these symbols to Baghdad where al-Khwarizmi (d. 850), the leading Islamic mathematician, explained and publicized their virtues. The unique value of these numerals derives from their arrangement in a place system built around the base ten, a scheme which vastly simplified multiplication and division. Because of al-Khwarizmi's reputation the West for a long time knew arithmetic as algorism. Al-Khwarizmi prepared important astronomical tables as well as the oldest work on algebra. Schoolboys may wonder about the practical value of this branch of mathematics; al-Khwarizmi did not. In his introduction he assured the reader that he had limited his presentation "to what is easiest and most useful in arithmetic, such as men constantly require in cases of inheritance, legacies, partition, law-suits, and trade, and in all their dealings with one another, or where the measuring of lands, the digging of canals, geometrical computation and other objects of various sorts and kinds are concerned. . . ."

In literature medieval Islam produced no poets of the stature of Dante, Petrarch, or Chaucer, nor any great prose literature beyond the Koran. This last, the Prophet's own "recitation," remains in terms of literary excellence and eloquence the finest piece of Arabic literature. To Westerners the best-known prose collection is that of the *Arabian Nights* which the Arabs themselves do not hold great literature. Many of the earliest stories are of Persian and Indian origin. Other tales from a variety of sources kept being added until the fourteenth century when the *Nights* acquired substantially its present form. What furnish the stories a distinctly Arabic and Islamic flavor are the continuous references to the almighty power of Allah, to the jinn, magic, and precious stones which fascinated the Bedouin's imagination, and to the court of Harun al-Rashid where many incidents described in the stories took place.

It is not easy for the non-Arab to judge the value of Arabic poetry. Poetry loses heavily in translation, a misfortune that applies especially to Arabic verse. The attractiveness of Arab verse depended on form and style for the most part and on the music of the words, values which almost defy transferal to another language. The themes, too, were romantic and imaginative rather than idealistic and intellectual. Arabic bards sang about the stars, the colors of the desert, the virtues of horses, love, girls, and deeds of valor. The narrow appeal of such themes rarely extended beyond the unsophisticated Arab for whom they were composed. While contact with higher cultures encouraged the refinement of literary forms, the Arab continued to prefer his sensual themes. The greatest Islamic poet was abu-Nuwas (d. 810), who entertained Harun al-Rashid and his harem with his exquisitely beautiful verses. His broad repertoire included lascivious, irreverent, and satirical themes, poems extolling the virtues and magnificence of his patron Harun, and, as he grew older, even ethical and religious subjects.

Some of the better literary prose of medieval Islam appears in the writings of chroniclers and historians. This is less true of the early writers who adopted a starkly annalistic pattern even though the best of these annalists remains one of Islam's leading historians. He was the Persian, al-Tabari (d. 923), who carried his chronicle of events from the Creation down to 915 A.D. His voluminous works—he is said to have written forty, some say eighty, pages a day for forty years—include a commentary on the Koran and *Annals of the Prophets and Kings*. For his information al-Tabari consulted what written sources existed and supplemented these with oral traditions he gathered on his travels through Syria and Egypt. Only an abridgment remains of his principal historical work. In this book he describes one of the rare non-hostile exchanges between Nicephorus and Harun al-Rashid. It appears that when Harun's troops overran Heraclea they had captured a girl who was the intended bride of Nicephorus' son. Nicephorus asked Harun for her release and at the same time requested some perfume and a tent. "And al-Rashid ordered the slave [girl] to be sought," wrote Tabari, "and she was brought and decked out and seated on a throne in his tent in which he was living; and the slave was handed over, and the tent with all the vessels and furniture in it, to the envoy of Nicephorus. And he sent him too the scent he had asked, and . . . some dates, figs, raisins, and treacle." Nicephorus gave al-Rashid's envoy in return 50,000 drachmas, 100 silk and 200 embroidered garments, 12 falcons, 4 hunting dogs, and 3 horses.

A second leading Islamic historian was the Arab, al-Masudi (d. 956). Because of the interesting variety of information he gathered on his extensive travels and which he incorporated into his writing, he has earned the name the "Herodotus of the Arabs." Few scholars in their lifetime have acquired his broad erudition. Of his thirty-volume *History of the Times* little remains. His masterpiece, the *Golden Meadows*, contains many anecdotes which he gleaned from the reigns of the caliphs. Though he is no more dependable as a historian than al-Tabari, the ordinary reader prefers his narrative, which he organized around kings and peoples, to the other scholar's annals. Less scholarly although valuable are the biographies which ibn-Khallikan (d. 1282) prepared of leading Moslems.

The most famous of Islamic historians was ibn-Khaldun (d. 1406).

Probably no writer of history has ever held so prominent a position. He served first the king of Morocco, then the sultan of Granada, finally the ruler of Egypt. It was as a member of the Egyptian court that he accompanied an embassy to Damascus to meet the dread Tamerlane. (See below, p. 375.) That Mongol world-conqueror, it appears, was impressed with ibn-Khaldun, and, partly because of his counsel, decided to withdraw from Syria. What sets ibn-Khaldun far above contemporary historians was the extraordinary perceptivity with which he wrote. When they explained the course of history as the product of men's decisions, fortune, and divine providence, ibn-Khaldun looked for equally powerful factors in the physical environment and social institutions of peoples. Most peoples, he believed, had a life cycle somewhat similar to individuals and dynasties. They are born as nomadic states, pass through an agricultural stage to urban culture, then inevitably decline as luxury and the relaxation of moral values deprive them of their originally strong fiber.

Of the peoples in ibn-Khaldun's day who had scarcely advanced beyond the nomadic stage with whom the historian was best acquainted were the Arab Bedouins and the Berber tribes. (He was himself from Tunis.) These hardy desert folk, ibn-Khaldun maintained, had chosen to retain their rough ways since only these mores enabled them to escape political domination by more advanced civilizations. For that reason, when they had need for stones to prop up their cooking vessels, ibn-Khaldun pointed out, they demolished a building and used its materials. Because of this mode of life, they made themselves the enemies of buildings, "which are the very foundation of civilization." Arnold Toynbee described ibn-Khaldun's philosophy of history as "undoubtedly the greatest work of its kind that has ever been created by any mind in any time or place."*

Medieval Islam made a signal contribution in the field of philosophy. Her scholars had a solid base upon which to work: first the writings of Plato and Aristotle, then the critical studies of later Greek and Syrian commentators who were scattered throughout the eastern Mediterranean world, many of them having fled to Persia in the sixth century to escape Byzantine persecution. Of the two ancient philosophers, Aristotle received by far the greater attention. Platonic thought seeped in by way of Neo-Platonic scholars and other thinkers who mistakenly attributed to Aristotle writings which actually belonged to Plotinus. The Abbasid caliphs in particular encouraged the study

* A Study of History, III, 322.

of philosophy although not necessarily as a discipline apart from knowledge in general. Islamic scholars drew no sharp line between philosophy and learning in general. Their most eminent philosophers were usually men of such encyclopedic learning that they distinguished themselves in a number of fields of learning. To the Arabs, indeed, philosophy meant essentially the knowledge of the true cause of things, whose answer might lie in metaphysics, medicine, mathematics, or even history.

The broad erudition of Islamic scholars was one respect in which they differed from those in the West. Their different approach to the problem of reconciling faith and reason represented another. The scholastics in the West, who were all members of the clergy, started with faith and ended with faith. What tenets of faith they could explain rationally, they accepted; what tenets they could not rationalize they still accepted. The most eminent Islamic scholars who delved into philosophical questions, on the other hand, were principally laymen. Not only was it their wont to start with Aristotle (or what they deemed Aristotelian) rather than the Koran, in their attempt to reconcile faith and reason, but when they discovered that they could not rationalize certain fundamentals of the Moslem religion, they either became agnostics or took refuge in what is known as the principle of the double truth. This principle, which is associated with Averroës, would permit the scholar to accept some matter of Koranic faith as truth, such as the creation of the world, yet leave him to deny this as a philosopher.

One of Islam's leading philosophers was al-Kindi (d. 850), one of the few Arabs to attain eminence as a scholar. He lived most of his life at Baghdad where he served as court physician and astrologer. Though he wrote on many subjects and with unusual erudition, his writings lack originality. In company with other Islamic scholars he expended much thought on Aristotle and much effort in an attempt to harmonize his thought with that of Plato. His commentaries on Aristotle were prized in the West, which preserved them in more Latin manuscripts than the Islamic world did in Arabic.

The leading philosopher of the following century was al-Farabi (d. 950). He studied at Baghdad but lived most of his career at Damascus. There the eminence of his scholarship earned him the title "second teacher." (Aristotle was the first.) Like al-Kindi he too sought to harmonize Aristotle and Plato. So comprehensive was his learning that he wrote authoritatively in the fields of medicine, mathematics,

and alchemy. And so profound was his knowledge of music, according
to ibn-Khallikan, and so proficient was he with the lute, that he was
able to put his hearers to sleep (including the doorkeepers), or, if
he chose, cause them to laugh, or make them weep.

Ibn-Sina (Avicenna), the distinguished scholar of medicine, was
also an eminent philosopher. For some years, however, he must have
wondered whether he was cut out to be a thinker. He tells in his
autobiography of having read Aristotle's *Metaphysics* forty times, of
having actually learned the work by heart, without gaining any com-
prehension of its contents. Then by chance he happened across one
of al-Farabi's commentaries and read it, whereupon its meaning immediately became crystal-clear. Ibn-Sina's writings reveal an intimate
understanding of Aristotle although a willingness to depart from him
on questions of time, movement, and the divisibility of matter. His
notion of God was similar to Aristotle's, that is, a first being who possessed no freedom of the will, therefore the creator of the universe
not by choice but by necessity. Ibn-Sina exerted most influence upon
subsequent Islamic, Jewish, and Christian thinkers through his success
in harmonizing Neo-Platonism and Aristotle.

Of all Islamic philosophers none enjoyed a higher reputation in the
West than ibn-Rushd, or Averroës (d. 1198). He was born in Cordova,
served as a judge in Seville, later as court physician to the king of
Morocco. His rationalism led to his being charged with heresy, judged
guilty, and exiled for a number of years. All his philosophical writings
were ordered destroyed. (He was reinstated shortly before his death.)
So profound and influential were his Aristotelian studies that Western
scholars referred to him traditionally as the "commentator." Though
ibn-Rushd knew no Greek and so was obliged to depend upon translations, some of them faulty, his reverence for Aristotle was extreme.
"Aristotle's doctrine is the sum of truth because his was the summit of
all human intelligence," he affirmed. As indicated above, so great was
his devotion to Aristotle and reason, that he took refuge in the principle of the double truth when confronted with a theological dogma he
could not rationalize. He was more responsible than anyone else for
introducing the cult of Aristotle to the medieval West.

One of the philosophers ibn-Rushd influenced was his contemporary
Moses Maimonides (d. 1202). Maimonides was also born in Cordova
though he left Spain when about thirty years of age and spent most
of his active years in Cairo. There he served as court physician to the
sultan. His best-known work, entitled *Guide to the Perplexed*, repre-

sented the most learned attempt by a Jew to harmonize faith and reason. He was in agreement with Thomas Aquinas in maintaining that Scripture was always true, and that in case of a conflict between Scripture and philosophy, it was the latter that must be made to conform. So renowned was Maimonides for his knowledge of medicine that even today poor Hebrews are said to spend the night in the synagogue he served as rabbi in Cairo, in the hope of being cured of their maladies.

One of the most outspoken critics of what many religious leaders deprecated as rationalism among Islamic intellectuals was al-Ghazali (d. 1111), Islam's leading theologian. Al-Ghazali was born in Khurasan where his unusual intellectual talents had already aroused wonder when he was still only a boy. He moved to Baghdad and in time gained great fame as a professor of law and philosophy. Then something happened. He lost confidence in the validity of his subjects, became a skeptic, his health broke, he abandoned his career, family, and possessions, and finally took up the life of an ascetic. For a dozen years he divided his time between prayer and the study of religious books. In the end he became convinced that both knowledge and truth came from God, and both of these God bestowed gratuitously. Though al-Ghazali found no conflict between faith and reason, he gave reason an inferior position. He returned to Baghdad, resumed lecturing, but now in theology rather than in law, and in a short time he had regained all his earlier fame. He eventually retired to his birthplace at Tus where he founded a monastery and school. Scholars consider him the brightest light in the history of Sufism (Islamic mysticism). Even though his writings were religious in character, they were not without interest to Western mystics. In the history of Islamic theology, his influence remains second only to that of the Koran.

The art of Islam, by reason of its own distinctive character, helped accentuate the distinctiveness of Islamic culture. The horseshoe arch in Spain, Egypt, and the Middle East informs the visitor to those lands, for instance, that a common civilization once spread itself over that immense expanse. Several factors collaborated to encourage the evolution of similar art forms throughout the Islamic world. One could properly credit the dry, hot climate which prevails over North Africa and the Near and Middle East with influencing the art of that area. The Kaaba, which was open to the sky, together with the open courtyards of many mosques could not have become popular in the Islamic world were its climate not one of the driest on the earth.

Art historians discover a common and persuasive influence upon Islamic art in the Koran's denunciation of idols and in the Prophet's warning contained in the Hadith where he threatened painters and those who depicted men and animals in color and stone with Allah's special vengeance on the day of judgment. Not only were representations of men and animals banished from mosques but from private homes as well. Only after Persian influences had weakened the faith of Islam during the Abbasid period did such forms appear. The absence of images in stone, painting, and mosaic provided a striking contrast between the interior decorations of Christian and Islamic houses of worship. In fact, the peculiar kind of interior decoration which Islamic artists developed in order to compensate for their inability to show the forms of men and animals sharpened its dissimilarity from the Christian world. This was an interior art consisting of a complex design of intertwined patterns, leaves, and flowers painted or carved in low relief. So characteristic was this kind of decoration of Islamic art that it acquired the name arabesque. The function of arabesque was exclusively decorative, which reveals yet another contrast with the Christian West where painting and sculpture frequently assumed a didactic or inspirational role.

Another art form that is peculiar to the Islamic world is the high slender tower called the minaret. The minaret which is commonly attached to the mosque provides the muezzin a prominent place from which to summon the faithful to prayer. As indicated, some of Islam's mosques (place of prayer or prostration) remained open to the sky. Over other mosques the Islamic architect erected a dome, frequently more bulbous than hemispherical, which provided protection against the sun. The only essential departure, perhaps the only permissible departure, from the puritan simplicity of the interior architecture was furnished by the qibla. This was the semicircular recess placed in the wall closest to Mecca. Other characteristics that distinguish Islamic architecture are cusped door and window openings, richly decorated arches, and various kinds and groupings of columns. Some of the finest examples of Islamic art are found in its illuminated manuscripts and calligraphy.

CHAPTER 6

The Dark Ages and
the Dawn of a New Era

It now comes time to return to western Europe of the sixth century which we left in the hands of rough Franks, Angles and Saxons, Burgundians, Visigoths, and Lombards. From point of view of culture and intellectual life, this century ushered in the period known as the Dark Ages. (See above, p. 102.) As Gregory of Tours had lamented, "Woe to us, for the study of letters has disappeared from amongst us!" For most people, however, Gregory's lament would have been equally expressive of the times had he simply said, "Woe to us!" These centuries from the sixth to the close of the tenth were the most turbulent and misery-laden that Europe has ever experienced. It is not an accident that the three "Greats" who lived during the period, Gregory the Great, Alfred the Great, and Charlemagne, earned most merit for having halted further deterioration of conditions during their lifetimes and for having achieved some improvement.

Nevertheless, the Dark Ages were not just a period of strife and turmoil, of renewed invasions and more plunder. Those were melancholy times to be sure, and there were many men who feared the very bases of society would dissolve before the terrifying onslaughts of the fierce Vikings, Saracens, and Magyars. Still, when the smoke from their widespread and pitiless pillagings had cleared, the outlines of a new and vigorous Europe stood clearly to view. By the close of the eleventh century the new Western states that were aborning had even acquired sufficient strength and maturity to mount a powerful attack against the world of Islam. A large measure of the darkness of the Dark Ages was, therefore, relative, not unlike the unproductive years it requires to make a young man out of a boy.

Among the countries whose culture and people had suffered most during the period of the Germanic invasions, few were in a sorrier

state than Gaul. There let us begin the political story of the Dark Ages
in the land where the youthful Clovis (481–511) had succeeded his
father to the throne of the Merovings, legendary kings of the Salian
Franks. Though Gregory of Tours hailed Clovis as a doughty champion
of Christianity, his level of moral development appears to have been
no higher than that of his semicivilized neighbors. He was as savage
and treacherous as they were, although more cunning and ambitious.
He displayed his savagery by eliminating, by means mostly foul, all
who opposed him in his quest for power, or whose lands he coveted,
whether they were friends, relatives, or enemies. He demonstrated his
sagacity by being baptized a Catholic Christian. Gregory of Tours provides a miraculous setting for this baptism. According to his account,
Clovis' army was on the point of suffering a disastrous defeat at the
hands of the Alemans and the situation looked hopeless. The king in
desperation called on the God of his Christian wife Clothilda and promised to accept baptism were He to turn destruction into victory. While
Clovis was yet praying, God had intervened, so Gregory declared,
caused the Alemans to give way, whereupon the Franks won a great
victory. After the victory the saintly Remigius, bishop of Reims, baptized Clovis and three thousand of his warriors.

It may, indeed, have happened as Gregory describes the incident.
Still the wily Clovis must have appreciated how valuable it would be
for him to have the Catholic hierarchy and clergy of Gaul on his side in
his battle with his Arian neighbors, the Visigoths, Ostrogoths, and Burgundians. Whatever the circumstances that attended Clovis' baptism,
of the fact of his conversion there is no question, nor of the important
contribution the Roman church made to his victories.

Clovis' first success was over Syagrius, last representative of what
may still have remained of Roman authority in northwestern Gaul. This
victory enabled him to annex the territory to the Loire, including the
cities of Soissons, Paris, and Reims. He then extended his control over
his neighboring Salian chieftains and later over the Ripuarians, the
other great branch of the Frankish nation. Against the Burgundians
he was less successful although they became his allies. His "miraculous"
victory over the Alemans at Tolbiac (Zülpich) shattered that powerful nation. When he attempted to pursue the last disorganized groups
that had fled for safety to the territory of Theodoric, king of the Ostrogoths, the latter had remonstrated. He warned Clovis to be moderate:
his long experience had taught him that "those wars of mine have been
most profitable, the ending of which has been guided by moderation."

Clovis was not moderate, although Theodoric was too strong to trifle with. A few years later when Clovis annexed Aquitaine at the expense of the Visigoths and was minded to take over the Provence area as well, Theodoric inflicted a sharp defeat on his army and kept this land for himself. Yet when Clovis died in 511 at the age of forty-five, his Franks had established their rule over two-thirds of Gaul, and they were there to stay.

While the Merovingian dynasty continued on for almost 250 years, its history after Clovis' death was in the main a chronicle of internecine wars, royal incompetency, and progressive decline. Before 638, the year King Dagobert died, cruelty and treachery marked the reigns of most monarchs; after that date only moral and physical degeneracy. Dagobert's son was the first of the *rois fainéants* (do-nothing kings), as a contemporary referred to them. "Nothing was left to the king. He had to content himself with his royal title, his flowing locks, and long beard. Seated in a chair of state, he was wont to display an appearance of power by receiving foreign ambassadors on their arrival, and, on their departure, giving them, as if on his own authority, those answers which he had been taught or commanded to give." In 751 the Franks tired of this pretense, cut off the locks of Childeric III, the last of the Merovingians, and immured him in a monastery.

Not the entire fault for the decline of the Merovingian dynasty need be laid to the deficiencies of its monarchs. So violent were the times, indeed, that the very barbarity of many of its kings might be considered an asset since fierce men about them responded only to fear. These kings had so few circumstances working in their favor and so many against them. A small measure of strength flowed from their character as hereditary monarchs, and the dynasty could usually count on the support of the church, for what this was worth. Generally the church was in as much need of help as the king. Arrayed against the ruler were a multitude of arrogant, brutal counts and dukes, all of them eager to exploit any possible royal weakness they might detect.

The turbulency of the times also made ruling difficult. So much were war and turmoil the normal order of things that the chronicler relates as an item of real interest that "the whole land had peace for two years [749–750]." Conditions never remained peaceable sufficiently long to permit the establishment of those social and economic ties which furnish stable regimes their foundation, nor for many centuries to come would there appear any sense of national feeling to bind together peoples so diverse as those which made up the population of Gaul. Most disturbing of all circumstances was the poverty of the Merovingian kings. They drew their revenue from plundering raids for the most part and from their own estates. Yet plunder was irregular and their own estates kept dwindling as successive kings continued to alienate more and more of the crown estates in order to gain the adherence of greedy, unscrupulous nobles.

A significant factor in the decline of the Merovingian monarchy was the custom Frankish (Salian) kings had of partitioning their realms among their sons. Even though the sons might view their individual portions as part of a Frankish kingdom and, on occasion, might cooperate against a foreign foe, more frequently greed had them at each other's throats. When Clovis died, his four sons assumed control of their respective parts of the kingdom, then proceeded to fight among themselves for larger shares. (They did manage to complete the conquest of southern France by driving the Goths across the Pyrenees and by annexing Burgundy.) From out of these wars and the deaths of his three brothers emerged the brute Chlotar as sole ruler, but with a trail of corpses in his wake that included two young nephews whose throats he personally cut, and the charred bodies of his eldest son, the latter's wife, and their two children whom he had watched die. A third nephew was spirited away, grew up a monk, and eventually found his way into the liturgical calendar as St. Cloud. Even the cruel Merovingians could produce a saint!

The principal victors in these wars among the Merovingian kings were the counts and dukes, more especially the mayors of the palace. The latter were royal officials who administered the king's estates and supervised his other officials. As the king grew weaker, the mayor of the palace grew stronger, particularly after 614 when he succeeded in making his office hereditary. The first mayor to actually replace his king as ruler was Pepin II (687-714). When he died, he passed on his office to his illegitimate son Charles Martel, called the Hammer because of his impressive victories over the Moors. As noted above, Charles defeated them at Tours in 732 and subsequently drove them across the Pyrenees. He also defeated the Bavarians, expelled Saxon and Frisian invaders, and re-established Frankish authority throughout the kingdom—all this simply as mayor of the palace. Had he consented to lead an army against the Lombards as the pope begged him to do, and had he been successful, Christian chroniclers might have acclaimed his deeds as only less glorious than those of his distinguished grandson Charlemagne.

The mayor of the palace who finally regularized his position was Pepin III (741–768), the son of Charles Martel. In 751, upon the approval of the Frankish princes and Pope Zacharias, he ascended the throne and was crowned by St. Boniface. In answer to his plea, the pope had assured him that "It is better that the man who has the real power should also have the title of king, rather than the man who has the mere title and no real power." A few years later the next pope, Stephen II, crossed the Alps to beg Pepin to use that power against the same Lombards who were again pressing about Rome, and Pepin accommodated. He drove them from Rome—a second expedition became necessary when the Lombard king failed to honor his promises—and from the exarchate of Ravenna as well, then turned these territories over to the pope. For himself he retained the position of protector of the church and patrician of Rome. At long last, after centuries of anxious dependence upon capricious, tyrannical Byzantine power, the pope had found a strong, loyal Frankish arm upon which to lean.

In 768 Charles, the most renowned of all Frankish kings, perhaps of all medieval kings, followed his father Pepin to the throne. Time has been harsh with the title "Great," which a dozen men have borne from out of the past. Of the few remaining "Greats," Charles should be the last to relinquish his title, at least in the English-speaking world. There tradition has incorporated "the Great" into his name of Charlemagne. That two modern states, France and Germany, both count him their most heroic ancestor, will also prolong his fame. His dominion included all of France, western Germany and the lands to the east, as well as part of Spain and more of Italy. Across the Channel kings extended him tacit recognition as lord, and even proud Byzantium for a time acknowledged his title emperor.

The account of Einhard, Charlemagne's secretary, expresses some of the awe in which the king's contemporaries held him. "Charles was large and strong, and of lofty stature, though not disproportionately tall (his height is well known to have been seven times the length of his foot); the upper part of his head was round, his eyes very large and animated, his nose somewhat long, hair fair, and his face was bright and pleasant. Thus his appearance was always stately and dignified, whether he was standing or sitting. . . . His meals ordinarily consisted of four courses, not counting the roast which his huntsmen used to bring in on the spit. . . . While at table he listened to reading or music. The subjects of the readings were the stories and deeds of men of olden time: he was fond, too, of St. Augustine's books, and especially of the one entitled 'The City of God.'"

By temperament Charlemagne was a man of moderation, firm without being cruel, in his dealings with men frank and straightforward. Given his powerful position and his conviction that no human authority stood above his, he might have been arrogant or despotic, but he was not. His demeanor resembled that of an Old Testament patriarch, and he ruled his large household at Aachen with the paternalistic benevolence of a Jacob. Of his own children he was especially fond of his daughters, so much so that he would not permit them to marry. There were stories, as a consequence, of moral irregularity on their part which Charlemagne, if he knew, accepted without complaint. The fault may have been his, he might have argued, or he might have accepted such conduct with the same tolerance as he did the easy moral atmosphere that prevailed at Aachen. It would require several centuries more before Frankish mores would approach the moral level set by monastic reformers. After the death of his fourth wife, Charlemagne kept several mistresses of his own, although the austerities he practiced in his last years, it is said, were meant to atone for his earlier laxity.

Charlemagne remained nonetheless a dedicated Christian. Contemporaries, including churchmen, took little heed of his moral laxity. To them he was the great strong arm of God, the terror of the Infidel, the scourge of the pagan. Charlemagne too believed his foes were God's foes. His was a sacred responsibility to destroy these enemies, to bring to pass in his own lifetime the City of God of which Augustine had written. His first major victory was over the Lombards, a people the papacy had never ceased to abominate despite its conversion to Catholic Christianity. Yet when Pope Hadrian begged him to come down to Rome to drive them off, Charlemagne at first hesitated. The daughter of their king Desiderius had once been his wife—that marriage had been annulled—and the Lombards had given him no provocation. When Desiderius refused to withdraw from territories the pope claimed and to accept lands elsewhere, however, Charlemagne marched across the Alps, captured Pavia, Desiderius' capital, placed him in a monastery, and put an end to Lombard history. He took over their iron crown for himself.

Against the Moslems in Spain he won a magnificent victory if one accepts the romantic tale in the *Song of Roland*. Actually he suffered a sharp, though not serious, setback. In this instance he had committed the one blunder of his career. He had permitted himself to accept the assurances of several Abbasid emirs that they would join him in an attack on the Umayyad emir of Cordova should he march an army across the Pyrenees. When he did come south, they failed to show, and the discomfited Charlemagne, after several reverses, returned to Gaul. On his retreat Basques attacked his rear guard as it was passing through a defile and "in the struggle that ensued, they cut them off to a man." Some years later Charlemagne avenged this earlier defeat and annexed the territory to the Ebro River.

The most stubborn of Charlemagne's enemies were the Saxons, the last of the powerful German tribes that had once harassed imperial Rome's northern frontier. Frankish kings before Charlemagne had won temporary victories over scattered groups of Saxons when these ventured west of the swamps and forests that covered their homeland. Charlemagne also gained victories, secured promises of subjection, and took hostages, yet to no avail. Once the summer was over and the Frankish army had returned home, the Saxons would revolt and massacre the officials, missionaries, and bishops Charlemagne had left behind. Year after year, for thirty-three summers so Einhard writes, Charlemagne fought the Saxons. Even his execution of 4500 of their leaders, following upon a particularly serious revolt, did not bring them to heel. What finally broke their indomitable spirit was the policy of deportation Charlemagne finally adopted, when he moved thousands who "lived on the banks of the Elbe and [settled] them with wives and children, in many different groups here and there in Gaul and Germany."

Charlemagne also extended his rule over the Bavarians, forced the Slavs between the Elbe and Oder to recognize his authority, then destroyed the barbarous Avar nation to the southeast. This brutal people had failed to acquire, during the two centuries since coming from Asia, even sufficient culture to make use of the horde of booty it had since accumulated. "All the money and treasure it had been years amassing was seized, and no war in which the Franks have ever engaged within the memory of man brought them such riches and such booty." Charlemagne also extended his rule over Brittany, but against the Danes who were just beginning their raids along the North Sea, he and his Franks could do little but throw up defenses and pray. As an old man, it is said, he wept over the misery these savage Northmen would cause his people after his death. The tale may be true, for the aged Charlemagne had lost his youthful vigor, his two ablest sons had died, and when his own death came in 814, his empire appeared on the point of disintegrating.

Historians attribute part of the ineffectiveness of most Frankish kings to the primitive administrative machinery with which they had to rule. Despite long contact with imperial Rome and Byzantine rule, the personal character of the Frankish government had remained almost unchanged from tribal times. Custom continued to expect the king to administer the kingdom from what revenues his own personal estates produced. Charlemagne did nothing to alter this custom, although among the most valuable documents from his reign is the detailed directive he sent to his stewards (Capitulary *de Villis*) concerning the efficient administration of his estates. Fortunately for Charlemagne and the peace of his realm, he possessed more extensive estates than his Merovingian predecessors, and he also captured more booty. His counts and margraves were also expected to bring gifts with them in the spring when they met and advised with him concerning matters dealing with the empire. It was at these Mayfields, as they were called, that he generally issued his capitularies after consultation with these men. In a country that had few roads and no postal system, no better opportunity presented itself for publicizing such proclamations. Charlemagne experienced little trouble from his counts. They held him in fear if not respect, and they also were wary of the *missi dominici*, the two royal inquisitors Charlemagne sent to each county each year "to report to him any inequality or injustice . . . and to render justice to all, to the holy churches of God, to the poor, to widows and orphans, and to the whole people."

What strikes the modern scholar who examines Charlemagne's capitularies as most unusual is the wide variety of problems he made his concern. He legislated on education, on roads and trade, on justice and military service as might be expected. But with equal freedom he issued decrees touching theology, the liturgy, and monastic reform. His father Pepin had cooperated with the papacy in fighting the pagan and in pushing church reform. Charlemagne did not cooperate so much as dictate. He did not follow the lead of the pope; he ignored or led him. He appointed bishops and abbots, convened synods to discuss doctrine and liturgy, and even lectured the pope on his failure to introduce the Filioque clause in the Nicene Creed. Still it was not arrogance but faith that drove him, not pride but love of God, as when he personally attended the baptism of thousands of pagans in the waters of the Elbe. Above all cities he loved Rome the most, the city made holy by Peter

and Paul and so many martyrs. When he learned of the death of Pope
Hadrian, "he wept as much as if he had lost a brother or a very dear
son."

There was one occasion when the pope undertook to act without first
securing Charlemagne's approval. That was on Christmas Day in the
year 800. Charlemagne happened to be in Rome at the time. He had
come there in answer to the pope's urgent plea for help against enemies who wanted to unseat him. Charlemagne confirmed the pope in
his position; then some days later, on Christmas, as the king knelt in
St. Peter's, Leo placed a crown on his head. The assembled faithful
must have been aware of what the pope planned, for they promptly
cried out: "To Charles Augustus, crowned by God, great and peaceful
Emperor of the Romans, life and victory." Charlemagne, for his part,
was so annoyed at the pope's action, so Einhard insists, that he declared he would not have gone near the church that day had he suspected what the pope had in mind.

Because of Einhard's testimony, historians have long puzzled over
the incident. Surely Einhard must be in error, some have argued, for
what man should not have been pleased with so noble a title. Scholars
reason, furthermore, that Charlemagne should have appreciated the
greater propriety of the title emperor over the tribal "king of the
Franks" in dealing with his polyglot subjects. If Charlemagne was irritated as Einhard declared, scholars suggest that it was over the pope's
own decision to do the crowning himself. Such action could be dangerous in an age which set such high store on precedent. Some years
later, in 813, as if to undo this precedent, Charlemagne had his son
Louis crowned emperor without benefit of any ecclesiastic. Charlemagne's coronation made official, incidentally, the alliance between
the Latin church and the Frankish monarchy, while it severed by implication the pope's political subordination to Byzantium.

Among Charlemagne's other achievements was a revival of learning
which he inspired. No doubt his personal interest in learning provided
him strong motivation, although what aroused his greatest concern was
the low level of learning among churchmen. The letters he received
from monasteries which should have been penned in quite scholarly
Latin, he found full of grammatical errors and "uncouth expressions.
Hence we began to fear," he explained, "that being too little skilled
in writing, there might also be far too little wisdom in understanding
the holy Scriptures." He accordingly issued instructions to the bishops
and abbots of his empire that they improve and expand their schools

and libraries, and that they keep these schools not entirely to themselves but open them to the sons of the laity who had no intention of becoming monks. And "let them learn psalms, notes, singing, computus (arithmetic), grammar, and let the religious books that are given them be free of faults because often some desire to pray to God properly, but they pray badly because of faulty books. And let care be taken that the boys do not damage them [books] either when reading or writing."

As if to dramatize his efforts at elevating the level of learning in his kingdom and, at the same time, to provide himself teachers and scholarly companionship, Charlemagne invited leading scholars of the day to come and make their home at Aachen. Alcuin, England's brightest light, came from York and spent fifteen years at Aachen. For a somewhat shorter time came the grammarians Peter of Pisa and Paulinus of Aquileia from Italy, Theodulf from Spain, the leading poet of the day (*Glory, Laud, and Honor*), and Paul the Deacon, who later composed a history of the Lombards. Charlemagne proved himself an apt scholar, learned to speak Latin "as well as his native tongue, but he could understand Greek better than he could speak it. . . . He most zealously cultivated the liberal arts, held those who taught them in great esteem, and conferred great honors upon them." His favorite teacher and mentor was Alcuin, with whom he "spent much time and labor . . . studying rhetoric, dialectic, and especially astronomy; he learned to reckon, and used to investigate the motions of the heavenly bodies most curiously, with an intelligent scrutiny. He also tried to write, and used to keep tablets and blanks in bed under his pillow, that at leisure hours he might accustom his hand to form the letters; however, as he did not begin his efforts in due season, but late in life, they met with ill success."

Had the empire of the Franks remained at peace following Charlemagne's death, his encouragement of learning might have inaugurated an intellectual revival which would have anticipated that of the eleventh century. As it was, when Charlemagne died, so did peace; and within a century conditions in Frankland had sunk almost to the low level of the Dark Ages. Still some good lived on from the work of the great emperor. The bishops he had carefully selected for their learning and worthiness worked with his son Louis and the reformer Benedict of Aniane in effecting a general improvement in the condition of the church. Charlemagne's renaissance could also claim credit for a harvest of textbooks, principally by Alcuin, improved monastic schools, renewed attention to the collection of books and the copying of manuscripts, a much more legible script (Carolingian minuscule), an improved Vulgate (this had suffered considerable corruption), and a more scholarly Latin. What in particular assured his work endurance were the monasteries whose cultural life he had helped stimulate. "The great abbeys, such as St. Gall and Reichenau, Fulda, and Corbie, were not only the intellectual and religious leaders of Europe, but also the chief centers of material culture and of artistic and industrial activity. In them there was developed the traditions of learning and literature, art, and architecture, music and liturgy, painting and calligraphy, which were the foundations of medieval culture."*

Shortly after Charlemagne's death, what had happened to the empire of Alexander the Great when he died, also happened to his: it disintegrated. For the moment fortune seemed to smile. Only one legitimate son, Louis, survived the emperor, so there had been no need for Charlemagne to divide his dominions among several. Yet Louis proved to be a weak king, not at all in the tradition of strong rulers the dynasty of Pepin had been producing for more than a century. Virtuous he was, to be sure, and history remembers him as Louis the Pious. No sooner had he succeeded his father in 814 than he sent packing the loose women about the court, and these included his own sisters. Louis could do without these women, not without his father's old ministers whom he also expelled for their immoral lives. His puritanical ways, his forgiving nature, and his scrupulousness may have pleased the pope— on one occasion he even did public penance for his sins and shortcomings—but they alienated his counts who despised any ruler they did not fear.

Louis made his most grievous mistake just three years after his accession. This was his decision to divide his empire among his sons. What prompted him to do this was a serious accident he had suffered which he feared would cause his early death. He had three sons, Lothair, Pepin, and Louis, all full-grown and greedy. Then to complicate the situation, he married a new wife, as imperious as his first one who had died. She bore him a fourth son, Charles. Even Solomon would have had difficulty handling the situation, although unlike Louis, he would probably not have aggravated tensions by lavishing his affection, plus lands, on his youngest son Charles. The result was civil war for the greater part of Louis' reign, with sons fighting sons, then when

* Christopher Dawson, *The Making of Europe*. New York (1938), pp. 231–32.

tiring of this, fighting their father. Twice they deposed him and would have finally confined him in a monastery had not their monstrous ingratitude been too much for the aristocracy to stomach.

When Louis died in 840 the sons continued to quarrel, now only three since Pepin had died. So great was the slaughter at Fontenay in 841 when the three kings fought that "the strength of the Franks was so cut down, and their fame and valour so diminished, that for the future they were not merely unable to extend the bounds of their realm, but even incapable of protecting their own frontiers." Reason did momentarily assert itself in 843 when, upon the prodding of the bishops, the three brothers agreed to divide the empire (Treaty of Verdun). To Charles (the Bald) went the western third of the empire, to Louis (the German) the section to the east, and to Lothair, the eldest son, the central portion including Italy and the imperial title.

The settlement held for ten years, then civil war broke out again despite the constant raiding of Saracens and Danes. The reader of the chronicles of the period feels pity for the helpless peoples, anger for the Carolingian monarchs who could have driven the Vikings off the islands and headlands they had seized had they joined hands against them. Their fratricidal wars brought western Europe instead to the point of anarchy. When Lothair died in 855, his three sons divided his realm and continued the wars against their uncles. Then Louis the German announced a division of his kingdom among his three sons, the result being still more wars. Louis died in 876, Charles the Bald in 877, and shortly after a number of their successors, one on a hunt, another when he failed to lower his head when riding his horse through a passageway after a girl. During the winter of 881–882 the Danes plundered Aachen and stabled their horses in Charlemagne's cathedral! In 884, with almost all the Carolingians dead and no one else to choose, Charles the Fat, son of Louis the German, received by default the allegiance of all parts of the Frankish empire. Charles proved himself a coward in his dealings with the Danes and in 887 his disgusted subjects forced him to abdicate. The proud Carolingian dynasty sputtered on here and there for a few more generations* within the frontiers of Charlemagne's great empire, then faded out completely. Its end proved almost as inglorious as that of the Merovingians.

Before continuing with the history of the two new states of France and Germany which emerged from the wreck of the Carolingian em-

---

* The ablest of Charlemagne's great-grandsons was Louis II, son of Lothair. He prevented the Saracens from overrunning Italy. See below, p. 211.

pire, it will be well to introduce the Vikings or Northmen who were partly responsible for the collapse of that empire. Their homeland was Scandinavia and the lands about the Baltic. From these cold, bleak regions many Germans had preceded them—Goths, Vandals, and Burgundians among others—who had lived along their rugged shores before migrating southward. Those Germans who remained in Scandinavia took to the sea for fish and plunder in order to supplement the meager harvests they could wring from their unproductive lands. One of the earliest recorded raids was that which carried kinsmen of Beowulf against the Franks early in the sixth century. Not until the close of the eighth century, however, did these Vikings adopt raiding on a large scale. The first raid noted by the Anglo-Saxon chronicler came in 787. His cryptic entry pictures an unknown, barbarous folk. "And in his days came first three ships of Norwegians from Horthaland: and then the reeve rode thither and tried to compel them to go to the royal manor, for he did not know what they were: and then they slew him."

This was just the beginning. In 793 the Northmen sacked Lindisfarne, and Jarrow the following year. Reports of the ease and lucrativeness of these raids spread quickly through Scandinavia. In a few years Vikings in their "dragon ships" were harassing shorelines and rivers all over western Europe. They attacked Ireland in 795, then Aquitaine and Frisia. Since most of the leading towns of western Europe lay on the sea or navigable rivers, all suffered sacking and burning, the fortunate ones only once, including Utrecht, Antwerp, Rouen, Paris, Cologne, Nantes, Hamburg, Bordeaux, Ghent. In their depredations the Northmen observed a rough division of regions to be despoiled. The Danes preferred the inner route along which they harried the German coast, the Channel areas, France, Spain, and southern England. The Norwegians took the outer route to the north of Scotland, to Ireland, the Shetland and Orkney Islands, Iceland, Greenland, and, about the year 1000 A.D., to Vinland in North America. The Swedes crossed the Baltic to Russia, then to Novgorod, thence to the Dnieper and Volga, finally with Slavs in their company against Constantinople in 860.

What impelled this exodus of raiders from Scandinavia? Scholars suggest overpopulation which the barrenness of the region would surely have made a sensitive factor. Many jarls may have left the land to make their fortunes elsewhere rather than submit to the rule of stronger chieftains who had begun to make good their claims to rule. Until the fierce Saxons had accepted Frankish domination, they had prevented Viking raids from carrying beyond the periphery of the Carolingian empire. Shortly after Charlemagne's death, when word reached Scandinavia of the weakly ruled lands to the south in Germany, Gaul, and England, these raiders came pouring out of the north. Where they encountered resistance they fled; where opposition failed to materialize or collapsed they burned, looted, and slaughtered. In time they began to stay over the winter, then to establish settlements, first on islands in rivers, then along the coast which they gradually expanded. In England they acquired the Danelaw; on the Continent, Normandy and, for a time, Frisia; in Ireland, Dublin and other port cities. Then suddenly, within a generation or two of establishing their new homes, they were often assimilated, their ferocity a memory only to the older folks and the chroniclers who had recorded their pillagings.

Two other invaders, Magyars and Saracens, joined the Northmen in spreading destruction over western Europe during these terrible centuries. The Magyars were nomadic people from central Asia, not unlike the hordes of Avars and Bulgars that had earlier moved into Europe to plunder and enslave. By the late ninth century the Magyars had established their authority in the area of the middle Danube where they absorbed what remained of the Avars Charlemagne's armies had destroyed. While the Magyars were similar to the Avars in mores, military usages, and savagery they settled down in time and accepted civilization. For the moment, however, they rode their horses on raids over Bavaria, Lorraine, Saxony, the Provence, and northern Italy, killing the older people and carrying off the young women, girls, and boys for their own pleasure or to sell to others. In southern France and in Switzerland their raids brought them into conflict with Saracen marauders from the south. These Moslems had started moving from Tunis and Algiers into Sicily early in the ninth century, crossed over to Italy, then moved north to burn Monte Cassino and St. Peter's outside the walls. Though Pope Leo was victorious over them, as were the armies of Byzantium and Louis II, more Saracens kept swarming in. Moslem pirates came also from Crete, attacked Pisa and Genoa, built a stronghold in the Provence at Fraxinet, from which they raided north Italy, Switzerland, and the upper Rhine country. On one of their raids they shot down with their arrows the monks of St. Gall as they marched in procession round their church to beg God's succor. Never until the recent war have these lands of western Europe, from England through Germany, France, to Italy, suffered such untold and universal misery!

Britain also suffered grievously from the depredations of the North-men, but first we shall take a brief glimpse at the four centuries of its history that preceded the appearance of these Vikings. Actually so little light remains concerning these centuries that one cannot help but be brief. Particularly dark are the two hundred years which followed Emperor Honorius' hollow charge of 410 A.D. to the islanders who had appealed for assistance to take what measures they could to meet the invasions from Scotland and across the Channel. About all that is clear is the ineffectiveness of these measures, if any measures were taken. The identity of these early invaders who harassed Britain is all that is clear. They were Angles and Saxons for the most part, some Jutes and scattered Frisians and Swabians. From raiding expeditions with which these Germans had plundered British shores in the third and fourth centuries, they turned to actual invasions in the fifth. Small groups came at first, then late in the sixth century more powerful thrusts that carried all the way to the highlands of Cornwall, Wales, and the Cumbrian Mountains. Some Romans who had not followed the legions back to Gaul must have fled with the Britons to the west, but their numbers were too small to leave any lasting influences. All that remained of a more cultured era were some agricultural practices together with the Christian religion which hung on here and there among the Celtic refugees and in Ireland. Meantime in their part of Britain the German invaders extinguished the whole of the Roman cultural heritage.

The obscurity of the period of Anglo-Saxon invasions lifted only slightly as Germanic Britain progressed into the seventh century. Older historians wrote somewhat confidently of a heptarchy of Anglo-Saxon kingdoms where more recent scholars see principally confusion. One hard fact of considerable significance was the arrival in 597 of St. Augustine to Kent with his band of monks. One of Augustine's very first converts was Aethelbert, ruler of Kent. Aethelbert's Christian wife, a princess from Merovingian Gaul, had already prepared him for this step. When Aethelbert died, his brother-in-law, King Edwin of Northumbria, also a convert to Christianity, fell heir to Kent's dominant position. So blessed was the land during the reign of this God-fearing monarch that "if a woman should have wished to walk with her newborn babe over all the island from sea to sea, she might have done so without injury from any." Some years later Christianity suffered a temporary setback when the heathen king of Mercia extended his rule over much of Britain. In the second half of the seventh century when Northumbria recovered its independence, Celtic missionaries "came daily into Britain, and with great devotion preached the word to those provinces. . . ."

A curious problem developed when the Christianity which these Celtic missionaries introduced from the north and west came into contact with that the monks from the south had brought with them from Rome. Certain differences in liturgical practice between the two groups came to view, due no doubt to the fact that for almost two centuries the Germanic invaders of Britain had severed Celtic connections with the Continent during which period various "eastern" practices had persisted without challenge. While these differences were of no great consequence—Celtic monks used leavened bread, for instance, instead of unleavened, and shaved their heads differently—to unsophisticated minds such diversities were apt to appear large. And they could occasion inconvenience. Bede tells of the confusion in the household of King Oswy of Northumbria where the king followed the Celtic liturgical calendar while the queen observed the Roman. The result was such "that Easter was kept twice in one year, so that when the king had ended Lent and was celebrating Easter, the queen and her followers were still fasting and keeping Palm Sunday." A council of churchmen met at Whitby in 664 to resolve the difficulty, and King Oswy gave judgment in favor of Roman usages. What most impressed Oswy was the importance both Celtic and Roman representatives at Whitby attached to St. Peter's role as keeper of the keys. Such reverence prompted Oswy to announce his adherence to Rome and to St. Peter, "otherwise, when I come to the gates of the kingdom of heaven, there should be none to open them since it will be my adversary who holds the keys."

The outlines of British history become clearer with the rise of Wessex early in the ninth century although the times themselves were evil. This was the century that bore the worst of the Danish invasions. Had it not been for Alfred (871–900), the Northmen would probably have overrun the entire country. Even Alfred suffered several defeats at their hands, but he won more often than he lost and eventually forced them to be content with the country northeast of the Thames (Danelaw) and to accept Christianity. Alfred's victories over the Danes gained him his title "the Great," although his peacetime activities, like those of Charlemagne, might themselves have earned him that distinction. He encouraged learning, invited scholars to come to England—dismal testimony to the destructiveness of the Danes—in the hope that the products of improved schools would effect both a reform in the church and in the administration of his kingdom. Alfred also translated a number of books which he considered of special importance for the spiritual and cultural well-being of his country. These included Bede's *History*, Orosius' history, Pope Gregory's *Pastoral Care* and *Dialogues*, the *Soliloquies* of Augustine, and Boethius' *Consolation of Philosophy*.

For some seventy-five years Alfred's successors prosecuted the war against the Danes. Danish pressure persisted, however, and under Ethelred the Redeless (without counsel) Britain finally succumbed. Sweyn, king of Denmark, took over most of the country; his more famous son Cnut (1016–1035) completed the task. At the height of his power Cnut ruled as king of Denmark, Norway, and part of Sweden. Above all he wished to be considered an English king. For that reason he married Emma, widow of Ethelred, although his hope of founding a dynasty through her proved in vain. She did bear him a son, but both this son and a second by a concubine proved weak men, so after their deaths the succession went to Edward, Emma's son by Ethelred. History knows this last Anglo-Saxon king as Edward the Confessor—and little else did he do but be pious. His piety led him to devote much effort to rebuilding Westminster Abbey. It may also have inspired him to lead a celibate life although he appears never to have wasted much affection on his wife Edith from the beginning. This proved unfortunate, for when he died childless in 1066, three ambitious men came forward to press claims to his throne. One was Harold, who was Edith's brother, the choice of the Anglo-Saxons and, it appears, Edward's choice as well. Harold first defeated Harold Hardrada, who claimed succession through Cnut, in a battle at Stamford Bridge in the north. Then he hurried south to Hastings to meet the army of William, duke of Normandy, the other pretender. When darkness fell on the field about Hastings the evening of October 14, 1066, Harold lay dead and "the Frenchmen had possession of the place of slaughter."

William deserved his title "the Conqueror." Beyond this initial victory of 1066 which gave him the crown, he put down several rebellions so ruthlessly that he well nigh exterminated the old Saxon aristocracy. No native chronicler remained to lament the passing of the old order, although the peace William forced upon the country drew from the author of the Anglo-Saxon Chronicle the reluctant admission that "a man of any substance could travel unmolested throughout the country with his bosom full of gold." More enduring testimony to William's strong hand is the Domesday Book which his commissioners compiled in 1086, an inventory of the value of all the lands of Britain and its chattels. So thorough was this survey that "there was not a hide of land in England which he did not know who held it and how much it was worth. . . ."

William's most valuable contribution to England was the bases of strong government which he introduced. In the first place he brought much knowledge of statecraft from Normandy, which was already one of the best-administered feudal states in western Europe. Then, true to the Norman tradition of adapting the practices and institutions of subject peoples to serve their own use, William also preserved a good measure of what he found in Britain. He retained the Anglo-Saxon shire and hundred courts, as well as the office of sheriff. Both courts and sheriff would provide him the means of blocking complete control of the countryside by the Norman aristocracy. William also retained the fyrd, the Anglo-Saxon militia, which he used on one occasion to good advantage against his Norman vassals. More effective in preventing his proud vassals from growing too powerful was his decision to retain as royal prerogatives the right to license the building of castles, the coining of money, and the punishment of serious crimes against the king's peace (viz., murder, treason, counterfeiting, robbery). And probably upon the advice of Lanfranc, his learned and able archbishop of Canterbury, he removed ecclesiastical cases from the shire courts and established separate church tribunals for their adjudication.

By designating his second son William as heir before he died in 1087, William made certain that a strong hand would continue to rule England. In his judgment his eldest son Robert lacked the sternness the job required. His foresight proved correct, and for thirteen years William II (Rufus, the red) maintained an iron grip on the country. Yet while he possessed all the firmness his father had wished, he lacked the Conqueror's concern about justice. His people took to the hills, a chronicler wrote, when the king went about the country. Some of the rapacity and cruelty with which monastic contemporary writers charge him may have sprung from their bitterness over the harsh manner he treated the church. William's archbishop of Canterbury, the learned and saintly Anselm, whom he appointed during a serious illness when he feared he would die, spent half the years of his office in exile. No one cared to investigate the circumstances that led to William's death on a hunt in the year 1107, least of all his younger brother Henry who hurried off instead to Winchester to seize the royal treasure and assure himself the succession.

So powerful were these Norman kings of England, William I and William II, that it is easy to forget that in France they remained simple dukes of Normandy. Which raises the question what their lords, the kings of France, were doing meantime. Had they approved of what their dukes of Normandy had undertaken? As a matter of fact, they had not approved, although they could have done little to prevent it. For France's kings during this period were among the weakest monarchs in Europe, not so powerful as a dozen of their own feudatories. That would remain their condition until the twelfth century. The deposition of Charles the Fat in 887 for his pusillanimity in dealing with Vikings had not effected any great change in the character of French monarchs. True, the new king was the valiant Count Odo of Paris who in 885 had directed the heroic defense of Paris against an army of forty thousand Northmen. Despite his fame, however, and new title, Odo remained barely more than a count, as did the kings who succeeded him. Several of these were Carolingians, others Capetians, that is, drawn from the family of Odo. In 987, upon the death of the last French Carolingian, the French nobility elected Hugh Capet to be their king. And while that family held the throne from that time until the French Revolution, it was more than a century after Hugh's accession before these early Capetians did anything more than reign.

Even for the modest success of being able to reign during this period, these first Capetians had more fortune and circumstance to thank than their own limited talents. The central position of their capital Paris, its commercial advantages, even the prestige of their titles, were distinct assets whose value only later generations of Capetians would be able to exploit. For their part Hugh Capet and his immediate successors did nothing more spectacular than produce sons, then live such long lives that these sons were fully grown, even middle-aged, before their fathers died. These early Capetians did something more. Being normal fathers and wishing to leave their titles with their sons, they succeeded in persuading the French nobles to elect these sons and have them crowned before they themselves passed on. In this way they managed to establish the hereditary character of the French monarchy, no mean accomplishment in an era when jealous vassals would not have permitted anything more ambitious.

This was the sole achievement of the early Capetians. The chroniclers record nothing further. Little is known of Hugh Capet, not much more of his son Robert except that he was a pious monarch. Henry I did bestir himself and engaged the duke of Normandy in two minor, unsuccessful campaigns. The fourth of these undistinguished Capetians, Philip the Fat (1040–1108), spent the greater part of what energies he had in eating, wenching, and sleeping. It was principally the concentration of the more powerful French nobles on objectives nearer home and the willingness of the Capetians to lead unobtrusive lives within their own domains about Paris, that kept them their thrones. As traditional dispensers of justice and defenders of law and order these Capetians also enjoyed the support of the church, but that institution was itself quite powerless at the time. The church did seek to impress upon the new king, by means of an elaborate coronation ceremony, the magnitude of his royal responsibilities, and, upon the nobles who attended, their duties as loyal subjects to respect his authority. A more tangible aid to the growth of royal power came from the church by way of the right the Capetians exercised of nominating candidates to some two dozen bishoprics.

In sharp contrast to the mediocrity and quiescence of the French kings of the tenth and eleventh centuries stood the aggressiveness of the German monarchs to the east. It was not only that these Germans were generally abler men. They could conduct themselves more like kings because the base of their power was infinitely stronger than the relatively weak Île-de-France from which the Capetians had to operate. The German monarchs were dukes before they became kings, lords over fairly large, compact territorial units to which historians have given the name "stem duchies." As the term suggests, these duchies presumably represented ancient German nations which had somehow preserved their homogeneity, and their vigor as well, during the turbulency of the *Völkerwanderung* and the wars since. What were often the most powerful of these duchies, Saxony and Bavaria, lay along the eastern frontier against which pressed the Northmen, Slavs, and Magyars. Next to the Rhine and to the south in the area of the Alps, stretched Swabia, while about the middle Rhine lay Franconia. Less important, since its people were not so homogeneous, was the duchy of Lotharingia or Lorraine. The greater part of this duchy lay to the west of the lower Rhine.

After the incapacity of Charles the Fat led to his deposition in 887, the different parts of the Carolingian empire never again reunited. The West Franks, as noted, elected Odo; those of Germany selected Arnulf, duke of Carinthia. What recommended Arnulf as their choice was his Carolingian blood, for which reason they also chose his son Louis the

Child when he died. When the latter died in 911, the German princes turned their backs permanently on the Carolingians and chose a man of their own. Their first new king was Conrad I, duke of Franconia, who spent his reign in a fruitless effort to gain ascendancy over his dukes. That lesson of failure was not wasted on his successor Henry I of Saxony. Instead of concerning himself with his position as king, he devoted his efforts to driving back the Slavs and Magyars and fortifying his eastern frontiers against them. His title, Henry the Fowler, originated, it is said, from his indifference to the office of king. Instead of being with the other princes who had gathered to elect a new monarch, he was out hunting with his birds!

Henry's son Otto I (the Great) proved himself the ablest and most ambitious German monarch since Charlemagne. The powerful position which his father left him tempted him to subordinate his dukes. After some years of hard fighting he accomplished this, then discovered that the relatives he placed in charge of those duchies were no more loyal than the former dukes. What proved more successful in strengthening his royal position was his policy of extending royal control over the German church, then favoring it with privileges and estates. Such a church could provide him a powerful counterpoise against the hereditary nobility. He dared not risk interfering in the hereditary process by which dukes, counts, and margraves acquired their positions, but he could, and did, control the election of bishops and abbots. So he built up older ecclesiastical principalities and created new ones at Magdeburg, Oldenburg, and Brandenburg, then demanded heavy military assistance from them in return. Earlier kings recognized the value that would accrue to the crown from a royally controlled hierarchy, although no monarch before Otto had ever gone to the lengths he did in influencing elections. And so long as the pope in Italy remained helpless or unwilling to take a stand against such interference, no policy promised richer returns to the monarchy.

Otto's most ambitious undertaking was the annexation of Italy. Both sentiment and ambition drove him on. He would emulate the role of his illustrious predecessor Charlemagne in the peninsula, and he would also block the plan of Berengar, king of Lombardy, to create a new kingdom in Italy that might threaten his own. On Otto's first trip to Italy he married Adelaide, the young widowed princess who had appealed to him against Berengar who had planned to marry her. On his second trip, he rescued Pope John XII from this same Berengar who was threatening Rome. A few months later Pope John rewarded Otto with Charlemagne's title of Roman emperor. Then when John, who had finally awakened to the fact that Otto wanted more in Italy than just a title, began undermining Otto's position, Otto drove him from Rome, set up a new pope, and warned the Romans "never again to elect or ordain any Pope without the consent and choice of the Emperor Otto and his son Otto II."

Otto judged the extension of his authority to Italy to be his principal accomplishment. In the judgment of his contemporaries, his most impressive achievement was the resounding defeat he inflicted upon the marauding Magyars in 955 at Lechfeld. Never again would these Asiatic horse-archers carry their devastating raids into Germany. A few years later, in fact, they accepted Christianity and settled down in the great plain which lay between the Carpathians and the Danube. Otto also gave German civilization its first major push eastward since Charlemagne when he drove the Slavs from the lands between the Elbe and Oder. He also forced the Czechs to acknowledge his overlordship, and he arranged the marriage of his son to Theophano, daughter of the Byzantine emperor, in the hope that this alliance would someday bring southern Italy within the empire.

Otto's son and grandson, Ottos like himself, were not without ability and ambition, although their accomplishments bulk small by comparison with his own. Two items of interest attach to the reign of Otto III. One was his appointment of Gerbert, his tutor, reputedly the leading scholar of his day, as Pope Sylvester II. The other was Otto's dream of reviving the Roman empire of the ancient Caesars somewhat as Frederick II was to contemplate this possibility in the thirteenth century. (See below, p. 305.) Henry II (1002–1024), Otto III's successor, earned canonization by his piety and by advancing church reform throughout Germany. When Henry died the Saxon line died with him, so the German princes turned to Conrad, duke of Franconia, who inaugurated a century of Salian (Franconian) rule. Conrad was an able king, as was his son Henry III. What has most impressed modern historians was the extent of royal authority under Henry III whom some considered the most powerful of the medieval kings of Germany. In Germany he held the duchies of Swabia, Bavaria, and Franconia; in Italy he appointed four successive popes; in eastern Europe, Poland, Bohemia, and Hungary all acknowledged his overlordship.

Henry III's early death jeopardized the bright future of the German monarchy. During the minority of his young son Henry, most German princes, lay and ecclesiastical, hurried to grab what they could of royal rights, estates, and monasteries. Not surprising, therefore, was the wide-spread opposition Henry IV encountered when he came of age and proceeded to take steps to recover what prerogatives and properties the crown had lost. He set out to erect a compact domain in southern Saxony and Thuringia, to develop the silver mines in the area, and to gain the adherence of the towns that were making their appearance in Germany. These policies promised to provide him a solid economic and popular base upon which to establish his authority. Then to bypass the power of the nobility and to assure himself a loyal bureaucracy, he expanded the use of *ministeriales* in the government. These were low-born men who had been taken into the royal household, where their efficiency and loyalty could be counted upon since without royal favor they counted for nothing.

The use of *ministeriales* infuriated Henry's nobles while his policy of appointing bishops and abbots friendly to the crown aroused the indignation of reformers. The result was fairly continuous conflict in Germany, on occasion civil war, during the greater part of his reign. In time his eldest son Conrad joined the rebels, then Conrad's brother Henry who succeeded in 1106. Only one king in German medieval history has suffered the vilification that was Henry IV's lot, and that was Frederick II. (See below, p. 304.) In both instances scholars have difficulty dividing truth from calumny. Both kings were men of great talent and ambition, both pursued objectives that begot conflict and war, both engaged in bitter struggles with the papacy, and both died having accomplished little but the weakening of Germany.

Two additional lands deserve attention during these formative centuries when western Europe struggled to establish new civilizations. These were the lands of Spain and Italy. Except for the mountainous region of the Asturias in the northwest, all the Spanish peninsula had fallen to the Islamic conquerors. Until 750 A.D., when the Abbasids seized the empire, an Umayyad emir ruled the land from Cordova. Then a new Abbasid emir took over and all seemed quite secure until Abd al-Rahman, one of the few Umayyad princes to escape the purge, appeared five years later and, after considerable fighting, took over the country. Five years of harassment, deprivation, and flight had made this Abd al-Rahman a tough, determined young man. When al-Mansur, who was caliph back in Baghdad, sent his own governor to Spain, Abd al-Rahman had him decapitated, put his head in camphor and salt, and sent it back to the caliph wrapped in a black flag. The warning was not lost on the caliph. "Thanks be to Allah," he is said to have observed, "for having placed the sea between us and such a foe."* Baghdad never bothered with Spain again.

Abd al-Rahman made Cordova his capital, then made it the rival of Constantinople and Baghdad in magnificence, while building an army and navy that were the most formidable in western Europe. Moslem power reached its zenith during the reign of Abd al-Rahman III (912–961), who was the first emir to assume the title caliph. The year 1031 marked the end of the ruling dynasty and the breakup of the emirate into smaller principalities based upon Toledo, Valencia, Seville, Cordova, and Saragossa. Meantime Spain under Moslem rule had become one of the wealthiest, most populated, and culturally advanced states in Europe. No Western state exported a greater volume or variety of agricultural and industrial products: olives, cotton, sugar, grapes, figs, wheat, oil, leather, glassware, metalwork, gold, and silver. Nowhere in Europe, except perhaps in Constantinople, could one find so many libraries, scholars, and artists. And it was principally by way of Spain that Moslem learning made its greatest impact upon the West.

Even before the breakup of the Cordovan caliphate, Christian states to the north had been slowly enlarging their holdings. León expanded from its base in the Asturias, then gave birth to Castile which later broke off to form a separate state. By this time the county of Barcelona, later Catalonia, had thrown off control of the Carolingians—it had constituted the Spanish march—while the Basque state of Navarre had come into existence. The first important Spanish conqueror was Ferdinand I, who extended his authority over most of the Christian princes and even forced tribute from several Moslem emirs. When his son Alfonso VI (1072–1109) annexed Toledo, the Moslems sought the assistance of the Almoravides, who had established a militant Moslem state in Morocco. Their appearance halted Christian expansion for a half-century, although not the fighting. This was the era when Rodrigo Díaz de Bivar, the renowned Spanish warrior, worked the spectacular feats that gained him immortal fame in *El Cid*, the best-known of Spanish epics. His name, El Cid Campeador (the champion), he earned from his Moslem soldiers. For Rodrigo, like occasional other Christian warriors, now fought on the side of the Infidel, now with the Christians, though always for himself. When he died in 1099 as ruler of Valencia, the First Crusade was already under way.

The Moslems were also active in Italy, the other land that merits

* Quoted in Hitti, *History of the Arabs*, p. 507.

attention during these centuries. To recapitulate the history of Italy during the years before the appearance of the Moslems: the Lombards who crossed the Alps shortly after Justinian's death had never been able to conquer the entire peninsula. They almost succeeded, however, during the reign of their most able monarch Liutprand (712–743). So close, indeed, did they come to attaining their objective that the pope in desperation called in the Franks. Pepin responded, drove them away from Rome, but left their destruction to his son Charlemagne. It was only a few years after Charlemagne's death that Saracens from Tunis began their attacks on Sicily, took Palermo in 831, then crossed over to Italy proper, and a few years later were plundering the churches of St. Peter and St. Paul outside Rome (that is, outside the Aurelian Wall). Louis II, son of Lothair, first slowed their progress, then after his death Basil I sent over troops and ships from Constantinople. Though Basil drove the Saracens from Italy, he could not prevent their overrunning the whole of Sicily.

After the death of Basil, the political situation in southern Italy rapidly deteriorated. Byzantine governors, Lombard dukes, and independent city-states such as Amalfi and Naples contended for control. In 1016 a group of Norman pilgrims stopped there on their return from Jerusalem to visit more shrines. They found the country so inviting and so many wealthy lords eager to pay them for their services, that they decided to stay. Shortly more of their Norman cousins began streaming in, principally from Normandy, when they learned of this new land of opportunity. At first they were content to serve others—Lombards, Byzantium, even Saracens—whoever could pay for their services. Then they began to acquire holdings of their own, finally appropriated the entire area for themselves. The most aggressive of these Norman visitors were the sons of Tancred of Hauteville, and of these the most formidable was Robert Guiscard, called the Crafty. When Pope Leo IX attempted to curb their depredations, they defeated and captured him. Later the papacy recognized the potential value of these barbarians in any struggle with the German king to the north, and accepted them as vassals. In 1070 Guiscard captured Bari, the last Byzantine foothold in Italy, seized several cities in Greece, and began to drive the Saracens out of Sicily. His younger brother Roger completed the conquest of the island in 1091. That year marked the expulsion of Islam from Italy and Italian waters, to which end Pisa, Genoa, and Venice among others had also collaborated. Here in Italy as in Spain, well before the First Crusade, Europe had taken the offensive against Islam.

During these unsettled five hundred years, from the days of Gregory the Great to the close of the eleventh century, the only institution that preached law and order and held before western Europe the prospect of a happy era when all men would live together in peace in the service of God, was the church. Yet the church herself was not immune to the same vicissitudes that had harried the world about her. The invasions of the Vikings, for instance, had destroyed the majority of churches and monasteries in western Europe, and in so doing had severely crippled as well the spiritual and intellectual agencies she administered. The collapse of the Carolingian empire and the weakness of kings in general enabled an unprincipled aristocracy to seize control of the hierarchy and use it for its own purpose. From the late ninth century for about a hundred years the papacy itself fell upon such evil times that only the efforts of reformers who remembered an earlier day, prevented it from foundering. Though a revitalized church emerged at the close of the eleventh century under the leadership of a rejuvenated papacy, that victory only came after the institution had passed through an era as dangerous to its existence as any it had experienced during the persecutions of pagan Rome.

Perhaps the most significant development in the history of the church during the seventh and eighth centuries had been the growing estrangement between papacy and Constantinople. Justinian had been sufficiently strong to force compliance upon Rome; his successors had not. Because of Byzantine involvement with the Lombards in Italy, with the Persians, then Moslems, in the east, and a series of dangerous enemies along the Danube, popes over in Rome discovered that they could resist, occasionally even defy, pressures from Constantinople. It was during these centuries, beginning with Gregory the Great, that there began to emerge what is commonly referred to as the temporal power of the popes, that is, the growing ability of the popes to exercise authority in civil and political matters. While Gregory the Great might deplore the nonreligious responsibilities this growing independence from Constantinople brought with it, his successors gradually came to regard the freedom this furnished them, for example in dealing with the iconoclastic emperors, as the *sine qua non* of the existence of the church. For that reason the allegiance of the popes to Byzantium always remained an unknown quantity, nor were they any more willing to accept Lombard hegemony instead when this threatened to become a fact. They never trusted these former Arians; for one reason they were too close. They preferred rather to accept the status of a protectorate under control of the distant Franks whose interests north of the Alps promised to keep them sufficiently engaged elsewhere to prevent their assuming too powerful a position in Italy.

This was not true of Charlemagne, however, who ruled Rome with an uncomfortably firm hand. Still Charlemagne was only human. When he died the situation might improve, and it did. Louis the Pious reversed, in fact, the relationship between king and pope. The pope directed him, not he the pope as Charlemagne had done. The resurgence of the papacy reached its height under Nicholas I (858–867), who interfered in the election of the patriarch of Constantinople and even ordered the Frankish king Lothair II to take back his divorced wife.

Yet Nicholas was premature in announcing that the day of king-priests and emperor-pontiffs was past. Almost overnight the grand prospect he had contemplated for the papacy faded and died. Instead of dictating to kings what kind of lives they should lead and to Byzantine emperors who should be and who should not be patriarchs, the papacy found itself the prisoner of factions within the city of Rome. Ambitious men and women now sat in judgment, and made and unmade popes as it pleased their sordid fancies. Never had the character and prestige of the papacy fallen to so low a point. Its deficiencies need not detain us except to point up the fact of how much the medieval church during these rough times stood in need of a protector.

The Merovingian period had already demonstrated the need of royal protection. When Brunhild and the Frankish aristocracy, for instance, had completed their corruption of the hierarchy in Gaul, Boniface had to start almost from scratch with rebuilding the church. With the help of the Carolingians, the church had managed to extricate itself from that morass, only to sink into a deeper pit when Carolingian power disintegrated. No authority remained that could check the aristocracy in its scramble for church lands and revenues, and, what was worse, in its practice of filling the offices of bishops and abbots with friends and relatives. That the mere investment with these sacred offices did not transform their unworthy incumbents has only surprised later myopic scholars who apparently credited the holy oils with greater powers than even theologians claimed for them. If the new bishop had been an avid hunter, warrior, or debauchee before his consecration, the probability was great that he would remain so afterward. Practices that were considered unhealthy which followed upon the feudalization of the church included simony (traffic in church offices), clerical marriage and concubinage, and the consequent degradation of the sacramental character of the priestly office.

The tenth century, which witnessed the general decline of the church throughout western Europe, also welcomed the first solid evidences of reform. Where the wellsprings of this reform movement were located is difficult to say. The very extensiveness of the movement suggests that its roots were widespread. Kings had their part in the movement; so did rough warriors whose consciences were touched, along with bishops and monks, not to forget the many commoners who found a new attractiveness about monastic life. So many abbeys sprang up from the labor of monks and the benefactions of non-monks, that the new style in which they were constructed, commonly called Romanesque, also bears the name monastic. Because of the widespread interest in reform one had best view the movement as a popular reaction to the low moral conditions of the times.

In a search for the first overt signs of the movement three places in particular receive special mention: England, principally in the person of Dunstan, abbot of Glastonbury (later archbishop of Canterbury); the monastery of Cluny in Burgundy, with its series of great abbots; and Lorraine, especially the monastery of Gorze. Of these reform centers that at Cluny is best known. The reform movement that originated there owed its rise to William, duke of Aquitaine, who in 910 announced that he was surrendering all control over the life of the community. "It has pleased us," he proclaimed, "to set forth in this testament that from this day forward the monks united in congregation at Cluny shall be wholly freed from our power, from that of our kindred, and from the jurisdiction of royal greatness, and shall never submit to the yoke of any earthly power"—an implied acknowledgment that the source of infection from which much monastic corruption sprang at the time was lay interference.

The specific evils, or what passed as evils, that the reformers wished to correct were generally three: simony, clerical marriage (concubinage), and lay interference in the selection of bishops and abbots. This last was generally known as lay investiture from the practice of kings of investing bishops and abbots with the insignia of their offices. In the case of the bishop, it involved investiture with ring and crozier; in that of abbot, simply with ring. As practiced by such kings as Henry II and Henry III of Germany, lay investiture was not universally viewed as an evil, even by reformers with the zeal of Peter Damian. For the tradition that kings should invest bishops was an ancient one and one that possessed some justification. Bishops were royal officials, not greatly different from counts in the services they owed their lords; furthermore, kings possessed a kind of priestly character. The emperor, for example, wore a particularly high hat in order to make room for a cloth miter underneath. Nevertheless, few kings were so careful in their selection of bishops as were the two Henrys, while more members of the aristocracy ignored than followed the example of William of Aquitaine. In any event, whatever the record of individual kings, reformers condemned the practice of lay investiture on two counts: first, the sacred insignia should be conferred only by churchmen; second, only members of the clergy or hierarchy should have a hand in the selection of bishops and abbots.

The man who traditionally receives credit for pushing through the reform program of the eleventh century was Pope Gregory VII. This may be doing an injustice to Gregory's predecessor Leo IX whose solid work in reorganizing the papacy made possible Gregory's achievement. Until Leo's time the papacy, following its degradation in the late ninth and early tenth centuries, had remained hardly more than a Roman institution. Leo reorganized the chancery, greatly expanded its activities by conducting correspondence with all the important men of Europe, and sent out legates everywhere to champion the cause of reform. He spent as much time traveling about western Europe as he spent in Rome, preaching reform, investigating monasteries and dioceses, even stopping long enough at Reims to censure its archbishop and several bishops of the vicinity for simony. He also laid the foundation for the important role the college of cardinals was to play by inaugurating the policy of bringing able men to Rome from all corners of Christendom, where they were to assist the pope in administering the church. This policy of appointing men from different countries as cardinals continued, incidentally, on down to the Great Schism (see below, p. 381). Then Pope Urban VI, in order to assure himself its loyalty, transformed the curia into an Italian institution. It has remained that up to the present time.

The first dramatic step taken by the reformers was the announcement in 1059 of a new papal electoral law. This new procedure was intended to strike a blow at lay investiture where it was most solidly entrenched, namely, at the German court. For the past century, ever since the interference of Otto I, the kings of Germany had almost regularly placed their man in the papal office. This pronouncement of 1059 aimed at changing this. From now on, the cardinal clergy of Rome, which included bishops, priests, and deacons, were to select the new pope, then after his election announce his name to the king of Germany. In effect, therefore, the role of the German king was to be no different from the rest of the laity, simply one of giving approval to the action of the church. Although the new law did not eliminate all German interference, it represented a major move in that direction. What it did accomplish immediately was to introduce the cardinals as an important body into the administrative machinery of the church.

The reformers' second dramatic step came with the election in 1073 of Hildebrand as Pope Gregory VII. Hildebrand's origins remain obscure. He appears to have been of Roman birth and, for a short time, a monk, although not associated with Cluny as generally assumed. Leo brought him back to Rome from Germany where he had gone with the exiled Gregory VI whom Henry III had deposed. This incident may have left a deep impression upon Gregory. At least as pope, all his efforts appear to have been dedicated toward the objective of depriving the king of Germany of any voice in church affairs. He had already been of great assistance to Leo, and his leadership in the curia, following the death of Cardinal Humbert (see above, p. 133), had been unquestioned.

Gregory's goal as pope may not have been greatly different from that of Leo, but he pressed it with inflexible determination. His enemies said he had a demon; his admirer Peter Damian referred to him as "my holy Satan." Nothing must stand in Gregory's way, not cardinals nor other advisers who pleaded moderation. What Gregory willed, that God willed, so Gregory was convinced. His practice of punctuating his pronouncements with texts from the Bible has led scholars to liken him to Elijah. Yet for all his holy anger, Gregory was prudent in one respect. He crossed swords with but one king. The gross immorality of Philip I of France put him beneath notice. Over in England William the Conqueror was too strong and too distant to make protest practical. Gregory's logical enemy was Henry IV of Germany. Not only was the king of Germany the worst offender in the practice of lay investiture; he was also the closest. As Holy Roman Emperor he made appointments in Italy.

The issue came to a head in 1075 when Henry's nominee was selected for consecration as archbishop of Milan. Since this followed on the heels of Gregory's formal condemnation of lay investiture, the pope promptly warned Henry to withdraw his appointment or suffer deposition. At the moment Henry happened to feel more secure on his throne than he had reason to be, so he convened a council of German bishops which just as promptly deposed Gregory. Gregory countered by excommunicating and deposing Henry as he had threatened to do, and releasing the king's subjects from their obedience. All this would have passed as mere shadowboxing between pope and king had not the German princes taken a hand. Some had already revolted against Henry, others were waiting for just such a development as papal condemnation of Henry before joining the rebels. So when they learned of Gregory's action they notified Henry that unless he secured absolution from the pope by February 22, 1077, the anniversary of his excommunication, they would proceed to carry out the papal decree of deposition. They then blocked Henry's passage southward out of Germany in order to prevent his dealing independently with Gregory, and invited Gregory to come to Augsburg to advise with them concerning the matter.

At this juncture, when Henry's fortunes appeared beyond mending, he made a move which confounded his enemies. Despite the bitter cold and the grave danger involved, he and a small party made their precarious way across the Alps, then hurried south to make his peace with Gregory. When Gregory heard of Henry's approach, he turned aside and took refuge in the castle of the Countess Matilda at Canossa since he feared Henry's hostile intent. When he learned that Henry was coming as a penitent and wished only to submit, he was even more fearful. For if Henry confessed his crime and asked for pardon, he would be obliged to recall his anathemas, even though he was convinced that Henry would be lying. And that is precisely what happened. For three days Gregory kept Henry "weeping" outside the castle gate, as he later wrote in defense of his action, then finally had to loose "the chain of anathema" and receive him "into the favor of our fellowship."

The German princes condemned Gregory's "treachery" for pardoning Henry, then went ahead with their revolt. By 1080 Henry's continued defiance enabled Gregory to convince himself that he could finally support the anti-king the rebel princes in Germany had set up, but then it was too late. The anti-king died and the revolt collapsed. When Henry later approached Rome with an army to punish Gregory, the pope appealed to Robert Guiscard who came up with his Normans and Saracens, looted the city, and took Gregory back south with him to Salerno where he died (1085 A.D.).

Several years later Henry died in as deep a gloom as had Gregory. It remained for Henry V to agree with Pope Calixtus II in 1122 to a compromise of the conflict over lay investiture known as the Concordat of Worms. According to the terms of this compromise, the election of bishops and abbots was to follow proper procedure, that is, the canons of the cathedral were to elect the bishop, the monks choose the abbot. This was the minimum that the church had demanded. The compromise consisted in the pope's agreeing that the king or his representative should have the right to be present at such elections in order to decide in case of any dispute between candidates. What this meant in effect was that the king would have the bishop he wanted, although some prelate would invest the new bishop with the insignia of his office. As William of Champeaux had assured Henry V, he had nothing to lose by surrendering the right of investiture. In the Concordat of Worms the church had accepted a face-saving compromise; the king retained substantially what he already possessed, that is, the power to fill bishoprics with men of his own choice. Nevertheless, Gregory's dramatization of the issue did produce a significant improvement in the character of men raised to the episcopacy. Kings no longer interfered so frequently in their election, and when they did they generally nominated more worthy candidates for the office.

CHAPTER 7

The Feudal Age

"After the death of Charles [the Fat] the kingdoms which had obeyed his rule fell apart and obeyed no longer their natural lord Arnulf whom they had elected, but each elected a king from among its own inhabitants. This was the cause of many wars, not because there were no longer any princes among the Franks fitted by birth, courage, and wisdom to rule, but because of the equality of those very traits among so many princes, since no one of them so excelled the others that they would be willing to obey him."

What the chronicler was writing of here in the late ninth century was the dissolution of the Carolingian empire. His words, "no one of them so excelled the others that they [meaning the counts] would be willing to obey him," described the condition of the Frankish monarchy. To such a low estate had it fallen that none of the few remaining representatives of the Carolingian dynasty could exercise any greater authority than many members of the landed aristocracy. These counts, dukes, and margraves might choose a king in order to preserve traditions, and they did. Such kings would ordinarily reign, however, not rule. They would bear the usual titles and they might preside at larger gatherings of the aristocracy when these took place. Of actual authority, of the ability to command loyalties, they had little. This was the feudal age, a time when the landed aristocracy, not kings, dominated the political and social life of a large part of western Europe. This age stretched roughly from the beginning of the tenth century to the close of the twelfth.

The factors which had conspired to bring Western monarchies to such a low condition passed under review in the preceding chapter. To recapitulate: there were first and ever present the economic and social circumstances which severely blocked effective exercise of royal

authority. These included the lack of roads and trade, and of traditions
that might have provided stability and cohesiveness to a people or
region. The poverty of the king rendered impossible the maintenance
of a royal bureaucracy or army. Instead the monarch had no choice
but to rely on an increasingly independent aristocracy for both his officials and his army. Only rarely could a king rise above such unfavorable circumstances and rule with a reasonably firm hand as did Pepin
and Charlemagne. Then, shortly after the death of Charlemagne, conditions became even more critical as Vikings, Saracens, and Magyars
poured into western Europe from the north, south, and east. The responsibility of ruling which had become an enormously difficult task
now became an impossibility. Before the onslaught of these destructive
invaders, the weakening states of western Europe broke up into frag-
ments, and over the scattered bits the local aristocracy extended what
control they pleased. Such was the feudal age.

Fortunately for western Europe certain practices had evolved during the centuries following the decline of Roman power which attained
full development during the feudal age and helped provide a measure
of stability to that period. Three of these deserve particular attention
since they characterized the organization of society during that age.
They also furnished the cement which prevented the complete dissolution of social life in the west and the advent of anarchy. There was,
first, the wide system of personal arrangements which existed among
men and bound them together. Since these extended from the lowest
peasant to the most powerful lord in a region, they helped stabilize
conditions in the area while promising some protection to its people.
A second practice was that of using land, in lieu of money, which was
in low supply, for procuring administrative and military services. A
third practice was the tendency for members of the landed aristocracy
to exercise increasing control over the people in their immediate vi-
cinities.

Human society has two basic needs, the one food, the other protection. The neolithic revolution which introduced agriculture and the
domestication of animals provided man the means of solving, within
limits, the problem of food. The rise of organized states satisfied for
extended periods the need for protection. For several centuries, for
example, the mighty Roman state had assured peace and tranquillity
to the millions who lived within its frontiers. When that happy age
ended in the third century and Roman power declined, western man
again resumed his search for protection. The first group to do so were

the most helpless, that is, the members of the peasant class. They surrendered their holdings and freedom to influential landowners in the vicinity in return for protection against the imperial tax collector. Curial refugees might join the peasants on such estates, along with the *coloni* who had already been frozen by imperial decree, as well as other poor people whom an aggressive proprietor might simply have forced under his control. For such proprietors were powerful men. They usually belonged to the senatorial aristocracy. They lived apart from the city and its magistrates, had secured or seized exemption from most of their traditional responsibilities, and maintained bands of warriors with which to defy marauders that might wander their way or an occasional imperial official who might dare show his face. The administration they exercised over their extensive estates and over the people living on them constituted the institution which historians have called patrocinium. (See above, p. 35.)

During the troublous Merovingian centuries when most kings were weak, and brutal men fought over power and booty, ordinary folk, as well as many who were not so ordinary, again found themselves in desperate need of protection. The result was the appearance and wide extension of a practice called commendation. This involved a formal act by which one person offered his services, together with his lands if he had any, to a stronger man in return for his protection. The individual peasant might ask a more powerful man in his neighborhood to accept him and his holdings and take them under his protection. That man in turn might approach one stronger than himself, perhaps the count or duke, and request a similar kind of protection. Given the weakness of kings and the turbulency of the times, most men stood in need of protection, from the meanest peasant to members of the landed aristocracy.

Place was made in the practice of commendation for landless men as well as for farmers, since what was of most pressing need was not land to be exploited but men. So if the man who commended himself had land to bring with him, the protector (lord) directed him to continue to use it; if he had no land, the lord gave him some (usually called a benefice or *precarium*). What the lord wanted from both men was work and services. In either case, the status of the commenders now came to resemble that of unfree *coloni*. The group composed of these commoners ordinarily remained below the level of feudal society, properly speaking. The fortunate few of these men who had commended themselves, those who had been of greater importance to begin with or who proved their value as warriors or advisers, might retain their status of freemen. Some of them would, in fact, join the ranks of the new feudal aristocracy. What is significant in both cases, that of the unfree and the free commender, is that these personal arrangements between themselves and their powerful neighbors supplemented, if they did not actually replace, the traditional relationship between king and subject which had failed to provide protection.

While the practice of commendation was erecting a social, semipolitical structure outside the state based upon arrangements between the strong and the weak, so also within the monarchy itself a practice was emerging, this one involving an arrangement between the king and his subject, which represented a similar adjustment to the weakness of government. This was the institution of vassalage. The first vassals were boys and young men, members of the king's household, who served him in a variety of capacities. Since they were drawn from the lower classes, the king found them quite faithful and dependable, and for that reason made increasing use of them. Some of their assignments might involve expense, for which reason the king would provide them with lands from which they derived the resources they needed to carry out their missions. Especially during late Merovingian times did the Carolingian mayors of the palace make a practice of distributing lands among their vassals in order to enable them to secure horses and what military equipment they might need to serve them as warriors. Some of these vassals might belong to a rank higher than that of commoners. In fact, when the aristocracy learned that the king was granting his vassals lands in this manner, they came forward and indicated their willingness to become his vassals. The king for his part was most willing to accept them as vassals since they would then swear oaths of loyalty to him, thereby affording him added assurance of their loyalty.

There was a third practice which combined with those of commendation and vassalage to produce the feudal system. That was the practice of immunity. Its historical antecedent might be considered the institution of patrocinium which had found the late Roman landed proprietor exercising extensive control over the people living on his estates. Where a Germanic king did not interpose his authority, which he usually found impossible to do, the tradition persisted into Merovingian times that large landowners would continue to enjoy wide authority over their servants and tenants. During Merovingian times kings actually encouraged the increase of such autonomous units by extending to monasteries and to bishops exemption from the jurisdiction of their officials. As an expression of their favor they would grant them immunity, which meant that their crown officials were barred from trespassing upon such lands in order to carry out their duties. As time passed, such grants of immunity were extended to members of the aristocracy, either to secure their pledge of support against hostile kings, or because the king would have been helpless to prevent the arrogation of such privileges had they been demanded. The consequence, whatever the particular circumstances, was the exercise of wide autonomous powers by the greater part of the landed aristocracy by the end of the ninth century.

One other development beyond commendation, vassalage, and immunity demands consideration in a discussion of the origins of feudalism. That was the change in the art of war. The feudal age was the age of the armed horseman, of the soldier on horseback, of the knight. His appearance in the eighth century in the west heralded the coming of the feudal age, when he would so dominate the battlefield that for several centuries the foot soldier would be rendered obsolete. Of itself this development would not have had serious repercussions on the organization of society had it not been for the fact that horses were expensive. Since peasants preferred the ox as a draft animal, horses were few in number and consequently expensive. They were the property of the wealthy who used them principally for travel. An important consequence, therefore, of the change-over in the west from the foot soldier to armed horsemen in the eighth and ninth centuries was to make the wealthy class also the military elite. Only they had or could afford horses. And since the king could no longer depend upon a militia of foot soldiers where this had been at hand, he found himself wholly dependent upon his already powerful aristocracy for an army.

Scholars are still debating the circumstances which led to the evolution of the knight. Several writers have recently focused attention on the stirrup. Their theory is that something of decisive importance must have happened during the eighth and ninth centuries which made the horseman a truly formidable warrior. The use of horses was surely not new. It went back many centuries beyond the feudal age. The Sarmatians and Goths used horses, so did the Avars and Magyars, and, of course, the Moslems who crossed into Spain. Yet it is significant that Charles Martel and his Franks who defeated these Moslems at Tours fought on foot for the most part, not on horseback. It appears, therefore, that while horses had a place in the annals of European

warfare before the feudal age, that place was limited to the greater
mobility horses provided mounted archers with their bows, arrows,
swords, and darts. The stirrup, which came into use in the late eighth
and ninth centuries, provided the warrior a vastly improved footing
from which to hurl his lance or swing his sword, mace, or battle-ax.
This period also witnessed the introduction of horseshoes, which greatly
facilitated the use of horses over rough ground.

[margin note: why horses were good for battle]

While the knight on horseback serves as the symbol of the feudal
age, of more fundamental importance to the stability of that age were
the arrangements of personal dependence that bound together the different classes which made up feudal society. It was from the agree-
ments which peasants made with landed proprietors and these
proprietors with counts, dukes, and kings, that the feudal age derived
the greater part of the equilibrium it enjoyed. A consideration of the
peasant's relationship with his lord or seigneur will appear later when
the manor comes in for discussion. Most critical to the feudal system
was the relationship which existed between the king (lord) and his
vassal. As noted, the vassal may have started out as a servant in the
royal household. By the close of the eighth century he was more frequently a man on horseback ready to fight the king's battles. Whatever
the vassal's particular responsibilities, the king could provide for him
in one of two ways. He might feed, clothe, and equip him and keep
him at his castle. This he did with a select few, a sufficient number
to guard himself and his family from ordinary danger. To have maintained any more than necessary in this fashion at his home was apt
to be both expensive and dangerous. For this reason the king normally
gave lands (benefice or *precarium*) to most of these vassals, who were
then expected to provide for their own maintenance from what resources these lands returned. When these early vassals died, their
lands reverted to the king, who might distribute them in turn to other
vassals under the same arrangements as before. *[margin note: → the son of the deceased would become usually the new vassal]*

Within a few generations the king lost his ability to take back these
lands when the vassal died. In certain instances he preferred not to do
so. If the vassal had been a loyal official and left a grown son when
he died, why not let the benefice continue in the family? More frequently the growing hereditability of benefices came about in another
way. The grown son or nephew or uncle of the dead vassal might
simply notify the king that he was taking over the deceased's lands
and responsibilities. If the king were prudent, he accepted the new

arrangement. To have objected would have invited a general revolt of his other vassals who were also hoping that their sons would inherit their lands. By the reign of Charles the Bald (d. 877) the hereditary character of benefices was considered normal. Then it was usually only the lands of a vassal who died without heirs which would revert to the lord. When this happened, the king might keep the lands for himself if his vassals did not object, or give them out again as before. By the close of the ninth century the term "fief" came to replace that of benefice or *precarium* in order to give emphasis to its hereditary character.

Another practice evolved during these early feudal years which kings found even more unpalatable than the growing hereditability of fiefs. That was the practice of subinfeudation. By subinfeudation is understood the granting by one vassal of part of his fief to another man who then became his vassal (the original lord's sub- or rear vassal). Generally the same factors prompted the vassal to subdivide his fief as had led the king to parcel out his domain in the first place. These would include the vassal's inability to administer a particularly extensive fief, when he might welcome the assistance of a vassal or two of his own. Or it might have happened that stronger men in the outlying reaches of the fief simply appropriated the land for themselves. Lest the vassal lose these lands completely, he would regularize such seizure by acknowledging the intruder as his vassal.

Still the most common explanation for the practice of subinfeudation was the relatively simple means it provided the vassal for meeting his military obligations to his lord. If he owed his lord the service of ten knights, he might set aside ten parcels of land, turn these over to ten men, who would then maintain themselves as horsemen equipped to perform military service. To illustrate: when William the Conqueror introduced feudalism to England he exacted the service of fifteen knights from the abbey of Tavistock in Cornwall. The abbey met this heavy assessment by endowing fifteen knights with lands, from which resources they then were expected to fit themselves out with horse and gear. A close look at the map of feudal France would, therefore, reveal not only the outlines of fiefs as large as Normandy, Toulouse, and Champagne, but of hundreds of smaller domains as well, the extent of each of them being computed, at least in theory, in terms of a given number of knights they would supply. Again in theory, this process of subinfeudation could proceed until the last fief created produced resources just sufficient to fit out a single knight.

While the practice of subinfeudation was wholly consistent with feudal principles, whatever these were, and represented an extension of the decentralizing tendencies inherent in feudalism, the practice, if permitted to go too far, promised, nevertheless, to subvert the very society feudalism presumably aimed to preserve. First, it severely limited the king's authority. He might claim the loyalty of his vassals, but feudal law had it, at least in France, that he could not claim obedience from his subvassals, that is, the vassals of his own vassals. His jurisdiction might begin and end with his own few immediate vassals. It was the desire to correct such a situation that prompted Louis IX to give his loyal friend Jean de Joinville, who was the vassal of the count of Champagne, a royal fief in order to make him one of his own "men." In England, William the Conqueror required all vassals, whether his immediate or rear vassals, to take an oath of loyalty to him (Salisbury oath). A second evil associated with subinfeudation was the practice of holding multiple fiefs. By the twelfth century it had become common for members of the feudal aristocracy to hold fiefs from several lords, to each of whom they had promised loyalty. There is, indeed, a record of one vassal's having had forty-three lords. If the oath of loyalty which the vassal swore his lord helped stabilize society, what happened to that society when he swore forty-three oaths?

The monastic chronicler introduces a story from the early tenth century which serves to illustrate the relative helplessness of the king during this period, either to direct or to prevent the evolution of feudal practices. It describes how the arrogant Rollo became the vassal of Charles the Simple. Though the circumstances do not exactly fit local conditions in feudal Europe since Rollo was a Viking invader and not a Frankish count, still his haughty demeanor toward Charles surely typified that of the feudal aristocracy. And the voluntary character of Rollo's decision to accept the status of vassal was probably typical of the French aristocracy in the ninth and tenth centuries.

The incident took place in 911. By this time Charles and his advisers had agreed to face up to the fact that they could not drive the Viking intruders from the area later known as Normandy. To put the best possible face on a sorry situation, they decided to turn the area over to Rollo, the Viking chieftain, but to require of him that he hold the land as a fief from Charles, in other words, that he become Charles' vassal. So the archbishop of Rouen went off to Rollo to apprise him of Charles' wish and to work out the arrangements. The Viking warrior appeared quite willing to accept the terms described until the prelate

explained that as Charles' vassal, he would be expected to kiss the
king's foot. "I will never bend my knee to anyone," stormed Rollo,
"and I will never kiss anyone's foot." Fortunately for the fiction of
Charles' royal authority, Rollo proved as much a man of reason as he
was brave, and "moved by the entreaties of the Franks, he ordered one
of his warriors to kiss the king's foot instead. The warrior immediately
lifted up the king's foot, threw the king on his back, and kissed the
foot, while he was standing and the king was flat on his back. At that
there was a great roar of laughter and much excitement among those
present."*

The requirement that Rollo kiss the foot of Charles did not ordinarily
form part of the feudal ritual by which a free man became the vassal
of his king (lord). This ritual dated from Merovingian times when
men of all stations were seeking the protection of those who were
stronger and asking to become their "men." In a simple ceremony,
called the act of homage (from *homo,* Latin for man), the one who
sought the protection of the other would place his hands, palms together, within those of his lord-to-be and promise to be his "man."
When he made this acknowledgment, he would kneel in order to give
clearer expression to his subordination. After he had performed the
act of homage, however, he arose and the two men would then kiss
each other on the mouth as a token of the bond of friendship that
now existed between them.

The act of homage, which all classes performed during the Merovingian period, came to be limited under the Carolingian kings to
members of the aristocratic class. The Carolingians also witnessed the
introduction of a second rite, known as the oath of fealty, to supplement the act of homage. When this had become part of the entire
ritual, the man would rise from his knees after performing his act of
homage and while standing, as befit a free man, swear on the Bible or
holy relics to be loyal to his lord. What led to the addition of this
second rite was not the insistence of the feudal aristocracy for a more
dignified ceremony to offset the demeaning implications of the
act of homage. It was the desire of the church and of the Carolingian
monarchs for a more Christian ritual and one which would hopefully
impress the vassal in a special manner with the sacredness of his
promises. For this reason, lords might demand that their vassals repeat
such oaths of fealty a number of times, particularly when the lord had

* Quoted in R. G. D. Laffan, *Select Documents of European History.* New York
(1930), I, pp. 14–15.

reason to suspect his vassal's loyalty. The act of homage and oath of fealty were held binding until the death of one of the parties.

During Merovingian times when the act of homage came into use, society was content that the mutual responsibilities of the two parties remain quite general. It was the duty of the one to provide protection, of the other to furnish services. When Carolingian usage limited the act of homage to the upper classes and combined with it a more formal oath of fealty, it was not long before the nature of the services expected of the vassal became more clearly defined. Because the lord was the benefactor, the vassal the beneficiary, and his fief an administrative unit, it was only reasonable that the lord's, not the vassal's, responsibilities, should continue somewhat undefined. Usually nothing more precise was required of the lord than that he defend his vassal "against all men who may live and die." Since the vassal was the lord's official and the vassal's fief part of his own domain, this was only to be expected. Men assumed, of course, that the lord would not reduce the size of his vassal's fief, nor declare it forfeit without just cause, nor molest his wife. And if the vassal died and left only minors, the lord would provide for their sustenance. The one specific obligation feudal tradition imposed upon the lord was to furnish his vassals justice, which, according to feudal usage, meant trial by his peers (fellow vassals).

When the vassal swore to be his lord's man during the feudal period, he assumed three major responsibilities. He swore to provide his lord military service, to furnish him counsel (court service), and to administer the fief which he received on this occasion. His military obligation required him to serve his lord as a knight forty days each year, and to supply additional knights in rough proportion to the size and value of his fief. A decree of Louis IX read: "The baron and all vassals of the king are bound to appear before him when he shall summon them, and to serve him at their own expense for forty days and forty nights, with as many knights as each one owes. . . . And if the king wishes to keep them more than forty days . . . they are not bound to remain if they do not wish it. And if the king wishes to keep them at his expense for the defense of the realm, they are bound to remain. And if the king wishes to lead them outside of the kingdom, they need not go unless they wish to, for they have already served their forty days and forty nights."

The obligation to give counsel imposed upon the vassal the duty of meeting with his lord, usually in company with the lord's other vassals, whenever the lord might summon him. Tradition limited such gatherings to two or three a year, often on great feasts such as Christmas and Easter. Then the vassals would advise with their lord concerning matters touching the realm. They might also serve as a court of justice in the adjudication of disputes among its members. The third obligation, that of administering the fief, was symbolically conferred upon the vassal when, on the occasion of swearing his oath of fealty, the lord tendered him a small stick, lance, or clod of dirt.

Beyond these three basic obligations which the vassal owed his lord (king), there were special occasions when he was expected to come to his financial assistance by contributing an aid. The three most common and traditional aids were paid when the lord's eldest son was knighted, when his eldest daughter was married, and when he was held for ransom. All were occasions of heavy expense. When Frederick Barbarossa celebrated the knighting of his two eldest sons in 1184 at Mainz, he invited thousands of knights from all over Europe to join him in extended festivities. Unfortunately for Frederick, the payment of an aid in Germany had probably not passed beyond the stage of a gift, whereas in England and France it had become an obligation. That contributing to the ransom of one's lord became a traditional aid during the feudal age provides more convincing proof of its turbulency than the melancholy descriptions a dozen chroniclers may have given of the times.

The vassal made other payments to his lord. The heaviest of these was a fee called a relief, which he paid when he took over the fief of his deceased father. In France and England payments of relief constituted a major source of crown revenues in the twelfth and thirteenth centuries. Since the relief was paid individually, never collectively by all vassals at the same time, harsh lords could impose heavy assessments without fear of provoking a revolt. English barons considered that practice among the most offensive of John's tyrannies. He once attempted to force a vassal to pay a relief payment of 5000 marks (approximately 3333 pounds before modern devaluations!). The vassal owed his lord hospitality (*droit de gîte*) when he stopped in with his retainers on his travels about the country. If the vassal died and left a minor, the lord appropriated the income of the fief until the son came of age, that is, until the youth would be capable of discharging the obligations incumbent upon him as vassal. Should the vassal leave only a daughter, the lord had the right to select her husband on the principle that such a man would be his new vassal and owe him military service. If the lord were generous, he might, in return for a considerable fee, grant the woman "license to marry where she wishes, so long as she does not marry herself to any of the enemies of the king."

It is no accident that the knight serves as the symbol of the feudal age. In no other age did a warrior class so dominate society, nor was there ever an age when warriors were so much on the move. Although the modern world has suffered its share of wars, it continues to consider the first responsibility of government, not the protection of frontiers, but the economic and cultural advancement of its subjects. During the feudal period the principal business of those who ruled was war. The most frequent demand which the lord made, therefore, upon his vassal was for military service. The vassal and the knights he owed his lord must be ready to fight, and they must know how to fight. So from boyhood this class began preparing itself for its future role. The boy first served his lord as page, then squire, and finally as knight. As he advanced in years, his skill and confidence in his arms progressed, not his willingness to accept the arbitrament of his disputes or the judgment of his peers. The aristocracy during the feudal age insisted instead upon what it considered its God-given prerogative of settling its disputes by force of arms, the so-called right of private warfare. When Louis IX and other kings forbade the exercise of this "right," the feudal aristocracy denounced such action as tyranny.

Until kings as strong as Louis IX appeared on the scene, turbulency and conflict were the order of the day. During the feudal age kings were usually too weak to prevent fierce, cruel men from attacking villages and pillaging the countryside, or from fighting among themselves over lands and booty. Yet though violence was prevalent, the actual number of men slain in combat was not great. Hostile groups of warriors ordinarily did little more than skirmish with each other, then after a sharp exchange of blows, ride off in their different directions. Armies in the feudal age were comparatively small, normally not counting more than several hundred on each side. Only the threat of dangerous attack that might arouse an entire region would lead to larger concentrations. Another circumstance that helped keep the number of casualties down was the knight's hope of capturing his opponent and holding him for ransom. Finally, the armor the knight wore provided him effective protection against most blows.

It is, nonetheless, no mistake to conceive of the feudal age as a period of violence and suffering. If the knight enjoyed his routine of fighting, all other elements of feudal society abominated it. The knight might return from a skirmish with nothing worse than bruises. For the villages in the vicinity of the battle, the day might have brought pillage and destruction, death to peasants who resisted or got in the way, and the slaughter or driving off of the stock. For many knights, indeed, plunder constituted their principal source of income, and what they could not carry off they might destroy out of sheer wantonness or in order to weaken a worsted foe who might attempt reprisals. Almost unending is the lament of contemporary chroniclers over the suffering of the peasantry from the violence of the feudal age.

The church, which also suffered severely in this age of violence, took the initiative in curbing feudal warfare. Late in the tenth century local groups of bishops began to meet to discuss steps for reducing violence. From such discussions emanated a proclamation known as the Peace of God. God wanted peace, such proclamations warned, and upon lawless men who attacked holy places, the clergy, peasants, travelers, and pilgrims, the church called down the curse of God. The early eleventh century saw another approach to this problem, that of the Truce of God, which prohibited fighting on certain days—first on Sundays and holydays, then on Saturdays as well, then finally for an extended weekend that ran from Wednesday evening until Monday morning. Here and there nobles formed sworn associations and pledged themselves to observe and enforce these proclamations, and an occasional king incorporated them with his own decrees. Still the success of neither the Peace nor the Truce of God was substantial. Peace only dawned for the helpless countryside with the rise of a strong king. Peace came to England during the reign of William the Conqueror, and when Frederick Barbarossa left Italy for Germany, "his presence there restored peace, but denied it to the Italians whom he had left."

Some credit for reducing violence during the feudal period may be credited to chivalry, in other words, to the institution of knighthood. The first knights were fierce warriors who lived by their arms in an age which knew no higher law than might. Slowly, very slowly, and principally through the appeals and denunciations of the church, did these rough men come to accept the propriety of setting some limitation on their freedom to fight. They must fight for their lords; they must fight for the church; they must fight evil men. Gradually a code of chivalry evolved. In theory, at least, the knight became the protector of the weak and poor, always ready to serve God, his lord, and society. The true knight was brave. "Unless a knight be brave," wrote the poet in the *Song of Roland*, "he had best be a monk." The true knight was also loyal to his lord, contemptuous of pain and death, the protector of widow and orphan, who, like Chaucer's knight "followed chivalry, truth, honor, greatness of heart, and courtesy." Unfortunately the feudal age produced few knights who measured up to that ideal. For that reason people welcomed the coming of a crusade which would siphon off these fighters and permit others to live in peace.

The gap between Chaucer's warrior and the historical knight of the feudal age was no larger than between the life he led in his "castle" and that which romanticists have imagined. Life was hard for the lord and his lady. His fare was notable more for quantity than quality, and there were times when a crop failure caused even the noble's larder to run low. The servants of his household made his clothes, of a finer quality of wool perhaps, and trimmed with sable and ermine. He sat on a bench, not a chair, ate from a plank table that rested on trestles, and slept on a straw mattress on the floor. Privacy during the feudal period was almost as much at a premium as peace, for the "castle" consisted almost exclusively of a large central hall where all ate and slept together. Only the more fortunate lord and his lady had a small room to themselves and their children, away from their servants and retainers.

When the knight was not fighting, he might be jousting with his friends or taking part in a tournament. The first tournaments combined sport with the serious business of training horsemen for combat. The church consistently condemned them because of their violence and Henry II prohibited them as being too bloody. By Froissart's day, that is, the late fourteenth century, they had "degenerated" into mere pageants, where knights hurled blunted lances at each other in order to gain prizes, as well as the favor of beautiful women who were in attendance. Next to fighting, the knight's principal sport was hunting. Hunting also served a second purpose of providing game for his table. Indoors the knight might join in dancing, playing cards, backgammon, and chess, or listening to the minstrel who happened by. And he took a far longer time at his meals than does modern man.

While romantic literature has erred in extolling the virtues, often imaginary, of the feudal knight, many modern critics have been quite as remiss in dismissing him out of hand as a wholly negative force. Actually the knight's apologist can present a good case for him and his role in the feudal age. What stability existed in that age was his work. Granted that he contributed his share to the violence, the fact remains that he subdued the Vikings and Magyars and helped drive out the Saracens. He responded with enthusiastic fervor to the pope's call to fight the Moslem in far-off Syria. To the serfs and villagers who lived on his domain he furnished a reasonably just administration while he protected them from the attack of marauders and hostile lords. Feudalism may even deserve credit for keeping alive the idea of monarchy in an age so hostile to all institutions that that institution might itself have otherwise disappeared.

Alongside the knight and feudal aristocracy that dominated western Europe during the feudal age was the mass of peasantry who made up the greater part of its population. The one class ruled society and provided it protection; the second group labored with its hands to furnish the food and services the landowning class required to perform its work. Feudal society had need of both classes to maintain itself, and for that reason God had so ordered. "It is seemly," wrote the saintly Ramón Lull, "that men should plow and dig and work hard that the earth may yield the fruits from which the knight and his horse will live; and that the knight who rides and does a lord's work should get his wealth from the things on which his men are to spend much toil and fatigue."

Peasants had, of course, existed long before the feudal age, and they would continue to constitute the largest group in society long after strong kings had deprived the feudal aristocracy of its authority and purpose. The kind of toil, too, that the peasant performed, chiefly that of working the soil in order to raise food, did not alter appreciably during the feudal age to justify setting his group off from the husbandmen of preceding and of subsequent centuries. Nevertheless, the peculiar term "serf" by which this peasant is traditionally known during the feudal age suggests that he was not just another farmer. Circumstances were present, such as those affecting his relationship to his lord for instance, that gave him a distinctly different character. In many respects his status, rights, and obligations bore strong resemblance to those of his aristocratic superiors, even though an impassable barrier marked off the one class from the other. Both knight and serf were typical of the feudal age.

Two features of peasant life during the feudal age that come readily to mind bore no immediate relationship to the presence of a feudal aristocracy. One was the large percentage of people who lived as peasants in this feudal period; a second, the tendency of these peasants to live together in villages. When Ramón Lull wrote of the men who "spend much toil and fatigue," he was probably speaking of more than 90 per cent of the population of western Europe. The percentage in Italy where there were towns, would be lower; in England it might be higher. The Domesday Book survey which William the Conqueror ordered in 1086 (see above, p. 214) revealed more than 95 per cent of England's population living in the country and drawing its livelihood from the soil. Seldom in recorded history has so large a percentage of an area's population pursued nonpastoral agriculture.

More unique was the practice for peasants, during this age, of living *living together in villages* together in villages and hamlets, rather than in individual homesteads scattered about the countryside. In the larger villages several hundred families might be gathered together; in the hamlets no more than a score. Where the community was a large one, it might actually represent two or more manors belonging to as many different lords. Here in this custom of peasants living together there is evident some link with feudalism, since the manorial village or manor was most common in the most highly feudalized parts of western Europe. In those areas, as we shall note, agriculture was also most highly developed. Why peasants chose to live together in villages may require no explanation *Protection* beyond their need for protection. As we have seen, that was the crying need of the time, and where better to assure oneself of the lord's protection than living in the shadow of his fortified manor house or castle.

The organization of the economic and social life of the peasantry about the village and the isolation of this community from other villages and towns introduces another feature of manorial life during the feudal period which was probably unique. The manor during that period was a self-sufficient institution. Because of the absence of roads and the great difficulty and danger involved in moving about, the peasant village depended upon its own resources to satisfy its need for food and services. What it required to exist, it raised or produced, and what it could not produce, it normally did without. Because of *self sufficient* the prevalence of this agricultural economy throughout the area, even the presence of roads would not have greatly altered the situation since the peasants of a wide region ordinarily raised the same kind of crops. The typical peasant community lived a life all its own. The lord would provide it some connection with the outside world, or an occasional pilgrim, the bishop of the diocese, or a representative of the crown. Other visitors—marauders and enemies—the lord of the manor would hopefully drive off.

The most unusual feature of the manorial village, from point of view of the modern world, was the unfree status of the greater number of its inhabitants and their complete dependence upon their local lord. The great majority of the peasants could not leave the community without the lord's permission; they owed him obligations which suggested a servile status; in the most highly feudalized parts of Europe they had, indeed, no existence apart from their lord. They were dependent upon him for justice and protection, for the use of his land, even for the spiritual services of a priest whom he might appoint. So much was he their lord, that the authority of the king and of the church, when this reached them, did so through his permission.

The circumstances which gave birth to the unfree village and its subordination to the local lord are obscure. Because of the paucity of records, the historian who seeks a complete answer, according to Marc Bloch, "might as well try to follow a track by night." Still, two historical antecedents for the practice of unfree people living together on the manor come readily to view. The most ancient was the colonate of late Roman times. Surely the unfree *coloni* and hutted slave who worked the latifundia strongly suggest the people who worked the medieval manor. There existed some differences between the late Roman villa and the medieval manor. On the villa the word of the Roman proprietor was law; on the manor it was commonly custom that fixed the peasant's place in the community. The villa, furthermore, could be viewed as a semi-capitalistic institution even during the centuries of Rome's decline, which did not become true of the manor before the late twelfth. Yet most of the people on both villa and manor were unfree, and to the modern world that characteristic appears to have outweighed all other considerations.

One may trace the other principal source of the manor's unfree population to the troubled conditions of the sixth, seventh, and eighth centuries. As noted above in the discussion of the origins of feudalism, those were centuries when men sought protection. To the lord who might furnish them protection, many men were willing to surrender ownership of their lands and their personal freedom as well. Everywhere men were commending themselves. The more fortunate, generally those who had more to offer, might serve their lord in some military or administrative capacity. The humbler sort, simple tillers of the soil, would remain farmers. They would continue at the same occupation as before, but now on land which belonged to the lord and on terms that left them unfree. In many instances, these unfree peasants had never had the opportunity to choose between freedom and the surrender of that freedom for protection. A powerful lord might simply have taken over control of them and their village. Whatever the circumstances, the end was the same. They now had the status of serfs.

Now, while the great majority of villagers during the feudal period were unfree, there were some who dwelt in the village who were free. These would include the lord of the manor, for instance, and his family, who might spend extended periods in the "big house" on the hill. How many weeks or months they spent in the village would depend upon a number of circumstances: the comfortableness of the manor house, the depth of its larder, the friendliness of the villagers, the abundance of game, the proximity to danger from attack, and the number of manors the lord might possess. In the course of the year, he would normally spend some time in each of his manors, if for no other reason, in order to consume the stores his serfs had provided him. However great the amount of time he spent at any one manor, he never ceased being something of an outsider, a member of the second estate as it came to be called, not of the third to which the unfree villagers belonged.

Another free man who lived in the village and who was not a member of the third estate of the commoners was the priest. His clerical rank placed him with the first estate, that is, with the group which concerned itself with spiritual matters. To this class the Middle Ages granted precedence, at least officially. By birth, however, and culture the village priest did not differ appreciably from the serfs among whom he labored. What may have explained his rise above that class was perhaps his intelligence as a boy which had attracted the attention of an earlier "parson" who had ministered to that community. This man taught him a little Latin, brought him to the attention of the lord, who in turn had the bishop ordain him and assign him to the village. The house that the priest occupied in the village was not different from the others, neither was his fare, and he might work his acres when they worked theirs. If his store of erudition was meager, neither the lord nor the villagers would have been apt to notice since theirs was no higher. Rarely does any great gulf separate the literacy or, for that matter, the morality of a native clergy from that of the people it serves.

Apart from the lord of the manor and the priest, there might be other freemen living in the village. These would be commoners, members of the third estate, of the class that constituted the bulk of the manor's population. By some fortunate circumstance, they had never surrendered nor been deprived of their freedom. That their number was small, given the turbulent conditions of the feudal age, is understandable. If the manor's population included very few slaves, that is also easy to understand. What services the lord of the manor required, he could demand of his serfs; so why have slaves in his household whose food and shelter he would be expected to provide?

This centers attention on the last group, the great mass of serfs, the unfree, who made up most of the population of the manor. In terms of rights and obligations, they stood between the minority of freemen who were above them and the few slaves who were beneath. What these rights and obligations might be varied with province and century, and, above all, with the arrangement entered in between the individual lord and villager. The latter might be a free villein, that is, one who paid a rental yet could not leave the village without the lord's permission. He might be a cottar, own only a cottage, and have no acres either of his own nor any others to rent, and limited for his livelihood to what he could earn working as a day laborer for his fellow serfs or for the lord. The scholar who attempts to spell out in precise terms the rights and obligations of each rank between the free villein and cottar and to note how these not only might differ from province to province but how they underwent constant change, will find that he has buried both himself and his reader in hopeless confusion. Suffice it to say that by the close of the twelfth century, the common terms of serf and villein, which were applied to the great majority of these villagers, had come to be largely synonymous.

The word "serf" is derived from the Latin *servus* which in classical times meant either slave or servant. The medieval serf was no slave even though two circumstances have left many people the impression that he was. One circumstance was the fact that he worked the demesne of the lord. The demesne was that part of the manorial lands, frequently one-third, which the lord kept for himself. The other circumstance was the serf's inability to leave the manor. To a modern generation both circumstances connote slavery; to the Middle Ages they did not.

The serf worked the land of his lord because he had none of his own. He had surrendered his farm to his lord in return for the latter's protection. What the serf continued to do, however, was to retain use (not ownership) of his land, as did the lord's other serfs. So while they worked the acres they had been permitted to use for themselves, they also worked the lord's demesne, partly to compensate him for the protection he was affording them, partly as a kind of rental for the acres which they were using for themselves. Had land possessed capitalistic value in the feudal age and had the serf money in sufficient quantity, he might have paid this rent in coin rather than labor. That would have saved modern students from the pitfall into which many of them have fallen in assuming the serf's labor charge made him a slave.

The other circumstance that leads some readers to ascribe a slave status to the serf, namely, his inability to leave the manor, no more denoted a servile condition than the labor rent he paid. One might ask first, why should the serf wish to leave the manor if he had just turned over his lands to the lord in return for his protection? The conclusion is, therefore, inevitable that the serf (tenant, the man who commended himself) had lived for a number of generations on the lord's lands before the thought of leaving had ever occurred to him. By the time it did, in the late eleventh century for instance, tradition had already established the rule that he was not to leave the manor. By that time, too, the lord had come to consider the serf as much a physical asset as the acres he worked, since without men to work the land the latter would have been of no value. The modern student should also keep in mind that mobility and freedom did not bear the same relationship in the Middle Ages as they may today. One last observation: if the serf did decide to leave the manor, he could flee to a distant town without great difficulty in a country such as France where the authority of the local lord lapsed at the confines of his land and where no effectual royal authority existed prior to the thirteenth century which might have worked to return the serf whence he had come. In England it would have been difficult to flee by the twelfth century, although custom then prescribed that a lord could not reclaim a serf who had been away for a year and a day.

The point of this discussion is to present the status of the serf as fundamentally different from that of the slave despite the serf's inability to leave the manor and the obligation upon him to work the acres of his lord. This last, called the *corvée*, represented the serf's heaviest burden. The lord might require two days of his time one week, three another, or even four. During the summer the serf spent his time in the fields; during the winter, at such tasks as repairing roads and walls, or cutting and transporting wood. Some serfs might be occupied summer and winter in the mill or smithy or about the manor house. At the peak of the harvest season, the serf could expect to put in a few extra days, called boon work, when his older children and his wife might join him. (Medieval women usually helped with the harvest and with the chores around the barn.) While the *corvée* might appear excessive, and the serf was sure it was, the days he put in working for his lord did not normally exceed half-days, while boon work was not without its pleasant features. The entire community joined together in bringing in the harvest, while the lord provided most of the food and drink from his own larder. Many serfs never ate white bread except on such occasions, nor could their vintage match that of the lord.

The serf bore a variety of charges in addition to the *corvée* that kept reminding him he was a serf and that all he possessed, including his land, belonged ultimately to his lord. Relatively common was the tallage (taille), which was ordinarily a tax on property and, like most taxes, paid in kind. The first tallage had been a gift, then became a regular charge, not an uncommon development in the Middle Ages when the temptation was strong to proclaim what was done once, surely twice, as custom. In France the taille gradually replaced the labor charge (*corvée*) since the seigneur in that country had parceled out most of his demesne among his serfs by the thirteenth century. The serf also paid a head tax (*chevage*), a *formariage* when his daughter married off the manor, and his family a mortuary gift (heriot, *mainmorte*) when he died. This was often a heavy payment and, in this respect at least, paralleled the relief paid by the vassal. In the case of the serf, the heriot might constitute his most precious chattel. The serf also paid a tithe to the church (unless the lord had appropriated this), one fourth of which was to go to the bishop, part to maintain the church building, part for the priest, and part for charity.

Though the serf complained about the heavy burden his lord laid upon him in taxes and prestations, and in his somber moments might have likened his status to that of a slave, he did possess important rights which furnished him a substantially higher status. He had the right to work the acres of his father (after paying the mortuary gift) and, in proportion to the extent of these acres, to share the use of the pasture lands, the commons, and the forest. The lord could not expel him from the manor or deprive him of his home. The serf had both the duty and privilege of attending the manorial court which settled disputes, property claims, and minor infractions of the peace and moral tranquillity of the village. If a senior member of the court, he would advise with others in matters that pertained to the well-being of the community.

He also had the right to marry, to raise a family, and to worship. And he ordinarily did no field work on Sundays and holydays.

While the manorial village population included men and women who were occupied with a variety of tasks—masons, cobblers, tailors, millers, smiths, food processers of all kinds—the larger part of its laborers spent their active lives working the land. Lack of agricultural knowledge and the inefficiency of agricultural methods, at least by modern standards, made such concentration inevitable. Two agricultural practices in particular, both basic to farming in the Middle Ages, explain the great demand for manpower and, at the same time, reveal the wastefulness of medieval techniques. These were the two- (three-) field and open-field systems of agriculture.

The medieval husbandman inherited the two-field system from his ancient ancestor. The system derives its name from the practice of dividing the arable soil into two fields which the farmer alternated in cropping. One year he would raise a crop from one of the two fields, while he permitted the other field to lie fallow, then the following year reverse the process. What prompted him to crop but half of his tillable soil in any one year was his knowledge that constant use of soil would deplete its fertility, and he knew of no practical means of correcting that situation short of the wasteful practice of fallowing half of his land. He was aware of the usefulness of animal fertilizer and marl, and even of the principle of crop rotation. Still, fertilizer existed in inadequate quantity, and he lacked sufficient legume crops to make rotation workable.

The three-field system which the medieval farmer introduced on a large scale in France, western Germany, and England, represented a distinctly more efficient method of handling the problem of soil depletion. In this case the tillable soil was divided into three fields. The farmer planted one of these fields in the spring, a second in the fall, while the third field he would leave fallow. The significant increase in food production realized under the three-field system was not its only advantage. Since the fallow field required at least two plowings to keep down the weeds, it meant that the farmer had less plowing to do under that system since the amount of ground left uncropped was smaller. The three-field system also made possible the planting of such spring crops as oats, peas, beans, and barley, which was not practical under the old system. The two-field system continued in use in those parts of

Europe where insufficient rainfall or the inadequacy of the soil made a shift to the three-field impractical.

As peculiarly medieval as the three-field system of agriculture was the open-field. The system has its name from the absence of fences on any of the great fields—two if the two-field system was followed, three if the other—into which the tillable soil of the manor was divided. The modern farmer ordinarily owns a compact farm of his own which he encloses with a fence or hedge. During the greater part of the Middle Ages individual compact farms were unknown. Instead the individual peasant (serf) had his land divided into small acre or half-acre strips which were scattered somewhat indiscriminately about the two (three) large fields. If the average holdings of a serf numbered thirty strips, he would have ten of these in each of the three fields. Partitioning of the land into such small strips made fencing impossible, whence the term open-field.

What circumstances led to this unusual division of the tillable soil into small strips is not clear. Few phases of medieval life are more obscure than that of agriculture. Alexander of Neckham, who supplies a variety of useful information in his *On the Nature of Things*, dismissed details concerning farming with the observation that those who knew the subject should tell about it. Apparently only the serf had any knowledge of agriculture, and he could not write. About the actual size of the strip there is little question. It was forty rods (furlong from furrow long) in length since that was presumably as far as oxen could pull a plow without stopping to rest. It was four rods in width which would then set off an acre. That amount represented a day's plowing. A plausible explanation for the use of strips is traced to the wish of the community that all its members have a fair share of the good and inferior soil. If this is true, it would tend to emphasize the character of the manorial village as a social unit here in the feudal age rather than one concerned with capitalistic advancement.

The medieval farmer contributed a solid chapter to the history of agricultural technology. If he did not introduce the heavy wheeled plow, he was the first to put it to extensive use. Such a plow was better suited to the heavy soil of north Italy and of west-central Europe, although quite unnecessary in the lighter soils of the ancient Mediterranean world. The heavier soil of western Europe also created a need for the harrow with which to break up the clods after plowing. The common draft animal on the medieval farm was the ox, although the horse came into extensive use in France, western Germany, and England. Until the tenth century, the horse had been a luxury reserved to the rich and for the battlefield. What had militated against its previous use was the manner the ancient world had harnessed the beast: the heavier the load the horse had to pull, the deeper would grow the pressure of the harness on the horse's windpipe. The introduction of the horse collar which rested on the horse's shoulders corrected this problem, while the use of the horseshoe further increased the horse's usefulness as a draft animal. The horse remained, nevertheless, an expensive animal. It required oats to supplement its hay, and when the beast grew too old to work, the peasant could not eat it as he did his ox. The great advantage of the horse was its speed. The less prosperous farmers stayed with their oxen in much the same way that poorer and more conservative farmers of the 1930s clung to their horses after their more venturesome neighbors had invested in tractors.

Most serfs had a garden plot to supplement the staples raised in the great open fields. There he and his wife might raise onions, cabbage, turnips, peas, and beans, as well as such strong-tasting herbs as sage, parsley, garlic, and mustard. These last substituted for the expensive spices that might grace the lord's table in the manor house but which he could not afford. Barring bad seasons, which might cause famine conditions to prevail over a wide area, the peasant had enough to eat, although the modern European would demand greater variety and succulency in his food. The peasant's principal dish was a gruel which his wife found went further than bread, although a dark bread of barley or rye was common. For meat he depended upon salt pork for much of the year, fowl for special occasions, and what game he might take by chance in the woods. Despite heavy penalties, poaching was common. The villager might be permitted to catch fish in the millpond or neighboring stream or purchase stockfish at the market. Eggs and cheese provided the bulk of his proteins. In warmer climes he raised grapes for wine, in colder countries hops and barley for beer, or he fermented honey and made mead.

The peasant built his own house, first putting up a frame consisting of heavy branches and posts, then filling in the walls with wattle and mud. In colder areas he might prefer a house of sod, but the roof in either case was thatched. Trodden earth served as a floor in what was usually a one-room dwelling. Doors and shutters provided for entrance and for light, and all were fixed tightly in place at night against intruders. The smoke from the hearth made its way out as best it could, usually through a hole cut toward the top near the gable, until the later Middle Ages when fireplaces and chimneys came into use. Furnishings, which were rough-hewn, included a plank table, benches, a chest which might hold the Sunday finery, and a bed of straw on the floor. The mistress of the house made all the clothes. They were of wool or linen and included a tunic, bound about the waist with a cord of leather, a cap, and long hose which the peasant turned into trousers. In the summer he went barefoot or used wooden clogs; in the winter he might wear shoes fashioned from leather. Night clothes and undergarments only came into use in the late Middle Ages.

Social life on the manor during the feudal period was secluded and provincial. Frequently only a trail connected it with a larger community, yet even this might not have anything more sophisticated to offer in the way of entertainment than additional taverns. Only the more venturesome would attempt to visit a distant city, although one is constantly amazed over the many thousands of people who undertook pilgrimages to far-off shrines. Should a fair be held within a distance of twenty or thirty miles, it would draw many of the curious in the village, as would the visit of an important dignitary to a neighboring city. The isolation of the village might be disturbed by the appearance of an occasional peddler, or a pilgrim, even traveling minstrels, jugglers, and entertainers with their trained bears and monkeys. Apart from these exceptional visitors the community depended principally on the many feast days in the liturgical calendar, including patron feasts, on weddings, and on funerals, to break the monotony of its existence.

The manor began to undergo significant change during the latter part of the feudal period. As this change progressed and grew more marked, it left the character of manorial organization and agriculture completely altered by the close of the Middle Ages. What happened, to express this change in the briefest terms, was the transformation of the manor from what had been fundamentally a social into an economic institution. The manor of the tenth century had been a self-contained unit, its economy one of sustenance, without outlets for its products, and dependent almost wholly upon its own efforts for the food and goods it required to exist. What the manor produced, it consumed, and what it did not raise, except for such items as salt and iron, it did without. The manor provided the villagers food and shelter; the villagers, in turn, furnished the lord with what he required to maintain himself in his station in feudal society. One might view the manor as a large family that sustained itself by its own efforts, almost completely cut off from the rest of the medieval population.

With the revival of trade and the rise of towns which began to affect the economic life of Europe in the tenth century, the manor's social and economic isolation began to crumble. The manor had geared its production, up to that time, to the satisfaction of its own needs. Any surplus crops simply rotted away or helped maintain the rat population. When townspeople appeared in the vicinity, however, who devoted their labor, not to the production of food but of wares, the villager suddenly found a market for his surplus products. He could now dispose of the extra grain he raised, of his wool and vegetables, of his bacon, butter, and cheese. For the first time in his life he began to sense a capitalistic urge. What could he not do, he wondered, were he to acquire more land and, above all, be able to spend all his time on his own acres.

The breakdown of the economic isolation of the manor affected the serf's lord in similar fashion. In the past the labor and ingenuity of the villagers had provided him what food, clothing, and supplies he needed. In the noncapitalistic feudal age that was all he expected; in fact, he could dream of nothing beyond that. The rise of towns changed his prospects as it had those of his serfs. He, too, could now anticipate realizing more than just a livelihood from his land. The manor had been a way of life for him; he would now make it a source of revenue. Many lords were, of course, not affected by these developments. This included those whose manors were too far removed from towns or who preferred to continue in the ways of their forebears.

But change was in the air. It became clearly apparent by the twelfth century, first in France, then in England, less so as one moved east of the Rhine. The lord of the manor began to commute the labor charge of his serfs to a money rent, to permit them to purchase their freedom from servile obligations, to hire farm hands to cultivate his demesne, even, in his lust for more gain, to enclose the commons for his own exploitation. The serf began to pay a rent, to exchange strips with his neighbors in order to have a compact farm, to buy more land when he could afford to do so, in short, to become a free farmer. The amount of arable soil meantime increased with the demand for more land. Forests were cut down and a frontier movement that spread northward and westward continued on to the close of the medieval period. Areas began to capitalize on certain advantages the quality of their soil or climate or location furnished them, by specializing in the cultivation of grapes or flax or wheat or in raising sheep.

These and other changes that transformed the agricultural patterns of western Europe covered many generations. In some countries they required more time than in others. In eastern Europe little was altered before early modern times. And, unfortunately, these changes took place only midst considerable travail as demonstrated by peasant revolts in Flanders, France, and England. By the end of the Middle Ages, however, the medieval manor had disappeared, and in most of the grain-producing regions of western Europe, the peasant was practicing a kind of agriculture that would persist without basic change to the nineteenth century.

When Ramón Lull described the duties of the three groups which composed medieval society, he wrote only of the clergy, the knightly class, and the peasantry. Had he taken a sharper look at the latter group, he might have identified as distinct from it a class whose economic and subsequent political importance earned it special consideration. This was the class of townspeople. They were commoners, of that no one had any doubt. Still, the gap which separated their way of living and their aspirations from those of the peasantry was just as broad and deep, in most instances, as that which divided the landed aristocracy from the people who worked their lands.

It is entirely possible that Ramón Lull was aware of this merchant group but preferred to ignore it. The Middle Ages in general felt uncomfortable about this new element which made its presence increasingly felt from the eleventh century onward. There was no place in medieval society for townspeople. They were not peasants even though they were commoners. Yet given the medieval habit of swearing by tradition and accepting a God-ordered and relatively unchanging universe, it seemed safest to treat them as the peasants their ancestors must surely have been. In time, and only with reluctance, western Europe came to accept these townspeople as something different and assigned them a separate status. The first to do so were kings who early discovered a means of tapping their money. The aristocracy hung back and so did the church. The aristocracy recognized the towns as the natural allies of the king against themselves. The church knew that the merchant brought with him from ancient times the reputation of dishonesty, a reputation many medieval merchants made no effort to correct. Even when honest, the merchant bought and sold for a profit,

which theologians condemned as sinful. And because writers viewed
the profession and its activities with distaste, they had little to say
about it, a fact which complicates the task of the economic historian
who wishes to discuss it.

It is customary to preface a consideration of towns and merchants
with a discussion of the revival of trade which began to affect the pattern of medieval economy in the late tenth century. That trade began
to revive at about that time is generally accepted, even though it is
no longer customary to view this revival as constituting a sharp break
with an exclusively agrarian economy which had prevailed during the
preceding centuries.* Present opinion holds that trade did not decline
so drastically from Roman times as scholars once believed, nor sink to
the point of disappearance. The West continued to import such commodities as spices, liturgical goods, papyri, and silk from the eastern
Mediterranean, even during the worst of Merovingian times. People
during those centuries also satisfied, to a degree, their need for such
basic items as iron and salt, while grain, wine, and dried fish undoubtedly moved along the rivers and coastal waters in the West.

Still there was so significant an increase in the volume of trade during
the latter half of the tenth century that historians commonly refer to
the development as the revival of trade. Because of the unobtrusive nature of the phenomenon and the lack of documentary evidence, scholars hesitate to assign a narrower period to this revival, nor are they
entirely positive in their explanations why this trade revival took place.
Certainly one factor must have been the rise in population which had
become apparent by the year 1000 A.D. and which was to continue until
1300. During those three centuries the population of western Europe
doubled and rose from approximately thirty million to twice that figure.

The impact of such an increase of population upon industry and
trade requires no elaboration, although what caused the increase itself
is not clear. In the absence of any more concrete factor, scholars suggest the relative stability of those centuries. Rollo and his Norsemen
had settled down in Normandy, Otto I had driven the Magyars back
to Hungary where they remained, while Basil I had expelled the Saracens from Italy (not Sicily). No doubt more young men and women
were marrying under promise of a future of peace, and of employment
as well, now that Europe could put its hand to repairing the dreadful
scars left by these barbarous invaders. More immediately linked with

* For a discussion of this matter and the Pirenne thesis, see above, p. 101.

THE MIDDLE AGES

the revival of trade was the success of the Normans and of Venice, Pisa, and Genoa in driving the Moslems and their ships completely out of Italy and Sicily and the waters in that part of the Mediterranean.

The fact that trade showed first evidences of revival in Italy lends credence to Pirenne's position that it was the Moslems who had destroyed the industrial life of the West with their seizure of the Mediterranean. With the ending of Islamic power in Italian waters in the eleventh century, trade could expect to flow again, and the first people to engage in it were the Italians, who had broken that power. From the beginning Venice took the lead and, as it proved, held that lead until the close of the Middle Ages. Few cities have had so colorful a history. Tradition has it that refugees from invading Huns, Goths, and Lombards fled to the barren islets upon which Venice rose, where they maintained themselves by peddling fish and the salt that they refined from sea water. From its very origins the community depended upon trade, and no nation in medieval times devoted itself more exclusively to its expansion. Venice's insular position also protected it from conquest by Charlemagne and later German invaders of north Italy, while her consequent isolation gave her no alternative but to develop connections with Constantinople and the Levant. In the ninth century she acquired the relics of St. Mark, which enhanced her attractiveness to pilgrims as a port of departure on their way to the Holy Land. In the eleventh century she received valuable trade concessions from Constantinople in return for assistance against the Normans.

Merchants from other Italian cities, from Bari, Taranto, Amalfi, Brindisi, Pisa, and Genoa, joined the Venetians in the eleventh century in establishing trade relations with the cities of the eastern Mediterranean. None of these eastern cities matched Constantinople in the volume and variety of commodities she made available to merchants. Beyond extensive industries of her own (see above, p. 150), Constantinople had direct trade routes which linked her with the markets of China, India, and the East. One of these crossed the Black Sea to the Sea of Azov, then overland to Sarai on the Volga, thence eastward to Turkestan and China. Another route crossed the Black Sea to Trebizond, and from there continued overland through Armenia and Persia to China and India. Antioch and Damascus offered Italian merchants ready access to the products of the Islamic world by way of the Euphrates to Baghdad—the Euphrates and Tigris connected by canal at Baghdad—and from there via the Persian Gulf to India. The Genoese dominated trade with Alexandria and Cairo in Egypt, where their ships could load cargoes containing most of the commodities available in Antioch, in addition to those that hailed from Arabia and east tropical Africa.

Whatever the origin of these commodities, whether from China, India, Arabia, or Africa, or even the factories of Constantinople, to the less culturally advanced Westerner they appeared strange and fascinating. They included silks, muslim (Mosul), damask (Damascus), brocades, tapestries, rugs, and carpets; glassware, mirrors, metalwork, precious stones, ivory, fragrant woods, and perfumes; figs, dates, almonds, apricots, rice, and sugar; and, above all, spices, cloves, pepper, ginger, drugs, and alum. Not only were most of these commodities exotic, they were expensive, so costly, indeed, that the masses in the West could only admire them at fairs, in shrines and cathedrals, or on the backs of great lords and ladies.

Because of the expensiveness of these Eastern commodities and the relative poverty of the West, the volume of Eastern imports remained low until the high and later Middle Ages when the rise of a prosperous bourgeoisie greatly expanded the demand. Another circumstance, beyond the high cost of Eastern commodities, which discouraged the expansion of this trade during the tenth and eleventh centuries was the difficulty the West experienced in creating an Eastern demand for its products. Some European products did move eastward—furs and hides, for instance, together with woolen and linen goods, iron, copper, tin, lead, pitch, tar, armor, wine, fish, honey, wax, and slaves—but never in sufficient quantity, because of the bulkiness of many of these exports and the high cost of transportation, to permit the development of a strong and natural flow of products east and west.

This trade in Eastern commodities, even though it did not reach sizable proportions until the high Middle Ages, did serve the function of a catalyst in shaking the West out of its economic lethargy and stimulating the growth of European industry and trade. For once these Eastern commodities had reached Italian ports, it was not long before ambitious merchants began carrying them northward through the Alpine passes to Austria, southern Germany, and the Rhineland country. There a series of rivers—the Rhine, Weser, Elbe, and Oder—were ready at hand to provide them cheap passage to the north and west, to the lands served by the Baltic, the North Sea, and the English Channel. Meantime merchants from Pisa and Genoa were shipping their goods to Marseilles and Narbonne, and up the Rhone River to east central France or by way of short portages to the Loire and Seine.

With the advent of these Eastern wares, industry and trade seemed suddenly to become alive all over western Europe. The Englishman found that people wanted his wool, the Scandinavian discovered he could sell his fish and iron, the Russian his furs, the Frenchman his wine, the German his grain and timber, the Spaniard his copper and lead. Other products of European origin began moving along the network of waterways with which that continent is blessed. These included butter, cheese, cabbage, onions, apples, beer, hops, pitch, tar, potash, soap, madder, woad, coal, salt, tin, amber, wax, honey, hawks, and feathers. Above all other European products in volume of trade were fish, grain, wine, timber, and wool.

A glance at these commodities will reveal a number of significant differences from those that came from Asia. They were inexpensive for the most part, yet possessed greater utility, in sharp contrast to the imports from China and India, which fell generally in the category of luxuries. Many of them, such as timber, wine, and even fish, commanded much space in shipment. Without the availability of cheap water transportation, they could not have moved in any volume. Some of these products, such as fish, grain, wine, and salt, for example, required no processing. Where processing was required, as in the case of wool, they encouraged the growth of industrial centers. Flanders, which enjoyed certain geographical and climatic advantages, developed into the world's leading textile-producing region. Florence later became an important textile center, Spain became famous for its leather, Montpellier for dyes, Dinant for copper, Nuremberg for wooden wares, and Sweden for its high-grade steel.

A description of the trade routes and waterways of the eleventh and twelfth centuries, of Oriental commodities and Western goods, and of industrial centers scattered over western Europe, invariably leaves the impression of a widespread and vigorously expanding industrial economy. Such was certainly not the case, nor would Europe approach that stage of industrial development before the nineteenth century. About all these early medieval centuries accomplished was to point the European economy in that direction. Several unfavorable circumstances, both physical and man-made, hampered the expansion of industry and commerce. Quite universal, for example, was the lack of roads and bridges, a fact which made travel slow and difficult. Because of their slow pace oxen were suited only for short distances, while the absence of roads discouraged the use of horses except as pack animals where the surer-footed mule was more popular. Where something approaching a road existed, two-wheeled carts came into extensive use. They actually remained the ordinary conveyance until the eighteenth century even though the four-wheeled wagon had appeared as early as the thirteenth century. England had the best highways, but there were occasions even in the fourteenth century when bad roads necessitated the postponement of parliament.

More satisfactory than land transportation was shipment by water although this also held its dangers. Light boats used shallow streams, heavier boats and heavily laden barges plied the deeper rivers. On the sea shipping usually stayed close to shore until the fourteenth century when the compass came into general use. Most ships were carvel-built, while galleys remained popular into the thirteenth century and later. They grew longer and roomier, however, reaching more than a hundred feet in length and having as many as three decks. Meantime a steady improvement in sails, masts, and spars, coupled with the introduction of fore-and-aft rigging, encouraged greater reliance on sails, which permitted more of the hold to be reserved for cargo. Greatest advance in sea-borne shipping waited for the thirteenth and later centuries, although what knowledge seamen acquired during the crusading twelfth century provided the basis for much of this later advance.

Man-made obstacles proved even more of a deterrent to the expansion of trade than did the lack of roads and bridges. Of these the most grievous were war and brigandage. War, even the threat of war, entailed a serious reduction, usually a total cessation, of trade. The presence of brigands forced merchants to make long detours in their travels. Even when no marauders were known to lurk in an area, merchants ordinarily traveled in groups with armed escort. Ocean travel was also unsafe. On the Atlantic there existed danger from pirates, in the Mediterranean from both pirates and Moslems. Ships generally moved in fleets and under convoy. Those carrying English wool to Flanders crossed over twice a year. So dangerous did the cities of north Germany find trading that they organized gilds, called hanses, to provide themselves protection. The absence of codes of maritime law discouraged trade as did the failure of countries to enact legislation to protect the foreign merchant and his cargo. There were instead such traditions as the law of wreck which permitted the local lord to seize any cargo that might remain after a passing ship had foundered.

Another obstacle to the flow of trade was the practice of levying tolls on a merchant's goods as he traveled through the country. Such a toll might be collected at a country's frontier, by each lord through whose land the merchant passed, or by the town where he stopped to dispose of his wares. In England royal power suppressed all but a few local tolls. Most numerous and annoying were those demanded in large sections of France and western Germany where royal authority did not extend. On the Loire the merchant might stop and pay a toll seventy times, on the Rhone sixty times, and on the Elbe thirty-five times. The prevalence of tolls in Germany prompted Thomas Wikes, an English traveler in the thirteenth century, to write of the "raving madness of the Germans." In England when the merchant paid a toll, he could expect some corresponding good, viz., improved road conditions. On the Continent the right to collect a toll generally represented a simple privilege.

A commercial institution that appeared with the revival of trade and which was uniquely medieval was the fair. For its origins one might go back as early as the fifth century, although the fair had scarcely developed into an institution with regular meetings, laws, and traditions before the twelfth. Most fairs evolved from a village or town market which by some happy circumstance, usually its accessibility, began to attract merchants and goods from distant provinces and countries. When this happened the king or local lord might grant a special charter and declare it a fair. Fairs were especially popular and useful in the twelfth and thirteenth centuries when they served as the principal emporia for commodities from distant provinces and countries. The most prosperous fairs were located in the county of Champagne in northeastern France where rivers and roads converged to bring together goods from all over Europe. At such fairs one could also expect to find spices, silks, and other precious goods from the Orient. The rise of large cities in the later Middle Ages deprived the fair of its unique role in European trade and it slowly disappeared. Yet Daniel Defoe could still acclaim that of Stourbridge in the late eighteenth century as the greatest in the world, while several of the German fairs, as at Dresden and Nuremberg, have had a continuous history up to the present.

Almost as uniquely medieval as the fair was the town, as historians use the term. They define the town, as opposed to a village of peasants, as a populated place where many residents engaged in industry and trade. Towns appeared with the revival of trade. While a few, called "new towns" (ville neuve) were towns from birth, the majority developed from villages whose favorable location from point of view of trade had bred or attracted craftsmen. The names of many towns reveal the reason why people came to live there in the first place. If the reason was protection, and this was a common one in the tenth, eleventh, and twelfth centuries, the root *burg* (*bourg*, borough) might appear in its name: *viz.*, Hamburg, Strasbourg, Peterborough. Some towns grew up near cathedrals because of the protection or employment such large institutions might offer. Whatever the circumstances, if a site were to develop into a town, it must possess commercial advantages, which explains why towns so frequently appeared near bridges (Bruges, Cambridge). Should an industry establish itself in a particular area such as did the manufacture of textiles in Flanders, towns (Ypres, Ghent, Arras, Bruges, Saint-Omer) would spring up in considerable number. The "new town" owed its origin to the ambition of a king or lord who offered inducements of freedom and other privileges to attract peasants and craftsmen to live in his domain. Dresden, Berlin, and Lübeck started out as "new towns."

As villages grew into towns and the number of smiths, bakers, butchers, tailors, and other men engaged in nonagricultural occupations multiplied, so did the dissatisfaction of the people grow over their condition. In the eyes of their lord they still remained serfs. They did not work his land (*corvée*) as did the traditional serf, but the lord continued to exact certain prestations, he restricted their movement, and he imposed tolls on their market. All these actions of the lord betokened their servile status, a condition they found intolerable. The townspeople of such Italian cities as Milan and Lucca, where the position of the local lords was often insecure, did not wait for time and reason to improve their lot. They rebelled, proclaimed their independence, and, because of their ability to exploit the conflict between papacy and Holy Roman emperor, were generally able to maintain their freedom. Other towns in northern France and Flanders fared less successfully in their bid for freedom since the king of France proved himself a more formidable lord to defy than the king of Germany.

The movement among townspeople took a more peaceful course for freedom in England and in those countries where the power of the lord was too mighty to be challenged. The usual procedure was for the leading citizens, ordinarily the merchants, to take the initiative in seeking an improvement in their status. They would present the lord their requests, which included the right to regulate their market, the privilege of selecting their town magistrates, and the liberty to come and go as freemen. If their lord needed money, they would encounter little difficulty reaching a settlement since they were willing to pay well for a charter. Should the lord be a monastery or a proud and prosperous nobleman who had no sympathy for commoners anxious to rise above their appointed station, they would be denied. Kings generally sympathized with townspeople since they could count on their loyalty and since the growth of towns meant more trade and, therefore, more taxes for their coffers.

A fairly constant provision in the charter which the lord would grant his townspeople was one authorizing them to maintain a merchant gild. These were trade associations which the leading merchants in the community would organize for the purpose of providing its members protection and promoting their common interests. Few gilds appeared earlier than 1000 A.D., although by the twelfth century they were common throughout western Europe. The earliest gilds may have sprung from religious or fraternal associations, which would have given them an origin not greatly different from the ancient Roman colleges (see above, p. 36). No doubt the need of merchants to travel in groups when visiting other towns on business encouraged the kind of cooperation which led to the formation of these gilds. As the number of merchants grew, those engaged in a particular trade might organize their own craft gild, a rather natural step since men engaged in the same occupation often lived on the same street. The names of some streets in European cities—Hutmacher Strasse, Rue de Drapiers, Ironmongers Lane—reveal the presence of such groups in the Middle Ages.

The principal objective which motivated the merchants of a town to seek a charter was to secure the exclusive right to buy and sell, unburdened by the lord's imposts and secure from the intrusion of foreign merchants. Theirs was to be a tight monopoly over the trading in the community. They would permit local peasants to bring their farm produce, their eggs, butter, and poultry into town and offer them for sale, since these did not compete with their own merchandise. Foreign merchants, however, if permitted to do business, must pay a fee.

This rule concerning foreign merchants eliminated competition from without the gild. Within the association a similar hostility toward competition prevailed. Members of the same craft gild were all members of one economic family and they must treat each other accordingly. All were to pay the same price for their raw materials, the same wages to their journeymen, they were to keep their shops open the same length of time, and they all sold their wares at the same price. They were not to advertise their goods since this might do injury to a fellow gildsman. One of the Rules of Saint-Omer forbade a merchant to greet passers-by, even to blow his nose in order to arouse attention. (The tradition that physicians and dentists do not advertise their skills is a legacy from the medieval gild.) Should a member of the gild propose to adopt a new style of shoes, for instance, he must secure the approval of the gild. Should an ingenious gildsman hit upon a labor-saving device, the gild might authorize its use if all members could afford to introduce it, as the gild of weavers in Speyer decided to do in 1297 in the case of the spinning wheel.

The gild undertook the training of its own craftsmen. In the Middle Ages it was the rule, less a tradition today, for a son to follow the trade of his father. The boy learned this trade, however, as an apprentice in the household of another gildsman, a master gildsman. Usually at the age of twelve he would go to live with the master, remain with him for five years in France, a year or two longer in England, during which time the master would teach him his trade, while at the same time providing him with "suitable clothing, shoeing, board, bedding, and chastisement," much as any father might do for his son.

At about the age of nineteen, the youth would rise to the status of journeyman (journée–day) and work as a day laborer in the shop of some master. If he proved ambitious, was successful in amassing the necessary capital, and was able to convince the gild supervisors, by means of a masterpiece, that he was a master at his trade, they might authorize him to open a shop of his own—provided the gild felt the community could use another shop. During the eleventh and twelfth centuries this might not be difficult. Town populations were growing and masters had not yet discovered how profitable they could make their positions if they restricted the number of gildsmen holding that status. For the moment the gild was happy to subscribe to the general philosophy of the Middle Ages that a properly ordered institution in a stable economic world was most conducive to peace and tranquillity.

For the sake of this tranquillity, the members of the gild bound themselves to sell their wares at a "just price." This was a price which other merchants, even the townspeople and theologians, would consider just. For despite the monopoly the gild might in theory have exploited, what determined the price of a commodity, such as a pair of shoes, was not the particular preference of the gildsmen but the cost of the leather and thread, the labor involved in the production of the shoes, and other cost items that the modern entrepreneur would classify as overhead. There the price stopped. It did not advance beyond the point which would have permitted the gildsman to make a "profit" on his investment. Had he charged more than this "just price," this would have disturbed the economic equilibrium of the small economic family of which he was a member. Had the cobblers charged more than they needed to maintain themselves in their place in society, the medieval economist would have argued, and with some validity, that the townspeople would have had less money to spend for clothes, meat, and other necessities. The cobblers' "profit" would, consequently, cause other merchants to suffer. So Thomas Aquinas was simply expressing the views of most medieval theologians and economists when he announced: "Trade is rendered lawful when one seeks a moderate gain in trading for the sustenance of his own household . . . and when he seeks gain, therefore, not as an end but as the reward of his labor."

That Thomas cautioned his readers by implication against the sin of seeking profit makes it evident that merchants were charging more than a "just price" in his day. This suggests that by the thirteenth century the noncapitalistic character and philosophy of the gild had begun to decay. Until the rise of capitalism the gild had resembled the early manor. Although both institutions were economic in their concern with the production of food, clothing, and similar necessities, they were organized for home consumption only. They were nonprofit-minded largely because of the "family" nature of the communities they served. We have seen that the revival of trade and the rise of towns eventually caused the manor to lose its noncapitalistic character. One would scarcely say that this same revival transformed the gild, since until trade had revived, there had existed no towns nor gilds. Yet when trade did revive to a point of destroying the relative isolation of towns, it exerted the same influence upon gilds as it had upon the manor. Gilds in many towns began to expand their activities in order to serve (exploit) the needs of people in other towns and outlying provinces. This opportunity to extend their activities into areas where the "just price" lacked its social rationale, had the effect of gradually transforming the gild into a capitalistic institution.

With the rise of capitalism another development took place within the organization of the gild itself which was equally destructive of its original "family" structure. As long as the gilds of a town limited their sales to the home community, the opportunity to make profits was minimal. For this reason, as the population of a town grew, the gild masters authorized journeymen to open new shops whenever the demand so warranted. Once a capitalistic philosophy invaded the gild and the gilds sought markets in other communities, however, masters quickly realized the advantages of their position and sought to exploit it. They began to limit the number of masters by raising the initiation costs and by requiring expensive robes of new masters, and they restricted promotion to their level to their own sons and friends. Within a brief period such policies had changed the "family" atmosphere of the gild to one of bitterness, as ambitious journeymen without the proper connections found no room for themselves at the top. Instead of the general tranquillity of the early gild, riots, strikes, and other forms of industrial strife mar their history in the late Middle Ages.

The rise of capitalism did not occasion difficulties for all gilds. Where the product was such as to demand highly skilled laborers, or where the gild continued to serve only a local market, it managed to adjust with a minimum of trouble. The gilds which suffered most dislocation under the impact of capitalism included those that produced goods which were in general demand, whose production required only modest skills, and whose nature lent itself to shipment to distant towns and countries. The textile industry was one of these, and it is significant that most industrial strife in the late Middle Ages centered in the textile-producing areas of Flanders and northern Italy. A word of comfort for those readers who resent the "selfishness" of the gild masters in destroying the "family" fabric of the gild: as trade and industry expanded and came to require greater investments of capital, financiers and bankers such as the Medici gained control. Their operations might become enormous and extend all the way from purchasing the raw wool, to arranging for its processing into cloth, then to the distribution of this cloth to the markets of the world. Before so broad an organization of his industry, the local master found himself helpless. From his once proud, independent position he now slipped to depending upon others for his orders. He was still more fortunate than his journeymen, however, who became members of the proletariat.

Of all the factors which contributed to the destruction of the non-capitalistic character of the manor and gild, none was more influential than the Crusades. To these we shall now turn our attention.

CHAPTER 8

The High Middle Ages—
Political History

THE CRUSADES

The occasion was one of the most memorable in the history of the Middle Ages. It was the year of our Lord 1095. Pope Urban II had come to Clermont in Auvergne (east-central France) to address a large gathering of French bishops and princes on "the imminent peril which threatens you and all the faithful [and] which has brought us hither.

"From the confines of Jerusalem and from the city of Constantinople a grievous report has gone forth . . . that a race from the kingdom of the Persians, an accursed race, a race wholly alienated from God . . . has violently invaded the lands of those Christians and has depopulated them by pillage and fire. They have led away a part of the captives into their own country, and a part they have killed by cruel tortures. They have either destroyed the churches of God or appropriated them for the rites of their own religion. . . . The kingdom of the Greeks is now dismembered by them and has been deprived of territory so vast in extent that it could not be traversed in two months' time."

The great peril which faced the Byzantine empire and, should that fall, then western Europe itself, was the first critical consideration the pope emphasized. The other, which he pressed with greater eloquence as the one more likely to sway his audience, concerned Jerusalem and the holy places. These last were in the hands of the Infidel, who "treated them with ignominy and irreverently polluted with the filth of the unclean." As for Jerusalem, it was "now held captive by the enemies of Christ and is subjected by those who do not know God to the worship of the heathen." In order to arouse the Frankish knights in his audience he appealed to their pride in the valiant deeds of their ancestors, of "King Charlemagne and his son Louis," who had fought the Infidel and had "extended the sway of holy Church over lands previously pagan." This was their opportunity to emulate the deeds of their forebears and to prove that they were a "race beloved and chosen by God" by reconquering these territories from the Infidel. And he assured his listeners that by their efforts they would conquer for themselves a glorious land that "floweth in milk and honey," win forgiveness for their sins, and "the assurance of the reward of imperishable glory in the kingdom of heaven."

A year after Pope Urban made his address, the First Crusade was under way. Two circumstances that prompted it had drawn Urban's principal attention. The first concerned the rise of the Seljuk Turks. These people had moved out of Turkestan late in the tenth century under the chieftain who gave them their name. For a time they were content to serve Persian princes as mercenaries, but in 1055 they seized Baghdad whose helpless caliph bestowed upon their leader the title sultan (one with authority). Under Alp Arslan they moved west into Armenia and at Manzikert in 1071 annihilated the Byzantine army. What cost Emperor Romanus the victory he should have won was the desertion of his Turkish mercenaries and his blundering into the same kind of trap which Asiatic armies had set before. This tactic had the troops falling back in order to simulate flight, then regroup and envelop the enemy when it broke rank in its eagerness to exploit its "victory."

As a result of the disaster at Manzikert, almost the whole of Anatolia fell to the Turks, who set up their capital at Nicaea, hardly fifty miles from Constantinople. Alexius Comnenus, who came to the throne in 1081, managed by nothing short of a miracle to save the crumbling Byzantine empire. He bought off the barbarous enemies along the Danube or set them to fighting one another, confiscated church revenues to organize a new army, and then sent an appeal to Pope Urban for western mercenaries. It was this request of Alexius' that had led to the council at Clermont.

Beyond this first objective of shoring up the faltering Byzantine empire, Pope Urban had stressed as the second objective of a crusade the liberation of Jerusalem and the holy places which were in Moslem hands. To what extent the Moslems had desecrated the holy places as Urban charged or interfered with pilgrims on their way to and from the shrines, is difficult to ascertain. One thing is certain, however, and this point deserves some emphasis since the modern world is not

given to making pilgrimages, namely, the large number of pious men
and women who made the long trip to Jerusalem. The practice of
making this pilgrimage to Jerusalem started back in the days of Constantine, who had restored the holy places and had erected several
large churches in the city. With the rise of Islam, the flow of pilgrims
was halted, but not for long. Moslem merchants and innkeepers early
learned how much revenue these pilgrims brought them, so local authorities generally adopted a policy of benevolent tolerance. In the
late tenth century Italian ships began taking pilgrims directly to Moslem ports, while those who preferred to travel by land followed a satisfactory route through the Balkans, Anatolia, and Syria. Members of
all classes, including the aristocracy, assumed the garb of the pilgrim
and journeyed to Jerusalem. Some went to do penance for grave
crimes, as did Fulk Nerra of Anjou who was obliged by his confessor
on three different occasions to make the trip. By the eleventh century
thousands of pilgrims were making their way to Jerusalem. We read
of one pilgrimage from Germany in 1064–1065 which is said to have
numbered more than ten thousand persons. This appears an exaggerated figure, but there is no question that the emotions aroused over
the holy places and the mistreatment of pilgrims represented the most
effective weapon preachers employed to recruit crusaders. Peter the
Hermit, the most eloquent of these preachers, had himself been roughly
handled by the Moslems and turned back.

A few other considerations deserve mention in a background discussion of the First Crusade. Some scholars view the Crusades as an
expression of Western imperialism. Islam was on the defensive; it had
now come the turn of the Christian West to go on the offensive. Fief-
hungry nobles from France already for some years had been crossing
the Pyrenees to help the Spanish drive back the Moslem. In the middle
Mediterranean aggressive Normans and ambitious Italian cities had
expelled them from the area and had even wrested a foothold at
Mahdia in Tunis. Now Italian cities together with Western knights like
Bohémond who had been disinherited by his father, were looking to
Syria for trade concessions and estates.

Pope Urban may have harbored other motives beyond the deliverance of Jerusalem and bringing aid to Constantinople when urging a
crusade on the West. Surely the departure of thousands of warriors to
Syria would effect a significant reduction in feudal warfare in Europe.
"Let those who have formerly been accustomed to contend wickedly
in private warfare against the faithful," Urban admonished them, "now

fight against the infidel. . . . Let those who have formerly contended against their brothers and relatives now fight against the barbarians as they ought." Finally, a crusade undertaken under papal leadership would strengthen Urban's position in his struggle with Henry IV of Germany. (See above, p. 226.)

So much did Pope Urban and preachers like Peter the Hermit and Walter the Penniless fire western Europe with their talk of a crusade that several months before the First Crusade got under way, a motley army of some forty thousand disorganized peasants, a scattering of knights, some women, and children, started out early in the summer of 1096 for Constantinople. This was the Peasant Crusade. So many were coming that Constantinople was worried. Anna Comnena, daughter of Alexius, wrote how disturbed the city was over all the barbarian tribes of the West that were moving in a body to Asia. Zeal these peasants had in excess, but no plan or organization. Because they lived off the countryside, continuous clashes with the native populations marked their march through the Balkans. On one occasion they slew four thousand Hungarians, then suffered that many casualties at the hands of the governor of Bulgaria. Although Alexius was disturbed over their numbers and their lack of usefulness when they reached Constantinople, he advised them to wait for the main crusading army, but they refused. All but a few thousand of those who crossed over to Asia Minor were slaughtered by the Turks. These few were rescued by Alexius' troops. Other peasant groups marched eastward from Germany, murdered many Jews on the way, and were themselves decimated by the Hungarians.

The different leaders of the regular crusade started moving eastward with their armies of knights in the late summer and fall of 1096. They included Godfrey of Bouillon, duke of Lower Lorraine, and his brother Baldwin. Baldwin had his wife and children with him since he planned to make his home in the East. Bohémond led an army from Norman Italy, Raymond of Toulouse a host from southern France. Robert, duke of Normandy, Stephen, count of Blois, and Robert, count of Flanders, led contingents of knights from northern France and Germany. Urban did not appoint a commander-in-chief, although he entrusted the spiritual guidance of the army to Adhemar, bishop of Le Puy. Altogether the crusaders may have numbered as many as one hundred thousand men, a truly formidable army for those times. Even though the main bodies of knights reached Constantinople at different intervals and Alexius had an opportunity to deal with their leaders individually, it required all his diplomacy and a lavish distribution of gifts to induce them to recognize his overlordship for any territories they might seize from the Moslems. Alexius had wanted mercenaries, and he was most uneasy about all these bold knights and their arrogant leaders. But once the army crossed over to Asia and headed south through Anatolia, he could breathe easy in the thought that his Constantinople was now at last secure from the Turks.

The crusade started auspiciously. Nicaea, the capital of the sultanate of Roum, fell to the crusaders and was immediately occupied by Alexius. As the army turned southward, it split into two groups in order the better to cope with the critical problems of food and water in that semiarid region. At Dorylaeum the sultan of Roum attacked the army under Bohémond and might have ended the crusade at that point had not the other army come up in time to rout the Turks. This opened the way to Antioch, although extremely difficult terrain immediately ahead slowed the crusaders and caused them to lose most of their horses and baggage. Still, Turkish power had suffered a serious blow, which Alexius exploited by reconquering parts of Anatolia, while Baldwin led an expedition to Edessa where the Armenians helped place him in command.

The key to the success of the First Crusade was Antioch. This was the largest city in western Asia and the best fortified city the crusaders ever attacked. So it surely appeared to them in the fall of 1097 after they had spent several hopeless months before its powerful fortifications. Their suffering from lack of food and water was intense, while discouragement sharpened the bitterness among their leaders. One of these, Stephen of Blois, took his knights with him and returned to France, where his mortified wife ordered him back. (He returned with another group in 1101.) Even Peter the Hermit despaired and attempted escape before it was too late. And news from the outside was all bad. The army that Alexius was bringing to relieve them had turned back when Stephen reported the hopelessness of the situation. Instead of relief for them, reports had it that the sultan of Mosul was bringing up a huge army to relieve the defenders in the city. Meantime Bohémond, who had his heart set on keeping the city for himself, had contacted a former Christian captain inside the city, who offered to betray his part of the wall. So after Bohémond had secured a promise from the other leaders to let that one have the city who first entered it, the traitorous captain did his part, Bohémond and his soldiers stole inside the walls, and shortly after the city was in Christian hands.

Barely were the crusaders inside the city than the army from Mosul moved in and the Christians now assumed the role of the besieged. Again Bohémond proved his sagacity. He managed to persuade the other leaders that their only hope lay in attacking the larger Turkish force outside the walls, which they did and successfully. With the rout of the Turkish army the success of the crusade was assured. The invincibility of the "Franks," which had been established at Dorylaeum, had now been confirmed. Many cities opened their gates, the garrisons of others took to flight, and several emirs came forward and bought their neutrality. Still the crusade was losing its momentum. Only Raymond of Toulouse with an army of five thousand foot soldiers and one hundred knights left Antioch in January 1099 for the final leg of the journey to Jerusalem.

Meantime the Fatimid rulers in Egypt who had seized Palestine and taken Jerusalem from its Turkish commander offered the Christians free access to the holy places if they remained where they were in Syria. The Christians refused—they could hardly have done otherwise now that they had come so far. Furthermore, their cause was again looking up as Bohémond and other stragglers from Antioch joined them to swell their numbers to about twelve thousand foot soldiers and thirteen hundred knights. With this army they invested Jerusalem on June 7. Nevertheless, the prospects looked bleak. Water was hard to find since the Turks had poisoned the wells, while the blistering summer heat made the walls of Jerusalem appear positively impregnable. But the crusaders remained and set to work constructing siege equipment—mangonels, movable towers, ladders—no easy task in the treeless country in which they found themselves.

When the situation continued hopeless, a "council was held, and the bishops and princes ordered that all should march around the walls of the city with feet bare, in order that He who entered it humbly in our behalf might be moved by our humility to open it to us and to exercise judgment upon His enemies." After the procession, the crusaders gathered on the Mount of Olives where Peter the Hermit, back again in good graces, delivered a moving address. Five days later, on the night of July 13–14, the Christians attacked from their movable towers and in the morning entered and captured the city. In their frenzied exhilaration the crusaders showed no mercy but massacred all the Jews and Moslems they could find. Some ten thousand of them, according to one chronicler, were beheaded in Solomon's Temple alone, and "had you been there, your feet would have been stained up to the ankles with the blood of the slain." (Another chronicler described the blood of the victims here in the temple so deep that it reached the bridle reins of the horsemen who did the slaughtering!) When the crusaders learned of the large army that the vizier of Egypt was bringing up, they decided their best hope lay in attacking it by surprise, which they did. The annihilation of this Egyptian army assured the permanent success of the First Crusade.

During the course of the crusade, Western leaders committed many errors, although none so great as the manner in which they disposed of the territories they conquered from the Turks and Fatimids. At Constantinople they had agreed to hold what territories they might conquer in the name of the Byzantine emperor. And they had not objected when Alexius took over Nicaea. As they moved farther away from Constantinople, however, particularly following Alexius' failure to relieve them in their desperate straits before Antioch, the feeling grew general that the emperor had forfeited any hold he might have had over them. What lands they might seize they would keep for themselves. So they set up four states from the land they conquered. These included the County of Tripoli, the County of Edessa, the Principality of Antioch, and the Kingdom of Jerusalem. All four were held independently of the Byzantine emperor. The result was a deepening of the suspicion that had already existed between the emperor and the crusaders, which in turn sharply reduced the potential success of subsequent crusades.

This friction between Constantinople and the crusaders contributed to the dismal failure of the Second Crusade. What prompted this crusade was the fall of Edessa to the Turks in 1144 and the threat which resurgent Turkish power held for the other Christian states to the south. Pope Eugenius took the lead in arousing Europe and prevailed upon St. Bernard, which was not easy, to preach the crusade. Bernard, who objected to the use of force, even against heretics, to bring men to the belief of the Christian God, must have gone through much soul-searching before agreeing to the assignment. And the failure of the crusade may have convinced him that he was right in the first place to oppose the idea. Two kings, Louis VII of France and Conrad III of Germany, hearkened to Bernard's eloquence. Only a saint like Bernard, so Conrad declared, could have persuaded him to go. He, too, must have had afterthoughts. The armies moved separately over the route followed by the First Crusade. At Dorylaeum the Turks mauled Conrad's army so severely that it ceased being an effective force. Conrad and what was left of his army joined Louis, then moved down to Attalia where the two kings took ship to Antioch. The ships that the Byzantine emperor Manuel should have supplied to ferry the army across never showed up, so the Turks cut them to pieces.

Western writers blame the perfidy of Byzantium for the failure of this crusade, although Manuel could argue that the crusaders were interested only in their own states; that open assistance would involve him with his Turkish neighbors; furthermore, that the Christian Normans were planning an attack on his own territories in Greece. A last desperate and foolhardy attack on Damascus by remnants of the crusading army and local Christian knights failed with heavy losses. The only positive consequence of the Second Crusade came over in Portugal. There a fleet of crusaders from England, the Low Countries, Germany, and Scandinavia stopped to assist a local Christian count to capture Lisbon and lay the foundations of modern Portugal.

The Third Crusade (1189–1192) was the Christian West's response to the fall of Jerusalem. The man responsible for the new threat in the East was Saladin, vizier of Egypt, who had overrun Syria after annihilating a crusading army at Hattin in July 1186. Jerusalem fell to him a year later. This crusade is the best known of the seven or more major expeditions which the West fitted out to take or hold Jerusalem, thanks to the presence of Saladin, three European kings who took part, and the manner Sir Walter Scott and other writers have woven the subject with romance. Frederick Barbarossa, king of Germany and Holy Roman emperor, led an army from Germany along the old pilgrim road through the Balkans. Richard the Lion-Hearted, king of England, and Philip Augustus, king of France, took ship directly to Acre. Religious motives may have warmed Frederick's soul. Philip Augustus went because it was the proper thing to do, while Richard hoped for military glory. Saladin was most concerned about the powerful army Frederick was bringing through Anatolia, and well he might. Had Frederick reached Syria, the Third Crusade would in all probability have gone down in history as the most successful of the crusades. But Frederick was drowned while crossing the Seleph River in Asia Minor, and only a portion of his forces ever reached Acre. There the two constantly quarreling kings, Philip and Richard, scored their greatest success when they captured the city in July 1191. Philip returned to France shortly after, and although Richard defeated Saladin on several occasions, he lacked the manpower and siege equipment to take Jerusalem. So the two finally drew up a treaty which reconstituted part of the kingdom of Jerusalem and permitted Christian pilgrims free access to the city.

The Fourth Crusade (1202–1204), which followed ten years after the Third, was the work of Pope Innocent III. No kings responded to his appeal. Richard and Philip were busily fighting over Normandy, while Germany had no king at all. Still, a good many knights indicated their willingness to take up the cross, and Innocent's hopes were high. According to plans, the crusaders were to gather in Venice, which had contracted to transport them to Egypt. Unfortunately, many knights took ship at other Italian ports, and only a third of the expected thirty-five thousand men showed up at Venice. These, Venice refused to transport to the East until the full eighty-five thousand marks which had been promised were delivered. So the crusaders and Venetians argued and haggled. Finally, it was agreed that in return for the crusaders' assistance in capturing Zara, which belonged to the Christian king of Hungary, Venice would advance the necessary credit. After a few days of fighting, the crusaders and Venetians captured and pillaged Zara, much to the indignation of Pope Innocent, who excommunicated them all when he learned of it.

Meantime Alexius, son of the deposed Byzantine emperor, had been attempting to convince the crusaders that they should help him and his father to get back in control in Constantinople. He would contribute a huge amount of money to the cause, an army of ten thousand men, even heal the schism, if they would help him. Some of the crusaders refused to consider the offer and left directly for Syria. But the majority accepted Alexius' proposal, stormed Constantinople, and restored his father to his throne. Then during the winter months while the crusaders waited for spring before proceeding on to Syria, a revolt took place in the city, Alexius was strangled (his father had died), and a new emperor acclaimed. This provided the Venetians their opportunity. Under their prodding the crusaders attacked the city a second time, captured it, then for three days subjected it to one of the most savage lootings in the history of warfare. Pope Innocent, who was not wholly disappointed over the miscarriage of the crusade since the schism was now ended, accepted the new Latin empire as a papal fief and set about organizing a new expedition.

Before this Fifth Crusade materialized, the strange, tragic episode of the Children's Crusade intervened. During the summer of 1212 a shepherd boy by the name of Stephen came to Philip Augustus with a letter he claimed he had received from Christ. According to the letter

Stephen was to lead a crusade of children to Syria, that God would show his favor by opening up the Mediterranean and provide them dry passage to Jerusalem. Philip told the boy to go back to his sheep, but he refused, stayed on and preached. Within a few weeks many thousands of children, perhaps as many as thirty thousand, most of them twelve years old and younger, had gathered at Vendôme. From there they trudged southward to Marseilles with Stephen riding along in his cart. When the sea did not open up, a fortunate few managed to make their way back home. The majority crowded into seven vessels and ended up in the slave markets of Islam. A similar movement in Germany, this one headed by a Nicholas, recruited somewhat older children, including a sprinkling of what the modern world might classify as juvenile delinquents. This group made its way to Genoa and Pisa, but again the sea refused to open up. Some of the youths stayed and made their home in Italy. Two shiploads of them left port and were never heard from again. A few made it back to Germany where irate parents hanged the father of Nicholas for having permitted his son to dupe their young ones.

Two years after Pope Innocent's death, the Fifth Crusade (1218–1221) began its equally futile course. The Fourth had planned to land in Egypt; this one did, and during the summer months of 1218 a powerful host gathered there recruited from many countries of Europe and from Acre as well. Egypt was in a weakened condition, and its sultan was old and tired. Had the crusading army possessed one capable leader in place of the half-dozen who aspired to that position, the crusaders might have been able to conquer the delta region and Cairo. But "sane counsel," as the chronicler wrote, "was far removed from our leaders," which was especially true of the papal legate Pelagius who usually had his way. They did occupy Damietta, which the sultan did not attempt to hold, but they turned down his offer of Jerusalem in return for their evacuating his country. Without the surrounding fortresses, the Templars and others argued, Jerusalem could never be held. In July 1221 an army of some fifty thousand men advanced up the Nile despite a warning that the river, which was nearing flood stage, would imperil their retreat should this become necessary. Within a few days the crusaders found themselves completely cut off by the Nile and the Egyptian fleet. The humane sultan agreed to let them go home.

Many people, including the pope, placed the onus for the failure of this crusade on Frederick II of Germany, who had kept promising to join the army in Egypt. In 1227 Frederick was finally ready to go, and in September an army of some forty thousand men embarked with him from Brindisi. Dysentery had already caused many of the knights who had gathered at Brindisi to succumb, so when Frederick became ill, he promptly turned back and retired to a spa to recuperate. When Pope Gregory IX, who had good reason to mistrust Frederick, learned of his action, he excommunicated him for again reneging on his promise. In 1228 Frederick did finally go, regardless of his excommunicate condition, less as a crusader, however, than as a claimant to the kingdom of Jerusalem through its heiress whom he had married. One of the reasons he had delayed going up to this time had been to permit negotiations to mature which he was conducting with the sultan of Egypt. The sultan had an admiration for Frederick and had also need for Frederick's alliance against the sultan of Damascus. So he promised him Jerusalem and other cities, but then the sultan of Damascus died, and Frederick found his bargaining value reduced to zero. However, the sultan agreed to honor part of his promise—had he done more his subjects would have overthrown him—and by the Treaty of Jaffa (1229) turned over Jerusalem and Bethlehem together with a corridor to the sea. Moslems were to retain free access to their shrines in Jerusalem.

Christians retained control of Jerusalem until 1244 when the Khwarizmian Turks, in alliance with Egypt, captured the city. The fall of Jerusalem prompted Louis IX of France to undertake what proved the last major crusade (1248–1254). He landed a powerful army in Egypt, but there suffered the same fate that had ended the Fifth Crusade. Since the resources of the entire eastern Mediterranean had been drawn upon to the point of exhaustion to fit out this expedition, its destruction constituted a near-fatal blow to the Christian position in Syria. For four years after his release as a prisoner of the sultan of Egypt, Louis remained in the East in order to reorganize the defenses of what remained of Christian territories, even though there was desperate need for him back in France. In 1270 Louis undertook a second crusade which his Machiavellian brother, Charles of Anjou, persuaded him to lead against Tunis, rather than Syria (or Egypt), because of his interests in the area. Louis and a large part of his army died in Tunis of dysentery. In 1291 Acre and what remained of the crusading states fell to the Turks, although Cyprus remained in Western hands until the latter half of the sixteenth century.

Louis' death marked the close of the crusading era. Popes, even kings, continued to talk of crusades, and Edward I led a small army to Syria in 1271. He stayed long enough to convince himself that further crusading efforts were useless under the circumstances, and returned. One circumstance that particularly shocked Edward was the manner the Venetians and Genoese were shipping to the Moslems the very materials they needed to fight the crusaders. For these Venetians and Genoese the crusade had long ago lost its religious character, if it had ever had one for them. The most serious circumstance that doomed the crusade was the small response papal appeals were evoking. Louis had managed to organize a strong army but solely on the weight of his authority and prestige. Edward could induce only a thousand men to accompany him. Knights were no longer ready to mortgage their estates and their future in a cause that looked hopeless. And who could blame them! The long history of crusading failures left the prospect of victory increasingly bleak, while it even raised the question in men's minds whether God was pleased with such expeditions. Less than a hundred years after Louis' death, Moslem Turks crossed over into the Balkans, after which there was no further talk of taking Jerusalem. From then on crusades were preached and organized to stem the spread of Islam in southeastern Europe.

The Crusades extended over the greater part of the twelfth and thirteenth centuries. In the judgment of many scholars, these were the most progressive of the Middle Ages, the centuries when western Europe made its greatest advances in economic, political, and cultural growth. In view of the hundreds of thousands of men and women who participated directly and indirectly in these military operations, of the many popes and churchmen, of the kings and scores of powerful lords who took part, of the Italian cities which capitalized on the expeditions, it is not too much to affirm that the Crusades exerted a profound influence upon the economic, political, and cultural developments which took place during those centuries.

An area where the Crusades exerted especially heavy influence was that of economic development. In 1096 when the First Crusade got under way, trade was already reviving, towns rising, and the first evidences of the future giant that capitalism was to be, coming into view. To these movements and developments the First and later Crusades provided the most powerful stimulus. Actually no single factor proved more potent than the Crusades in the expansion of trade, the growth of cities, and the evolution of efficient methods of organizing capital, of financing large undertakings, and of transporting money to distant places. It is significant that the Templars who had amassed fortunes in Syria took the lead in developing new banking methods during the thirteenth century. Venice and Genoa became the leading maritime and commercial states of Europe as a direct consequence of the crusades. And because of the more sophisticated tastes the crusaders brought back from Syria, a vast expansion took place in the importation of the luxuries from the East.

The impact of the Crusades upon the development of political institutions or upon the course of political history is less apparent. Because many knights and members of the aristocracy never returned to Europe or came back with depleted fortunes, the Crusades may have served to strengthen indirectly the position of kings who could better afford such operations—when they went. Since towns contributed significantly to the rise of monarchy, the impetus the Crusades provided their growth must be viewed a political consequence. Without question the fatal blow the Fourth Crusade struck the powerful Byzantine empire must be judged the most serious single political consequence. Although the empire was revived in 1261, it never recovered its earlier importance. The rapid expansion of the Italian cities which bore a direct link to the Crusades enabled these cities to win their independence from the kings of Germany in the thirteenth century and prepared the way for the brilliant "Age of Despots" which was to follow. (See below, p. 373.)

In terms of religious consequences, one clear-cut result was the estrangement of the Latin and Greek churches; the capture of Constantinople during the Fourth Crusade made them irreconcilable. Another development which must be associated with the crusades was the expansion of the doctrine of indulgences and the use of its promise of spiritual benefits by the papacy as a means of gaining the support of the faithful for its projects. It may be significant that the Orthodox church, which had severed its ties with Rome prior to the First Crusade, never developed the doctrine of purgatory. Whether the crusades enhanced papal leadership over western Europe remains a moot question. Had all these expeditions followed the pattern of the First, from being preached by the pope to sharing its success, that would certainly have been the case. Contacts with the Mongols who came within the sweep of the Crusades as possible allies against the Moslems encouraged missionary activity in their part of the world. While the work of such missionaries as John of Plano Carpini and William of Rubruquis proved impermanent, their accounts of distant Mongolia and China stimulated the interest that brought men like the Polo brothers and Marco to follow in their footsteps.

The land which supplied the greatest number of crusaders, even kings to lead a crusade, was France. Let us begin our consideration of the leading countries of western Europe with that land. In a real sense, the history of the medieval French monarchy begins with Louis VI (1108–1137), father of the Louis VII who had been one of the leaders of the Second Crusade. Until Louis VI came to the throne, historians pay little attention to the Capetian dynasty which began its long history with the election of Hugh in 987. (See above, p. 216.) These earlier Capetians were an unambitious lot. They surely had little inkling of how powerful future members of their dynasty would make their sleepy throne. Of course, an arrogant aristocracy hemmed them in on all sides, and perhaps all that could be expected of them under the circumstances was that they grow old and fat. For even that negative kind of existence helped establish, as we have seen, the hereditary character of the French crown.

Things began to happen under Louis VI whose activity belied his dubious title of "the Fat." It is said that he was so heavy by the age of forty-five that he could no longer mount a horse. (The chronicler does not say whether it was Louis who found it impossible to mount a horse or whether the horse objected.) Louis devoted his reign to taming the insubordinate baronage in his Île-de-France who had been a law to themselves and a scourge to everyone else. So Suger, his adviser, wrote: "He provided for the needs of the Church, and strove to secure peace for those who pray, for those who work, and for the poor. And no one had done this for a long time." The shrewd Louis paid especial attention to the towns, which his farsightedness enabled him to recognize as the crown's best friends. He protected them from their lords, granted them charters, and encouraged the establishment of "new towns." His Lorris was one of the first of the *villes neuves*. Suger, who was abbot of the famous Abbey of St. Denis, was but one of a number of clerks he took into his service. Louis hoped with these clerical assistants to provide himself a royal bureaucracy more responsive to his wishes and more efficient than the hereditary councilors (chancellor, seneschal, chamberlain) he had inherited.

His son Louis VII (1137–1180) is not so well known as the latter's wife Eleanor. One of Suger's prime successes, or so it appeared to contemporaries, was that of arranging the marriage of the young Louis to

Eleanor, heiress of the vast duchy of Aquitaine. Despite the promise of the marriage—man and wife were about the same age and apparently in love—the union only led to the most famous annulment in the history of the Middle Ages. There was some talk of moral irregularity on Eleanor's part, although Louis' principal reason for having a council of French bishops declare the marriage null on the ground of consanguinity was Eleanor's failure to bear him a son. Less than two months after the annulment, Eleanor, either from spite or because she could read the future better than her ex-husband, married Louis' most powerful vassal, Henry of Anjou and Normandy, who shortly after became king of England. Eleanor's action turned what might otherwise have been a simple mistake by Louis into a blunder of the first magnitude, and French historians have never forgiven him.

Louis' name is also linked with the fiasco of the Second Crusade, so little wonder that the historian must dig deep if he is to redress the king's sad image. Still Louis was not all a failure. He continued the enlightened policy of his father toward the towns and earned Pope Alexander III's deep gratitude by befriending him when the emperor Frederick Barbarossa drove him out of Rome. Toward his vassal Henry II who was more powerful than he was, he adopted the policy of making Henry's unfilial sons his allies and succeeded in keeping him out of Toulouse. His love of justice, his good will, and his sincere piety remind one of his saintly great grandson Louis IX. Walter Map tells the story how the count of Champagne once found Louis taking a nap in the woods with only two knights to guard him. When the count chided him for his carelessness, Louis replied: "I sleep alone, quite safe, because nobody wishes me ill."

Philip II (1180–1223), Louis' son, was probably France's greatest medieval king. His personality lacked the warmth and openness of his father, and though he was just in his dealings with his subjects and generous to the poor, he never won their affection. That he assumed the heavy burdens of government at the early age of fourteen might account for the cynicism, even unscrupulousness, with which he dealt with members of the aristocracy and with other kings. The loss of one eye and his generally poor health did not enhance his physical attractiveness. He did not attain a high level of education, but in the business of being king his practical mind and common sense saved him from committing any serious mistakes while they enabled him to take full advantage of the errors of others and of any happy circumstances that happened along. And he was above all industrious and ambitious.

THE HIGH MIDDLE AGES—POLITICAL HISTORY

Though he became involved in a long contest with the pope over his marriage (see below, p. 316), he was personally generous to the church and a reasonably devout Christian. His grandson, the sainted Louis IX, once told this story about Philip. It seems one of Philip's councilors reminded him on one occasion of the grave wrongs the clergy were doing him, "encroaching on his royal rights and obstructing his justice, and that it was astounding that he should put up with such treatment. The good old king answered that he believed this to be true, but that considering all the favors God had shown him, he would rather forfeit royal rights than quarrel with God's priests."

Philip goes by the title Augustus which a French historian gave him for his success in expanding the royal domain. This surely proved his most enduring achievement. By way of his wife's dowry, Philip acquired the rich fief of Artois, and, after a short war with the count of Alsace, the upper Somme Valley with the cities of Vermandois and Amiens. Though these were heavily populated areas, they bulk small compared with the noble acquisitions Philip made at the expense of the king of England. When still in his teens, Philip had seen the wisdom of his father Louis' policy of befriending the undutiful sons of Henry II, and he looked to the day he could rectify what in his eyes was an intolerable situation. This was the possession by the king of England of more than half of France, which he held as vassal of Philip, in his capacity as duke of Normandy, count of Anjou, and duke of Aquitaine, to mention only the most important of his fiefs.

During the ten-year reign of Richard (the Lion-Hearted), who succeeded his father Henry II in 1189, Philip should have bided his time. True, Richard was no match for Philip in sagacity and statesmanship, but he compensated for this deficiency by his superior military prowess. So while Philip had hoped to detach Normandy during Richard's absence on the Third Crusade by enfeoffing John, Richard's brother, with the fief, the maneuver had not succeeded, and the intermittent warfare he carried on with Richard in Normandy netted him just a few border fortresses. Fortune smiled on Philip when Richard, who was only a few years older than he, and who had kept him out of Normandy for as long as he lived, was struck by an arrow and died of the wound, whereupon John succeeded him. Unlike Richard, John possessed no military ability to compensate for his many deficiencies. Within a few years Philip had seized all of the English king's fiefs north of the Loire and part of Poitou to the south.

John had simplified Philip's task by marrying Isabella of Angoulême,

a girl of fourteen who had caught his fancy, but who was already betrothed to one of his vassals. John's act, therefore, constituted a serious
violation of his vassal's rights since such precontracts had all the force
of marriage. The vassal promptly appealed to Philip who was his and
John's common lord, and Philip hailed John to his court to answer to
the charges. When John refused to appear, Philip declared his possessions forfeit and proceeded to overrun Normandy.

John's act in marrying the betrothed of one of his vassals had alienated some of his French barons. Hardly had the war broken out with
Philip when he gave many other barons reason to turn against him.
This was over his treatment of Arthur, his nephew, who was holding
several French fiefs directly from Philip. Arthur had sided with Philip,
and in the ensuing fighting John captured him and probably had him
murdered. At least John's contemporaries were convinced that he had
authorized Arthur's murder, so within a few years John had nothing left
of his Continental fiefs save Aquitaine. The unruly vassals in that distant fief sided with him since they preferred an overlord in faraway
England to one closer by in Paris. John's desperate efforts to recover
Normandy and his other French possessions ended with Philip's magnificent victory over Otto IV of Germany and the count of Flanders,
both of whom were John's allies, on the battlefield of Bouvines in July
1214. The small army that John had been able to recruit had suffered
defeat shortly before.

The acquisition of these territories did more than just double the
French royal domain, that is, the territory under direct control of the
crown. In Normandy and Anjou Philip acquired an administrative system which was distinctly superior to his own. It was largely what he
learned of English practices there that guided him in his reorganization
of the administrative machinery in his own possessions. The royal
prévôt whom he had inherited from the earlier Capetians was quite
unsatisfactory as an agent of royal authority. What made him unreliable was the hereditary character of his office. Some *prévôts* might
be loyal and efficient; more of them were irresponsible and incompetent and chiefly concerned with advancing their own fortunes. To take
their place Philip created two new officials called bailiffs and senes-
chals, whom he appointed, paid salaries, and kept in his service so long
as they proved themselves useful. In time they assumed full management of the royal estates and handled the crown's judicial and financial
responsibilities. Many areas of France now for the first time began to
feel the presence of royal authority.

The annexation of John's English fiefs necessitated a major expansion of Philip's central royal administration as well. The principal instrument of royal government had remained substantially the traditional Curia Regis which had advised with early feudal monarchs and had assisted them with the simple tasks of feudal government. By the thirteenth century that assembly of untrained councilors meeting irregularly had demonstrated its inability to handle the crown's growing volume of judicial and financial business. With the acquisition of the English fiefs, this inadequacy became quite manifest. In his need for a more efficient body of men to assist him in the administration of the government, Philip found himself depending more and more upon a select group, usually drawn from the body of the Curia Regis, who possessed particular competency in matters dealing with justice and finance. During Philip's reign, these professional specialists were already becoming distinct from the Curia Regis, although they only became identified as separate bodies after his death. Those whose business was judicial acquired the name *parlement de Paris,* while those who dealt with fiscal matters constituted the *chambre des comptes.* Incidentally, Philip also deserves credit for a significant expansion of the crown revenues. This he accomplished by carefully exploiting aids and incidents, by collecting scutage from both knights and towns, by the sale of charters, from fees realized from the control of tolls and coinage, and from Jews whom he protected. Especially noteworthy was the protection he afforded the towns.

Philip's son Louis VIII (1223–1226) ruled too briefly to leave any deep mark on French history. With the blessing of his father he had taken part in the crusade against the Albigensians in southern France (see below, p. 314), and led another as king. The fruit of that intervention would come later with the absorption of Toulouse into the royal domain. His premature death provided his wife, Blanche of Castile, the opportunity to demonstrate her ability as regent during the minority of their son Louis IX. A number of restive French nobles, in addition to Henry III across the Channel, hoped to exploit the presence of a "foreign woman" on the throne to grab off parts of the royal domain. Blanche proved more than their match. She moved so energetically against the first coalition of enemies that it disintegrated before serious trouble developed. The other coalition she defeated, then forced one of its principals, the count of Toulouse, to agree to surrender his domains ultimately to the crown.

Although Louis took over in his own right in 1226, he continued to

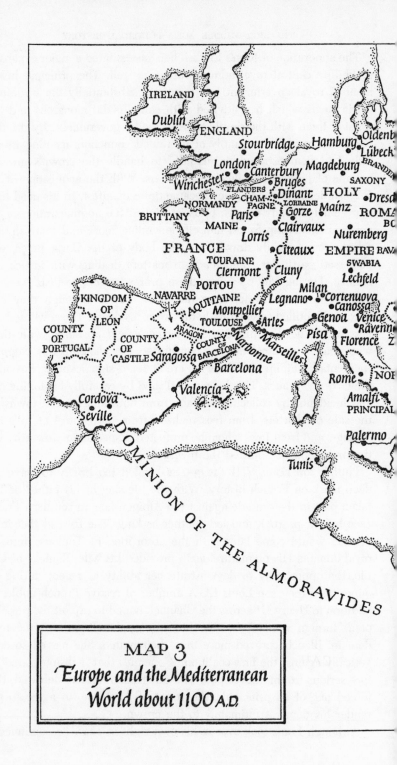

IRELAND

Dublin

ENGLAND

Stourbridge • Hamburg • Oldenb

London • Canterbury • Magdeburg • Lübeck

Winchester • Bruges • Dinant • SAXONY • BRANDE

FLANDERS • HOLY • Dresd

NORMANDY • CHAM- • LORRAINE • Mainz • ROMA

BRITTANY • PAGNE • Gorze • BO

Paris • Clairvaux • Nuremberg

MAINE • Lorris • Citeaux • EMPIRE • BAV

FRANCE • SWABIA

TOURAINE • Cluny • Lechfeld

Clermont • Milan

POITOU • BURGUNDY • Legnano • Cortenuova

NAVARRE • AQUITAINE • Canossa

KINGDOM • Montpellier • Arles • Genoa • Venice

OF • TOULOUSE • Ravenn

LEÓN • ARAGON • Pisa • Florence • Z

COUNTY • COUNTY • COUNTY • Narbonne

OF • OF • BARCELONA • Marseilles

PORTUGAL • CASTILE • Saragossa • Barcelona

Rome • NOR

Cordova • Valencia • Amalfi

Seville • PRINCIPAL

Palermo

DOMINION OF THE ALMORAVIDES • Tunis

MAP 3
Europe and the Mediterranean World about 1100 A.D.

LITHS
RUSSIANS

RUSSIANS

Kiev •

• Sarai

CUMANS

KHAZARS

GARY

BULGARIA

Trebizond

BYZANTINE
EMPIRE

Constantinople

Nicaea

Manzikert

Dorylaeum

SULTANATE
OF ROUM

TURKS

COUNTY OF
EDESSA

Mosul

Attalia

Edessa

P. OF ANTIOCH

Antioch

KINGDOM OF ARMENIA

C. OF
TRIPOLI

Tripoli

Baghdad

SULTANATE
OF
DAMASCUS

• Damascus

Acre •

Hattin

Alexandria

Damietta

• Jerusalem

K. OF
JERUSALEM

Cairo

CALIPHATE OF
CAIRO

• Medina

• Mecca

lean heavily upon his mother for counsel. When he left on his crusade, he placed her in charge. Of Louis' character we have an unusually vivid picture from the pen of his loyal fellow-crusader Jean de Joinville. Louis was handsome as a young man and possessed of a charming and open manner. In his early manhood he suffered a serious infection, probably malarial, which he never quite threw off. This illness, together with the rigor of his austerities, left him emaciated and weakened during the greater part of his life. He was in such poor health when he set out on his last crusade that Joinville declared those people "committed a deadly sin who encouraged his going." Three of his traits above all impressed Louis' subjects: his extreme piety, his love of justice, and his concern for the poor and infirm. All three virtues sprang from his deep faith which he inherited from his mother. She it was who "taught him to love and believe in God, and who set men of religion about him. Child as he was, she used to make him repeat his Hours and hear the lessons on feast-days, and often told him, as he recorded later, that she would rather he were dead than that he should commit a mortal sin."

Louis was generous in his distribution of alms, erected a number of homes for the aged, the blind, for orphans, and for fallen women. Much of his alms he distributed personally, waiting on beggars at table, and even feeding by hand lepers who were no longer able to feed themselves. He was most liberal in his donations to religious orders, in particular to the friars, for whom he had the greatest admiration. While his courtiers grumbled over the amounts he spent on charity which they felt might better be spent on court festivities, they could not help but be impressed with his faith. And though no king had ever dared to interfere more frequently with the manner they used their "prerogatives," only once did they attempt to organize a revolt against so holy a man, and that buckled almost immediately before his vigorous countermeasures.

Louis viewed his first responsibility that of providing his people a just rule. So he instructed his son: "Fair son, I pray you, win the love of the people of your kingdom. For truly I would rather that a Scot should come out of Scotland to rule the people of your kingdom well and justly, than that you should govern them unwisely." In the administration of justice, Louis permitted neither blood ties nor favor to sway his judgment. He directed his haughty brother, Charles of Anjou, to pay his honest debts to the Parisian merchants and to restore an estate he had appropriated for himself. When Charles protested his rights as a member of the nobility, Louis reminded him: "In France there can be only one king." He ordered one of his nobles to spend three years with the crusaders in Syria and pay a huge fine for having hanged three poachers. When his barons who had taken the part of this noble remonstrated and protested that he had grown so autocratic that he might hang them all if he chose, he told them in reply that what they said was nonsense, "but I shall punish them if they misbehave."

The one new official, the *enquêteur,* who appeared during Louis' reign was a direct product of the king's concern over just administration. Whenever he encountered corruption or tyranny among his officials, he punished with a heavy hand, but he could not be everywhere. And so when reports reached him that royal agents were defrauding people of their rights and property, he dispatched *enquêteurs* throughout the country with instructions "to receive in writing and examine all the complaints . . . against us . . . as well as statements concerning the injustice of which our bailiffs, *prévôts,* foresters, sergeants, and subordinates have been guilty."

Louis' concern for justice extended to kings and princes beyond his frontiers. In fact, his love of peace prompted him to make concessions beyond those which justice might demand. So he ceded several small territories to Henry III, his brother-in-law, when history, even perhaps justice, might have recommended that he take advantage of the weakness of the English and expel them from the Continent. In the interest of peace, he arranged a generous rectification of the frontier between France and Aragon. So eminent was his reputation for justice that foreign groups asked him on several occasions to arbitrate their disputes. The most famous of such arbitraments was the one he gave in favor of Henry III against the English barons. (See below, p. 299.) Toward the pope, Louis assumed an attitude of deep respect yet reserve. When the pope pleaded with him that he assist him against Frederick II (see below, p. 306), he refused. He was not convinced that the pope's position was a just one, and, furthermore, even against the papacy the rights of kings must be upheld. When the bishops of France asked him to order his officials to force excommunicates to make their peace with the ecclesiastical authorities, he agreed to do so but only after he and his courts had verified the justice of the sentences pronounced against these excommunicates. When Louis died, "he was mourned as no other king has ever been mourned. People did not wait for his canonization by the church before they began to adore his memory. His reign—the times of good King Louis—lived for centuries in the memory of French-men as a sort of golden age which would never come back."*

"[William II] was slain on a Thursday and buried the next morning. After he was buried, those councillors who were near at hand elected his brother Henry as king. . . . He then . . . went to London. On the following Sunday, he made a promise to God and all the people before the altar at Westminster, that he would abolish the injustices which prevailed during his brother's reign, and that he would maintain the most equitable laws established in the time of any of his predecessors. And after this Maurice, the bishop of London, consecrated him king, and all the men of this land submitted to him and swore him oaths of allegiance, and became his liege-men."

In these words the Anglo-Saxon Chronicle announced the election of Henry I to succeed his brother William Rufus in 1100. (For William II, see above, p. 216.) Though it was not unusual for a new monarch to pledge his subjects the correction of all injustices, in Henry's case it was a necessity. According to the same chronicle, William for his tyranny and crimes "was hated by almost all his people and abhorred by God." Henry also hoped by this pledge of just government to block any sentiment in favor of his older brother Robert, whose easygoing disposition would have made him more acceptable to the feudal aristocracy. Fortunately for Henry, Robert had not yet returned from the Third Crusade. When he did in 1101, he invaded England, but after no great difficulty was prevailed upon to leave England to Henry in exchange for Normandy and money. A few years later Henry took Normandy away from Robert and confined him for the remainder of his life.

The incident reveals one of Henry's traits: he could be hard and ruthless. Toward his subjects he was generally fair. In later years, during the lawlessness that reigned while Stephen was king, people even spoke of him as the "Lion of Justice," a title that probably did him more than justice. He was prudent, however, and so married an Anglo-Saxon princess in order to please his English subjects. To conciliate the church he invited the exiled Anselm back to England, and though they exchanged many bitter words over the same issue of lay investiture which was rocking the Continent (see above, p. 225), they hammered out at Bec in 1107 substantially the same compromise as later provided in the Concordat of Worms.

* Robert Fawtier, The Capetian Kings of France. London (1964), p. 31.

In the administration of his kingdom, Henry displayed much the same sense of responsibility and love of efficiency and order as had characterized his father the Conqueror. Were it not for the greater achievement of his grandson and namesake Henry II, historians would pay more attention to the steps he took to expand the jurisdiction and authority of royal administration. The first itinerant justices, of whom there will be more later, date from his reign, as does the emergence of the exchequer as a distinct division of the administrative machinery. Henry's hopes for the future of his dynasty all but foundered with the "White Ship" when this went down in the Channel carrying his only son (legitimate) William and other revelers with it. To salvage what he could from his years of hard work, Henry had his widowed daughter Matilda marry the son of the count of Anjou, then forced reluctant oaths from his vassals to accept her as his successor. Shortly after, he ate a meal of lampreys "though they never agreed with him" so the chronicler observed, and died of indigestion.

The holy oaths Henry wrung from his vassals did little good. The majority of Henry's barons gave their support instead to Stephen of Blois, grandson of William the Conqueror. Most of them knew him personally and liked his amiable, generous nature. What they had seen of the imperious Matilda suggested a continuation of her father's stern rule. When London, too, declared for Stephen, the pope announced his approval, and Stephen was crowned. The nobles never regretted their decision, but the people did. "For when the traitors [that is, Stephen's barons] understood that Stephen was a mild man, soft, and good, and no justice executed . . . they filled the land full of castles. They cruelly oppressed the wretched people of the country. . . . This lasted the nineteen winters while Stephen was king, and it grew continually worse and worse. . . . And men said openly that Christ and His saints slept."

While one must discount somewhat the heightened reports of medieval chroniclers, scholars accept in substance the picture of near-anarchy which they describe. That Henry II who became king in 1154 destroyed over a thousand adulterine castles attests to the weakness of royal authority and the supremacy of feudal rule. Meanwhile Matilda, who was a most resolute woman, never wavered in her determination to place her young son Henry on the English throne. She managed to hold on to Normandy where her son assumed control when he was seventeen. Shortly after, he inherited Anjou from his father, then in 1152 married Eleanor of Aquitaine. The following year he negotiated a settlement with Stephen that named him his successor. Stephen died in the fall of 1154 and Henry II was king.

Even before Henry was crowned, men knew he would be a different kind of king from Stephen. "No man durst do other than good for the micle awe of him" wrote the observant chronicler. Henry combined the mental and physical vigor of the Norman and Angevin (Anjou) dynasties, two of the most robust among scores in Europe, with a heavy sprinkling of their vices. At his accession he was a sturdy, broad-shouldered young man of above medium height, barrel-chested, with powerful arms and legs. Reddish hair and complexion, together with a violent temper, conveyed the image of the strong, rough character that his was. He loved to hunt, was ever on the go, and never liked to sit down—lest he grow corpulent, it was said. His courtiers were ever in a state of exasperation over the regularity with which he moved about the country and also the frequency with which he altered his plans and itinerary. One of these courtiers, Peter of Blois, finally decided he had enough of that hectic life and retired to a monastery to devote his last years to "study and peace." In the case of Henry, given his high-spirited wife Eleanor and his four unruly sons, peace only came when he died.

The extent of Henry's domain greatly impressed the kings of Europe. Henry claimed suzerainty over Scotland and Wales and an enclave about Dublin known as the English Pale. Most valuable were his fiefs in France—Normandy, Maine, Brittany, Anjou, Touraine, Poitou, and Aquitaine—which gave him possession of more than half that country. For a short time the count of Toulouse also accepted his suzerainty, and Henry even dreamed briefly of acquiring Savoy and Piedmont by having his son John marry a north Italian heiress. He used his three daughters to strengthen his ties with the duke of Bavaria (Henry the Lion), the king of Castile, and the king of Sicily.

What impressed Henry's fellow kings even more than the extent of his dominions was the depth of his purse. He continued to collect receipts from the royal estates, aids and incidents, and fees and fines from the hundred and shire courts. Because of the unpopularity of the Danegeld which dated back to Ethelred's day, he replaced that tax with a new land tax known as hidage (carucage). A new source of revenue which he introduced to England was scutage (shield money), which the baron or knight could pay in lieu of the actual forty days of military service he owed the crown. Henry also imposed taxes or tallages upon towns on the royal demesne, and at irregular intervals required "gifts" from Jews, monasteries, and the clergy. In 1188 in order to raise money for the crusade which he planned to lead, he ordered collection of the Saladin tithe, England's first experience with an income tax. Of all the new sources of revenue, most lucrative were the fees and fines collected by the royal courts. Evidence of the extent to which he expanded royal revenues is seen in the emergence of the exchequer, which up to this time had existed only in outline form, into the first distinct branch of the royal government.

The expansion of the royal judiciary represents the most enduring phase of Henry's work. This came as a natural extension of two of his ambitions: one, to rule with greater authority; the other, to establish peace and justice throughout England. In Henry's judgment, these objectives could not be disassociated from one another. Only by means of an effective system of royal courts could he hope to reduce the power of the feudal aristocracy which, in turn, constituted the chief obstacle to the rule of law and justice. Such courts, in addition to curtailing the jurisdiction of the feudality, would also bring in a steady flow of revenue, which in its turn, in the final analysis, would provide him the ultimate means for advancing his authority. That the great majority of the peasants, gentry, townspeople, and even barons subscribed to his methods and objectives became evident in 1173. Then a rebellion which his sons had organized against him in France in order to secure a greater voice in administering their fiefs, spread to England, where it found only a few supporters among the upper aristocracy.

Henry's new judicial system was not new so much in its components as in the manner the king combined these and established them as regular procedure throughout the land. William the Conqueror had already reserved to the crown the right to adjudicate serious crimes that disturbed the king's peace. In 1166 by the Assize of Clarendon Henry ordered men accused of murder, larceny, robbery, and the harboring of criminals to be tried by royal justices. Ten years later another assize added the crimes of forgery and arson. In these assizes Henry also introduced as regular procedure a precedent from the reign of his grandfather Henry I. This was the practice of sending members of the Curia Regis as itinerant justices into the different shires to preside over the trial of men accused of these crimes. Finally, in order to facilitate their work and to aid in the ferreting out of criminals, the Assize of Clarendon provided that twelve men from each hundred (township), together with four from each village, should serve as a jury of presentment, that is, present to the court the names of men in the area who might be guilty of these crimes. At this point reason halted. The final judgment itself, whether the defendant was guilty or innocent of the charge, was still decided by ordeal. Henry could do nothing about this, although he did order into exile men of notorious reputation even when the ordeal had "proved" them innocent.

Henry was also much concerned about suppressing another kind of crime, the fairly common one of seizing another man's property. The normal procedure in questions of land tenure had been wager of battle. Apart from being an irrational method, it was expensive since most men hired a "champion" to represent them. Henry now made provision that under certain conditions, when a man had been dispossessed, for instance, he could purchase a writ which would instruct the sheriff to summon a jury of twelve men who would then deliver the judgment in the case. Because this procedure, essentially the petit jury as it functions today, had both reason and speed to recommend it, it soon became popular, and early in the next century became standard procedure in criminal cases as well. One of the indirect consequences of Henry's legal reforms was the establishment of a uniform legal system, a common law, for all of England.

That a king as strong and ambitious as Henry should run afoul of the church is what one would expect in the Middle Ages when the paths of church and state so frequently intertwined. Henry's clash proved one of the most dramatic in history. While Henry was a faithful son of the church (although not a very faithful husband as he grew older), he objected to the extensive authority the church possessed in what he considered civil matters. He objected to church courts probating wills, to deciding certain kinds of property disputes, to trying clerks charged with serious crimes. What disturbed his sense of royal prerogatives, too, was the practice of taking appeals from English church courts to the papal curia. There were additional practices to which he objected, practices which were based upon rights he insisted the church had not possessed during the reign of Henry I but had arrogated to herself when the weak Stephen was on the throne.

Before moving to restore what he claimed had been custom during the reign of Henry I, he made sure, or thought he made sure, that a man of kindred spirit occupied the powerful office of archbishop of Canterbury. So he hand-picked his loyal and efficient chancellor, Thomas Becket, for the position. Too late he discovered to his chagrin that he had misjudged Becket. Once installed as archbishop, Becket abruptly left off his previous life of "worldly subdeacon," and assumed instead the role of doughty defender of the rights and prerogatives of the church. When Henry, therefore, came forward with a series of propositions, known as the Constitutions of Clarendon, which would have redefined the rights and position of the English church, Becket first gave a hesitant approval, then unqualifiedly rejected them. He based his rejection on the provision concerning criminous clerks. According to the Constitutions, such clerks were first to be tried in the church courts, then if found guilty, were to be degraded and turned over to the royal courts for punishment. This procedure, Becket argued, was tantamount to punishing a man twice for the same offense, something which even God would not permit. Then rather than be browbeaten or forced to submit, Becket fled to France and laid his cause before Pope Alexander III.

Alexander had his own troubles. He was in exile at the moment and Frederick Barbarossa's "pope" was in Rome. Had he thrown Becket his full support, that might have driven Henry to join Frederick. So he cautioned Becket to adopt a more flexible position; but the archbishop refused. After several years of further bitter debate, a hollow reconciliation was arranged, and Becket returned to England. Shortly after on Christmas Day he solemnly excommunicated those English bishops who had taken part in the coronation of Henry's son. (To crown an English king had always been Canterbury's prerogative.) When Henry learned of Becket's action, he exclaimed in his anger: "What a parcel of fools and dastards have I nourished in my house, that none of them can be found to avenge me on this one upstart clerk!" Four of his knights took him at his word and murdered Becket in his cathedral.

It would be difficult to single out any crime in the Middle Ages which caused greater shock than Becket's murder. Henry, who was as horrified as everyone else, disavowed all responsibility, but thought it prudent to go over to Ireland where he remained for six months. That gave tempers all around time to subside. In the end the actual impact of Becket's death on church-state relations in England was small. Henry was obliged to abandon a good part of the Constitutions, at least officially. This included the provision concerning criminous clerks. In substance, however, he did secure about what he wanted, especially the right to jurisdiction over disputes involving property. One might suggest, too, that many Englishmen, once over their shock, were not entirely unhappy over what had happened. Now they could boast a saint and a shrine as holy as any in Christendom west of Jerusalem—and men and women

from every shire's end
In England, down to Canterbury they went
The holy blissful martyr for to seek.

Richard, Henry's son, holds a warmer place in the hearts of the English than he deserves. Of the ten years of his reign, he spent fewer than six months in England and then was there merely to raise money. Still, romantic literature has treasured his handsome features, his tall, powerful build, his red-gold hair, his charming, generous manner, and, above all, his real prowess as a warrior and general. By his "settlement" of the affairs of Sicily, Cyprus, and Syria, and his dominant role in the Third Crusade, he did more than any medieval English monarch to make the Continent, and the world, aware of England's existence. Less well-known is Richard's hatred of his father, his selfish will and violent temper, and his cruelty. He ordered the massacre of twenty-seven hundred survivors of the siege of Acre, men, women, and children. Later while fighting Philip in Normandy, he blinded fifteen of his opponent's knights and left a sixteenth with one eye to lead them back to their king. For such a monarch England paid the largest ransom in medieval history, 100,000 solid medieval pounds! One of the enemies Richard's arrogance had made on this Third Crusade was the duke of Austria, who captured him on his return when he was seeking to make his way back to England in disguise and turned him over to Henry VI, the emperor. Had the ransom not been raised, England would never have missed Richard.

In the case of John, romantic literature, even history, has recorded only an evil side. There may not have been any other. John was cruel, lecherous, faithless, and unprincipled. Yet he was shrewd and as concerned as any good king should have been over preserving the rights of the crown. Under different circumstances, he might have fared better in history. Had Philip Augustus not seized Normandy and other Angevin lands (see above, p. 284), John would not have had occasion to resort to the criminal lengths he did to recover those possessions.

Scholars may even grant John a case in his bitter controversy with Pope Innocent III over the selection of an archbishop of Canterbury. This grew out of the action of the monks of Canterbury in disregarding John's voice when, upon the death of the archbishop, it came time to elect another. They did this, but in secret, then hurried their man off to Rome to secure Innocent's confirmation. When John learned of their action, he insisted upon another election, so the pope had two "archbishops" on his hands. He had no difficulty persuading both men to accept Stephen Langton, a learned English cardinal, as a compromise archbishop, but with John it was another matter. For seven years neither pope nor king would budge, even though Innocent used first interdict (the banning of all church services in England except baptism and the shriving of the dying), then excommunication to bring John to terms. Finally, when Innocent threatened John with deposition and angry English barons appeared prepared to do this with the assistance of Philip Augustus, John submitted and accepted Stephen.

What had angered John's barons was the king's tyrannical conduct. In order to raise money and recruit troops for his war against Philip, John had resorted to desperate and cruel measures. He had imposed frequent and heavy scutages, demanded untraditional aids, and exacted excessively heavy incidents. To enforce payments he confiscated estates, arrested those who objected, and from others seized their children as surety of good behavior. Since few barons held fiefs in Normandy and did not greatly mind the loss of John's French possessions, they resented the king's measures as doubly vicious. When he ordered a new tax after the defeat of his allies at Bouvines in July 1214, baronial opposition began taking overt form. The following June at Runnymede his barons confronted him with their demands. Since the alternative was deposition, John accepted them, and affixed his seal to the document which history knows as the Great Charter (*Magna Charta*).

In its final form, the Great Charter presented the demands of the barons in the form of a series of privileges which the king was pleased to grant, as it were, of his own free and good will. Actually only the first provision bears out that fiction. "In the first place, we have granted . . . that the English church shall be free, and shall hold its rights entire and its liberties uninjured. . . ." The sixty provisions which follow are of a much more specific character. Though expressed in the manner of privileges, they quite clearly represent in large part violations by John of his powers as feudal lord which he now solemnly declared he would correct. For example, provision number 40 stated: "To no one will we sell, to no one will we deny, or delay right or justice." Even more to the point was number 12: "No scutage or aid shall be imposed in our kingdom save by the common council of our kingdom, except for the ransoming of our body, for the making of our oldest son a knight, and for once marrying our oldest daughter; and for these purposes it shall be only a reasonable aid. . . ."

John's affirmation represented in substance a confirmation of the feudal contract that existed between him and his vassals. Still, John's barons had no intention of going beyond matters which pertained to their immediate position. About rules or principles which should guide feudal lords in the exercise of their powers, they had no concern. They wanted an end to specific abuses. Nevertheless, in forcing the king to promise to observe the limitations on his power expressed in the sixty some affirmations, they outlined in effect a definite body of law to which the king was himself subject. Not just the royal subjects, but the king as well, was beneath the law.

The Great Charter singled out two areas in which the king's behavior had been particularly reprehensible, namely, in the administration of justice and the imposition of financial exactions. In securing John's sacred promise that "no free man may be arrested or imprisoned . . . save by the legal judgment of his peers or by the law of the land" and that "no scutage or aid shall be imposed in our kingdom save by the common council of our kingdom," the Great Charter supplied, at least historically, two basic principles of constitutional government, namely, the right of the citizen to justice and parliamentary control of taxation. The qualification "historically" is worth noting. The Great Charter as the classic expression of English liberty did not evoke in the thirteenth century anything approaching the reverence its champions extended it in the seventeenth. Shakespeare could even write an entire play about John and omit all reference to Runnymede.

Several months after John had accepted the Great Charter, a French army landed in England. It had come to assist the barons in ridding England once and for all of the false king whose conduct since Runnymede promised no permanent redress of their grievances. Fortunately for all concerned, John died in October 1216, which happy event cleared the way for the accession of his nine-year-old son Henry III (1216–1272). Henry was a good man, a devoted son, and a faithful husband, and he possessed aesthetic interests for which his predecessors had either no time or taste. He also had ambitions—dreams might be a more proper term—since he lacked the vigor and statesmanship to see them through. His invasion of France failed, as did his wild Sicilian venture. These foreign enterprises, coupled with his subservient policy to the papacy and his dependence upon French advisers who flocked to England with his French mother and wife, convinced the barons that they must have a direct voice in the government. The indirect rights guaranteed them under the Great Charter were not enough. Under the leadership of Simon de Montfort, a French noble who had come to England and married Henry's sister, they forced the king to accept the Provisions of Oxford which subordinated the crown to the control of a Council of Fifteen. When Louis IX, who had been asked to arbitrate the conflict, decided in favor of Henry, Simon headed a revolt, defeated the royal army, and captured the king. Then in 1265 when the war broke out anew, Simon was slain and the revolt collapsed. While the revolt, even Henry's entire reign, was of little consequence, it did provide at least the historical setting for the origins of parliament. (See below, p. 354.)

In both France and England the twelfth and thirteenth centuries witnessed a considerable growth of royal power. The prospects for the German monarchy during those centuries were not good. The fifty-year reign of Henry IV had proved disastrous to the crown. It will be recalled that the feudal aristocracy sided with Pope Gregory VII in his contest with Henry IV over investiture, not for any love of the papacy, of course, but because they feared Henry, who was bent on building up royal power. So when Henry V (1106–1125), who had joined the revolt against his father, succeeded with the blessing of the German feudality, they forced him to promise to respect their rights. This meant in substance that there would be an end to further efforts to establish permanent bases for royal authority. Henry would not attempt to recover rights of jurisdiction and taxation, once belonging to the crown, which the aristocracy had appropriated.

During the next fifty years the German aristocracy took additional steps to weaken the monarchy. When Henry V lay on his deathbed, he nominated as his successor his nephew Philip, head of the Hohenstaufen family in Swabia. The princes chose Lothair, duke of Saxony. What recommended Lothair was the fact that he was not related to Henry. The princes wanted to prevent, if possible, the establishment of a hereditary monarchy as had happened in France. Furthermore, Lothair had no son and was not likely to have one. When he died, the German princes elected Conrad III (1138–1152) since he appeared less a threat to their position than Henry the Lion of Saxony, the other candidate. In Germany, therefore, in contrast to France and England, the monarchy continued elective, and the princes might use their option to deliberately choose a weaker candidate. In Germany, too, because the crown kept moving from family to family, no one place emerged as a capital city about which certain centralizing forces might have been able to gravitate. The crown could not assume leadership in German expansion eastward beyond the Oder; neither, because of its weakness, was it in a position to gain the adherence of the towns which had proved so valuable in the rise of the French monarchy. During the century, therefore, that elapsed between the accession of Henry IV in 1056 and the death of Conrad in 1152, the German aristocracy had so crippled the monarchy that even the genius of a Frederick Barbarossa could not restore it.

Frederick I (1152–1190) gained the votes of the majority of the German princes since his father was a Hohenstaufen and his mother of the Welf family of Bavaria. These two, the Hohenstaufens and the Welfs, represented the most powerful factions among the German feudality. The Hohenstaufens generally went by the term Ghibellines, from the name of one of their castles, while in Italy, at least, the opposing Welfs were usually known as Guelfs. Up to the time of Frederick's election in 1152, each group consisted of a loose coalition of feudal families, nothing more. Beginning with Frederick I, however, the Hohenstaufen dynasty kept the throne in its possession for the greater part of a century. For this reason, their faction came to be identified in men's minds as imperialist, that is, favoring a strong monarchy. Since the Guelfs made up the opposition, they quite naturally acquired the reputation of being anti-imperialists, that is, as favoring the aspirations of the German aristocracy. Since the ambitions of the Hohenstaufens extended to Italy where they posed a threat to the independence of the papacy, the pope consistently numbered himself with the Guelfs.

Frederick I was one of the most imposing figures of the Middle Ages. To many of his contemporaries Frederick was the perfect knight, the ideal crusader. When he celebrated the knighting of his two eldest sons in 1184, thousands of nobles from all over Europe gathered to felicitate him, while minstrels sang the praises of the new Arthur, the new Caesar and Alexander. Like Richard of England he was powerfully built, a courageous warrior, and an able general. In point of character and statesmanship, he was Richard's superior. The Italians, who felt his cruelty when they objected to his claims to rule them, called him Barbarossa because of his reddish-blond hair.

Frederick's ambition in Germany was to strengthen the royal authority, but there he had to move prudently. As indicated above, royal power had fallen to a low level. Few resources remained in Frederick's hands which he could have exploited. He did insist upon strict recognition of what imperial rights he still retained over feudal dues, roads, markets, and coinage. By the purchase or exchange of territories, and by persuading various monasteries to become crown lands in return for imperial protection, he made a beginning at establishing a more compact domain. He granted privileges to a number of Rhineland cities, expanded the use of *ministeriales,* and exercised a power over the German episcopacy reminiscent of the days of the Ottos. He also broke the power of his most formidable vassal, Henry the Lion of Saxony and Bavaria. After Frederick's defeat in Italy at the hands of the Lombard League (see below, p. 302) when Henry failed to show with his army, Frederick summoned him to answer to charges brought against him by his neighboring vassals, declared his duchies forfeit, and crushed his army. Had Frederick been able to keep Bavaria and Saxony, the future of the German monarchy might have been as bright as that in France. This the German princes would not permit, and although Frederick parceled these territories out among his supporters, the ultimate result was a victory for German particularism and a defeat for German unity under leadership of a strong king.

Frederick spent far more effort and resources south of the Alps where there were no mighty dukes to oppose him. His aim there was to recover the regalian rights his predecessors had once exercised but which had lapsed during the century preceding. At first he discovered an ally in the pope, Adrian IV, who shared his distaste for the cities of Lombardy (north Italy). Their anticlericalism disturbed him, and so did the manner in which these cities, and some of his own in the Papal States, had cast off the authority of their lords. Adrian also hoped Frederick would eliminate his most pressing problem, which was the presence of Arnold of Brescia, a "demagogue," who had made himself dictator of Rome. Frederick did seize Arnold and had him burned at the stake, but that was the extent of his and Adrian's cooperation. At their very first meeting there had been a painful incident. Since the ceremonial forms they would observe on that occasion might be construed as revealing and establishing their official relationship—whether Adrian was Frederick's vassal, for instance, or the reverse—Frederick refused to hold the pope's bridle and stirrup when he dismounted, although indicating his willingness to kiss the pope's foot. To do the first would imply feudal subserviency, to kiss the pope's foot simply betokened his respect for the head of the church. After much bitter wrangling, mediators convinced Frederick that holding the pope's bridle was only a custom, whereupon the emperor brought himself to do this, although he stated, loud enough for all to hear, that he was doing this for "Peter, not for Hadrian."

302 THE MIDDLE AGES

On Frederick's next trip to Italy he brought with him his army, forced Milan to surrender, and deprived the city of its autonomy. He also announced that imperial authority and the exercise of full regalian rights which included the right to levy tolls and customs, would again be the order of the day throughout Lombardy and Rome. And he would appoint the podesta in each city, the man who would enforce the recognition of those rights. When Milan rejected his claims Frederick invested the city and after a siege of three years, took and razed it. This should have frightened all Italy into quiescence, but it accomplished the reverse. Their hatred of Frederick caused the quarreling cities to close ranks, and even the new pope, Alexander III, joined the rebels. They organized the Lombard League, confronted the imperial army at Legnano in 1176, and defeated it with their crossbowmen. All Frederick salvaged from his grand dream of ruling Italy was acknowledgment of his imperial title, in recognition of which the Italian cities made him an annual payment. For the sake of peace, Frederick's position in Rome, together with his relationship with the pope, were left undefined.

A few years later fortune smiled on Frederick. In 1186 he arranged the marriage of his son Henry to Constance, aunt of the king of Sicily. There existed a small possibility that she might inherit the kingdom, but only if her young uncle, who was in his thirties, and his wife, who was still younger, died childless. The improbable happened, and when Frederick died on the Third Crusade, Henry VI (1190-1197) proceeded to take over his wife's inheritance. With the help of the huge ransom Richard had paid (see above, p. 296), he defeated a powerful coalition composed of rebellious Guelf princes in Germany, many Norman lords in Italy, and the pope as well, who wanted no imperial German authority hemming him in from both the north and south. Henry's next move, now that he had established imperial rule from the North Sea to the tip of Italy, was to organize a crusading expedition. Part of this had already sailed for Syria when he died.

Germany again faced a critical situation. The succession of Henry's young son Frederick, who was not yet three years old, was out of the question. But who should be king? For the next eighteen years Germany quarreled and fought over that question. Each of the two traditional factions brought forward its candidate. The Guelfs nominated Otto of Brunswick, son of Henry the Lion. The Ghibellines pressed the rights of Philip of Swabia, brother of the deceased emperor. Because John of England supported Otto, who was his nephew, Philip Augustus of France backed Philip of Swabia. So the contest went on year after year, with Pope Innocent III insisting from Rome that for a number of reasons, one the Donation of Constantine, he was entitled to a decisive voice in the matter. (For Innocent III, see below, p. 315.) Had it not been a foregone conclusion that Innocent would throw his vote to Otto, the Guelf candidate, the German princes, that is, the supporters of Philip of Swabia, might have paid him more attention. For Innocent had no other choice. The Ghibelline Henry VI had already made clear his claim to all of Italy, including Rome. Eventually the majority of German princes came around to accepting Philip, but then he was murdered (not by Otto or an accomplice), whereupon the weary princes decided on Otto. In October 1209 Pope Innocent, with complete satisfaction, crowned Otto Roman emperor.

Innocent's satisfaction over Otto lasted less than a month. No sooner was Otto on the imperial throne than he acted quite as aggressively as any Ghibelline. Despite his solemn promise to Innocent to respect the rights of the church wherever they existed, he marched directly across the Papal States in order to take southern Italy and Sicily from the young Frederick, the late Henry VI's son, who had established his rule there. Innocent promptly repudiated Otto, and since there was no one else about, urged the cause of Frederick as a new emperor even though there was a good bit of Ghibelline blood coursing through his veins. Since a number of German princes were also willing to make the change, and inasmuch as Philip Augustus had never wanted a nephew of John's on the throne in the first place, Otto's days were numbered. Philip's victory at Bouvines in 1214 destroyed both his hope of empire as well as his uncle John's plans for Normandy.

The story now turns back to the young Frederick who was just twenty-one years old in 1215 when he was crowned Roman emperor. Few kings have possessed so great and varied talents, few able monarchs have accomplished so little that was constructive and permanent, few have proved so much a puzzle to historians. Even his contemporaries found Frederick an enigma. The Franciscan Salimbene wrote of him: "Of faith in God he had none. He was a crafty man, deceitful, a voluptuary, malicious and wrathful. And yet at times he could be a worthy man when he wished to show his benevolence and good will. Then he was solicitous, merry, pleasant, and diligent. He knew how to read, write, and sing, and to compose songs and verses. He was a handsome man and well-formed, yet only of middle stature. For I myself have seen him and at one time was even fond of him. He wrote on my behalf to Brother Elias, minister general of the order of friars minor [Franciscans], that by his grace he might send me to my father. He also knew many and various languages. In short, had he been a good Catholic and have loved God, the church, and his own soul, there would have been few among the rulers of the world who would have been his equal."

Salimbene and Frederick's enemies accused him of being an agnostic. Without doubt he uttered irreligious and blasphemous statements, although he may have made these in order to scandalize his listeners. His enemies also charged him with keeping a harem. They offered as evidence the dancing girls his friend, the sultan, sent him from Egypt. Frederick had three wives, all in proper succession, but his only interest in them was for the children they might bear him. He kept them immured in solitary isolation in southern Italy, guarded by eunuchs, where they died of loneliness. He was cruel and vindictive and had eyes that sent chills up a man's spine. Men who turned against him he had sewn in bags with poisonous serpents, and thrown into the sea. So vindictive was he that had he one foot already through the door of Paradise, he once declared, he would return to earth, God permitting, to revenge himself on Viterbo.

A more pleasant side of Frederick was his interest in mathematics, astronomy, metaphysics, and literature. He kept a circle of scholars and literary people about him and carried on a correspondence with the sultan of Egypt about metaphysical and religious matters. The most scholarly book ever written on falconry was his *Art of Hunting with Birds*. He experimented with incubators in Sicily, introduced sugar cane, cotton, and indigo, and even attempted to acclimatize the date palm. When he traveled he took with him the most interesting zoo medieval Europe ever saw. Some of the more exotic beasts were the gift of the sultan. He learned six languages and a number of dialects, and helped his circle of versifiers compose the first poetry in the Italian language. He was tolerant of all views and religions—except heresies. To his contemporaries he was indeed "the wonder of the world."

Frederick revealed another side of his genius in establishing an autocracy in southern Italy and Sicily. The early Norman rulers there had provided him a strong organization and traditions upon which to build. Their state has, in fact, been called the "first modern state." What was "modern" about it was the government's dependence upon taxes and tariffs, rather than feudal aids and incidents and crown estates, for its revenues; its reliance upon an efficient bureaucracy which those Normans recruited wherever they discovered competency, rather than upon hereditary feudal councilors.

When Frederick fell heir to Sicily, civil war and anarchy had destroyed a good portion of the old Norman administrative machinery. He may have considered this a blessing since he could build from bottom up. One objective he had clearly in mind, and that was to establish an absolute monarchy. There would be no freedom in his kingdom except what he would permit. He introduced a legal system based upon Roman imperial law, then appointed a hierarchy of officials, all responsible to him ultimately, but immediately to the man above them, then trained them in the university he established at Naples. Any inefficient official would suffer dismissal; any corrupt one would suffer mutilation or death. He raised revenues by eliminating all interior tolls while maintaining a rigid system of collection at all ports. He established monopolies over the production of salt, iron, steel, hemp, tar, and silk, and permitted none but his own personal merchant marine to transport exports from his kingdom. The core of his army were Saracen mercenaries to whom he had given his protection. He introduced the first gold coin to be minted in the West, and he did, truly, establish the autocracy he wanted. As Pope Gregory protested: "In your empire no one may dare, without your leave, to move hand or foot."

Frederick's public career as crusader, king, and emperor was near tragic. His participation in the crusade has been noted (see above, p. 278). It will be recalled that he went to Syria as an excommunicate. He had broken his promise to lead a crusade in 1227, for which failure Pope Gregory IX had excommunicated him. The pope's real reason for the excommunication went deeper, to his conviction that Frederick would stop at nothing short of complete domination of all Italy including the Papal States. That was also the conviction of Innocent IV (1243–1254), who as cardinal had been numbered among Frederick's friends in the curia. Frederick knew full well what papal policy must be. When someone congratulated him upon the election of Innocent IV in 1243, he is said to have observed: "No pope can be a Ghibelline."

Shortly after Frederick returned from Syria, he and Pope Gregory IX patched up their differences. For the moment, hardly more than a year, Frederick enjoyed peace. In the fall of 1231 a revolt broke out in Germany which his own son Henry had organized with the encouragement of the cities of Lombardy. Frederick had no difficulty squashing the revolt. Then, after spending a few years in Germany, he marched south to punish Lombardy for its insolence and to extend his rule over the north. By a brilliant maneuver, he caught the Lombard army of some ten thousand men in a trap at Cortenuova (1237) and destroyed it. Then he made a fatal mistake. In his exultation he dreamed he had conquered all of north Italy. He insisted upon unconditional surrender. To surrender to a man as vindictive as was Frederick, the Italian cities knew was no better than death. As Milan replied to his demand: "We fear your cruelty which we have experienced; so we prefer to die under our shields by sword, spear, and dart, than by trickery, starvation, and fire." So the war continued, year after year after year, growing ever more fierce and cruel. In 1239 Pope Gregory renewed his excommunication and joined the Lombard cities. In order that all Christian Europe might join in the crusade against the antichrist as he branded Frederick, he summoned a church council to meet in Rome. Frederick countered with a warning to the rulers of Europe to bar their prelates from going to Rome since the pope's intent was purely political. When these bishops and cardinals attempted to get there nevertheless, he captured the bulk of them and stuck them away in filthy jails. Battles, sieges, surrenders, revolts, massacres, devastation—now one side winning, now the other: such was the story of this bitter war until December 1250 when Frederick died of dysentery.

Frederick left a son, Conrad IV, who reigned for four years. It was Frederick's natural son Manfred who continued the struggle for a few years longer, until defeated and slain by the French whom the pope had finally persuaded to intervene. Manfred's death marked the end of the Hohenstaufens and of German power in Italy. The pope had won that war. Another he had lost. His repeated anathemas against Frederick had deeply disturbed many Christians. Was not Frederick a crusader, and a successful one? These Christians also asked themselves, as did Louis IX of France, whether the struggle between pope and Frederick was not a political one. So while the Hohenstaufens lost out, the prestige of the papacy suffered disastrously and never recovered the position it had enjoyed early in the thirteenth century. Germany was also the loser. Frederick had paid it little attention, principally because he could never have ruled it in the manner befitting a king. So he abandoned it to all intents and purposes to its feudal aristocracy and to particularism. The last hope of the medieval monarchy in Germany faded away completely.

CHAPTER 9

The High Middle Ages—
Religion and Culture

THE CHURCH

"Therefore, dearest brothers, snatch up the weapons of sobriety, humility, patience, obedience, chastity, charity, and all the virtues, and do not concern yourselves over fields and cities, sons and wives, but only about your own souls which rise above every other consideration. And that your youth may grow strong, you must above all else fast and pray, since fasting will tame the desires of the flesh while prayer raises the soul to God." So wrote Peter Damian in the eleventh century of the monastic ideal. Though Peter Damian is forgotten and his theme holds little meaning for a modern generation, it was his hard work and the zeal of other monastic reformers that enabled monasticism to attain the dominant position it held in the life of the church in the high Middle Ages.

Peter Damian was a spokesman for the spirit of reform that was sweeping the Latin church in the eleventh century. One of the origins of this movement was the monastery of Cluny. (See above, p. 225.) The impact of the Cluniac movement upon the times has been likened to that of the Jesuits in the sixteenth century. Yet its influence arose less from a modification in monastic principles than from its emergence as the symbol of religious reform. One significant shift of emphasis in the philosophy of monastic life which it introduced was the expansion of the liturgical life of the monastic community. The traditional image of the medieval monk who spent the greater part of his waking hours at prayer in the abbey church, singing and reciting the divine office, dates from the days of Cluny. Cluny also departed from the Benedictine principle that each individual monastery should be autonomous. William of Aquitaine, who granted Cluny its freedom from lay control, placed other monasteries in his domain under its direction. Within a short time the prestige of Cluny and the renown of its abbots led other monasteries to ask to be associated with the organization. This led to the Congregation of Cluny, which by the twelfth century numbered some three hundred monasteries. All the houses in the Congregation accepted the authority of the abbot of Cluny and recognized his right to make inquisitorial visits.

The usual history of reform movements—that they are born, flourish, then decline—was also true of Cluny. By the close of the eleventh century it had lost its momentum. Other reformers, including St. Bernard of Clairvaux, were accusing it of laxity. Even in the vigor of its youth, certain monks held aloof, individualists like Romuald (d. 1000) who preferred to live as hermits. For the sake of convention, they left their lonely cells long enough to pray in a common chapel, then returned to their own contemplation. The best known of these anchoritic communities was the Carthusian which the scholarly Bruno founded in 1084 near Grenoble. He and six followers had come there to seek the spiritual peace the busy world was denying them. Because of the extreme austerity of their monastic regimen, the Carthusians attracted only few candidates, but those who stayed were holy men. It has been said that the order never needed to be reformed because it had never permitted itself to become deformed. There were no defections when Henry VIII's headsman appeared with his axe. The English Carthusians all died for their convictions.

The monks of Cluny hoped to reform monasticism by placing greater emphasis upon liturgical activities and by concentrating authority in the hands of the abbot at Cluny. In 1098 there was established at Cîteaux in France another reform movement which deliberately modified these principles. The Cistercians, as this religious community came to be called, proclaimed a strict return to the original rule of Benedict. They restored much of the autonomy of the original Benedictine community. But what they deprecated most in Cluny was the elimination of physical labor. This was to become again an integral part of the rule. And since the Cistercians also insisted upon greater immunization from the corrupting influences of civilization, they withdrew to the forest and swamp where men had not settled. Because of this practice the Cistercians made a significant contribution to the agricultural development of Europe in the course of pursuing their own monastic objectives. Some observers will even say that so long as they served man by pushing back the forest and draining swamps, they best served themselves. When they permitted society to catch up with them, they declined.

Even though a saint founded the Cistercian order and another gave it its constitution, the high hopes of the new order would probably have died with its birth had it not been for the appearance of St. Bernard. In 1112 he came and asked admittance, together with thirty other young men whom he had inspired with the love of God and the monastic life. This became his driving passion, to make all men serve God, preferably within the walls of a monastery. Three years later his abbot sent him fifty miles north into the county of Champagne to found another monastery. There at Clairvaux (Valley of Light) he made his headquarters, although it was never more than a place to leave and to return to for short intervals from his travels, which took him across France and Italy, reforming, teaching, organizing new monasteries, composing hymns, writing hundreds of letters, taking part in church councils, ending a papal schism, denouncing the "heresies" of Abelard, and preaching a crusade. Not all men welcomed Bernard's enormous energies or the manner he spent them. They likened him to a frog that would not stay in his swamp, to which Bernard retorted that if they had observed God's commands he would have had no occasion to leave his swamp. The mark of Bernard's deep influence upon the spiritual life stands best revealed in the growth of mysticism which he inspired.

Although the Cistercians became the most influential monastic order of the twelfth century, they were obliged to share their popularity in Germany and in the lands to the east with another group known as the Premonstratensians. The name of this order derives from Prémontré in France where St. Norbert of Xanten founded his community in 1120. The Premonstratensians, who were called the white canons, followed in large part the rule of St. Augustine. Augustine had required his priests, when they lived together in groups, to observe certain monastic regulations. This practice, a feature of the Premonstratensian rule, represented one of the earliest attempts at combining the role of the contemplative monk with that of the priest. The Premonstratensian monk did parish work and preached to the laity. The Premonstratensians also introduced a rule for women (Second Order) and for the laity (Third Order). Men and women could continue to live in the world and at their various tasks, while observing as far as possible the monastic principles recommended at Prémontré.

The most revolutionary development in medieval monasticism appeared with the establishment of the orders of friars in the late twelfth and early thirteenth centuries. The term "friar," which distinguishes the members of these religious communities from the traditional monks, suggests an essential departure from the spiritual philosophy of historical monasticism. In theory at least, the monk, as a son of the desert hermit, followed the life of a recluse. He shut himself off from the society of men, first in complete isolation, then in a monastery, in order to pursue a life of contemplation. In practice many of these monks became active missionaries. An occasional one like Bernard had active careers, and exercised such direct influence in the public life of the church that they seemingly belied the very philosophy of monasticism.

The new orders of friars did not abandon the spiritual goals of contemplative life. What they hoped to do was to combine those goals and the monastic way of life with an active apostolate among the laity. Like the Premonstratensians, they sought to unite the two roles of monk and priest. In their judgment the times called, not for more men and women to withdraw from society and pray and worship by themselves, but for zealous souls who possessed the spiritual dedication of monks and the missionary zeal of Paul. The appearance of the friars, according to many scholars, was an answer to the failure of the secular clergy to perform its task. The friars also placed much emphasis upon the practice of poverty since they believed that it was wealth which was the principal source of corruption in the church. Because they, therefore, shunned wealth and had to depend upon day-to-day begging for their livelihood, they went by the name of mendicant orders.

The best known of these mendicant orders were the Franciscan and Dominican. St. Francis of Assisi, who was the founder of the first, was the son of a prosperous and ambitious merchant. He hoped his son would prove his valor as a knight and make his way into the aristocratic class above him. Francis was a disappointment. He preferred to mingle with merry youths of his own age and to sing songs and compose verse. When he did assume halfheartedly the guise of a knight to please his father, he was captured in a petty clash with the troops of a neighboring town. A short confinement, then fever, changed Francis. He still liked to sing, but no longer the romantic themes of the troubadour. He sang instead of the love and goodness of God, of Christ in the crib and on the cross. For the love of the good God, he abandoned his patrimony, lived for a short time as a hermit, then devoted himself to the care of the poor and lepers. Though his father disowned him in disgust, other men were attracted to his simple gospel of loving the poor for the sake of the Saviour who loved all men. In a world of suffering and misery, he preached the message of love which should turn every sorrow into joy. And he admonished his followers not to appear sad and gloomy like hypocrites. They were to be joyful in the Lord, merry and becomingly courteous.

Still, Pope Innocent III was troubled when Francis presented himself and asked confirmation for his order. The holiness of the man was patent, but Innocent could not help but consider his proposal lacking in reasonableness. Here was a layman who presumed to win souls simply by preaching the love of God and serving the poor and neglected, something great popes, bishops, and learned theologians had not been able to accomplish. One of Innocent's cardinals, the future Gregory IX who fought Frederick II so vigorously, urged the pope to make room in the church for such a man as Francis. Innocent need fear no anticlericalism as had happened with a similar lay group of Waldensians (see below, p. 313), he assured the pope, since Francis never attacked anything. Nor did Francis have the Waldensians' interest in preaching the Bible. His only sermon and those of his little brothers, as he called them, was to live as Christ wanted them to live, and to let learning and theology to their superiors. In his full pontificate, Innocent suffered many disappointments, the Fourth Crusade among others. Nothing he ever did turned out so much an unqualified success as the tentative approval he gave Francis. Within a century of Francis' death his order numbered some fifteen hundred houses, including those of the Second Order of Poor Clares which St. Clare, one of his devout followers, founded. Thousands of laymen and women joined the Third Order.

The Dominican order paralleled the Franciscan in many respects, yet presented significant contrasts. Its founder, the Spaniard St. Dominic, accompanied his bishop as a young priest through the areas of southern France where Catharism had made deep inroads. (For this heresy, see below, p. 313.) What Dominic saw there convinced him that the only solution for that deplorable situation was the establishment of a zealous, well-educated clergy, whose lives and eloquence would convince the heretics of the error of their ways. Almost the last act of Pope Innocent was to give the order his blessing. Since Dominic limited his order to priests, it did not spread so quickly or grow so popular as the Franciscan. Still, the four hundred houses which made up the order within fifty years of its founding represented the most formidable organization of preachers the world has ever seen. Dominican friars flocked to the universities to learn, then to southern France and other infected areas to preach and teach. Dominic called his community the Order of Preachers. So much was preaching the *raison d'être* of the order that it took precedence over the divine office and other monastic regulations when the need arose.

The contribution of the friars to the church of the thirteenth century was of enormous importance. They became the most loyal champions of papal power in its contest with the state. In Italy Frederick II had them expelled from his dominions. Their appearance may have prevented the rise of dangerous reform movements. To reformers who wanted a purer doctrine and a better-educated clergy, the church could point to the Dominicans. To men who demanded more virtuous living and a concern for humanity, they had their answer in the Franciscans. To laymen who wanted an opportunity for living more religious lives, they offered the Third Orders. Reforming bishops, like Robert Grosseteste, encouraged them to come to their dioceses to preach. For the first time the church commanded a well-organized body of trained and devoted men dedicated in a special manner to the sanctification of souls. The friars took the lead in the missionary work in North Africa, the Near East, and among the Mongols. In southern France they did yeoman service in combating the blandishments of the Catharists. They contributed in significant measure to the flowering of mysticism in the fourteenth century. The leading scholastics, scientists, and even poets (religious verse) of the thirteenth century were friars. If the thirteenth century was the greatest of the Middle Ages, substantial credit for achieving that distinction is owing the friars.

In view of the existence of two heretical groups in the early thirteenth century, the rise of the orders of friars could not have come at a more providential time. The twelfth century had sired a number of lay religious movements, no doubt echoes among the laity of the same spiritual urges that had produced the Cistercians and other religious orders. Many laymen and women were seeking a more religious life. In scattered places in western Europe "poor men of Christ" came forward, not unlike Francis and his early band of followers, to seek the church's approval for their work. Local bishops were generally unsympathetic. They had a sufficient problem with their poorly trained clergy without having to guard the orthodoxy of untrained laymen. It was usually in Rome, from the pope, that these groups received most comfort.

One such group that the pope befriended was the "Poor Men of Lyons." Their founder was Peter Waldo, a wealthy merchant of that city and a pious man. Both his daughters took the veil. Peter's love of God and his fellow men led him to give away his wealth, to take up a life of austerity, and work among the poor and infirm. In contrast to Francis, Peter had a deep interest in the Bible. He would translate portions of it and explain these to his friends. In 1179 he secured qualified approval from the pope. His group might work among the poor, even preach provided the local bishop was agreeable. In a very short time, however, the Waldensians had aroused the ire of the clergy by preaching, among other things, the necessity of apostolic poverty, whereupon the pope suppressed the order. Many of the members of the group heeded the pope's order and resumed their place in the body spiritual. For others papal condemnation served as a spur to greater anticlericalism, then heresy. They began to attack the spiritual authority of the church, the mass and sacramental system, the priesthood. Every person was a priest, they insisted, and everyone, including women, could preach and could explain the Bible, which was the sole source of truth.

In Catharism (from *Cathari*, the pure), the medieval church encountered a more militant movement than the Waldensian and one which was heretical from the beginning. Catharism had a long and confused history. Its origins might be traced back to ancient man's view of the universe as a dualism in which two antagonistic principles, one good, which was spirit, was eternally locked in conflict with an evil principle, which was matter. Since man combined both spirit and matter, he found within himself this same conflict between good and evil. Such a religious philosophy had many contacts with Christianity. In the early centuries, the Manichaeans had proposed substantially the same views. When these ideas appeared in Bulgaria in the tenth century, a priest by the name of Bogomil adapted them to Christianity and established a sort of revivalist faith. Upon their expulsion from Bulgaria in the twelfth century, the Bogomils carried their views to the west, particularly to the viscounty of Albi in southern France, whence the name Albigensians by which they are often known.

Catharism possessed a number of features which both the common people and aristocracy found appealing. Since the clergy was to have no wealth, the nobility could hope to deprive the church of what property it held. What attracted commoners was the use of the vernacular in a relatively simple liturgical service in which all could participate. The Catharist clergy, the "perfect," were frequently learned men who practiced the strictest asceticism in keeping with their conviction that matter was evil. They remained celibate, were vegetarians, and partook of only sufficient food to keep alive. Such a harsh regimen was, of course, beyond the ability of ordinary folk. All that was required of them was to venerate the "perfect," and to look to the day when they themselves would become "perfect." This would involve a "novitiate" of a year when they would test themselves with ascetical practices, after which, if they were ready, they received the *consolamentum*. This rite consisted of the laying on of hands by which they received the Holy Spirit. Thenceforth they must live the austere lives of the "perfect." Those who doubted their ability to remain steadfast, should commit suicide. If they did fall back into sin and die, they would be reincarnated and hopefully fare better the next time. Until receiving *consolamentum*, there was little point in leading moral lives. Actually, since Catharism condemned marriage as a formal defiance of the principle that all flesh was evil, it invited the practice of easy morals. This, too, was one of the attractions of Catharism.

So popular did Catharism become that the Third Lateran Council in 1179 promised indulgences to whoever participated in its extirpation. Pope Innocent, who was most distressed by the movement, sought every means of curbing its spread. When agents of the count of Toulouse murdered the papal legate in 1208, he proclaimed a crusade. Once this got under way, however, Innocent regretted the step because of the savagery with which the "crusaders" did their work. For many nobles from northern France this crusade became an opportunity to acquire fiefs and booty, all with the blessing of God. Several years after the conclusion of the crusade, Pope Gregory IX established a special tribunal, known as the court of the Inquisition, for the purpose of completing the eradication of the heresy.

The bitter criticism which the medieval Inquisition has evoked in modern times is not wholly justified. In all respects, in the principles upon which it justified its action, in the procedures it followed, even in the use of torture to expedite confessions, it introduced nothing which was not in conformity with the times. Both state and society demanded the suppression of heresy, and both anticipated the church in insisting upon capital punishment. In 1249 the count of Toulouse, by this time thoroughly orthodox, ordered the burning of eighty Cathari to whom the inquisitor had given lighter sentences. It will be recalled that the otherwise tolerant Frederick II executed heretics since he considered their views a threat to constituted authority. One must also bear in mind that the modern world's aversion to capital punishment is not old. England still hanged petty thieves in the eighteenth century. In the Middle Ages there was no more heinous crime than heresy. The record of the Inquisition was, furthermore, not so black as painted, even though there were madmen like Conrad of Marburg who burned at the stake most anyone who caught his fancy. Bernard Gui, the most "vicious" of all inquisitors, turned forty-five Cathari over to the state during the fifteen years he held his post. What has helped darken the image of the medieval Inquisition has been the ruthless efficiency of the Spanish Inquisition with which it has only a historical connection.

The pope whose name appeared in connection with the major religious developments of the high Middle Ages—the rise of the friars, the suppression of heresy, the organization of the Fourth Crusade—was Innocent III. Many scholars acclaim him the greatest of the popes. Upon his accession he was the youngest cardinal to have ever attained that distinction. He was thirty-seven years old. He had attended the universities of Paris and Bologna, and his work in the curia subsequent to that had gained him a reputation as an astute canonist. A few treatises, including one on the contempt of the world and another on the liturgy, earned him some distinction as a theologian. Many Christians continue to sing the beautiful hymn he composed in honor of the Holy Spirit (*Veni, Sancte Spiritus*).

There have always been men in responsible positions who have ignored problems to which they should have given attention, and other men who have dealt only with matters which were most pressing. In the case of Innocent, nothing of any moment appears to have missed his scrutiny, whether it was a crusade, curial inefficiency, corruption in the church, doctrinal confusion, theological controversy at Paris, or political turmoil in Germany. To these and other matters Innocent gave full attention during his pontificate, and near its end, in 1215, convened the Fourth Lateran Council for the purpose of providing wider acceptance and permanency to his work, for the work of this council was largely his. Papal commissions had most issues resolved and reports ready when some twelve hundred bishops, abbots, and delegates gathered in Rome. There they remained for a few weeks, and returned home.

The council considered a wide variety of issues. In the field of theology it defined the doctrine of transubstantiation. In other affirmations concerning Christian doctrine, it pointedly refuted the major tenets of Catharism. Among disciplinary pronouncements was one which required annual confession of the faithful. Reform measures received extensive attention. A canon which reformers hoped would correct many of the inadequacies of the clergy required bishops to maintain cathedral schools. Other canons barred the clergy from taking part in dramatic performances and ordeals, or in performing surgical operations. Priests were also required to preach regularly. The practice of pluralities was condemned, as well as that of accepting fees for administering the sacraments. All taxation of the clergy was anathematized although, given the permission of the pope, a king might ask a "free gift." The council also approved plans for a new crusade and ratified the election of Frederick II as Roman emperor.

What many scholars find most fascinating about the pontificate of Innocent was the pope's relationship with the kings of Christendom. No pope carried on such extensive correspondence with these kings; none engaged in more controversy with them, nor, in the judgment of many scholars, scored such spectacular successes; none made so extensive appeals to law and reason as did Innocent to justify his position. The best known of Innocent's contests was with John of England over Stephen Langton. (See above, p. 296.) In the end, it will be recalled, John accepted Stephen. A second controversy involved Innocent with Philip Augustus. Philip had married Ingeborg, a Danish princess, then found her so unattractive that he put her away the day after the wedding. A submissive council of French bishops annulled the union on the grounds of consanguinity, whereupon the king married Agnes of Meran, daughter of a Bavarian duke. Innocent took up Ingeborg's cause, and after a long struggle persuaded Philip to take her back. The third *cause célèbre* concerned Germany where Innocent intervened in the contest between Otto and Philip. When the fighting was over, Innocent had his ward, Frederick II, securely on the throne. (See above, p. 303.)

That no pope before or since Innocent III found himself involved in so much controversy with such important people, one would have to admit. One must also confess that at first glance Innocent does appear to have won several stunning successes. Yet before granting Innocent such authority in thirteenth-century Europe that he could force kings to bend to his wishes, it will be well to take a second glance at the circumstances under which he won these contests. In the case of Stephen Langton, John submitted only after seven years of stalemate. During that period he punished anyone who dared carry out Innocent's interdict, while he seized (and never returned) the revenues of the English church. And he submitted finally for fear the king of France and the English barons would depose him. With regard to Innocent's controversy with Philip, again the king only submitted because it served his interests. His second wife had died and he wished to qualify as leader of the crusade against John. In the case of Germany, Innocent had no alternative but back his ward Frederick, which he did with considerable misgivings. A few years later, these misgivings proved well founded.

On the basis of Innocent's record with John, Philip, and Germany, it is, therefore, a mistake to proclaim him the master and arbiter of Christian Europe. That he was a man of great influence is evident, but equally evident is his helplessness in the absence of happy circumstances that worked in his favor. His victories remind one of Gregory VII's initial success against Henry IV at Canossa. (See above, p. 228.) Which raises the question, what precisely was Innocent's position with regard to the state? Did he advance claims inconsistent with the Gelasian Doctrine,* which accepted the existence of two separate jurisdictions, in one of which the state was supreme, in the other the church? No, he did not. He did insist upon the traditional reservation popes made regarding kings and their conduct, that when monarchs erred morally, he had the right to intervene on the side of right. So when Philip divorced his first wife and married another, he committed a sin, wherefore Innocent had a right to interfere. Innocent also insisted that he could order kings to cease fighting one another, as he did in the case of John and Philip, on the argument that it was the pope's responsibility and right to defend the peace. And he justified his projecting himself into the controversy over the throne in Germany since, following Pope Leo's coronation of Charlemagne, he had the right to crown the emperor.

In this last case Innocent also urged another argument. In the instance of a controversy among kings which a civil court found impossible to resolve, and when there existed, accordingly, the danger of war, then the pope must be free to interpose his authority. For God

* This had been enunciated by Pope Gelasius (d. 496).

had so ordered the universe that there should be no war among Christians. If civil or feudal law could not prevent conflict, then appeal must be made to the highest spiritual authority, which was the pope. In order to provide some machinery by which Innocent could implement this position he was forever pressing kings to become his vassals. John was only the most important monarch to do so. Other kings who accepted his suzerainty included the rulers of Sicily, Portugal, Aragon, Hungary, Bohemia, and Poland. When the time came that all Christian kings accepted papal overlordship, then the pope could hope to abolish war among them. That was the kind of Christian commonwealth Innocent contemplated.

Innocent took time from his many cares to reform the papal curia. This, the pope's council or government, resembled in origin, purpose, and development the feudal monarch's Curia Regis. It consisted initially of those men who kept about the pope to advise and assist him in the administration of the church. As time passed and the work of the papacy grew in volume and complexity, the number of such advisers increased as did their degree of specialization. By the thirteenth century the papal curia included hundreds of clerks and officials—cardinals, secretaries, auditors, notaries—many of them from lands outside of Italy, and all of them occupied in some manner with the work of the curia.

As the curia's volume of business and its personnel increased, there appeared a tendency for the administration to divide into departments. The principal branch of the curia was the chancery, which handled official correspondence, issued formal pronouncements called bulls or decretals, and administered the general judicial business of the papacy. Its scribes were the most proficient in the Western world, their Latin the most polished, and their script the most legible. For it was of great importance that documents concerned with legal matters or doctrinal definition should say what they meant. An equally serious concern was the problem of thwarting the efforts of forgers. The papal seal, for instance, must contain seventy-three dots around its circumference, twenty-five around the head of St. Paul, twenty-six around St. Peter's head, with twenty-five to compose his hair and twenty-eight his beard.

The other major branch of the curia was the camera, which handled all fiscal business. Of a wide variety of revenues, the most lucrative were returns from papal estates. The camera also collected feudal dues from the aristocracy living in the Papal States and from kings outside who paid homage, the fees and fines that its judicial business brought in, fees for dispensations, a percentage of the income of newly instituted bishops and priests, legacies and gifts, fees from exempt monasteries, Peter's Pence from certain countries, and levies on the clergy for special purposes such as a crusade. Any enumeration of papal revenues, as is true of a listing of a feudal king's incomes as well, is apt to leave an unreal picture of their adequacy. Governments have always complained about the lack of revenue. Those of the Middle Ages had appreciably greater cause to do so since they were so hidebound by tradition.

Ably assisting the pope in their primary role as advisers were the cardinals. While the pope might place them in charge of the different branches of the curia or assign them to hear and determine disputes and appeals brought to his court, their principal function remained that of advising the pope. With the enactment in 1059 of the Papal Electoral Law they had also assumed official responsibility for electing a new pope. Up to that time the cardinal clergy were recruited in Rome or its environs. Once they acquired this new prerogative of electing the pope, kings insisted that their countries be represented in what came to be known as the college of cardinals. Within a short time most cardinals actually came to be non-Italians, although all took up their residence in Rome in order to be in a position to advise and help the pope. The degree to which the pope depended upon their advice varied with the individual pope. When Pope Urban VI let it be known that he would bypass his cardinals, his action helped precipitate the Great Western Schism. (See below, p. 381.)

There exists a general misconception concerning the power of the pope in the Middle Ages. Tradition accords him far more authority than he actually possessed. The source of the error is, of course, the powerful position the pope holds in the Roman church today. He did not enjoy that in the Middle Ages, not even when Innocent III was pope. In theory his position was indeed majestic. He was the vicar of Christ, God's closest representative. His power came from on high and no one could question him in the exercise of that authority. His claim to primacy received universal acceptance in the West. Only the pope could summon a church council, and of its decisions, only those of which he approved became binding. His pronouncements in doctrinal matters and the judgments of his court were considered definitive and final.

Of the factors which obstructed the pope in the free exercise of his theoretically unlimited authority over the medieval church, the primary and most unyielding was the opposing authority of the state. The struggle over investiture between Gregory VII and Henry IV had dramatized the clash of church-state authorities. The Concordat of Worms had eased the situation; from point of view of the church it had not provided a satisfactory solution. The king still retained a decisive voice in the selection of the hierarchy. All kings, for example, supported John's defiance of Pope Innocent over Stephen Langton. They generally had their way when they insisted upon having it. The pope did exercise a qualified check in his right to approve the consecration of bishops and to invest the newly elected archbishop with a special stole-like vestment called the pallium. In practice, however, papal approval of any bishop's or archbishop's election followed almost automatically once Rome had received notification of who the new incumbent might be. If this approval had not been forthcoming, most kings had effective means whereby they could force compliance.

What served the papacy most effectively in establishing the tradition of papal supremacy was the work of the religious orders, first the Benedictines, then the friars. The pope assured himself of their loyalty by generally exempting them from the jurisdiction of the local bishop. The evolution of canon law worked in the pope's favor since it accepted many of the same imperialist principles that underlay Roman law. The pope required bishops to make periodic visits to Rome, while he regularly sent his own legates to foreign countries in order to establish closer liaison with their hierarchies. The efficient and impersonal reputation of the papal court attracted a steadily growing number of appeals, while the pope kept reserving additional types of cases to his jurisdiction. And until the close of the fourteenth century, the number of appointments to benefices and parishes directly authorized by the papal curia tended to increase.

The medieval church served a number of purposes which the Christian of the Middle Ages considered vital. One was to worship God through the medium of a formal liturgical service. Another was to provide the means, principally the mass and the sacraments, by which the individual Christian could gain God's grace in his march toward eternity. A third purpose the church served was that of teaching the Christian what he must believe and what he must do in order to save his soul. In order to perform these functions, the church must staff its churches and monasteries with men of some learning. The priest (monk) must be able to read the Latin of the mass and the divine office, be able to sing, and to explain the gospel story. He must know how to reckon the date of Easter, even to do simple computation. In order to provide herself a trained clergy, the church maintained a system of education. For much of the period there was no other kind of education available.

The subjects studied in these church schools comprised the traditional liberal arts. Their content had been established in ancient times when Plato and Cicero discussed them. Who hit upon the number seven is not entirely clear. The number seven certainly recommended itself because of its unusual sanctity. So Cassiodorus in his introduction to the liberal arts wrote: "It is quite evident that the Sacred Scriptures frequently express by means of this number [seven] what they desire to be understood as continuous and perpetual." Varro (d. 27 B.C.), "the most learned of the Romans," composed lengthy descriptions of the nine liberal arts. To the traditional seven, he added medicine and architecture. Martianus Capella (d. 429) in his *Marriage of Philology and Mercury* introduced the liberal arts as so many bridesmaids at a wedding. As each appeared on the stage at the wedding reception, she took her turn telling the audience about herself. The lateness of the hour forced a curtailment of this part of the celebration, Capella explained, so that two other maids, medicine and architecture, were left waiting in the wings. By Capella's day these two subjects had apparently become professional and therefore omitted.

While the content of the liberal arts remained substantially in medieval times what it had been in the ancient world, its orientation was altered. In antiquity a liberal education, as the term suggests, was reserved, at least theoretically, to freemen. Presumably the unfree had no need for that kind of instruction. An educated man betokened, therefore, a citizen, one who could demonstrate his usefulness to society. Because of the severe limitations of educational facilities in medieval times, together with the presumed uselessness to most people of "book" knowledge, it became traditional to limit instruction in the liberal arts to those who had a positive need for education, namely, the clergy. There were many pious souls, indeed, who insisted that unless liberal instruction had some direct spiritual value, it was vain. During the Carolingian period it became customary to distinguish between the trivium, that is, the three ways to learning which included grammar, rhetoric, and dialectic; and the quadrivium, which consisted of arithmetic, geometry, astronomy, and music. In a broad sense the subjects of the trivium represented the arts: they provided the student the tools of learning. The subjects of the quadrivium might be equated with the sciences, that is, branches of learning which the student might approach after he had first acquired the proper tools to attack that knowledge.

The first of the seven liberal arts, and the most important in the early Middle Ages, was grammar. Alcuin defined the subject as the "science of letters and the guardian of right speech and writing." What the student learned was Latin grammar, how to read and write that language. He would begin with Donatus or Capella, then advance to Bede, the Bible, and the church fathers. For those who planned to become teachers of others, there would next be Vergil, Cicero, Livy, and Ovid. Such students would surely have commended themselves for their solidity of character, which was well. Not everyone should be exposed, so Alcuin warned, to the "dangerously smooth style" of Vergil.

Rhetoric, which had been the most popular of the liberal arts in Roman times, received scant attention. Cassiodorus defined the subject as the "art of speaking well on civil questions." For subject matter the teacher drew on pertinent treatises of Cicero and Quintilian. In addition to an introduction to law, the student acquired some skill at drafting letters and documents, as well as training in public speaking. In dialectic or logic, the student learned to construct an argument and to detect fallacies. For a manual he used Boethius' treatise. The more ambitious might turn to his translation of Porphyry's *Isagogue*, as well as the logical works of Aristotle which he had translated.

The earlier Middle Ages found the study of grammar, rhetoric, and dialectic easier and more rewarding than the study of the quadrivium. They, first of all, had less concern about these subjects. The Romans before them also evinced little interest in the sciences. Even in mathematics they had limited themselves to what was practical, which Cicero remarked was commendable. In arithmetic the Romans also passed on to the Middle Ages their use of letters as numerals, which rendered even simple addition and subtraction an arduous undertaking. Arithmetic included the study of chronology, which was useful, and the symbolic value of numbers, which was nonsense—a superstitious inheritance from antiquity. Only with the introduction of the abacus in the eleventh century did any significant progress in this subject become possible.

The loss of a knowledge of Greek was especially tragic in the study of geometry and astronomy. Until the eleventh century, when some of Euclid seeped in through the writings of Gerbert of Aurillac (see below, p. 326), geometry consisted of a little geography and surveying, and that was about all. The study of astronomy introduced the student to what Boethius and other transmitters had gleaned from Pliny the Elder, and what men like Bede may have added. What attached special importance to the study of astronomy was the reputed influence the moon and other heavenly bodies exerted upon plants, animals, and men. In music the student became acquainted with what Boethius and Cassiodorus had written on the subject. He also received some training in plain song. Early in the eleventh century Guido of Arezzo (d. 1050), a Benedictine monk, introduced the four-line staff and square notes, which facilitated the development of organum and counterpoint.

The spiritual orientation of medieval education becomes most evident when one moves on to consider the schools which provided instruction. All, or almost all, were maintained by the church. A few lay schools may have lingered on in the larger cities of Italy and Spain, but of these there is no firm knowledge. Of the existence of church schools there is no question, although much doubt concerning their quality. There were in general two kinds of schools, monastic and cathedral. Despite the clear need priests had for formal instruction, the number of cathedral schools which should have provided this was not appreciable before the thirteenth century. Monastic schools existed in all but the smallest religious communities since participation in the divine services made some knowledge mandatory. It would be a rare monastery which could not furnish both the time and a member or two of the community to give that instruction. In addition to the inner school where the novices received their instruction, some of the larger monasteries maintained an outer school for boys and young men who had no intention of becoming monks. Because of Charlemagne's encouragement, the number of such outer schools may have been significant during the ninth century. Thereafter their number dwindled. The troubled times that followed reduced their patronage, as did the rise of reform movements which generally regarded the presence of lay boys a dangerous intrusion into the religious life of the community.

Although the whole point of the instruction provided in these schools was religious, the subject that received most attention was Latin. It was that circumstance, not the spiritual objective of the instruction, which has appealed to modern humanists. They have enthused over the manner the monks collected ancient manuscripts during these centuries, how they copied them in order to have more available and to preserve them, and how they even put their hand to composing Latin verse. Some of the scholars who did this appeared in the list of transmitters of classical learning and in Charlemagne's palace school. Among the more prominent who appeared after Charlemagne's death was Hrabanus Maurus, known as the "first teacher of Germany." His presence at Fulda helped establish that monastery as the leading intellectual center of Germany in the ninth century. Maurus' pupil Walafrid Strabo, who spent his career at Reichenau, composed both religious and secular verse, as well as contributing biblical studies of real merit. Lupus, abbot of Ferriers, in his zeal for manuscripts was a prototype of the fourteenth-century humanist Poggio. And it is evident from his letters that he lived during times far less favorable to manuscript collecting. In a letter to a humanist friend and monk in the monastery at St. Gall, he warned him to be most wary and travel only in the company of a large group since "nothing occurs more frequently and constantly than robbery and violence." Should this friend come to Ferriers, Lupus asked him to bring with him "Sallust's Cataline and Jugurtha and the books of the Verrine orations (Cicero), and if there are any others you know we have either in imperfect shape or lack entirely, be good enough to bring to us that through your kindness those that are faulty may be corrected, and those that we do not have and can never have except through you may be acquired all the more gratefully because unexpectedly."

The most unusual humanist of the tenth century was the nun Hrotsvitha, member of the religious community at Gandersheim in Saxony. It is rare to read about any nun in the Middle Ages, let alone one who composed Latin poetry. The theme of her poetry was, of course, properly religious, that is, all except the hexameters she composed to commemorate the exploits of Otto the Great. (The abbess at Gandersheim was a niece of Otto's, which explains this "lapse" on the part of the pious Hrotsvitha.) Her best-known religious verse consisted of six moral dramas she composed after the model of Terence's comedies. She admired Terence's style, not the characters of his plays, especially the female ones who were often women of uncertain reputation. Hrotsvitha's heroines were all holy virgins who safeguarded their chastity even at the cost of their lives.

Two bishops of Chartres, one Fulbert and the other John of Salisbury, made that cathedral school probably the best in the West. Fulbert was a teacher by profession, and a great one, who found time to compose some verse. His most charming piece is entitled "Ode to the Nightingale." John combined broad learning and a polished Latin style with such wide acquaintance with the men of distinction in his day that he has been styled the Erasmus of his century. He was one humanist who appreciated the value of logic, although he condemned the futility of some of its disputations. In his best-known work, entitled *Polycraticus* or the *Statesman's Guide,* he discussed the character and duties of the ideal prince. His ideal ruler was an elected monarch who followed the advice of the church. It was from that institution that he received his authority.

Long before the death of John of Salisbury the popularity of grammar was already beginning to wane and its place of eminence among the seven liberal arts being appropriated by dialectic (logic). It is difficult to suggest any specific reason for this development beyond the general revival of learning that took place in the eleventh century. Scholarship had attained such a level of maturity that men no longer were content to digest what the transmitters of the Dark Ages had preserved. They began to give closer attention to the logical works of Aristotle which Boethius had translated, together with Porphyry's introduction to the *Categories.* This shift to the study of dialectic may also have some association, at least in terms of time, with the emergence of cathedral schools to positions of leadership. During the eleventh century Chartres, Reims, Paris, Orléans, York, and Lincoln came into prominence as centers of learning, although one could not deny the continued flourishing of the monastic schools at Monte Cassino and Bec.

The term "scholastic" is applied to this new scholar of the eleventh century who turned with special interest to the study of dialectic. In its simplest application, the designation "scholastic" might be given to any scholar or schoolman. As the term came to be applied, it referred more specifically to the scholar who pursued the study of logic and of metaphysics in his conviction that a knowledge of those subjects would facilitate his study of Christian theology. Scholasticism might therefore be defined as the system of thought that dominated the schools of the Middle Ages from the eleventh to the fifteenth century, which had as its objective the clarification of Christian faith with the help of reason.

Except for the premature scholar John Scotus Erigena (d. 880), who demonstrated his dialectical skill in his writings on Christian metaphysics, the era of scholasticism began with Gerbert of Aurillac (d. 1003). Gerbert was the most learned man of his day, master of the cathedral school at Reims, and later Pope Sylvester II. The breadth of his knowledge, which was remarkable for his times, embraced classical studies, dialectic, mathematics, and astronomy. Most of what he knew he acquired in Spain where scholarship was further advanced than in any other country of western Europe because of the introduction there of Islamic learning. Gerbert was successful in instilling in his pupils his enthusiasm for dialectic. One of these, Fulbert of Chartres, wrote of logic: "It is part of courage to have recourse to dialectic in all things, for recourse to dialectic is recourse to reason, and he who does not make use of reason abandons his principal honor, since by virtue of reason he was made in the image of God."

Berengar, one of Fulbert's pupils, took this instruction too seriously and applied it to the mystery of transubstantiation. According to the teaching of the church, the miracle of transubstantiation took place when the priest spoke the words, "This is my body," over the particles of bread. When Berengar approached this mystery through the eyes of a rationalist, therefore, he could only conclude that no miracle had taken place. After the priest's words, the bread still looked like bread, tasted like bread, smelled like bread. In short, Berengar reasoned, it remained bread.

Berengar's stand brought scholasticism to a crisis. Voices had already been raised in condemnation of this pagan emphasis on reason as an implicit denial of the validity of faith. Peter Damian had denounced it as a tool of the devil. Had Christ wanted erudite men to preach his gospels, he argued, he would have selected philosophers, not fishermen, to be his apostles. Lanfranc, the most influential teacher of the day, took up Berengar's challenge. He would have preferred leaving tradition and Scripture to solve theological questions, but if he was to save dialectic from ecclesiastical condemnation, he must answer Berengar on his own terms. For "dialectic," he explained, "is not an enemy of the mysteries of God if properly used; it rather confirms them." He proceeded to draw a distinction between the substance of the bread and its accidents, that is, its color, taste, and smell. Only the substance of the bread changed with the words of the priest, he explained, not the accidents. These remained the same after consecration even though a transubstantiation had taken place.

The scholastic whose learning, piety, and charm dispelled the misgivings and hostility of many churchmen and assured scholasticism honored reception in the church was Lanfranc's pupil, Anselm of Bec. For this, if for no other accomplishment, Anselm merits the title "father of scholasticism." He had gone to Bec from Italy in order to learn from Lanfranc, later became prior there, and still later archbishop of Canterbury. (See above, p. 215.) Despite his enormous debt to St. Augustine with whom his thinking is in complete harmony, Anselm is considered an unusually original thinker. In resolving issues such as that raised by Berengar, he charted the course that scholasticism adopted as eminently orthodox and reasonable. The Christian should never doubt what the church taught, so argued Anselm. Yet God gave man a mind and he was expected to use it. When confronted with some problem in faith which he wished to clarify, the Christian should "as far as he is able, to seek the reason for it. If he can understand it, let him thank God. If he cannot, let him not raise his head in opposition but bow in reverence."

Anselm also took a hand in another issue, the problem of universals, that was dividing thinkers in his day. No group of scholars disturbed Anselm more than did "those dialecticians, or rather dialectical heretics of our time, who maintain that universal substances are nothing but words." Such skeptics, he pleaded, "should not be permitted to take part in discussions of theological questions." The group which had aroused the gentle Anselm's ire was the nominalists. They had earned that designation for dismissing as mere words or names (Latin *nomen*, whence nominalist), such universal ideas as humanity, society, justice, and goodness. To the nominalist these and similar terms and concepts served no purpose beyond the purely semantic one of enabling men to discuss them intelligently.

Their position was the reverse of the realists, who maintained that universal ideas were much more than mere words, that they were indeed subsistent entities and possessed true reality. The realist would argue, for example, that it is only because the idea of justice has existence as a universal from all eternity, that man can judge acts as either just or unjust. For the realist, therefore, the general idea preceded the thing (*ante rem*). The nominalist reversed this sequence. Man started with acts, he reasoned. After judging these acts as to their merit and reasonableness, he had invented the term justice (*post rem*) in order to facilitate the process of evaluating behavior. While the term "justice" possessed usefulness, therefore, it remained nothing more than a term.

That the controversy over universals, far from being simply an exercise in dialectics, involved a fundamental issue became evident when the nominalist, Roscelin of Compiègne (d. 1122), proceeded to attack the doctrine of the Trinity. He was quite ready, he affirmed, to accept the existence of three persons, Father, Son, and Holy Spirit, even the value of the term Trinity to designate their oneness. But that the Trinity possessed any kind of entity apart from these three persons he refused to agree. Two centuries later another nominalist, William of Ockham (see below, p. 333), attacked the traditional view concerning the teaching authority of the church. To him the church was simply a term, nothing more, so how could it teach. If Christian man sought truth, he should go to the Scripture.

The leading scholastic of the first half of the twelfth century proposed a compromise on the issue of universals which most scholastics found acceptable. This man was Abelard and his solution of the issue conceptualism. Abelard started with the nominalist in agreeing that the mind first perceives similar objects, then abstracts what qualities they have in common, whereupon the idea comes into existence. But he disagreed with the nominalist, who simply treated this idea as a word. Abelard insisted that that idea was much more than a mere word, that it possessed intellectual reality, that it existed, not before (*ante rem*) nor after the thing (*post rem*), but in the thing (*in re*). The Trinity would, consequently, not have existed before the three persons, nor after the three persons, but in or with the three.

That Abelard should ever have exerted a moderating, even constructive influence, will strike some as curious. His name generally conjures up an image of turbulency and revolt. His father was a member of the lower aristocracy in Brittany, but Peter turned his back on his patrimony and went off to Paris to learn. In his search for an education, he had a number of distinguished teachers, including William of Champeaux and Roscelin. Still, Abelard disagreed with the manner these two handled the problem of universals; in fact, he appears to have been disagreeing with teachers and with ecclesiastical authorities most of his life. No doubt Abelard possessed a brilliant mind and was a master in dialectical argumentation. Yet he was vain, and many men who might have paid him a sympathetic ear, he alienated with his intellectual arrogance. Several times he set up a school of his own, then was offered a chair in the cathedral school at Notre Dame in Paris. There he became involved in an affair with Heloise, a young woman he was tutoring. Since marriage would have blighted his career, Heloise sought first to dissuade Abelard from marrying her, then agreed to a secret ceremony which her angry uncle and guardian accepted only because he had full intention of publicizing that fact. When Abelard subsequently sent Heloise off to a convent where she stoutly denied the marriage, the infuriated uncle had some ruffians attack and mutilate Abelard. In the end Abelard became a monk and Heloise a nun. Troubles continued to harass Abelard even as a monk. By temperament he proved unsuited to monastic life, either as a monk or abbot. Then his theological writings, particularly those concerning the Trinity, had St. Bernard and other unfriendly observers smelling heresy. He finally took himself off to Rome to defend his views, stopped on the way at Cluny, apparently made his peace with both the church and Bernard, and remained there to die.

Abelard's last active years which he spent teaching at Mont Ste Geneviève were his most productive. There he composed the *Sic et Non*, which is his best-known work. In this work he proposed some 150 doctrinal and moral propositions, then brought forward arguments in support of and in opposition to each. His purpose, as he stated in his preface, was to encourage questioning, since the "first key to wisdom is this, constant and frequent interrogation. For by doubt we are led to question, by questioning we arrive at the truth." That he based his arguments on testimony drawn from Scripture and the church fathers simply emphasized the point Abelard wished to make, namely, that one should not blindly accept on authority since the authorities themselves may not agree.

When Abelard died, scholasticism stood at the threshold of its most brilliant era. This was partly his doing and that of Anselm and the other early scholastics. Most effective, however, in opening the doors to the vast intellectual expansion of the thirteenth century was the introduction of Aristotle's works and the writings of Arabic and Jewish commentators. These began filtering into western Europe in the 1130s. By the close of the century all of Aristotle's works—those dealing with ethics, politics, rhetoric, metaphysics, physics, the natural sciences, and his more advanced logical writings—had become available. The impact of this learning on Western scholarship was staggering. Scholars, theologians, and ecclesiastical authorities all talked about Aristotle. Some condemned him out of hand as a pagan who maintained positions on creation, on the immortality of the soul, and on the eternity of matter to which no Christian could subscribe. Others, called the Latin Averroists because their devotion to the Greek philosopher was almost as unquestioning as that of Averroës, were ready to accept him as the final arbiter in all metaphysical questions not specifically blocked by dogma. The position of the majority lay somewhere between these extremes. They welcomed Aristotle and began an earnest study of his writings for what light they could throw on Christian faith.

The man who convinced the doubting that Aristotle offered much the Christian West could use was Albert the Great (Albertus Magnus). A long life of study and teaching, which he dedicated to making Aristotle intelligible to the Latin world, had convinced him that those ancient scholars like Aristotle, "despite their paganism, have none the less spoken in a wonderful manner of the Creator and His creatures. Virtue and vice they knew, and a great number of truths which faith as well as reason announce from on high." Possibly because Albert bit off too much for a trail blazer, his thinking is occasionally muddled and disorganized. He made his most valuable and original contribution in zoology and botany, although his principal distinction is that he was the teacher of Thomas Aquinas.

In Thomas (d. 1274) scholastic thought attained its highest perfection and discovered its most eloquent exponent. That he caused the philosophical basis of Christian thought to shift from Augustinian Neo-Platonism to Aristotle provides proof of his immense influence. Thomas was able to accomplish this revolution on the strength of his remarkable intellectual powers, his appreciation of Aristotle's profundity, his ability to adapt much of that pagan philosopher's thought to the service of Christian faith, and, finally, the superbly harmonious and convincing manner in which he presented his thought. His principal works include the Summa Contra Gentiles, in which he presented his theological system in rational terms a non-Christian might accept, and his Summa Theologiae, which he did not complete. This last provides, nevertheless, a near-complete synthesis of Christian faith and morals sustained by a sturdy fabric woven from Scripture, tradition, the teaching of the church, and reason.

Until the time of Aquinas, reason had constituted a useful, though not a major nor even independent, factor in elucidating the Christian faith. Thomas now distinguished it sharply from faith and assigned it an important role of its own. In the natural order its authority was pre-eminent, as was faith's in the supernatural order. Yet since God had made both the natural and supernatural orders, faith and reason were in complete harmony. This was, of course, only logical, since the omniscient God, who was the author of all things, could not teach one thing in revelation and another in nature. Faith and reason complemented one another. Faith drew its matter from revelation and dealt with divine truths which transcended reason. Reason started with what experience and observation taught. If man is to live intelligently, he must make use of both faith and reason. So while Thomas offered his reader five proofs from reason to demonstrate the existence of God, he immediately reminded him that, if he was to believe and to love God, it was necessary that he be in God's grace.

Thomas' deep faith helps explain his complete dedication to learning, for what he learned he did so for the honor and glory of God. There is a charming story which illustrates that dedication, about the occasion Louis IX of France invited the learned scholastic to dine with him and his court. Thomas had no appetite for such formal gatherings, and begged his prior to excuse him, but without success. So this particular day Thomas found himself sitting at the banquet table with scores of courtiers and their ladies in the presence of the king, all the others chatting gaily with one other, he in deep silence pondering a problem that had proved particularly vexing. All of a sudden he struck the table with his great fist—Thomas was a heavy man—and exclaimed: "That will refute the Manichaeans." His embarrassed prior grabbed him by the arm to wake him from his study, whereupon Thomas rose and bowed his humble apology to the king for having been so rude. That was quite unnecessary, Louis assured him, and lest Thomas happen to forget the happy solution he had come upon, the king sent an attendant to the learned man to make a note of the matter.

Meantime the Franciscan Bonaventure (d. 1274), who was the contemporary of the Dominican Thomas, was pointing out the course Franciscan thought, as opposed to Dominican, would generally pursue. That a Franciscan friar should have essayed the role of a formal scholar requires some explanation. St. Francis had already been aware of differences of opinion among his friars as to the propriety of holding corporate property and of attending the universities, both of which he had condemned. These issues came to a head after his death, and it was largely the skill and prudent leadership of Bonaventure, who was minister-general of the order, which prevented the Franciscan community from breaking up. He reorganized the constitution of the order, wrote a commentary on the rule, and, to the point of this discussion of scholasticism, convinced the order to recognize the intellectual discipline involved in study as worthy a form of asceticism as manual labor and physical mortification.

Bonaventure remained with the Augustinian tradition which had characterized scholastic thought before the advent of Aristotle. He subscribed without modification to the formula which Anselm had inherited from Augustine, *credo ut intelligam*, meaning, "I believe that I may understand." Faith sought understanding, but this would depend heavily upon God's grace. Because of the sin of Adam, man could no longer contemplate God directly. It required an effort of his will, and this will only God's grace could activate and sustain. Only by means of faith could man understand first principles and come to the knowledge of the existence of God. Bonaventure had little interest, therefore, in reason as based upon experience and natural theology as a means of arriving at spiritual truth and the knowledge of God. In this he differed from Thomas, and he also placed greater reliance upon God's grace than did the Dominican. He remained, in fact, fundamentally a theologian, rather than a scholastic, and his best-known work is a mystical treatise entitled *Journey of the Soul to God*. This journey man could make without the assistance of natural knowledge.

Duns Scotus (d. 1308), the most distinguished of the Franciscan scholastics, continued generally in Bonaventure's footsteps although he accepted considerably more Aristotelian influences. He studied at Oxford, then at Paris, but was expelled with other Englishmen by Philip the Fair and went to Cologne where he died. It is unfortunate that his death came at the early age of forty. Subsequent writing might have brought his work to full maturity and may also have furnished it greater polish. What further complicates the analysis of Duns Scotus' thought is the questionable authenticity of some of the works ascribed to him.

In agreement with Bonaventure, Duns Scotus limited the role of reason in the pursuit of divine knowledge. He went a large step further, indeed, and denied any complementary relationship between faith and reason. They belonged to different worlds. Reason and philosophy dealt with the natural order and with being; theology was concerned with God. Since revelation was a matter of faith and of divine origin, reason can contribute nothing to its confirmation. The theologian and the philosopher are different men and have different concerns. The truths that the theologian pursues depend upon faith and revelation for their proof, not on reason as based upon experience and natural theology. So he dismissed Thomas' five proofs of God's existence from sense experience as resting upon an untenable premise. In keeping with Augustinian tradition Duns Scotus also emphasized the primacy of the human will in human action. The will commanded the intellect, not the reverse, and the will in turn was motivated by God's grace.

The third great Franciscan thinker to appear within fifty years was William of Ockham (d. 1349). For most of his active career he was in open warfare with the papacy. His lectures on the *Sentences* of Peter Lombard had drawn charges of unorthodoxy, and he had gone to Avignon where the pope was making his home, in order to defend himself. There he met the minister-general of the Franciscan order, who bade him scrutinize papal pronouncements and the decrees of church councils on the subject of apostolic poverty. Both he and the minister-general sympathized with the view of the "radical" Franciscans that it was sinful for priests to hold property. When the pope declared that position heretical, Ockham fled to the court of Louis of Bavaria where he spent the rest of his life as an excommunicate, busily engaged in publishing pamphlets denouncing papal authority and urging the supremacy of the church council. (See below, p. 382.)

William of Ockham drove a still deeper wedge between faith and reason than had his predecessor Duns Scotus. He denied the existence of universals, attacked the moderate realism of Thomas, and even denied metaphysics an existence. He maintained that only by faith and revelation can man accept the existence of God. He further insisted that God does not work through reason, nor do the presumed intelligence and order reflected in the universe bind the divine will in any way. For the power of God was not only absolute; it also defied any kind of limitation. God might do what he pleased, and what he pleased to do was good. This was the reverse of Thomas' position that God only did what was good. So arbitrary could God be, in Ockham's judgment, that it was useless to speak of standards of good and evil. God may reward and punish as he sees fit.

Such attacks as Ockham's proved disastrous to scholasticism. They denied the basic premise of scholasticism that faith and reason complemented one another and that reason was useful in explaining the faith. Even without the appearance of Ockham's views, it was inevitable that scholasticism should have suffered decline. Thomas Aquinas, Bonaventure, Duns Scotus, and the earlier scholastics had resolved, to the satisfaction of their followers at least, most of the fundamental problems confronting theologians. The consequence was that a good deal of the scholarly activity of the late fourteenth century passed beyond the point of refining those solutions to sink to the level of hair-splitting. Because of this circumstance Ockham's views contributed to bringing about a shift of emphasis in scholastic thought. In the past God had been the center of that study. But if God's will was without limitation of any kind, why study God? So major attention swung to man, to grace, free will, sin, and sanctification.

Meantime as scholasticism rose and flowered, it witnessed, if it did not give birth to, another intellectual development. That was the medieval university. Both in origin and in interests, the university was so closely associated with scholasticism that it is impossible to separate the one from the other. What happened in substance was this, that as scholasticism grew more popular, its interests broader, and the new knowledge from the Islamic and Byzantine worlds permitted a vast expansion of its subject matter, the traditional cathedral school underwent a transformation: it became a university. This, then, was one of the major factors in the rise of the university, namely, the vigorous intellectual life of the cathedral schools of the twelfth century. The other principal factor was the higher learning that came to the West by way of Islam and Constantinople and which the scholars seized upon and sought to assimilate. This learning included the works of Aristotle, Ptolemy, and Galen, in addition the commentaries of Arabic and Jewish scholars, and the *Corpus Juris Civilis* of Justinian. From the interaction of these two factors, the intellectual vigor of scholasticism with this higher learning from the East, sprang the medieval university.

A glance at the institutional evolution of the university will confirm the manner in which these two factors collaborated to bring it into existence. It should be noted, first of all, that the university evolved from the cathedral rather than from the monastic school. Of the two, the cathedral school was the more responsive to the expanding intellectual, legal, and theological demands of the times. Furthermore, those cathedral schools grew most rapidly, both in number of students and fame, which had the most advanced instruction to offer. Such a cathedral school would shortly receive the name of *studium generale*. This meant, in effect, that it was offering instruction in one or more of the higher faculties of theology, law, and medicine, and that it was attracting students from beyond the immediate vicinity. By the thirteenth century the term *studium generale* also assured the student who completed his instruction there, that he could teach anywhere in Western Europe.

A third step in the institutional evolution of the university came with the appearance of the gild. This was the organization of the masters at such a *studium generale*, or of the students there or of both masters and students, into a gild, not unlike the more common trade associations that handled buying and selling in the town. Such organizations became a necessity in the early stages in the evolution of the university when church and state had as yet not come forward with charters to extend their protection. Until then the students or masters or both needed protection against the local authorities, who frequently lacked sympathy for the boisterous life occasionally displayed by the student body. They might need protection, too, against gouging landlords and landladies. Foreign students—and there were many more of these in the medieval university than is the custom today—were especially desirous of some protection since they were normally without rights of any kind. The university might itself feel defenseless against the interference of the bishop who was officially its head. In order to meet these needs, the masters or students or the two together might organize a gild in order to secure the necessary "rights." The conventional Latin term for gild was *universitas*, whether a gild of butchers or of students. By the late Middle Ages the *universitas* of students had managed to appropriate that term for its own use.

One of the earliest universities, if not the first, was the university of Bologna. When the outlines of the school appear in the eleventh century, it was municipally organized and controlled by laymen. This circumstance has led some scholars to suggest that its origins extended back into antiquity. Perhaps a tradition of legal studies had persisted there from Roman times. During the investiture conflict, the number of students grew as both pope and king made increasing appeals to the law. The presence at Bologna of the distinguished jurists Irnerius (d. 1125) and Gratian (*ca.* 1140) also attracted many students. In 1158 Frederick Barbarossa granted the institution a formal charter. What was most unique about the university of Bologna was the control exercised there by the students. They hired the instructors, prescribed the subject matter, and fined any master who might absent himself from class, might begin lecturing late or go beyond the stipulated class period, or might fail to cover all the material. Masters were also required to take an oath that they would not leave the city in search of more lucrative employment elsewhere.

The most renowned of all medieval universities was that which evolved from the cathedral school of Notre Dame at Paris. Two other schools, Mont Ste Geneviève and the abbey of St. Victor, also attracted students to Paris. Many flocked there to hear Abelard. By 1200 the school had spread from the island on which the cathedral was located, to the left bank of the Seine which has retained its name, the Latin Quarter. In that year Philip Augustus granted the institution a charter which provided the students benefit of clergy. They had threatened to leave the city after the brutal manner the local authorities had suppressed a riot. In 1210 the pope recognized the gild of masters and in 1229 gave it independence from the bishop. Paris retained its eminence as the theological arbiter of Europe until the Great Western Schism when most German and foreign students withdrew. The majority of English students had already left back in 1167, whence they moved north of London to establish Oxford. Oxford's permanent foundation dates from 1214 when the pope granted it a charter, although it was not entirely free from the authority of the bishop of Lincoln until 1367. The medieval university enjoyed a high degree of academic freedom, and both church and state were reluctant to interfere in its life. Even the "heretic" Wyclif was permitted to lecture at Oxford so long as he did not preach outside its halls.

The major components of the medieval university were its faculties; in modern parlance, its colleges. Few universities boasted all the four faculties of the arts, law (canon and civil), medicine, and theology. However many faculties existed, they were usually autonomous. Their masters might determine the subject matter, grant their own degrees, and elect the rector of the institution. Frequently the dean of the arts faculty was the most powerful of all officials since all students ordinarily enrolled in his faculty before proceeding on to the professional schools of law, medicine, and theology. Most students did not progress beyond the arts degree.

In theory the curriculum pursued in the arts faculty represented the old trivium and quadrivium. In practice the course of study did not venture far beyond Aristotle, his ethics, metaphysics, natural sciences, and logic. The principal matter studied by law students consisted of the *Digest* in civil law, of Gratian's *Decretum* in canon law. Galen provided the core of the matter in medicine, together with the *Canon* of Avicenna and the commentaries of other Arabic scholars. In theology the student studied the Bible, the writings of the church fathers, and the *Sentences* of Peter Lombard. After four years of study in the arts curriculum, the student received a bachelor's degree. Many of them stopped there. Those who wished to teach devoted another two years to study, after which they received a master's degree, that is, after they had convinced their examiners that they were masters at that trade. A graduate in one of the professional faculties received a doctor's degree upon completion of his work, although the Middle Ages insisted upon no more standardization in this matter than does the modern world.

An appealing feature of the medieval university was the generous assistance poor youths might receive from church, king, or wealthy benefactor to further their education. The church came forward with benefices; lay benefactors might establish lodging houses as did Robert of Sorbon at Paris. His was one of the first "colleges" of its kind. As the years passed, such a dormitory assumed an increasing share of the responsibility of educating the student. In the later Middle Ages when wealthy patrons founded colleges, such as Balliol and Merton at Oxford, these constituted complete educational institutions. Poor students who lacked other means might work their way through the university by copying manuscripts, or they might beg. One of the heritages of the medieval university is the verses which students continue to sing about the "wandering scholar" who probably never quite disappeared from that campus.

I, a wandering scholar lad,
Born for toil and sadness,
Oftentimes am driven by
Poverty to madness.

Literature and knowledge I
Fain would still be earning,
Were it not that want of pelf
Makes me cease from learning.

These torn clothes that cover me
Are too thin and rotten;
Oft I have to suffer cold,
By the warmth forgotten.

Scarce I can attend at church,
Sing God's praises duly;
Mass and vespers both I miss,
Though I love them truly.

Oh, thou pride of N_____,
By thy worth I pray thee
Give the suppliant help in need,
Heaven will sure repay thee.

Take a mind unto thee now
Like unto St. Martin;
Clothe the pilgrim's nakedness,
Wish me well at parting.

So may God translate your soul
Into peace eternal,
And the bliss of saints be yours
In his realm supernal.

The medieval university did not limit itself to the study of metaphysics, theology, law, and medicine. It also contributed significantly to the advance of science. That the curriculum in medicine concentrated on what passed as scientific studies is understandable. Yet even in the arts curriculum the student gained some acquaintance with astronomy, physics, meteorology, geometry, optics, mathematics, and what the Middle Ages called natural philosophy but the modern world knows as natural science in general. Roger Bacon even recommended the study of techniques employed by artisans and alchemists. And when he declared that the study of theoretical sciences was justified principally by the use man made of them, he sounded thoroughly modern.

Before commenting on the two most prominent scientists of the Middle Ages, a word about compilers of scientific lore. The Franciscan Alexander of Hales (d. 1245) gathered what he could find in Pliny, in bestiaries (see below, p. 340), in Aristotle, and from his own observations, and incorporated this along with other information in his massive *Summa*. Roger Bacon said the work "weighed about as much as one horse could carry," although in his usual uncharitable manner he denied that any of it was Alexander's own contribution. Alexander of Neckham (d. 1217) presented in *On the Nature of Things* a mass of scattered information, including valuable information about the compass which he had gathered from his reading and observations. In good medieval fashion he often saw God's hand in nature, and he delighted in drawing moral lessons. After telling the story of the wren that hid itself in the wing of the eagle, then perched on the eagle's head when that great bird had flown higher than any other and was about to claim supreme power for that feat, Neckham observed: "This fable touches those who enter upon the works of others and presumptuously appropriate the credit due elsewhere. As the philosopher says, 'We are dwarfs standing upon giants' shoulders.' We should therefore be careful to ascribe to our predecessors those things which we ought not to claim for our own glory, and not follow the example of that wren which, with little or no effort of its own, claimed to have outdone the eagle." The most impressive of medieval scientific encyclopedias was

Vincent of Beauvais' *Speculum Maius* (*Greater Mirror*). Its contents, he claimed, included "whatever has been made or done or said in the visible and invisible world from the beginning until the end, and also of things to come."

The two leading scientists of the Middle Ages were Robert Grosseteste (d. 1253) and his pupil Roger Bacon (d. 1292). Robert Grosseteste began his public career as chancellor of Oxford and ended it as bishop of Lincoln. Throughout his long and active life he encouraged his disciples to study Greek and Arabic, and mathematics as well, in order to assimilate what the Greeks had written in science and to build on that foundation a contribution of their own. What he found particularly intriguing was the study of astronomy and the physical problems associated with light, color, heat, and sound. Despite a full career as prelate, reformer, and statesman, he made a significant contribution in the fields of optics and calendar reform.

His pupil Roger Bacon is the more famous of the two, less because of what he achieved than the difficulties he encountered with his superiors and the spectacular technological advances he predicted would eventually come through science. Bacon had a sharper tongue than Abelard and, like that scholastic, few friends to take his part when he got into difficulties. Like his mentor Grosseteste, Bacon urged the study of languages and mathematics, and contributed knowledge from his own experiments in the study of the refraction and reflection of light. Though he had a mind of great critical power, he accepted the usual claims of his age concerning alchemy and astrology. These last led to his confinement for a time, although the circumstances attending this incident are not all known. Bacon had first been headed toward a career in theology, then returned to Oxford from Paris where Grosseteste persuaded him to devote himself to science. Later Bacon attacked the work of the scholastics as largely a waste of time, and pleaded instead for greater attention to the experimental sciences. In his *Opus Maius* he wrote that "there are two ways of learning, that is, through reasoning and through experience . . . [yet] reasoning does not suffice, but only experience."

From intellectual life to literature is a small step today. In the Middle Ages it was a longer one, although less so in the field of medieval Latin literature than in the vernacular. Among the names of medieval Latin poets, for instance, we meet with scholastics like Abelard and Thomas Aquinas. These men wrote only Latin, and if the fancy struck them to versify, they composed in Latin. The Latin they used, however, was not that of ancient Rome. To distinguish it from the classical Latin of Cicero, it goes under the name of medieval Latin. An excellent example of this Latin—and there are hundreds, most of them inferior—is that in Jerome's *Vulgate*. It will be recalled that Jerome chose a simple grammar and word order for his text in order to accommodate his less learned readers. These qualities of relative simplicity, together with a broader vocabulary to meet the needs of the new age, remain the distinguishing characteristics of medieval Latin. A scholar who knows classical Latin will read medieval Latin with the aid of a dictionary—but he will not enjoy it. Its style is functional, narrative at best. Still this same classical scholar might give grudging admiration to the polished, precise style in which papal letters and bulls were composed.

While medieval Latin prose generally lacked literary quality, to an unsophisticated age it could be immensely popular. Most popular were the lives of the saints. Such tales recounted the marvelous, heroic, and edifying in the lives of holy men and women about whom most people had heard. Another class of Latin prose went by the name of Gesta Romanorum. These included stories of a wide variety, about the only constant feature being the Roman name borne by this or that character and the moral which they usually preached. One such story presented an early version of "The Merchant of Venice." More factual and of far greater value to historians were the chronicles kept by many monasteries. The larger part of what the modern world knows about the history of medieval times it has derived from chronicles like those written by Matthew Paris of the monastery of St. Albans and Otto of Freising. Bestiaries make up a small but interesting group of Latin prose writings. These purport to present scientific descriptions of animals, birds, and insects, together with the spiritual or symbolic significance each of these subjects might have for mankind.

There also remains from the Middle Ages a rich store of medieval Latin poetry. This is not so massive in volume as the Latin prose literature but far superior in quality. The verse form these medieval poets employed was itself a contribution. In contrast to the classical quantitative verse of antiquity, the rhythm of medieval verse was based upon accent, upon the sequence of accented and non-accented syllables. Scores of poets, including St. Bernard and Innocent III, tried their hand at this verse. Many of their poems made their way into the liturgy. Adam of St. Victor has been acclaimed the leading medieval

Latin poet, while the best known of medieval hymns is the *Dies Irae* (day of wrath or judgment day) of Thomas of Celano. The twelfth and thirteenth centuries, which produced the finest religious verse, also witnessed the appearance of the best secular Latin verse. This bears the traditional name of goliardic verse since Golias, whoever he might have been, was accepted by university students and masters who composed this verse as their patron. An example of the light-hearted themes that characterized this verse is provided by the "Wandering Student's Petition." (See above, p. 337.)

While medieval Latin literature holds real interest for the historian and deserves the attention of literary critics, it affords little insight into the general life of the Middle Ages. Its themes were too narrow. Religious poetry reveals the faith of the period; the secular verse, what university students may have sung about in their frivolous moments. Furthermore, since Latin was the language of this literature, it was limited in its enjoyment to the small minority of people who knew Latin. The literature which told about the people of the Middle Ages, which expressed their thoughts, which they loved to read or have read (sung) to them, appeared in the vernacular. No facet of medieval culture is more uniquely medieval than the vernacular literature of the early and high Middle Ages.

The oldest vernacular literature of a people usually consists of songs about their ancient warriors. These songs—epic poems they are called —are frequently the first pieces of an ancient heritage that a people writes down once it acquires a script. Much of the epic poetry of the early Germans of the Middle Ages was never written down. The Germans themselves could not write, while the missionaries who converted them saw little value in those old pagan tales. If Charlemagne had had his way, some of these tales would have come down to us. For "He also had the old rude songs that celebrate the deeds and wars of the ancient kings written out for transmission to posterity." Unfortunately, these poems ran afoul of Louis the Pious' censorship. A few of the primitive epics have been preserved including *Beowulf* and the *Nibelungenlied* (*Song of the Nibelungs*). Less ancient and more historical are the sagas of Scandinavia. One can enjoy a recreation of the conditions they depict—the harsh life of the people, the first influences of Christianity, the moderately successful efforts of the *Ding* (court) to reduce the constant feuding among clans—in the novels of Sigrid Undset.

Such epics reflect an age almost primitive in its culture. The more advanced epic poems of the eleventh and twelfth centuries are literary productions. They do not represent tales from an ancient past. The principal Spanish epic, *Poema del Cid* (*Poem of the Cid*), glorifies the exploits, some of them probably authentic, of the Castilian warrior Rodrigo Díaz de Bivar (see above, p. 221). The most famous of all medieval epics, the *Chanson de Roland* (*Song of Roland*), also falls into this category. The hero of the long poem is the nephew of Charlemagne. According to the tale, Roland was in charge of the rear guard which the Moslems annihilated in the mountain pass at Roncevaux (see above, p. 203). Who composed the poem remains a mystery. Perhaps priests and minstrels who traveled the pilgrim routes to various European shrines, had a hand in gathering together different songs about Roland into one continuous piece. Both the *Poema del Cid* and *Chanson de Roland* glorify chivalry and heroism, and the virtues of courage and loyalty which every honorable warrior should possess. The few expressions of national pride which appear in these poems are among the earliest discovered in European literature.

As interest in the epic ebbed and tastes demanded something different, there appeared another kind of heroic poem called the romance (courtly). What was principally different about this poem was the presence of beautiful women—Queen Guinevere, Lunette, Isolde, and many others. They brought with them the elements of love and romance which were absent in the epic. A popular romance told the story of Tristan and Isolde. Tristan had brought the beautiful princess Isolde from Ireland to become the bride of his aging King Mark of Cornwall. By having Tristan and Isolde drink a love potion which had been intended for Mark and Isolde, the author of the poem brought more tragedy, and love too for that matter, into the story than most romances contained. Chrétien de Troyes (*ca.* 1180) popularized the romance in France, whence it moved to Germany where a number of distinguished poets, including Wolfram von Eschenbach, adopted it. His *Parzival* who goes in search of the Holy Grail is one of the finest of all medieval romances.

The twelfth century also welcomed lyric poetry in the *langue d'oc* of southern France. The composer of this kind of verse was the troubadour (one who composes verse). His theme was love, its joys and, when the Lady refused to unbend, its disappointments. As Vidal complained:

My loving heart, my faithfulness, myself, my world she deigns to take,
Then leave me bare and comfortless to longing thoughts that ever
    wake.

No medieval literary type has generated more controversy concerning
its origins, the kind of love it sang about, even the role of its author.
Was he first a poet, for instance, or a musician? Whatever else he was,
the troubadour was a versatile artist. He sang a variety of themes
—the dawn song about the nightingale who would warn the lovers of
the coming dawn; the *pastourelle* about the knight who chanced upon
the beautiful shepherdess; and many others—always in a stanza form
all its own and after a different rhyme scheme. The most popular
of all troubadour songs was the formal love lyric (*canzone*). The leading author of this kind of love poem, at least in his own judgment,
was Bernard de Ventadour. "It is no wonder," he boasted, "that I sing
better than any other singer; for my heart draws me more than others
toward Love, and I am better made for his commandments." The
best known of the German minnesingers (*Minne*, love) was Walther
von der Vogelweide (d. 1228).

The lyric poetry of the troubadour especially charmed the hearts
of the aristocracy. What the common people, the townspeople above
all, found most enjoyable, were short, humorous poems called fabliaux. Any anecdote might serve as the theme of the fabliaux, however
indecorous it might be, provided it was light and entertaining. Anecdotes that fit this definition have a tradition of long life as they make
their way from one century to another and from one culture and country to the next. Scholars have traced fabliaux back to ancient times, to
India, and to the *Arabian Nights*. The characters change to fit the
country and the times. The standard ones of the medieval fabliaux
included the prosperous though often duped merchant, the slow-
witted peasant, the unprincipled clerk, and the woman who was always willing to share her virtue for entertainment's sake (the reader's
too). One fabliau told of the stableboy who wandered into the street
of the apothecaries where the vile gases caused him to swoon away.
The only thing that could revive him was a forkful of manure that a
thoughtful bystander hurried to procure and hold in front of his nose!

As entertaining as the fabliaux, though possessing a wholly original
humor, was the *Roman de Renart*. The name Reynard was that of the
wily fox who was the central figure in this collection of animal stories.
The use of animals as characters is as old as the fables of Aesop, and

the Middle Ages also had its fables. In the *Roman de Renart,* however, the different episodes in which Reynard encounters Isengrim the wolf, Nobel the lion, Brun the bear, Chanticleer the cock, and others of his brother animals, are only intended to entertain. There is no thought, at least originally, of moral or satire. The modern world continues to find the incongruity of animals acting like human beings a delightful source of entertainment in such comic strips as Pogo and Peanuts.

The *Roman de Renart* is an allegory of a sort; that is, it presents ideas by means of characters that are not entirely lifelike. Since the theme of an allegory is ordinarily a serious one, a more representative medieval story of this kind is the *Roman de la Rose* (*Romance of the Rose*). This long poem of some twenty-two thousand lines had two authors, William of Lorris of the first part, Jean de Meun of the second. The story is of a youth who falls asleep and dreams of a rose, actually a young woman whom he seeks after until he finds and possesses. Such a simple plot should not have required so long to tell had not the authors introduced all manner of obstacles such as Danger, Evil Tongue, Jealousy, even Reason who seeks unsuccessfully to dissuade the young man from his search. What the reader finds most interesting in the poem are the digressive observations that Jean de Meun offers about the people, problems, and conditions of the thirteenth century.

As uniquely medieval as the romance and troubadour song was the mystery play of the high Middle Ages. This was a wholly religious dramatic composition that had its germ in the trope. This in turn represented an interpolation of a passage in the liturgy of the divine office or of the mass for the purpose of clarifying or dramatizing its meaning. One of the first tropes was the Easter play *Quem Quaeritis,* of the tenth century, which described the meeting of the holy women with the angel before the tomb of the risen Christ. In time the popularity of such tropes led to the evolution of formal dramatic performances called mystery plays. The theme of the mystery play was drawn from the Bible. That of the miracle play, which followed shortly after, concerned saints and their miracles. Morality plays, of which *Everyman* is an example, appeared in the late Middle Ages.

To many art historians, the crowning achievement of the high Middle Ages was the Gothic cathedrals of Chartres, Reims, and Amiens. All three churches were begun within twenty-six years of each other,

Chartres, the first getting under way in 1194. As it happened—or did it just happen?—all three were located in northern France, close to Paris where Gothic is supposed to have originated. Some scholars will affirm that Gothic represents a new stylistic movement whose innate principles of form need not have had their origins in earlier styles. The majority of art historians will maintain, however, that Gothic represents a logical extension of architectural principles present in Romanesque. In any event, since Romanesque preceded Gothic chronologically and, in the judgment of many critics, is quite as impressive and beautiful, it is only proper to take a glimpse at what passes as a typical Romanesque church of the twelfth century before passing on to Gothic.

A representative Romanesque church is St. Sernin in Toulouse. This church was begun late in the eleventh and completed early in the twelfth century, a time which is generally recognized as marking the height of the Romanesque period. Most characteristic of St. Sernin and all Romanesque churches is the massive barrel vault that spans the nave. In the case of St. Sernin, transverse arches that connect with piers directly opposite each other, support this vault. The use of transverse arches permitted the architect to reduce the weight of the vault while at the same time breaking its monotonous expanse. It did not solve the problem of light, for the nave of St. Sernin is quite dark. It could not be otherwise since the clerestory, which had introduced a wealth of light into the basilica of the early church, had all but been eliminated. The small windows that remained proved incapable of illuminating the upper nave area. The heavy piers of St. Sernin that divide the nave from the aisles were a feature of all Romanesque churches. About Romanesque there is, in general, an atmosphere of strength, solidity, and permanence.

What the Romanesque architect did do in order to bring light into his church was to use a groined or cross vault, instead of a barrel vault, over the aisle areas. The superiority of the cross vault for this purpose is quite evident. Because its weight is concentrated at four corners, it permitted the removal of the intervening wall and its replacement with windows. So the Romanesque architect placed windows in his aisle walls, though they were unfortunately too far from the nave to accomplish all that was hoped for in relieving the gloom. That the Romanesque architect did not replace the barrel vault over the nave with a cross vault in order to insert additional and larger windows in the upper nave area either stemmed from his preference for the unique, if somewhat darkened, beauty of the church, or from his inability to do so. For so long as he used a square cross vault whose arches were equal half-circles, it could not be fitted over the rectangular sections of the nave vault, which were not square.

In the simplest structural or architectural terms, what basically changed the Romanesque to a Gothic church was the introduction of the cross vault over the nave. The Gothic architect accomplished this by pointing the arches on the two shorter sides of the cross vault in order to bring their level to an even plane with the two arches along the two longer sides. And now that he had this cross vault over the nave, he did what the Romanesque architect had done with the aisle walls, he filled the upper nave wall, the clerestory area, with windows.

The pointed arch had solved the Gothic architect's problem but it had not satisfied him. He wanted still more windows and he wanted more height. He took yet another step. He brought his buttressing out from under the aisle roof where it had supported the nave wall, and placed it outside above the roof. He added what architects call a flying buttress. With the aid of this buttressing there was almost nothing now that would stop him from raising his nave ceiling to any height he desired. The nave of Chartres went to 120 feet, at Reims to 125, and at Amiens to 138—the chronological sequence in which the three naves were completed!

There is much more to Romanesque and Gothic than engineering. The sculpture of both churches has inspired countless treatises, while thousands of visitors have been enraptured by the stained glass of the Gothic cathedrals. Most of this glass, incidentally, is not the medieval, although in Chartres, of the original 186 windows, 152 still remain in place. It is at Chartres where the "supernatural" beauty of medieval stained glass can still be appreciated. Its interior "is bathed in a dark, reddish-violet light, which has a mysterious quality difficult to describe, and which, in particular, does not come from a single source, seeming to fluctuate in its brightness according to the weather of the natural world outside, now swelling, now receding, now filling the twilight colours with an unimaginable incandescence."*

* Hans Jantzen, *High Gothic*. Translated from the German by James Palmes. New York (1962), p. 69.

CHAPTER 10

The Late Middle Ages

"The king of France can do all that he wishes and he has the habit of doing it." When the count of Anjou muttered this observation in the late fifteenth century concerning the manner Louis XI exercised his autocratic authority over France, he might have included several other kings of western Europe in that description. For the emergence of the strong monarch who commanded the loyalty of an efficient bureaucracy which ruled the entire state is the principal development of the late Middle Ages. Before Louis XIV declared, "I am the state," Louis XI announced, "I am France." In Spain Ferdinand could have made the same statement and a little later Henry VII of England. Although these three were still medieval kings in the chronological meaning of the term, their near-absolutism suggested less affinity with medieval traditions than with political institutions of the sixteenth century that were to come. During the greater part of the Middle Ages three institutions competed for control: the monarchy, the landed aristocracy, and the church. Until the beginning of the fourteenth century the church could aspire to retain a significant voice in public affairs. And there were moments even in the fifteenth when the aristocracy appeared about to extinguish the monarchy in both England and France. But in the end the king emerged supreme over most of western Europe. By 1500 he had subordinated both church and feudal aristocracy to his will.

The principal opponent of royal power in the Middle Ages had always been the aristocracy. Since the appearance of the absolutist monarch was due probably more to the decline of the landed aristocracy than to the individual king's own talents, it is proper to consider first the decline of feudalism which brought about the decline of that aristocracy. What were the factors which weakened the position of the feudal aristocracy and thereby paved the way for the emergence of a strong king? Curiously enough, these were frequently the same factors which had been operative back in the ninth and tenth centuries, only now they were reversed. Then they had conspired to weaken, almost to destroy the monarchy, to the benefit of the landed aristocracy. Now being reversed, they accomplished the opposite. They crippled the aristocracy while they greatly enhanced the position of the king.

Developments in the art of war are a good case in point. It will be recalled how the shift from foot soldiers to cavalry in the eighth and ninth centuries had played into the hands of the landed aristocracy. Only they could afford to provide mounts for themselves and for their retainers. Since the king could no longer rely on the infantry his lower-class subjects could have furnished, he had no choice but to depend upon the independent-minded feudal aristocracy for his army. Until the late Middle Ages the feudal knight dominated the battlefield. Yet there had appeared signs that his proud monopoly was slowly eroding. Humble crossbowmen of the twelfth century had enabled the Lombard League to defeat Frederick Barbarossa and his feudal army at Legnano in 1176 (see above, p. 302). Had anyone asked Richard how useful were these archers to him in his contests with Saladin, he would have insisted that they were indispensable. A new weapon, the longbow, came into use in the British Isles in the thirteenth century which the English employed with deadly effectiveness against the French in the Hundred Years' War. A skillful archer could kill a knight at two hundred yards. The Swiss mountaineers contributed two weapons, the pike and the halberd. Pikemen with their twenty-foot spears could stop a charge of knights. If they took the offensive, they could throw a company of knights into panic. The halberd was a fearful weapon some eight feet in length, whose heavy head bore a sharp point at the top, a hatchet on one side, and a wicked hook on the other. When swung like a battle-ax it could cleave through helmet and armor as though they were matchwood.

To counter these new weapons, the knight kept putting on more armor. In the fifteenth century plate armor covered him from head to toe, and except for the well-aimed shot of a longbowman's arrow, he was reasonably secure. Yet while armor assured him considerable protection, it almost immobilized him in addition to bankrupting him. Only under ideal field conditions could he fight, and progressively fewer men could afford the necessary outlay. Against another development the knight was even more helpless, and that was artillery. This had reached a level of efficiency early in the fifteenth century that doomed the castle. And when the walls of his castle came tumbling down, little remained of the means by which the landed aristocracy had acquired his dominant position. It had come time for him to bow to the superior power of his king and retire to his château or manor house.

A second development, as much a threat to the position of the aristocracy as the change in the art of war, was represented in the rise of the townspeople with their trade and money. Had the king possessed ample revenues even in the turbulent ninth and tenth centuries, he might have blocked the rise of the feudal aristocracy by equipping horsemen of his own. But he had lacked revenue at that time. Had no development taken place which could have enabled him to circumvent the feudal tradition that the king should live off his own estates, he might have continued relatively helpless throughout the medieval period. The rise of towns promised to change this. As they grew in number and wealth, kings found in their trade a rich source of revenue. By 1300 Edward I of England was realizing more from duties than from other royal revenues combined. And given any struggle with his aristocracy, the king could depend upon help from his towns. What they wanted above all else was the peace that he could bring. Even the duties and taxes he might collect would be small price compared with the misrule and anarchy that feudal supremacy usually meant. With the money of the townspeople the late medieval monarch equipped a strong army of his own, led by captains of his choice, which he found a vastly more reliable force than the earlier feudal levy. With his greatly increased revenues, the king was also able to maintain a loyal and expanding bureaucracy with which to extend the machinery of royal administration throughout his realm.

The change in the art of war and the rise of towns helped the king destroy the political autonomy of the landed aristocracy. It might only be a careful observer like Commines (see below, p. 388) who would have appreciated that fact since counts, dukes, and their lesser cousins continued to dominate society. However prosperous a burgher might become, his fondest hope was to marry his daughter into the class above him. This was the period when knightly orders such as the Knights of the Garter and the Knights of the Golden Fleece were in their glory. Lords and their ladies never dressed more splendidly than in the late Middle Ages, nor were their homes ever more luxuriously furnished. A glance at the roster of high officials in the king's court would find titles still monopolizing the highest offices—with this significant difference. They now served the king, not as proud representatives of a powerful feudal class, but as private individuals. The king's subordination of the church will receive attention later.

Had it not been for the intrusion of the Hundred Years' War, the country that might best have demonstrated in its history the decline of the aristocracy and the rise of the monarchy would have been France. French kings since the time of Louis VI had been striving, and with success, to extend royal authority throughout the country. The prospects for attaining that goal never appeared brighter indeed than during the reign of Philip IV (1285–1314). He continued the tradition of strong monarchs, although the harshness of some of the methods he employed to advance royal power resembled those of early modern, rather than medieval, monarchs. Ably advising him in the application of Machiavellian principles were two professionally trained laymen, Pierre Flote and William Nogaret. Nogaret's parents had both been executed for heresy, for which reason he took special delight in helping Philip harass the papacy.

The most disagreeable facet of Philip's reign concerned the means he used to increase royal revenues. He was exacting in his collection of aids and incidents, levied heavy tallages upon towns, imposed sales taxes on wheat, wine, and salt, debased the coinage, expelled Jewish and Lombard bankers and seized their accounts, and even stooped to extorting money by judicial process. His most infamous act in his unprincipled search for revenue was the suppression of the order of the Knights of the Temple. The order had grown enormously wealthy and, now that the crusading period was past, relatively useless and with its earlier high repute somewhat tarnished by indolence and luxury. All that mattered to Philip was their money which he wanted. Upon his direction Nogaret trumped up vile charges against the order, with the help of torture extorted "confessions" from several of their leaders, then browbeat the pope into ordering its suppression. The pope gave instructions that the order's wealth be turned over to the Hospitalers, but Philip saw otherwise. Philip also forced large sums from the French church which lay prostrate before him after his brutal humbling of Pope Boniface (see below, p. 379). One constitutional development of some significance dates from Philip's reign. That was his summoning of the estates general. His purpose in calling this group to Paris was to assure himself the support of the aristocracy, the French church, and the towns in his attacks on Pope Boniface and the Templars.

Had the kings who succeeded Philip possessed his talents, the French monarchy would have gone on to establish by 1350 the kind of absolutism that came only a century later. As it happened, the century after Philip's death produced only one able monarch (Charles V), and what was worse, the terrible conflict known as the Hundred Years' War. The principal cause of this war was a legacy from the feudal past. This was the province of Guienne in southwestern France, roughly the old duchy of Aquitaine. This huge fief was all that remained in English hands of the vast expanse which Henry II had once ruled. Back in the twelfth century, kings of France might have accepted as tolerable the possession of French fiefs by the kings of England. In the fourteenth century such practice had become an anachronism, and a dangerous one. The French feared that unless they forced the English out, they would lose Guienne forever. The kings of England, for their part, had been in possession of Guienne for such a long time, they had begun to think it was theirs. They would insist upon holding on to it as tightly as they might Wales.

The war broke out in 1337 and continued on to 1453. That the war should have lasted such a singularly long time was due principally to the inability of France, which was the more powerful country, to drive out the English. Three times the French and English fought major battles, and on each occasion the French should have won. Instead, because of their overconfidence, their indifference to elementary rules of strategy, and the deadly accuracy of the English longbowmen, they suffered disastrous defeats.

The first part of the war proved an unqualified success for the English. Edward III destroyed a large French army at Crécy in 1346, while his son, the Black Prince, did the same to another large army at Poitiers ten years later. To add to the misery of the French, the Black Death struck in 1348–1350 and carried off at least one-fourth the population. Sporadic rebellions called *Jacquerie* broke out here and there during this dreadful period, led by peasants who could no longer suffer the terrible conditions under which they lived. Their lords burdened them with heavy impositions, yet could not protect them from bands of marauders, many of them unemployed soldiers, who roamed the countryside. The Treaty of Brétigny (1360), which closed this disastrous period of the war, gave the English sovereignty over Guienne.

The fortunes of war went to the French during the second period of the war, although without benefit of any splendid victories. The new French king, Charles V, called the Wise (1364–1380) gave strict instructions to his captains to avoid large-scale operations. The guerrilla warfare that they conducted instead proved highly successful, although the illness and death of the Black Prince and the senility and death of Edward must have contributed significantly to that success. There appeared no way the English could halt their reverses in any event, until they found themselves swept completely out of France.

Then the war lagged. Until Richard II grew up, the English government was too divided to undertake any major offensive, and when he did grow up, he was more concerned with establishing his authority in England than with fighting the French on the Continent. (See below, p. 357.) Richard's neglect of the war was most fortunate for the French. They had troubles of their own following the death of Charles V. His son Charles VI, known as the Mad, became insane in 1392 and remained in that condition for most of his long remaining years. He lived on until 1422. Meantime two factions came forward to take over direction of the government, the one headed by Charles' uncle, the duke of Burgundy, the other by Charles' younger brother, Louis, duke of Orléans. When the English king Henry V reopened the war, the Burgundians refused to fight, although the French should still have won at Agincourt in 1415. Their overwhelming defeat gave the duke of Burgundy pause, and he arranged to meet with the dauphin, Charles VI's son, to discuss a reconciliation. As he knelt to do obeisance to the dauphin, "unknown" assassins cut him down. Thereupon the slain duke's son, the new duke of Burgundy, allied himself with the English and in the name of France, agreed to the Treaty of Troyes (1420). According to the terms of the treaty, the dauphin was to be disinherited, and the succession to the throne of France was to pass to Catherine, daughter of the insane Charles VI, who was to marry Henry V.

The dauphin did not give up, although few causes which ultimately proved successful have ever had a less aggressive and inspiring leader. Once the dauphin's major stronghold of Orléans, which was under siege by the English, would fall, it was assumed his end would have come. It was at this juncture that Joan of Arc appeared, rallied the French soldiers with her claims to being God's messenger, and opened the way to Reims where the dauphin was crowned Charles VII (1429). The following year the Burgundians captured Joan outside Compiègne, sold her for a huge ransom to the English who "proved" her a witch in the most famous mistrial in history, and burned her at the stake.

The momentum of French successes continued on nevertheless. In

1435 the duke of Burgundy abandoned his alliance with the English upon Charles' promise of autonomy for his duchy. Next Charles VII borrowed heavily from Jacques Cœur, the richest merchant prince in France, while the estates general voted him the right to levy what tallages he might need to win the war. The future proved that the estates did a foolish thing when they granted the crown this right, for the crown never relinquished it. This meant that the estates had surrendered the one lever they might have employed to force concessions from the king. For the moment, however, their act helped win the war, and in 1453 nothing remained of the once extensive English holdings on the Continent except the city of Calais.

When Louis XI (1461–1483) came to the throne, he found France safe enough from the English, but his own position as king precarious. During his very first years as king, he had given the aristocracy cause to hate and to fear him. They might have been able to stomach his open contempt for their frivolous, extravagant ways. They could not stand idly by as he slowly but inexorably whittled away at their traditional privileges and rights. For though Louis was an unchivalrous-looking king, he was a most wily and ambitious fellow. The writer Commines, who left the service of the duke of Burgundy to join the king's household once he was convinced Louis would win out, declared that no one "was more capable of extricating himself from a difficult situation in time of adversity." One of the most adverse situations Louis ever found himself in came in 1465 when many French nobles, under the inspiration of the duke of Burgundy, formed the League of Public Weal and presented him an ultimatum. Louis might have defeated the coalition, but he preferred not to risk his throne on the battlefield. He was sure that time and his own cunning would eventually give him the victory. So he bent to the demands of the feudal aristocracy, gave the duke of Burgundy all he demanded, then retired to his gloomy castle to await the fruition of his schemes.

In these he depended heavily upon his horde of gold which he used to purchase allies and corrupt enemies. He also expected the foolhardiness of his principal opponent, Charles the Rash, the duke of Burgundy, to simplify his task. He was not disappointed. Charles had lofty ambitions but lacked moderation and good sense. He wished to establish a middle kingdom between France and Germany by uniting his Burgundian possessions with what came to be known as the Low Countries which he had inherited. Once he had united these two sections into the richest country of Europe, he would demand recognition of himself as king. Since many small princes would suffer if the duke of Burgundy had his way, Louis had no difficulty paying others to do his fighting. The Swiss who were in his pay defeated Charles three times; the last time they left him dead with his head cloven by a halberd. Louis promptly seized the bulk of the dead duke's possessions and with that move all but completed the work begun more than three centuries earlier by Louis VI. With his victory over Charles he had also broken the power of the French feudal aristocracy. When he died he passed on to his son Charles VIII a position of near absolutism.

The history of England offers interesting parallels and contrasts to the history of France in the late Middle Ages. The two countries fought each other in the Hundred Years' War, although the impact of the war on England was negligible compared with the devastation and misery it caused in France. Ironically, the loss of the war, which contemporaries viewed as a disaster, proved a blessing for the English. It insulated her from most continental problems and left her in a position to develop a larger industrial and colonial empire than would otherwise have been possible. The Black Death struck England with the same deadly force as it had France, and England also had a peasant revolt. In England, however, the peasants rebelled not out of blind rage over their abject condition, as was the case in France, but in order to improve a condition that was already on the rise. During the fourteenth and fifteenth centuries a few able kings sat on England's throne and more who were not able, in which respect the fortunes of the two countries were similar. England even had a mad king in Henry VI, who also reigned some forty years as had his maternal grandfather Charles VI in France. In both countries the crown passed through a dangerous period when a triumphant aristocracy might have reduced it to a position of impotence had they been able to agree among themselves. Yet both England and France emerged at the end of the Middle Ages with an absolute king. The most important development in late medieval England, something only later generations would appreciate, was the rise of parliament. Let us begin a brief survey of English history in the late Middle Ages with a look at this institution.

For the origins of parliament we go back to the middle of the thirteenth century, to the revolt which Simon de Montfort led against Henry III (see above, p. 299). Simon had just defeated the king, in fact was holding him a prisoner, when in 1265 he called a meeting of the great council (the king's direct vassals). What was most unusual about this summons was the invitation he sent to each of the shires and boroughs to send two representatives to meet with the council. Later when Henry and his son Edward recovered control, they considered it prudent to continue summoning such an enlarged council lest they antagonize the popular element in the country. Then they discovered that such a concession to the commoners offered advantages. It enabled the crown to give wider publicity to its proclamations, for instance; above all, it provided a convenient means for discussing the financial needs of the crown with the boroughs and gentry who were coming into an increasing share of the country's wealth. And since the crown's financial needs kept steadily increasing, it shortly became traditional that these commoners should keep on meeting with the great council. Actually it was not all the king's vassals who assembled at such gatherings. Only those who received personal summonses deemed it necessary to appear; the others remained at home. By some chance, the chronicler in describing the meeting of the great council in 1295 referred to it as the Model Parliament. In his judgment, apparently, its membership, composed as it was of representatives of the shires and boroughs, together with the peers of the realm, was precisely what it should be. The chronicler was also responsible for the adoption of the term parliament to designate that body.

Such were the origins of the institution of which the English are most proud. Yet the existence of parliament was still far from assured. Had Edward I and Edward III not needed funds so regularly in order to prosecute their wars, the vital growth which parliament experienced during the fourteenth century would not have taken place. And the absence of that vital growth might have proved fatal to its eventual development. It met rarely in the fifteenth century, only once during the twenty some years of Edward IV's reign. He would not have summoned it then, but he wanted its approval for the execution of his brother Clarence. This incident from the reign of Edward IV emphasizes the one essential ingredient in parliament's growth, namely, its control over taxation. Because Louis XI paid Edward IV a handsome annual pension to keep him out of France, Edward had no need to ask parliament for funds. Had Edward I and Edward III experienced no greater need for financial assistance, neither would they have summoned parliament. In that case, students might not be giving any greater attention to the history of parliament today than they do to that of the French estates general. Fortunately for the rise of parliament, these early Edwards did require funds and these with considerable frequency. When the king summoned parliament, it would consider the king's demands, but would usually not vote him a subsidy until he had met their demands. The Good Parliament of 1376 even obliged the crown to dismiss unpopular ministers before considering a grant. Still the Middle Ages witnessed only the birth of parliament. Its real history began in the seventeenth century.

Edward I (1272–1307), the son of Henry III, ranks second only to Henry II among England's leading medieval kings. His strongest ambitions were territorial, although his only solid achievement was the conquest of Wales. In two well-organized campaigns he defeated the Welsh and, upon the death of the last native prince Llewellyn, appropriated the title "Prince of Wales" for his son. He was less successful against the Scots. Henry II had forced King William to swear him homage in 1175, but the Scots had never taken that homage seriously. When the Scottish royal line died out during Edward I's reign, they did not object, however, when he insisted upon his rights as overlord to decide between the two leading claimants. But John Balliol, whom Edward selected, did object to joining the English when Edward ordered him to do so. Instead he made an alliance with the French which endured for several centuries to come—much to the grief of England. Edward had some success against the Scots, although he was on another trip northward to put down a revolt when he died.

Edward I made a solid contribution in the field of administrative reform. More than a century had elapsed since the death of Henry II. During the reigns of the weak kings who followed Henry, many abuses had crept into royal administration while the rights of the crown had suffered considerable erosion. Edward enacted laws against the practice of collecting excessive feudal dues, and he carefully defined the powers and duties of the crown's agents in order to prevent abuses on their part. On the other hand, he suppressed a number of private baronial courts which had encroached on the jurisdiction of the royal courts, and collected a heavy fee from those that he permitted to continue. He reaffirmed the crown's right to feudal aids and incidents, revived the ancient militia, and ordered the collection of duties on the export of wool. At the same time he encouraged foreign merchants to bring their wares to England by promising them the protection of the crown. So much legislation did Edward inspire that he has been called the "English Justinian."

Edward II's reign (1307–1327) was unfortunate except for the Scots. At Bannockburn in 1314 they defeated an English army three times theirs in size and won their independence. The victories of Edward III (1327-1377) over the French, and his own courteous, generous nature brought him much popularity during the greater part of his long reign. Later reverses in France, the fatal illness of his son the Black Prince, and financial and moral scandals in his household for which he was partly responsible, darkened his last years. The greatest misfortune of his reign was the Black Death. No accurate statistics report the number of casualties, nor can any positive statements be advanced concerning its social and economic impact. The church may have been the principal sufferer, especially the monasteries which could not afford the grave decline in their memberships. At St. Albans the abbot, prior, subprior, and forty-six monks died within the space of a few days. One piece of legislation furnishes official evidence of the effect of the Black Death on the peasant population. So many peasants (serfs) died, that those who remained could press for better terms and higher wages from the lords of the manor. Parliament stepped in to protect the lords from this kind of pressure in 1349 by enacting the Statute of Laborers.

When Edward died in 1377, his grandson Richard II (1377-1399), the son of the Black Prince, began his uneasy reign. During his minority years, his uncle John of Gaunt attempted to serve as regent. The ineptitude of the government during those years helped spark the Peasant Revolt, which erupted in 1381. This was a minor revolt which affected only a few eastern counties, but it did occasion a good bit of excitement. The rebels managed to get into London where they executed the chancellor and treasurer, whom they blamed for their troubles. The youthful Richard, only fourteen years old, left the Tower to confer with them, and promised an end to personal serfdom and the commutation of all services to money rents. Later, once the rebellion was broken, he also broke his promises. The nineteen years of his reign which lay ahead proved sterile, principally because of the contest between himself and the aristocratic faction that controlled parliament. In 1397 Richard finally seized control, executed those leaders of the opposition who had not fled, but was himself deposed and murdered in 1399. The victor was John of Gaunt's son Henry, who succeeded.

The fifteenth century remains the most barren in English medieval history and, until recent years, the most ignored. Since it appeared to offer nothing other than violence and futility, historians have generally avoided it. They did mention the insanity of Henry VI, the Wars of the Roses which this insanity helped precipitate, then hurried on to introduce Henry VII and the glorious era of the Tudors, delaying only long enough on the way to drop one last curse of their own on the corpse of the tyrant Richard III who fell on Bosworth Field. Because of this inattention, many questions about fifteenth-century England remain unanswered: questions about developments in agriculture and industry, questions about the social life of the people, about the English church, even the question whether Edward IV (1461–1483) was little better than a voluptuary or the man who established the administrative machinery upon which the Tudors based their absolutism.

The principal political events of the century require little attention. Henry IV, first of the Lancastrian kings—the dynasty has its name from Henry's father, John of Gaunt, who was duke of Lancaster—put down a Welsh revolt and had parliament enact legislation authorizing the execution of Lollards. These were a small group of revolutionaries who claimed to be followers of John Wyclif, although Wyclif showed no interest in their program of social and economic reform. The movement, which was always small, disappeared overnight. Henry V was the most popular and able of the Lancastrians. Had he lived beyond thirty-four, he might have saved England the misery of the civil strife it suffered during the long reign of his son Henry VI. This Henry was a pious, generous soul when he was in good mental health, but whether well or ill, he could not contain the rapacity of the feudal aristocracy. During his reign two factions surfaced, one called the Lancastrian, the other the Yorkist. In time the greater part of the English aristocracy committed itself to the contest for the throne, now adhering to one side, now to the other. The consequence was a significant weakening of its position during the generation of turbulency and warfare (Wars of the Roses) that spreads over most of the period from 1455 to 1485, since many were killed and many others impoverished. Henry Tudor, who claimed to represent both factions, had relatively little difficulty, therefore, in subordinating what remained of the aristocracy after he had defeated Richard III on Bosworth Field. In his bid for absolutism, Henry had the support of the gentry and towns who looked to him to provide them the peace and justice that aristocratic misrule had denied England for a large part of the century.

Germany, which had played a major role in west European affairs until the middle of the thirteenth century, dropped far behind England and France in the late Middle Ages. In England and France, these two centuries witnessed the growth of strong centralized states even though there were moments when the aristocracy appeared to threaten the monarchy. In Germany the position of the king was one of constant helplessness, so constant that there were not even moments of improvement. While the kings of France and England were consolidating their power, expanding royal administrative machinery, and, in the late Middle Ages, emerging as almost absolute monarchs, the king of Germany remained an elected official, with no capital of his own, and with no royal bureaucracy or judiciary to do his will. He did have a consultative body called the diet which was composed of members of the lay and ecclesiastical aristocracy. Later the imperial cities and a special group of electors joined to establish an assembly of three houses. Whatever its composition, the diet always remained a futile body. It would meet with the king, agree to some resolution which the king would then promulgate, after which the princes and others would return to their domains and do precisely as they chose. The king had no army with which to enforce his or the diet's will.

A look at the map of Germany in the late Middle Ages will reveal at a glance the root of most of the trouble. Late medieval Germany gives the impression of a quilt composed of hundreds of patches of varying sizes. It consisted of a conglomeration of some 1600 principalities, a few of them, like Bavaria and Saxony, of considerable extent, but many hundreds of them too small even to note on a map. The tiniest possessions were those of the imperial knights who supplemented the meager returns from their fiefs with what they could plunder from neighbors and travelers. There were imperial cities such as Hamburg, cantons in Switzerland, Teutonic Knights along the Baltic, the cities of the Hanseatic League, and now and then dynastic links with Poland and Hungary to add to the general state of confusion. Over all these the German king and Holy Roman emperor reigned in regal impotence.

A shrewd observer back in the thirteenth century might have predicted the gloomy prospects that awaited the German king. He could have pointed to the inability of even a talented monarch like Frederick Barbarossa to accomplish much in his ambition to establish in Germany something approaching the strong base upon which the power of Philip Augustus rested in France. All Frederick could hope to do was to hold fast to the imperial rights he possessed—the rights of mint, tolls, judicial prerogatives, rights over roads and streams—and trust that the future would bring more favorable developments. These turned out to be just the reverse. During the reign of Frederick II the crown abandoned all these remaining imperial rights and left the German princes *de facto* independent. Furthermore, while the crown now had nothing upon which to build its authority, the rulers of such states as Bavaria and Brandenburg were establishing strong, compact domains similar to those of France and England. They would never have tolerated the emergence of a strong king.

That the position of the king of late medieval Germany was so altered from that of earlier centuries is most manifest from the changed attitude of the papacy. Pope and German king had been bitter foes since the late eleventh century. Now the pope looked longingly north of the Alps to Germany for an ally. For once the Hohenstaufens had been destroyed and the French in control in southern Italy (see above, p. 306), they constituted as much of a threat to the independence of the papacy as the Germans had been. So the pope urged the princes of Germany to elect another king—they had not had one since 1254. They proceeded to do this in 1273, although they had in mind quite a different kind of king from what the pope wanted. The man they would elect would lack the power to threaten even them, let alone go south to fight the French. This man was Rudolf of Hapsburg, a small Swabian count who had no illusions about the meaning of his title. He behaved himself properly, that is, he minded only the business of his own estates. One move he did make which proved of great significance. As emperor he could claim by right of escheat any territory that became heirless. Back in 1246 the Babenberg house, which controlled Austria, Styria, Carinthia, and Carniola had died out. Ottokar II, king of Bohemia next door, had seized these territories. Once the princes had elected Rudolf, they gave him their blessing to take over these territories since they feared Ottokar. He drove Ottokar out and made Vienna his capital, where the Hapsburgs stayed until 1918.

Although the history of late medieval Germany is a tedious story of mediocrity and impotence, several kings deserve mention. Henry VII (d. 1313) permitted his foolish dream of restoring the Holy Roman empire to take him south of the Alps where Dante welcomed him but no one else. He died there of the fever. Louis IV (d. 1347) revived the equally anachronistic spectacle of German king quarreling with pope. Ably assisting Louis in the war of words that ensued—it amounted to little else—was William of Ockham and other antipapalist writers. To give emphasis to his feelings, Louis decreed the official rejection by the German princes of any voice the pope might claim in the selection of the king of Germany and Holy Roman emperor.

Charles IV (d. 1378) assured himself a mention in the histories of the Middle Ages by regularizing with his Golden Bull (1356) the procedures to be followed in the election of a German king. Seven princes were to elect the king. These included the three archbishops of Cologne, Mainz, and Trier, together with the duke of Saxony, the margrave of Brandenburg, the count Palatine of the Rhine, and the king of Bohemia. Sigismund (d. 1437) imagined his position much more powerful than it was, although he did dominate the proceedings of the council of Constance. (See below, p. 382.) His son-in-law, Albert II, by inheriting both the Hapsburg and Sigismund's extensive Luxemburg domains, acquired such a powerful position in Germany for the Hapsburgs, that they secured permanent control of the position of king and Holy Roman emperor. During the reign of the last German king of the medieval period, Frederick III (1440–1493), Germany reached a level of anarchy almost as dreadful as that which had prevailed during the period of Viking and Magyar invasions.

It comes as a relief to turn from this depressing tale to consider other developments in Germany, which proved more substantial and permanent. The most unique of these, given the prevalence of aristocratic and monarchical rule in the Middle Ages, was the rise of Switzerland. In this case a group of cantons, some peasant, others containing a sprinkling of towns, gained their independence from their feudal lords. The movement began with the three forest cantons of Uri, Schweiz, and Unterwalden which formed a confederation for the purpose of mutual assistance in 1291 in order to block the efforts of the Hapsburgs to take over control of the lucrative trade that passed through the St. Gothard pass. These cantons had secured trade privileges and exemption from the rule of their Hapsburg neighbors from Frederick II back in 1231. Since the emperor then left Germany to itself, such privileges carried no guarantee. The Hapsburgs soon after began to consolidate their control of the area in order to exploit its trade advantages, and when Rudolf became emperor, the threat to the privileged position of these cantons became a very real one. They did, however, not proclaim their Perpetual Compact until Rudolf's death in 1291 lest their action be viewed as open defiance of his authority.

The first major attempt the Hapsburgs made to humble the Swiss ended in disastrous defeat at the battle of Morgarten in 1315. Following this victory, more cantons joined the original three, whereupon the confederation began to assume an expansive policy. Unwilling districts were forced to join, others were detached from their south German neighbors, whereupon a full-scale war broke out between them and the Hapsburgs and their German allies. Again the Swiss were victorious, first at Sempach in 1386 and two years later at Näfels. The threat of rising Burgundy, together with the diplomatic efforts of Louis XI, served to reduce some of the hostility between the Swiss and their German neighbors, and by the Treaty of Basel (1499) the emperor reluctantly granted them an autonomous position within the empire. Their official independence came in 1648 with the Treaty of Westphalia.

By the close of the Middle Ages the original confederation had swelled to thirteen cantons which had alliances with other cantons, towns, and districts in the area. As such it was known as the League of Upper Germany. The cantons varied in political organization, the control in some being democratic, in others oligarchic. All exercised full control over their own affairs. For external affairs they had a federal diet, in which the thirteen cantons had two votes each. Though the diet lacked the means of enforcing its decisions upon recalcitrant cantons, the continued confused condition of Germany and the rugged terrain of the area protected Switzerland against any dangerous coalitions. One by-product of their victories was the military fame these brought their pikemen and halberdiers, which in turn led to their recruitment by kings during the sixteenth century as mercenaries and palace guards. The Swiss Guards at the Vatican date back to this era.

The history of the Hanseatic League provides further testimony of the weakness of the German monarch in the late Middle Ages. For the origins of this league one must go back at least to the early twelfth century when German merchants from Cologne and the surrounding country secured trade privileges from Henry II of England. Other German merchants were active at this time and in the century following, carrying the products of their own country and of northern Europe to the lands to the west and south. Actually in the rise and expansion of European trade in the twelfth and thirteenth centuries, the most active merchants were the Germans. Their middle position between the countries of northern and southern Europe afforded them an excellent position, while the backwardness of Scandinavia, the Baltic lands, and Russia provided them the opportunity to establish a monopoly over the trade in those regions. In Bergen, Novgorod, Bruges, and London they founded large trading colonies, and smaller ones in many other cities of western Europe. Foreign kings were generally pleased to grant them trading privileges since they brought commodities otherwise unavailable, they stimulated local business, and their trade netted some income by way of indirect taxes.

Merchants in Lübeck, Hamburg, Bremen, Danzig, Cologne, Dresden, and scores of other German cities were interested only in trade. There were occasions when they found it necessary to organize gilds or hanses in order to suppress brigandage or to compel a foreign state to grant it privileges. Once such a problem had been resolved, there was a tendency for such hanses to dissolve. Even in the fourteenth century when the Hanseatic League attained the peak of its influence, it did not constitute a sharply defined group of cities, nor did it ever establish a permanent executive or adopt a common seal or flag. Its greatest moment came in 1367–1370 when seventy-seven cities organized a fleet and made war on King Waldemar of Denmark who was threatening to take over southern Sweden and cut off their access to the North Sea. In the Treaty of Stralsund (1370) they forced him to confirm their privileged position in Denmark and Sweden, even to grant them the right to confirm the accession of any king to the Danish throne.

The Treaty of Stralsund marked the height of Hanseatic power. The League had already begun to feel the threat of foreign competition. States which had earlier welcomed the appearance of Hanseatic vessels began to encourage the building of merchant marines of their own. The first of the English navigation acts dates from the reign of Richard II. This required Englishmen who shipped goods into or out of England to employ only English ships. A more immediate threat to the power of the League came from within the organization itself, from competition and dissension among the member cities. Lübeck and Danzig, for instance, headed their own separate groups in the fifteenth century. An unforeseen blow came when the herring which provided one of the staples of Hanseatic trade, moved from the waters between Denmark and Sweden out into the North Sea. The Hanseatic League managed to stagger into the sixteenth century, but it was a dying institution.

A third development along with the rise of Switzerland and the operations of the Hanseatic League which revealed the weakness of the German king in the late Middle Ages was the movement of German power and influence eastward. Of all the achievements of late medieval Germany, this proved the most far-reaching in its consequences. Yet German kings had little to do with this development. It was the work principally of German missionaries and bishops, of German princes and nobles, and of German crusading orders. The German movement eastward began with Charlemagne who pushed the Slavs to the Elbe and established a series of marches to consolidate Frankish power east of the Rhine. Under Otto I the line dividing German and Slav moved to the Oder. There German kings dropped out of the picture. German counts and dukes along the eastern frontier took up the drive and during the twelfth century carved out for themselves the states of Lübeck, Mecklenburg, and Brandenburg.

Early in the thirteenth century the king of Denmark drove eastward up the Baltic and for a short time held most of the south shore under his control. When his power collapsed, Cistercian monks moved into the area to convert the natives with the word, while Livonian Knights of the Sword sought to accomplish the same end by force. A third group, the Teutonic Knights, joined them in the thirteenth century. Since this was primarily a German order, it had quite naturally transferred its activities to eastern Europe when the crusading period came to an end. In 1237 the Livonian and Teutonic Knights combined and together conquered Prussia. By the early fourteenth century the Knights had annexed the entire south Baltic shore from Pomerania to the Gulf of Finland. In their wake thousands of German peasants and merchants swarmed into the area, as well as younger sons of the German nobility who had aided their expansion and now took over fiefs as vassals of the Order.

The expansion of the Teutonic Knights had meantime aroused the hostility of the Poles and the Liths, who found themselves cut off from access to the Baltic Sea. In 1386 the two countries took a step which heralded the end of the Teutonic Order by arranging the union of the two countries through the marriage of Jagiello, grand prince of Lithuania, to Jadwiga, heiress of Poland. Jagiello also agreed to the conversion of his people, a step which deprived the Teutonic Order of any justification for further expansion in the area. In 1410 a huge army of some 100,000 Poles, Liths, Czechs, Tartars, and Russians annihilated the Teutonic army at Tannenberg (Gruenwald). Subsequent defeats led to the Peace of Thorn (1466) which deprived the Order of all its possessions with the exception of East Prussia. This it was permitted to retain as a fief of Poland.

The state that profited most from the decline of the Teutonic Order was Poland. The first of its nobles to secure the title king was Boleslav the Brave (d. 1025), who succeeded in uniting the western Slavs under his rule. When he died Poland's neighbors divided up the greater part of his possessions, deprived the king of his title, and left them a duke who did homage to the German king. Boleslav the Bold (d. 1078) regained the royal title and, in fact, proved so aggressive and successful that his nobles helped depose him lest he deprive them of their privileged position. Under Boleslav III (d. 1138) Poland regained its independence and an outlet to the Baltic with the conquest of Pomerania. Another period of decline set in after his death, followed by the loss of Pomerania and the invasion of the Mongols who overran most of the country.

Medieval Poland reached the height of its power and influence under Casimir III (d. 1370). His title, the Great, he earned less by conquest than by his peacetime activities. He founded the university of Cracow, issued the first code of Polish laws, abolished serfdom, and encouraged Jews and Germans to come to Poland to develop its industry and trade. So many Jews took advantage of his hospitality that they made Poland the leading center of Jewish culture in eastern Europe. Less wise was Casimir's policy of granting privileges to the landed aristocracy. In time they became so powerful that they could block any attempt on the part of the king to erect a strong centralized bureaucracy. What also hampered Poland's development was the fact that it was so frequently united, through the person of the king, with Hungary and Lithuania. The union with Lithuania in 1386 had, of course, resulted in the defeat of the Teutonic Knights. Casimir IV (1447–1492) completed the destruction of Teutonic power, annexed west Prussia, and gave Poland its famous corridor to the sea. Casimir placed a son on the throne of Bohemia and Hungary and another on that of Lithuania. A third son, John Albert (d. 1501), who succeeded him as king of Poland, was so generous with his privileges to the nobles, that he undid much of the progress realized since Casimir III's accession in 1333. Without natural frontiers to provide Poland protection against its powerful neighbors, and with a selfish aristocracy never willing to make sacrifices for Poland at the expense of its own privileged position, the future of that country after 1500 promised to be as gloomy as it had been for the greater part of the Middle Ages.

The Hungarians or Magyars were the only Asiatic nomadic invaders of the early Middle Ages who retained their identity and established a country of their own. When they appeared in the ninth century they were as savage as any of their Asiatic predecessors including the Avars whom they absorbed. For about fifty years they carried their plundering raids across central Europe from their headquarters in the land to which they gave their name. Here their first king, Arpad, ruled early in the tenth century. A few years after Arpad's death Henry the Fowler inflicted a severe defeat on them, then in 955 Otto I dealt them a crushing blow at the river Lech. They retired to Hungary, accepted Christianity from Latin missionaries, and placed their first Christian king, Stephen (997–1038), in the liturgical calendar. Stephen's son, as a bit of incidental information, was St. Emerick, whose namesake gave his name to America.

During the eleventh century Hungary annexed the greater part of the Dalmatian coast—it will be recalled that the crusaders on the Fourth Crusade took Zara from Hungary—but shortly after Mongols overran and ravaged the country. Fortunately, they did not remain long. Two able kings, Charles I and Louis I, whose rules covered most of the fourteenth century, encouraged immigration, industrial development, and the "Westernizing" of the country's culture. Under Louis I, Buda became a leading cultural center in eastern Europe. The rise of Turkish power absorbed much of Hungary's attention in the late Middle Ages. Sigismund, their king and also German emperor, led an unsuccessful crusade against the Turks, and one of their most renowned heroes, John Hunyadi, owed his fame to the victories he gained over them. That fame led the nobles in 1458 to elect his son Matthias Corvinus to be their king. This talented king might have altered the course of history had he concentrated his efforts on the Turks. Instead he wasted his country's resources on vain efforts to replace Frederick III on the throne of the empire. He still found time to subdue the powerful aristocracy, encourage industry, and, from expanded revenues, build up an excellent army. He also patronized scholars and artists. But he failed to inflict any decisive defeats upon the Turks. Thirty years after his death they conquered Hungary.

Shortly before the Hungarians settled down and accepted Christianity, the people of Scandinavia had started doing the same. Monarchies began to emerge in the late ninth century, although for many years no sharp distinctions divided the three areas. As noted above, Cnut ruled over Denmark, Norway, and part of Sweden. By the year 1000 Christianity had been generally accepted, although the sagas reveal the survival of a solid core of superstitious practices from the pagan past. In general kings and bishops cooperated with one another since they found a common foe in the powerful aristocracy which dominated that sparsely settled country. This circumstance may also have accounted for the greater freedom the peasantry of Scandinavia enjoyed as compared with that of the serfs of western Europe.

Somewhat strange was the failure of the descendants of the intrepid Norsemen to continue the trading traditions of their forebears. Rather it was German merchants who took the lead in the commercial development of the region. The Hanse established several of its most lucrative centers at Bergen, Stockholm, and at Wisby on the island of Gothland. Waldemar IV of Denmark made an unsuccessful attempt to dislodge the Hanseatic League, as we have seen. The most ambitious attempt to unite the three lands was made by his daughter Margaret. She married the king of Norway and for a time ruled all three countries as regent. In 1397 she proclaimed the merging of the three countries in the Union of Calmar. Fifty years later the Swedes withdrew, but Norway and Denmark remained united until the Congress of Vienna (1815). Scandinavia did not play the role in European affairs one might have expected on the basis of the enormous energies it had demonstrated back in the ninth and tenth centuries. Part of that failure may be traced to the dominant position of the Hanseatic League, part to the power of the local aristocracy which prevented the rise of strong monarchies.

The history of Russia in the later Middle Ages is joined with that of the Mongols who overran most of the country early in the thirteenth century. These Mongols were from east-central Asia where the modern province of Outer Mongolia is located. Europe knew little of the nomadic tribes that made up that nation before the advent of Genghis Khan (1167–1227), the greatest conqueror and butcher in all of human history. The Mongols were not unlike such earlier Asiatic tribes as the Huns, Avars, and Magyars who invaded Europe; in fact, the description of the thirteenth-century chronicler, Matthew Paris, might have been torn from the pages of Jordanes. They were "human monsters," aptly called Tartars since they appeared "like demons loosed from Tartarus." They "razed cities, burned woods, pulled down castles, tore up vineyards, destroyed gardens, and massacred the citizens and husbandmen; if by chance they did spare any who begged their lives, they compelled them, as slaves of the lowest condition, to fight in front of them against their own kindred. . . . They have no human law, know no mercy, and are more cruel than lions or bears. . . . They come with the force of lightning into the territories of the Christians, laying waste the country, committing great slaughter, and striking inexpressible terror and alarm into every one."

The last statement offers an explanation for their invincibility, namely, the speed with which they moved and the terror people had of them long before their approach. For they made deliberate use of terror in order to encourage cities and lands to submit on the chance of their being spared. This was, unfortunately, only a chance. Genghis slaughtered the entire population of Bokhara because that city had resisted, then that of Samarkand because they had not resisted. They were clearly unreliable for having deserted their sultan! A military factor in their success was the tight organization and discipline of their armies and the long years their warriors trained to fight and maneuver. Against such highly trained warriors, the feudal armies of Europe were helpless. The Mongols might well have overwhelmed the whole of Europe, some scholars maintain, had it not been custom for their chieftains to return to Karakorum in distant Mongolia when the khan died in order to elect another. Many months, even years, might elapse before Mongol expansion could regain its momentum. The Mongol empire was the largest land empire in history. At its height it encompassed China, central Asia, Persia, Mesopotamia, Poland, Hungary, Bulgaria, Serbia, and all of Russia with the exception of Novgorod.

One of Genghis' generals invaded Russia in 1223. His grandson Batu came in 1237 and in a few years had overrun the country except the region about Novgorod which was protected by marshes. Some years later a Franciscan passed by Kiev which Batu had razed and found about two hundred houses and an enormous mass of skulls and bones. Batu built a new city at Sarai on the Volga which served until the end of the Middle Ages as the capital of the khan of the Golden Horde. Once the Mongols had conquered the country, they were satisfied to leave the local princes in control, from whom they exacted an annual tribute. Although Mongol rule was not oppressive, the destruction of most of the cities of Russia and the powerful hold the Mongols kept on the land served to set back the country many generations culturally and economically.

The rise of Russia is linked with the practice of Mongols of entrusting the responsibility of collecting the annual tribute to one of the Russian princes. The first of these princes was Alexander Nevski, earlier a great hero of Novgorod, who became grand prince in his capacity as ruler of Vladimir, a province to the east of Moscow. His son became prince of Moscow. Early in the fourteenth century Ivan I (d. 1341), prince of Moscow, gained permanent possession of the office of grand prince. That office, together with the decision of the metropolitan to live in Moscow, as well as the city's position at the heart of Great Russia where it could command the river traffic of the area, assured the prince of Muscovy his position of leadership. In 1380 the prince renounced Mongol tribute, but Tamerlane sent his generals who sacked the city and reimposed Tartar rule. Yet nothing could halt the inevitable decline of Mongol power. Ivan III (1462–1505) (the Great) finally expelled the Mongols, then rounded out his possessions by conquering Novgorod and seizing what Lithuanian lands lay east of the Dnieper. Ivan also married Zoe, niece of the last Byzantine emperor. When Constantinople fell to the Turks in 1453, he announced that his Moscow had now become the third Rome, he the new tsar (Caesar), and the new protector of orthodox Christianity.

When the Middle Ages came to a close in 1500, one of the two most powerful states in Europe was Spain. This would have appeared a most unlikely development back in 1200 when the Moslem Almohades still held about half the country. (The Almohades had destroyed the empire of the Almoravides. See above, p. 221.) The critical break in Moslem power came soon after in 1212, when Christian armies won a tremendous victory at Las Navas de Tolosa. Still the division of Christian Spain into a number of states prevented the exploitation of that victory. In 1230 León and Castile merged, but the future lay with the smaller state of Aragon in the northeast. Aragon acquired footholds on the north coast of Africa, took over the Balearic Islands, occupied Sicily in 1282, then Sardinia, and early in the fifteenth century Naples and southern Italy. The most spectacular advance in the rise of Spain came in 1469 when Ferdinand of Aragon married Isabella of Castile. In 1492 the two sovereigns conquered Granada, the last Moorish province in the country, then a little later added the southern part of Navarre.

The territorial unification of most of the Iberian Peninsula represented one of the two major developments in late medieval Spain. The other was the rise of royal absolutism. Particularly important in the growth of the Spanish monarchy was the role of the towns. Different Spanish kings had, in fact, used towns as a means of holding the territories they took from the Moors. They would lay out new sites

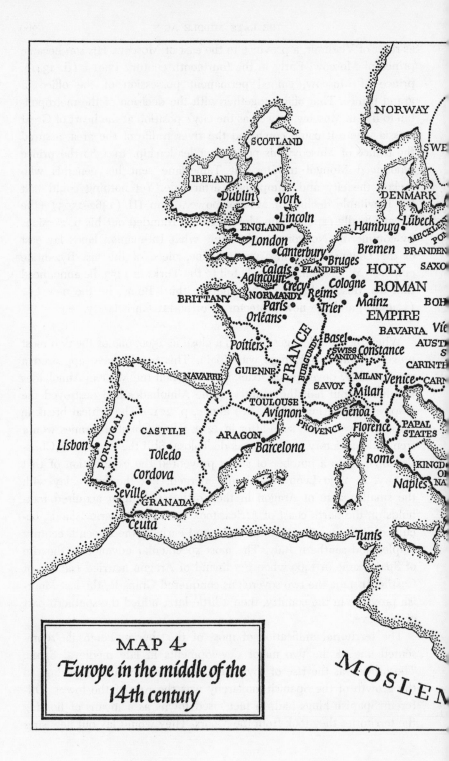

NORWAY

SWE

SCOTLAND

IRELAND

Dublin •York
•Lincoln
ENGLAND
London
•Canterbury
Calais• Bruges
-Agincourt FLANDERS
Crecy•
Cologne
BRITTANY NORMANDY Reims
Paris• Trier
Orléans•

DENMARK

Hamburg •Lübeck
MECKLE
Bremen POS
BRANDEN
SAXO

HOLY
ROMAN
Mainz
EMPIRE
BOH

Poitiers•

FRANCE
Basel
SWISS Constance
CANTONS

BAVARIA Vie
AUST
S
CARINTH

NAVARRE
GUIENNE

SAVOY
MILAN Venice CAR
Milan

TOULOUSE
Avignon•
GENOA
PROVENCE Genoa•
Florence

PAPAL
STATES

PORTUGAL
CASTILE
Lisbon•
Toledo•
cordova•

ARAGON
•Barcelona

Rome•
KINGD
O
NA
•Naples

Seville•
•Ceuta
GRANADA

•Tunis

MOSLEM

MAP 4·
Europe in the middle of the
14th century

Novgorod

RUSSIAN STATES

Moscow

TEUTONIC
KNIGHTS

TONIC
GHTS   LITHUANIA

Warsaw
OLAND   KHANATE

Kiev   OF THE   Sarai

Cracow   GOLDEN HORDE

dapest

UNGARY

WALLACHIA

GEORGIA

Nicopolis Varna

RBIAN   BULGARIA

RINCI-   BYZANTINE Constantinople

PALITIES   EMPIRE

Angora

OTTOMAN TURKS.   MOSLEM

STATES

SELJUK TURKS

ARMENIA

Athens

STATES

and promise liberal charters to any townspeople who might settle there. Representatives of Spanish towns met with the nobles and clergy in the first *cortes,* which date from the late twelfth century. (Spanish *cortes* anticipated the rise of the English parliament by three-quarters of a century.) The history of Spanish town charters and of *cortes* was short. After the towns had assisted the king through their organizations called *hermandades* to subdue the nobility, they found their turn came next. With the help of the Inquisition which Ferdinand revived in 1478, almost every form of independence and dissent was ruthlessly suppressed. Most sensitive was the Inquisition about religious non-conformity, and several thousand Jews and Moslems who refused to leave the country or who, in the judge's opinion, had not converted to Christianity, were executed.

Little Portugal to the west of Spain also rose to a position of prominence at the close of the Middle Ages. Her location on the Atlantic as well as the absence of internal strife enabled her to become the first of the European powers to seek an all-water route to the Indies. The rise of the Ottoman Turks (see below, p. 374) had affected the flow of goods from the Orient, although the principal obstacle to Portugal's ability to participate in that trade was the near-monopoly which the Italian cities had enjoyed since the twelfth century. Since Portugal lay so many more miles farther to the west, her only hope to share in that trade was to discover another route. The stories which travelers to eastern Asia brought back of the great wealth they found there, especially the marvelous account Marco Polo gave of his visit to the court of Kublai Khan (d. 1294), whetted men's curiosity and their acquisitiveness. Other motives stirred the spirit of exploration among the Portuguese, such as the discovery of gold and the capture of slaves as they moved southward along the coast of Africa.

By the middle of the fourteenth century, the Portuguese had acquired considerable knowledge of the ocean to the south through their occupation of the Canary, Azores, and Madeira Islands. To this store of information the center of marine study which Prince Henry the Navigator directed at Cape St. Vincent kept adding new knowledge through explorations which it conducted. Ever farther to the south the Portuguese kept venturing until in 1487 Bartholomew Diaz turned the Cape of Good Hope and proved that ships could circumnavigate Africa. Ten years later Vasco da Gama and his fleet of four ships turned the Cape and dropped anchor in the harbor of Calicut (1498). Meantime Columbus had discovered America, although that achievement caused nothing like the sensation of Vasco da Gama's feat. The cost of spices dropped by almost 50 per cent, while "all the city of Venice was greatly impressed and alarmed, and the wisest men held that this was the worst news that could ever come to the city."

The greatest period in the history of Spain and Portugal came with the end of the Middle Ages. In the case of Italy the situation was the reverse. Every country in that tormented peninsula was in decline at that time and would remain so. The one state most fallen from its earlier position of progress and prosperity was the kingdom of the Two Sicilies. It had once been the "first modern state" in Europe. (See above, p. 304.) Since the destruction of the Hohenstaufens in the middle of the thirteenth century, it had been moving backward. The political division of the area into two hostile sections must be considered a significant factor in this decline. In 1282 Aragon had seized control of Sicily, but a century and a half elapsed before she added southern Italy. By that time the economy of the entire southern peninsula was suffering.

To the north lay the Papal States, which were no better off economically or politically. The popes had never succeeded in holding the hostile factions in the city and area in check for any length of time. The reason was twofold. The hard business of subjecting proud, selfish lords belonged to a strong, aggressive king, not to a churchman who might be a mystic, a foreigner, an old man, or any number of things but a political administrator. The other explanation lay in the elective character of the pope's office. If no elective monarchy of the Middle Ages succeeded in erecting an efficiently administered state, why should that of the papacy have fared any better?

The most advanced and enterprising states in the peninsula were the city-states in the north. The revival of trade and the Crusades had brought them prosperity and population which only the county of Flanders might rival. Because they lay within the dominion of the Holy Roman empire, and since the emperor usually stayed north of the Alps, they had always enjoyed a high degree of autonomy. This became outright independence after the death of Frederick II in 1250. Of the states in the area, the most important included Genoa, Milan, Florence, and Venice. They shared a number of features: their prosperity depended upon trade; they had dictatorial governments; these governments prided themselves on patronizing the arts and learning. Most of the rulers of these states were "despots." The despot might be a member of the aristocracy, a banker, even a *condottiere* by origin, that is, a captain of a company of professional soldiers. The kind of rule these despots provided, or should have furnished their people, is what became the theme of Machiavelli's *The Prince*.

Representative of the prosperity and aggressiveness of these states was the "republic" of Florence. Cosimo de' Medici (d. 1464), head of the great banking house, made himself "boss" of the city. The most distinguished of all these despots was his grandson Lorenzo the Magnificent (d. 1492). How mercurial could be the tempers of the populaces of these city-states was demonstrated in the career of the Dominican friar Savonarola. So eloquently did he condemn the corruption and worldliness of the Medici and of the city itself, that the people made him their dictator, then when he was condemned for heresy, applauded as he burned at the stake. Milan to the north was ruled by the Visconti family for two centuries, then was seized by the *condottiere* Francesco Sforza who had been in their employ. Venice had no dictator, although there never existed a more dictatorial rule than that maintained by its oligarchy of leading families. Unswerving was its policy of expanding the city's trade. No consideration, no principle, was permitted to interfere with the attainment of its commercial objectives. It did business with Moslems as readily as with Christians, punished the family of any artisan who dared leave the city, and consistently used the Crusades to serve its own purposes. The passing of the city's maritime eminence, which did not long outlive the Middle Ages, arouses little sympathy.

On four occasions during the Middle Ages Europe suffered terrible invasions: those of the Germanic tribes in the fourth, fifth, and sixth centuries; those of the Vikings, Magyars, and Saracens in the ninth and tenth centuries; the invasion of the Mongols in the thirteenth century; and that of the Ottoman Turks in the fourteenth and fifteenth centuries which now comes time to consider. These Turks had been dislodged by the Mongols, whence they moved into Anatolia under their leader Othman or Osman (d. 1326), who established an independent state just south of the Black Sea. The Turks constituted an explosive force, partly because of the vitality they shared with other Asiatic tribes which had moved out of Turkestan, partly because of the decadence of the Moslem states in the area and the Byzantine empire. This Byzantine empire had been re-established in 1261 after its destruction during the Fourth Crusade, but had never recovered its former strength. And since Genoa and Venice kept draining off its economic resources, while relatives and other families struggled over the throne, there was little likelihood that the empire would ever recover.

The first of the Turks to move into Europe came on invitation of Constantinople. The city needed assistance against the Serbs. Here in the middle of the fourteenth century, the Serbs, under their renowned leader Stephen Dushan (d. 1355), seemed about to take over the entire Balkans. The Turks proceeded to destroy the Serbs, then the Bulgarians, next a huge crusading army under Sigismund at Nicopolis in 1396. The only thing that prevented their taking Constantinople at this time was the resurgence of Mongol power under Tamerlane (Timur the Lame). At Angora in 1402 he annihilated a Turkish army of some 100,000 troops, and dealt so disastrous a blow to Turkish power that it was a generation before the Turks were again ready to attack the city.

By this time Constantinople was in a desperate condition. The defenses of the city had been permitted to deteriorate, the Byzantine navy was pitifully small, the population had declined to less than half its original size, and the government was bankrupt. The last forlorn hope of aid from the Christian West went glimmering with the destruction of the crusading army at Varna on the Black Sea in 1444. For the assault on the city, the Turks brought up the most formidable cannon in the world. These could hurl stone balls of one thousand pounds' weight against any ship that might attempt to relieve the city while they pounded huge holes into its fortifications. Over a wooden track a mile long they transported seventy of their own ships directly into the upper harbor in the Golden Horn. The city fell on May 29, 1453, and Constantine XI, its last emperor, died with his soldiers. The Turks sacked the city, desecrated Hagia Sophia, then turned the church into a mosque. Though the fall of the city sent a shudder throughout Christian Europe, the only people who suffered loss were the Genoese and Venetians. To such a degree had the city fallen from its once proud condition, that it remained little more than a symbol of the role it had once essayed of protecting Christian Europe from Islam.

The fourteenth and fifteenth centuries witnessed a number of significant, several critical, developments for the medieval church. Included with the significant developments was a notable expansion of the papal curia. Ever since the pontificate of Innocent III, the curia had been assuming new responsibilities and administering old ones with greater efficiency, so that was no new phenomenon. Still, the practice of papal provisions, for example, which saw the curia making direct appointments to a large number of benefices (parishes and canonries) throughout western Europe, reached its peak in the fourteenth century. So also did the volume of judicial business as many more appeals reached its tribunals, perhaps the bulk of them the direct result of the mushrooming of this practice of papal provisions. The growth of canon law, based as this was on the centralizing principles implicit in Roman law, resulted in the inevitable extension of papal authority. Papal encroachment on the jurisdiction of local bishops, coupled with growing demand for more revenue which curial expansion necessitated, engendered growing hostility to Rome. The protest of the clergy of Cologne might have been made by the clergy of a score of dioceses in the West. "In consequence of the exactions with which the papal curia burdens the clergy," it announced, "the apostolic see has fallen into such contempt, that the Catholic faith in these parts appears to be seriously imperiled."

The late medieval church suffered three developments of such serious proportions that many contemporaries feared the institution would perish. The first of these chronologically was the Avignonese Residence. For almost seventy years the papacy directed the administration of Latin Christendom from France rather than Rome, with serious consequences for the church, which we shall note. Following upon the heels of this misfortune was the most dangerous schism ever to attack the Latin church. For almost forty years Europe divided its loyalties among two, then three, bitterly vituperative papacies. From this schism there emerged a third development, the conciliar movement, which almost succeeded in depriving the papacy of its supreme position and subordinating it to the general council.

There were also concerns of a less serious nature which absorbed much of the papacy's attention. One was the perennial problem of church reform. Like taxes and the weather, this elicited more talk than results. Until all Christendom, at least all men of influence from the aristocracy, through kings, hierarchy, and pope, actively threw their support behind reform, little could be accomplished. Two heresies appeared, of which one, the Hussite movement, outlived the Middle Ages. That the center of humanism (see below, p. 390) shifted from Florence to Rome in the fifteenth century suggests that individual popes of that century showed more than casual interest in that development. A more serious matter was the manner the papacy found itself caught up in the vortex of Italian politics. And the problem to which the papacy devoted possibly its greatest attention, and with almost complete lack of success, was that of stemming the flood of Ottoman power in the Balkans.

What proved the most momentous development to affect the position of the church in the late Middle Ages was the rise of the dynastic or national state. The evils of the Avignonese Residence and the Great Western Schism passed into history; the conciliar movement died almost without trace, while the problems of reform and the menace of the Ottoman Turks were left to the following century. But there was no ignoring or passing on to subsequent centuries the rising power of the state. The dominant position in society which it seized, it kept. From the fourteenth century that was a fact of life, and the church had no choice but to adjust to that fact.

The new order in church-state relations came with dramatic suddenness at the very beginning of the late Middle Ages. The issue which precipitated it concerned the right of the state to tax the clergy. Two powerful kings, Edward I of England and Philip IV (the Fair) of France, confronted the papacy on this issue. Because of the wars these kings were waging or planning, they needed revenue, and no place looked more likely to produce that revenue than church property. This was not the first time kings had imposed levies on the clergy. The Fourth Lateran Council, it will be recalled, had prohibited such levies, although it permitted the clergy to make a "free gift" to the king upon authorization of the pope. Actually the church had accepted the necessity of conniving at occasional levies in order to keep in the good graces of the state. But now Edward's and Philip's levies were coming so regularly, as the bishops complained in their appeal to the pope, that the clergy was being impoverished.

Because scholars attach special importance to the character of the pope who represented the church in this contest with Edward and Philip, it becomes necessary to give him a closer look. His name was Boniface VIII. For some years before his election in 1294 he had been a powerful figure in the curia. His enemies charged him, in fact, with forcing his predecessor, the octogenarian hermit Celestine V, to resign, in order to make room for himself. Boniface was seventy-seven years old upon his accession, with a reputation, it is said, for tactlessness and obstinacy. This may well have been, although it is doubtful whether a prudent pope would have salvaged anything more for the church in the end. Still one would have to admit that a more yielding character would have permitted the passing of papal power to be accomplished in less dramatic fashion.

When Boniface received his bishops' appeal for assistance, he issued the bull *Clericis Laicos* which bluntly condemned the actions of Edward and Philip. In the document he warned that "emperors, kings . . . who shall impose, exact, or receive . . . payments" from the clergy, "shall incur the sentence of excommunication." Boniface's strong language perhaps forced the issue and made compromise impossible. In any event, neither king offered to discuss the matter. Edward seized church properties owing the crown and outlawed the clergy. Philip placed an embargo on the shipment of gold to Italian bankers to whom Boniface was in debt. Since Philip's action placed the pope's political position in Italy in jeopardy, he capitulated, rescinded *Clericis Laicos*, and with a new bull authorized the kings to tax the clergy when, in their judgment, an emergency existed.

Boniface's concession satisfied Edward and he dropped out of the contest. He had secured what he wanted, namely, the right to tax church property. This in itself is significant, doubly so, however, the manner he had achieved his objective. Good Christian though Edward was, he had employed force. Philip, who was perhaps as good a Christian as Edward, was not satisfied. Exactly why he continued the contest with Boniface is not clear. Many scholars believe he hoped to so humiliate the papacy that he would be left free to deal as he chose with church appointments and taxes in France.

A few years later Philip precipitated a new crisis. He had seized church moneys which were to go to Rome for the purpose of a crusade, and Boniface appointed Bernard de Saisset, a French bishop, to investigate the matter. Philip ordered the bishop arrested, had him tried and judged guilty of treason, then demanded that Boniface defrock him so he could be punished. Instead Boniface summoned a general council to Rome to consider what steps should be taken against Philip. Philip countered with the first meeting of the estates general (see above, p. 350), at which session his trusted adviser Pierre Flote read a forged bull, purportedly Boniface's, in which the pope announced his intention of extending his civil authority to France. When Philip next prohibited French prelates from going to Rome, Boniface issued his most famous bull, called *Unam Sanctam*. Again in language as forthright as that of *Clericis Laicos* Boniface warned Philip that God had conferred upon him, the pope, the spiritual authority to judge the temporal "if the earthly power shall err." For that reason it was "altogether necessary to salvation for every human creature to be subject to the Roman Pontiff."

Philip paid not the least heed to Boniface's threat. When he learned that his own excommunication and deposition were imminent, however, he dispatched William Nogaret to Italy where he joined the Colonna faction in organizing a force to capture the pope. With some two thousand troops they occupied Anagni where the eighty-six-year-old Boniface was staying, seized and subjected him to indignities, then were driven off three days later by the aroused townspeople. The greatly shaken Boniface returned to Rome where he died within the month.

Christian Europe stood aghast at the "crime of Anagni." Even Dante, who hated Boniface, likened him to the crucified Christ, while he denounced Philip, Nogaret, and the leading Colonna representative as Pilate and the two thieves on Calvary. One might have expected a reaction which would have reduced French influence in the curia, but none came. Instead the incident set the stage for a long period of French control. This the simple-minded Celestine V had made possible when he added a dozen French prelates to the college of cardinals, which gave them a large majority in that body. After the death of the short-lived Benedict XI, the cardinals elected the archbishop of Bordeaux who took the name Clement V (1305–1314). Clement never reached Rome. Between the violence that was raging in Rome and his love for France, he decided to remain in France. He did make it as far as Avignon on the Rhone River by 1309, but there he stopped. Not until 1377, except for a brief visit by Urban V, did the pope return to Rome.

Few periods in the history of the papacy have drawn such unqualified denunciation as that of the Avignonese Residence. This was not the first time the pope had lived away from Rome. German emperors had forced a number to live in exile. This was the first time, however, that they had elected to live elsewhere. They gave, in fact, every indication of planning to remain in Avignon, for they proceeded to erect a sumptuous palace to house themselves and the curia. And to hear descriptions which critics brought to Germany, England, and Italy, of this palace, one would envisage something as luxurious as the fabled Hanging Gardens of Babylon. Petrarch did call the city the "guilt-laden Babylon, the forge of lies, the terrible prison, the hell on earth."

Petrarch was an Italian who resented in a special way the absence of the pope from Rome.

Men hostile to the Avignonese papacy maintained that it was not only the reputed luxury and wonderful climate that kept them in France. The papacy, they charged, was the captive of the French crown, a "French chaplaincy." The charge was not entirely, nor even in large part, justified, although the circumstances were not reassuring. The great majority of cardinals were French as were all the popes during this period. National consciousness was also becoming a factor in foreign affairs. The enemies of the French, the English in particular, were inclined to raise the charge of partisanship when some action of the papacy displeased them. It was partly for that reason that John Wyclif hailed the election of Urban VI, the Italian, in 1378, with so much satisfaction.

Most of the Avignonese popes left good records. Several introduced measures of reform; some sent missionaries off to China, India, Egypt, and Abyssinia. During this period the papal curia experienced considerable expansion, something which efficiency experts would have applauded, although the reaction elsewhere in Christendom was unfavorable. The best known of the popes was John XXII, who became involved in a bitter controversy with that group of Franciscans who not only insisted on observing their sainted founder's strict prohibition against holding property, but also maintained that anything less than mendicancy violated the rule of apostolic poverty set by Christ and his apostles. When John condemned that position as heretical, a number of the Franciscans, including William of Ockham (see above, p. 333), denounced the pope as a heretic.

Meantime reformers kept appealing to the popes to return to Rome. They warned them that the faith of the people was weakening because they had abandoned the city of St. Peter, that Rome itself was falling into ruins, and that the Papal States themselves would be permanently lost unless they returned. Two saintly and highly influential women, Brigid of Sweden and Catherine of Siena, added their entreaties. God was displeased, they admonished the popes, over their absence from Rome. After the pacification of the Papal States which Cardinal Albornoz carried out in the late 1360s, the popes could no longer justify their absence on the plea that Rome was too dangerous. So finally in 1377 Gregory XI made the break without enthusiasm and returned to Rome.

Pope Gregory XI died in 1378, the year after returning to Rome. His death helped precipitate the Great Western Schism, the most grievous of the evil consequences of the Avignonese Residence. The immediate cause, so the dissident cardinals charged, were the circumstances under which they had elected Urban VI, Gregory's successor. The French cardinals dominated the conclave, but they were divided; furthermore, the Roman populace was clamoring for the election of an Italian. One day, during the conclave, the mob had actually broken into the room where they were debating. This intrusion may have helped the cardinals make up their minds. At least they all agreed on the archbishop of Bari, an Italian, who took the name Urban VI. Since Urban was identified as a reformer, the choice appeared a popular one, and all the cardinals, without exception, acknowledged him as pope. That was in April. Two months later the majority withdrew to Anagni, announced they were repudiating Urban since the mob had forced their choice, then elected their most militant member, Robert of Geneva, who took the name Clement VII. He went off to Avignon, took most of the cardinals with him, and Europe settled down to a bitter schism.

Scholars still argue the cause for the cardinals' defection. All rule out the justification they offer, namely, pressure from the Roman populace. This was present, historians agree, but was no decisive factor. The real cause they trace to Urban himself, to the stern, even abusive manner he treated the cardinals—he condemned several in public for their deficiencies—to his evident determination to direct the curia himself without sharing control with them as had been traditional; worst of all, to his manifest intention of remaining in Rome.

The schism that followed divided Europe as never before. On several previous occasions when Europe had had two popes, one was clearly the antipope, generally the creature of the German emperor. Now honest men were confused. First the cardinals had informed their monarchs that they had been unanimous in their choice of Urban; next they had repudiated him. France and her friends generally supported the cause of Clement VII, while those who opposed France acknowledged Urban. Regardless of their sympathies all responsible men called for a quick end to the tragic situation. If the Avignonese Residence had disturbed people since the pope was not at Rome, how much more the spectacle of two popes, one heaping abuse on the other and calling on his adherents to destroy the antichrist.

Meantime theologians and canon lawyers had been busy presenting their views on the subject. Most of them endorsed what is known as the conciliarist position. This held that the authority of the general

council was superior to that of the pope. Until the coming of this
schism, the only writers who might have dared propose such views
were radicals like William of Ockham and Marsiglio of Padua, who
had drawn papal condemnation for their efforts. Now theologians began to take a closer look at their theories. William of Ockham, who
considered the pope a heretic for having condemned certain Franciscan views on poverty, maintained that God had vested divine authority in the people. They in turn could delegate this authority to a
general council, which in turn could judge a pope. If they found him
heretical, the emperor should depose him. The position of Marsiglio of
Padua was still more revolutionary. In his famous work entitled *De-
fensor Pacis* (*Defender of the Peace*) he subordinated the church to
the state, deprived it of all coercive authority over men, and gave it a
position not unlike that it holds in the modern state.

Two of the most respected writers to propose views on the subject
of the schism were John Gerson, chancellor of the university of Paris,
and Cardinal Zabarella. Gerson, who was a man of moderation, wished
to do as little violence to tradition as possible. He proposed that the
pope be viewed as a kind of limited monarch. Under ordinary circumstances, he should guide the church as in the past. When a crisis broke,
however, as was then the case, the general council should assert its
pre-eminent authority and decide the issue. Cardinal Zabarella, the
foremost canonist of the day, placed the ultimate authority of the
church in the *congregatio fidelium*, that is, the body of believers.
That body could not err, popes might; furthermore, just as that body
had invested the pope with his authority, so they could also withdraw
it, and they should do this through the machinery of the general council. Finally, failing action by the popes or cardinals to summon a council, the emperor should assume that responsibility. The cardinals had,
indeed, made such an attempt in 1409 when they convened at Pisa,
deposed the Roman and Avignonese popes, and elected Alexander V.
The consequence was, however, more confusion, for now there were
three instead of two popes.

In 1414 the Emperor Sigismund hearkened to men like Zabarella
and took the initiative. He prevailed upon the Pisan pope to summon
a council to meet at Constance, which was considered neutral territory, neither French nor Italian. As cardinals, bishops, abbots, and
theologians gathered from all over Europe, the Roman pope, Gregory
XII, took the decisive step that assured the success of the council. He
announced his willingness to resign his position provided the council

permitted him to issue a formal summons for its convention. Upon the council's acceptance of Gregory's proposal, he officially called it into session, then abdicated. The council then deposed the Avignonese and Pisan popes, elected a Colonna cardinal who took the name Martin V (1417), and the schism was at an end.

On the council's agenda at Constance was also the problem of heresy. Two men required attention, one John Wyclif, fortunately dead, the other John Hus, very much alive and with an active following behind him in Bohemia. John Wyclif (d. 1384) had been a noted theologian at Oxford whom John of Gaunt had employed on occasion at the court. (For John of Gaunt, see above, p. 358.) His association with Gaunt who was the most powerful man in England at the time, saved Wyclif from the efforts of the English hierarchy and the pope to prosecute him for heresy. His views were clearly heretical. He had first been a reformer when he attacked the wealth of the church, the political influence of bishops, and assorted abuses. Then he became a revolutionary, and in voluminous writings shifted his assault to such fundamental practices and doctrines as monastic vows, indulgences, the institution of the papacy, and transubstantiation. In these and other attacks he anticipated the position taken by the Reformers of the sixteenth century, even to their appeal to the Bible as the sole source of theological truth. Because of pressure from the hierarchy and pope, and because governmental circles had no real sympathy for Wyclif's views, the crown ordered him to halt his attacks on the church, shortly after which he retired from Oxford to his parish in Lutterworth where he died.

The council encountered no difficulties over Wyclif. They condemned his writings, ordered them destroyed, and directed that his bones be removed from consecrated ground. Hus posed a real problem. His views were substantially those of Wyclif; furthermore, because he was of peasant origin, he had been able to stir the hearts of the masses in Bohemia for whom he became a symbol of Bohemian nationalism against German influence which dominated their country. Like Luther a century later, Hus took his stand on the Bible. When the theologians at Constance could not shake his determination after several months of fruitless debate, the council condemned him as a heretic and he was burned at the stake. Unfortunately for the medieval church, his followers, the Hussites, refused to die with him. They carried his cause to the sixteenth century when it merged with the Protestant Reformation movement.

The men at Constance had no suspicion that the ideas of Wyclif and Luther would dominate the religious history of the sixteenth century. It was they, they were convinced, who were writing history with their successful attack on the thousand-year-old doctrine of papal supremacy. To make that victory permanent and to incorporate the principle of conciliar superiority into canon law, the council enacted two decrees. The first, entitled *Sacrosancta*, affirmed that the general council "has its power immediately from Christ, and every one, whatever his position or rank, even if it be the papal dignity itself, is bound to obey it in all things which pertain to the faith." The second decree, called *Frequens*, implemented the first decree by requiring the pope to call another general council within five years, then at regular intervals thereafter.

Although Pope Martin V gave only qualified endorsement to the decrees of the Council of Constance, he trimmed his sails to conciliarism to the extent of summoning a council in 1423 as required by *Frequens*. This council, which met at Pavia, accomplished little, nor was much in the offing at Basel where a council convened in 1431. Then representatives of the Calixtines, the more moderate Hussites, put in their appearance. They had their name from *calix*, the Latin word for chalice, which they insisted the priest share with them at communion. What brought them to Basel was an invitation from the council fathers, who hoped to win them back to the orthodox fold. This would split the Hussites, which would in turn enable the Emperor Sigismund to destroy the more radical Taborites. The demands this group of Hussites was making would have involved a revolution in both church and society. With them no discussion was possible, yet something must be done. Under the generalship of Ziska, then Prokop, the combined Calixtines and Taborites had defeated every army the emperor had sent against them.

The strategy of the conciliar leaders at Basel worked. The Calixtines accepted the so-called Compacts of Prague which conceded the right of communion in both kinds, then joined the imperial armies in breaking the back of Taborite power. As things turned out, the council gained this victory at the cost of its own conciliar supremacy. When Pope Eugenius IV learned of what was transpiring at Basel—namely, the concessions granted the Calixtines together with moves to abolish papal provisions and reservations—he removed the council to Ferrara, then Florence, ostensibly to accommodate the Byzantine emperor and his large delegation. They were coming west to discuss reunion with

Rome. The majority of the bishops at Basel, including many who were disturbed over the concessions to the Calixtines, moved to Ferrara as bidden. The confirmed conciliarist minority remained at Basel, deposed Pope Eugenius, and elected a pope of its own. This imprudent action lost it what support it still enjoyed, and in 1449 these conciliarists recognized their mistake, dissolved and went home. Pope Pius II formally anathematized conciliarism in 1460 with his bull *Execrabilis*.

Most developments in the history of the late medieval church proved dangerous, if not injurious, to that institution. One which revealed real spiritual maturity was the flowering of mysticism. The mystic seeks a closer union with the supernatural, the Christian mystic a more intimate communion with God. Men who aspire to attain the goal of the mystic maintain that an intense love of God and contemplation of the deity will bring that objective within the realm of the possible. Early Christian mystics included St. Augustine and St. Gregory the Great. The immediate factor which provided the inspiration for late medieval mysticism were the lives and example of St. Bernard and St. Francis. Both men dedicated their lives to the service of God; both men lived their whole lives, as it were, in the presence of God.

What is most remarkable about late medieval mysticism is the large number of clergy and laity caught up in the movement. Among the more prominent priests were four Dominican friars, Meister Eckhart (d. 1327) and his disciples John Ruysbroeck, John Tauler, and Henry Suso, who lived in the Rhineland. In their writings and sermons they preached the goodness of God, the joy of living in his presence, and the need to carry out Christ's command to love one's neighbor. In England Walter Hilton, who may have been a Carthusian, contributed *The Ladder of Perfection*, the most influential work of its kind to emanate from that country. There were also many laymen and women who aspired to lead more religious lives. A few, such as the strange Margery Kempe in England, did so as individuals. They held aloof from organized communities like the Beguines and Beghards, which cropped up here and there to harness this religious ferment. While the members of these communities ordinarily took no formal vows, they did practice chastity, poverty, and obedience. They also engaged in the care of the sick and needy, while the best known of such groups, the Brethren of the Common Life, also maintained schools. Luther and Erasmus attended such schools. Thomas à Kempis, who lived with the Brethren for some years before becoming an Augustinian canon, was the author of *The Imitation of Christ*, the most popular mystical writing of the period.

If the Gothic cathedral represents the apogee of the culture of the high Middle Ages, that of the fourteenth and fifteenth stands revealed in the literature of Dante, Petrarch, and Chaucer. Most unusual was the high literary productivity of that age. One might even argue that no period of comparable length in the history of literature produced such a galaxy of writers. Their presence alone should effectively annihilate the view, which still persists in certain circles, that the late centuries of the Middle Ages were decadent.

The first literary figure in point of time and, as it happens, the greatest of them all, was Dante (1265–1321). He was a member of the upper classes in Florence, wealthy and well educated, and might have lived a reasonably pleasant and uneventful life had he not entered politics. In 1302 he left Florence to go to Rome to plead with Boniface VIII to block the arrival of a French army which was momentarily expected. While he was on this mission, the French marched into Florence, and he and his fellow Whites, the faction of which he was a member, found themselves exiled with a price on their heads. Dante lived most of his mature life, accordingly, in exile and died in Ravenna.

Dante's minor works included two short Latin pieces. In the *De Vulgari Eloquentia* he appealed to his fellow scholars to stop despising Italian as the language of the illiterate. Given encouragement it could rise to the rank of a scholarly language, possessing a formal grammar and established syntax. Had Dante published this appeal in anything but Latin, scholars would have ignored it. As it was they waited until the sixteenth century to do what Dante had proposed. Dante's other minor work in Latin, *De Monarchia*, constituted a plea for the restoration of the Roman empire. History had demonstrated the need and value of such a universal empire, God wanted it, and the church should do nothing to prevent its rise. This was not an academic hope with Dante. Should the emperor Henry VII prove successful in his dream and re-establish imperial rule in Italy (see above, p. 360), Dante would be able to return to Florence.

Two minor works in Italian deserve comment. In the *Convivio* Dante planned to furnish his reader an intellectual "feast" of fourteen courses. Had he completed the work—he only finished three courses— this would probably have represented the most scholarly synthesis of the scientific, theological, and literary knowledge ever attempted of any one age. In his *Vita Nuova*, which was the first troubadour verse to appear in Italian, Dante sang the virtues of Beatrice. Although Dante had but a slight acquaintance with Beatrice, she seems to have made a lasting impression on him. He made her his guide through the mysteries of the *Paradiso*.

The *Paradiso* is the third part of his great poem the *Divine Comedy*. This is his *magnum opus*, some will say the greatest work in all of literature. With matchless rhythm and profoundly beautiful imagery it tells the story of sinful man's journey through hell where he acquires a hatred of sin, then through purgatory where he is cleansed of his vices, and finally to the highest point of heaven where he sees God. Dante's guide through hell is Vergil, the symbol of reason. As they climb down its precipitous sides, Vergil explains the reason why the damned souls they encounter on the way, the immoral, the hypocrites, the thieves, the heretics, and others, suffer the miseries they do. At the bottom they behold Lucifer, frozen to his waist in ice, where he stands gnawing in his three horrible mouths the world's leading traitors: Judas, who betrayed Christ, the church, and Brutus and Cassius who betrayed Julius Caesar, the founder of the empire.

As Dante and Vergil emerge from the dreadful regions of hell and start their climb of Mount Purgatory, the atmosphere brightens, they hear birds for the first time, they see people who smile. For purgatory is a region of hope, even though the souls there suffer as they slough off the mark of the seven deadly sins. These seven form the principal divisions of purgatory. Near the top, Vergil disappears since reason can no longer fathom the mysteries that beckon above. Beatrice, who is the symbol of divine faith and revelation, takes his place. She serves as Dante's guide through the spheres of the moon, planets, and stars to the beatific vision. On their way they meet the great saints and theologians of Christendom who discourse with them on the mysteries of the universe and the faith, while interjecting now and then bitter denunciations of the corruption which was soiling God's own church.

Petrarch (d. 1374) enjoyed even more fame than Dante among his contemporaries. This he could not understand, since it was his Italian poetry that they admired, not his Latin. "They may know why," he said, "I certainly do not." Let no one conclude that Petrarch was a humble man. He was most proud of his Latin verse which he felt more than matched Vergil's. (See below, p. 390.) His Italian poetry included 350 sonnets which he composed in honor of Laura, a married woman he had loved in his youth. As is evident from his verse, Petrarch was a restless soul. Although he wrote on sensuous themes, he revealed flashes of mysticism, and he counted himself with the reformers of the day. The musical, rhythmic qualities of his verse served European poets as a model for the next five hundred years.

The third renowned Italian literary figure of the late Middle Ages was Petrarch's friend Boccaccio (d. 1375). He lived his youth in the spirit of the amorous adventures that fill his *Decameron*, though religious scruples began to bother him as he grew older, and he turned toward mysticism. For a time he tried his hand at verse, then abandoned this for prose when he realized he could never approach Petrarch's genius. His masterpiece, the *Decameron*, represents the first great prose literature of the Middle Ages. Later students of style studied his prose in much the same way that budding poets analyzed Petrarch. Boccaccio drew the stories which make up his *Decameron* from a wide variety of sources, including medieval fabliaux, but he dressed them up in language with which they had never been adorned.

In François Villon (d. 1463?) France produced one of literature's greatest lyric poets. He was born in Paris, orphaned, then adopted by a priest who sent him to the university. There he earned a master's degree, then took to drinking, brawling, and, when his money gave out, to stealing. He may have been a murderer. What saved him from hanging was the visit of the young King Louis XI to Tournai, which happy occasion opened the gates of the city's jail to him and other criminals. No one knows what was his end, and charitable people hesitate to guess. The themes of his poems reflect the tumult of his life. He may pray to the Virgin in one poem and curse a debauched companion in the next. Both the beautiful and good in life drew his attention as well as the sordid and the pitiable. What gives his verse special attraction is his psychological insight into the motives that move men.

Another French writer of note was the chronicler Jean Froissart (d. 1410). His theme was the Hundred Years' War, more especially "the noble adventures and deeds of arms performed in the wars between England and France—to the end that brave men taking example from them may be encouraged in their well-doing." This suggests Froissart's principal bias, namely, a warm admiration for the chivalrous life of the knightly class. Though he did concern himself about cause and effect in his writing of events, his virtues are those of a narrative, rather analytical, historian. Almost the reverse is true of Philippe de Commines, Froissart's principal successor in the art of recording historical events. Commines was not unaware of his talent at analyzing men's motives nor the circumstances that influence the course of history.

He was not writing, he declared, to provide reading matter for simple folk; great men might well discover much of value in what he recorded. For he himself he had discovered that history held the "master key to all types of frauds, deceits, and perjuries." Commines' *Memoirs* cover the reign of Louis XI, for whose court he abandoned the household of Charles the Rash long before other men suspected what the outcome of that contest would be.

England, which had been suffering a literary blight since the arrival of the Normans, produced a pair of distinguished writers in the late fourteenth century. The first, William Langland (d. 1400?), was the author of a long allegorical poem entitled *The Vision of Piers Plowman*. Langland may have been a priest; he reveals considerable knowledge of the church and theology. He was a most perceptive man in other subjects as well. In his poem he considered almost every facet of English life and found little good. The church, the state, officials, even ordinary folk because of their lack of diligence, needed reforming. His penetrating insight, his sincerity, and the vigor of his literary style shine through the difficulty of his allegory.

The other English poet was Geoffrey Chaucer (d. 1400). Like Petrarch, he was one of the very few poets who basked in the warmth of men's praise while still living. They buried him in Westminster Abbey where his tomb gives its name to the "Poets' Corner." Chaucer's aim in his *Canterbury Tales* was that of Boccaccio's, to amuse and to entertain, although he employed a more subtle wit and greater dignity than the Italian in accomplishing this. The setting of his brilliant poem is the Tabard Inn at Southwark where a group of pilgrims had converged on their way to Canterbury. What interests the modern reader is less the tales each of these pilgrims tells to entertain the others—the prioress, monk, pardoner, friar, merchant, wife of Bath—but the charming descriptions with which the poet introduces these people. With such photographic accuracy does Chaucer paint his characters, that writers have been tempted to accept his poem as providing a true mirror of the times. This is dangerous. Chaucer was a poet, not a historian. As a poet he enjoyed sharpening the features of his characters in order to make them glisten the more. His knight and clerk, the latter worn and thin from study, were meant as ideals; Chaucer's monk and friar as the negation of the ideal.

Another group of men were busy writing, even composing verse here in the late Middle Ages. To some of their contemporaries, and in their own judgment, too, they were indeed stylists and scholars without peer. These were the humanists. As fate would have it, while the world has not forgotten them, it has forgotten their writings. As one modern critic has commented about Petrarch's pride and joy, the long epic *Africa*, of the twelve books he projected, we are lucky to have only nine! These humanists represent, nevertheless, a development of some significance in the literary and intellectual life of the late Middle Ages. To define the term humanist in terms of the Middle Ages, he was a student of classical literature. For practical purposes this meant Latin literature since few men had more than a working knowledge of Greek until the fifteenth century. Actually there were Latin humanists scattered throughout the Middle Ages, from Jerome through Hrabanus Maurus to John of Salisbury. What entitles the humanists of the late Middle Ages to special attention is their greater number, the presence of many laymen in their ranks, their excessive devotion to humanism, and their different approach. John of Salisbury was content with enjoying Cicero's language, although he may have found his observations on moral duties and old age of some interest. The humanists of the late Middle Ages also looked to Cicero for inspiration, for ideas that would enable them to acquire the presumed urbanity and cultural sophistication of those ancient Romans.

Had it not been for the rise of scholasticism which blighted the flowering of classical studies back in the eleventh century, it might be unnecessary to single out humanism here in the late Middle Ages for special attention. Its history would never have been interrupted. Humanists in that earlier period were also interested in style, in composing classical verse, in searching high and low for manuscripts. And when Petrarch and Poggio resumed this last task in the fourteenth century, they "found" most of their precious manuscripts in monastic libraries where they had been gathering dust during the centuries when scholasticism ruled supreme.

The success of humanists like Poggio in locating manuscripts led to the birth of such literary sciences as orthography, paleography, critical philology, and textual criticism. With the skills acquired through the study of linguistics, humanists were able to uncover a number of forged documents. The most spectacular discovery of that kind was Lorenzo Valla's success in proving the Donation of Constantine to be a forgery. The collection of manuscripts encouraged the growth of private holdings as well as laying the foundation for such famous institutions as the Vatican and Laurentian (Florence) libraries. Devotion to things ancient also led to the establishment of museums to house the physical relics of the past. An important landmark in the history of humanism was the year 1462 when Pope Pius II set aside the Colosseum and other ancient structures as national monuments.

Because scholasticism was already in decline and losing its hold on education, humanism was able to exert significant influence in liberalizing the new curriculum. Literature and history managed to establish a bridgehead by the late Middle Ages. Grammar, that is Latin grammar, had dominated the liberal arts in the early Middle Ages. Now it recovered its popularity. Its aim was no longer to supply the clergy the knowledge they would require to read the Bible and the prayers of the liturgy. The humanists hoped the study of Latin would open to them the treasures of ancient culture and endow them with the talent to write like Cicero. A necessary prerequisite was that of purging Latin of all words Cicero had not employed, a step which made Latin a dead language.

Many of the humanists put their love of classical Latin to use in composing letters, essays, poetry, even history after the manner of the ancient Romans. Petrarch and Boccaccio became so obsessed with the passion of the classics, that they abandoned their magnificent sonnets and prose to grind out long, dreary Latin productions. Mention has been made of the *Africa*, Petrarch's principal folly. Boccaccio's most ambitious venture into classicism, *On the Genealogy of the Gods,* was no more original or enduring. In terms of influence upon subsequent scholars, historical writings such as Leonardo Bruni's history of the Florentine people proved of considerable importance. What distinguished the historical works of these humanists from medieval chronicles was their secular tone, superior organization, and their denigration of all things medieval. In placing emphasis upon the same political and biographical factors in history as had Livy and other Roman historians, and ignoring the social and economic, humanistic historical writings may not have revealed any more of their age than the chronicles did of medieval centuries. Humanists showed no interest in science, nor did they welcome John Gutenberg's invention of the printing press in 1450 since this deprived their treasured manuscripts of much of their value.

The one deep regret of the humanists of the fourteenth century was their ignorance of Greek. All Petrarch could do with his precious manuscript of Homer was to identify the letters and translate a few words. A major event, therefore, in the history of humanism was the arrival in Florence in 1397 of the Greek scholar Manuel Chrysoloras from Constantinople. Important men of affairs dropped what they were doing to learn Greek from him during the six years he remained in

Italy. Some humanists went to Constantinople to learn Greek, while more Greek scholars came west, many to make permanent homes there when the fall of their city appeared imminent. In general it was not Greek science nor even philosophy with the exception of Plato's idealism that interested them, but rather history, biography, poetry, and drama. Under the patronage of the Medici, Florence became a center of Platonic studies. Its principal luminary, Marsilio Ficino (d. 1499), devoted his time to the study and teaching of Plato and the Neo-Platonists. Another member of the center at Florence, Pico della Mirandola, was one of a group of humanists whose interests were ethical, even religious. Pico studied scholasticism, for example, in addition to the religious writings of the Jews and Moslems. In his *Oration on the Dignity of Man* he set forth the humanist philosophy that man, being a free creature and master of his fate, may with the aid of his native talents rise to the level of the divine.

Surely the most impressive and permanent achievement of humanism came in the realm of art. Like literature, art had attained a high degree of maturity by the late Middle Ages. It had separated into its three major divisions of architecture, sculpture, and painting, and in each of these branches individuals were gaining reputations as distinguished architects, sculptors, and painters. A departure from the earlier Middle Ages was also represented in the extent to which towns, gilds, and wealthy laymen drew on the services of artists. Heretofore the modern student had little need to go beyond churches and illuminated manuscripts in his study of medieval art. In the late Middle Ages he finds it necessary to study gild halls, civic buildings, private palaces, together with portraits of individual men and women. In the layman's judgment the most striking development in late medieval art appears in the high degree of naturalism sculptors and painters were able to bring to their work.

Two significant developments come to view in late medieval architecture. One is the tendency of the Gothic architect to shift his attention from problems of structural refinement to the embellishment of the exterior of his structures. Where the classic Gothic church presented an identity of structural and ornamental forms, in late Gothic a rich overlay of lacelike stonework, tracery, and pinnacles tends to obscure the facts of construction. The two spires of the cathedral of Chartres furnish striking evidence of this shift of interest. The more ornate one on the left, which dates from the sixteenth century, replaced a simpler, more classic spire which had been destroyed by fire. The other development witnessed the emergence in Italy of a neoclassic architecture called Renaissance. Examples of the new art appear in private palaces in Florence, while the best-known structure to exemplify the new art at its height is St. Peter's in Rome. In their desire to revive the glories of ancient Roman architecture, these structures featured classical columns, pilasters, architraves, cornices, barrel vaults, coffered ceilings, rosettes, medallions, and similar art forms from the past.

The success of the late medieval sculptor to give naturalism to his subjects represents the culmination of the long efforts of his predecessors since the eleventh century to recapture the skills lost during the Dark Ages. Art historians can trace the development of those skills from early Romanesque where sculpture is part of the wall structure, through Gothic when the figures begin to move away from their architectural setting, to the late Middle Ages when they are completely freestanding. While the stone figure was thus moving out of and away from the masonry, it was acquiring over the centuries a higher degree of individuation and more lifelike features, until in the hands of a Donatello it became as much a living person as the subjects of the best Hellenistic and Roman sculptors. Most notable among the sculptors whose achievements grace the pages of the history of late medieval sculpture are those of Nicola Pisano, Claus Sluter, Ghiberti, Donatello, and Verrocchio.

A similar trend toward naturalism parallels the history of late medieval painting, most strikingly so from the time of Giotto (d. 1337), the "father of modern painting." A large number of artists, most of them from Italy, northern France, and Flanders, gained prominence in the closing centuries of the Middle Ages. Among these were Masaccio, Memling, Fra Lippi, Jan van Eyck, and Botticelli. Giotto and Masaccio employed the principles of foreshortening and the use of light and shadow to invest their subjects with the illusion of depth. Jan van Eyck and other painters of the fifteenth century used oil paints which set up more slowly to accomplish the same effect. For this reason they introduced on to their canvases a plethora of objects and detail, all set off in bright colors, which to the layman becomes the most striking feature of late medieval painting.

By 1500 when time ran out for the Middle Ages, Western Europe had attained in its universities, literature, art, learning, science, technology, expanding capitalism, and governmental institutions a level of cultural, political, and economic maturity no other part of the world, whether Islamic or Oriental, could match.

Bibliography

(The great majority of the following titles, which the student will find useful who wishes to pursue the subject, are paperbacks.)

Chapter 1

W. C. BARK, Origins of the Medieval World (Anchor)
J. B. BURY, History of the Later Roman Empire (2 vols., Dover)
J. CARCOPINO, Daily Life in Ancient Rome (Yale)
M. CARY & T. HAARHOFF, Life and Thought in the Ancient Greek and Roman World (Barnes & Noble)
The Fall of Rome: Can It Be Explained? ed. M. Chambers (Holt, Rinehart, Winston)
M. P. CHARLESWORTH, The Roman Empire (Oxford)
S. DILL, Roman Society: From Nero to Marcus Aurelius (Meridian)
———, Roman Society in the Last Century of the Western Empire (Meridian)
E. GIBBON, Decline and Fall of the Roman Empire (3 vols., Washington Square)
F. LOT, The End of the Ancient World (Torch)
H. MATTINGLY, Roman Imperial Civilization (Anchor)
Meditations of Marcus Aurelius (several editions)
H. S. MOSS, The Birth of the Middle Ages (Oxford)

Chapter 2

ST. AUGUSTINE, City of God and Confessions (Image)
H. DANIEL-ROPS, Church of the Apostles and Martyrs (2 vols., Image)
E. S. DUCKETT, The Gateway to the Middle Ages: Monasticism (Ann Arbor)
The Essential Eusebius (Mentor)
A. FREEMANTLE, Treasury of Early Christianity (Mentor)
E. J. GOODSPEED, A History of Early Christian Literature (Chicago)
H. M. JONES, Constantine and the Conversion of Europe (Collier)
H. MARROU, Saint Augustine and His Influence (Men of Wisdom)
J. MC CANN, Saint Benedict (Image)
The Fathers of the Primitive Church ed. H. A. Musurillo (Mentor)
New Testament (several editions)
H. POPE, Saint Augustine of Hippo (Image)
E. K. RAND, Founders of the Middle Ages (Dover)
H. WADDELL, Desert Fathers (Ann Arbor)
J. WEISS, Earliest Christianity (Torch)

Chapter 3

W. C. BARK, Origins of the Medieval World (Anchor)
J. B. BURY, History of the Later Roman Empire (2 vols., Dover)
C. H. DAWSON, The Making of Europe (Meridian)
M. DEANESLEY, A History of Early Medieval Europe, 476–911 (London, 1960)
S. DILL, Roman Society in the Last Century of the Western Empire (Meridian)
A. DOPSCH, The Economic and Social Foundations of European Civilization (New York, 1937)

C. D. GORDON, The Age of Attila (Ann Arbor)
A. F. HAVIGHURST, The Pirenne Thesis (Heath)
F. LOT, The End of the Ancient World (Torch)
H. S. MOSS, The Birth of the Middle Ages (Oxford)
TACITUS, On Britain and Germany (Penguin)
H. O. TAYLOR, The Emergence of Christian Culture in the West (Torch)

Chapter 4

N. H. BAYNES, The Byzantine Empire (London, 1946)
N. H. BAYNES & H. MOSS, eds., Byzantium: An Introduction to East Roman Civilization (Oxford)
J. B. BURY, History of the Later Roman Empire (2 vols., Dover)
F. DVORNIK, The Slavs: Their Early History and Civilization (Boston, 1956)
D. J. GEANAKOPLOS, Byzantine East & Latin West (Torch)
R. GUERDAN, Byzantium (Capricorn)
J. M. HUSSEY, The Byzantine World (Torch)
D. A. MILLER, The Byzantine Tradition (Harper & Row)
G. OSTROGORSKY, History of the Byzantine State (Oxford, 1956)
PROCOPIUS, The Secret History (several editions)
MICHAEL PSELLUS, Fourteen Byzantine Rulers (Penguin)
S. RUNCIMAN, Byzantine Civilization (Meridian)
A. A. VASILIEV, History of the Byzantine Empire (Wisconsin)

Chapter 5

T. ANDRAE, Mohammed: The Man and His Faith (Torch)
E. DERMENGHEM, Muhammad and the Islamic Tradition (Men of Wisdom)
H. A. GIBB, Mohammedanism: An Historical Survey (Galaxy)
G. E. VON GRUNEBAUM, Medieval Islam: A Study in Cultural Orientation (Phoenix)
A. GUILLAUME, Islam (Penguin)
P. K. HITTI, Arabs: A Short History (Gateway)
———, History of the Arabs (New York, 1956)
Koran (several editions)
B. LEWIS, The Arabs in History (Torch)
J. J. SAUNDERS, A History of Medieval Islam (New York, 1965)
Islamic Literature, ed. Najib Ullah (Washington Square)
W. MONTGOMERY WATT, Muhammad, Prophet and Statesman (Oxford, 1961)
W. MONTGOMERY WATT & PIERRE CACHIA, A History of Islamic Spain (Anchor)

Chapter 6

BEDE, A History of the English Church and People (Penguin)
J. BRONSTED, The Vikings (Penguin)
C. BROOKE, Europe in the Central Middle Ages, 962–1154 (New York, 1963)
Z. N. BROOKE, A History of Europe, 911–1198 (London, 1951)
M. DEANESLEY, A History of Early Medieval Europe, 476–911 (London, 1960)
EINHARD, Life of Charlemagne (Ann Arbor)
H. FICHTENAU, The Carolingian Empire (Torch)
GREGORY OF TOURS, History of the Franks (2 vols., tr. O. Dalton, Oxford, 1927)
M. L. LAISTNER, Thought and Letters in Western Europe, 500–900 (London, 1957)
H. PIRENNE, Mohammed and Charlemagne (Meridian)
E. K. RAND, Founders of the Middle Ages (Dover)
G. TELLENBACH, Church, State, and Christian Society at the Time of the Investiture Controversy (Oxford, 1940)
J. M. WALLACE-HADRILL, The Barbarian West, 400–1000 (Torch)
R. WINSTON, Charlemagne: From the Hammer to the Cross (Vintage)

Chapter 7

H. S. BENNETT, Life on the English Manor (Cambridge)
M. BLOCH, Feudal Society (2 vols., Phoenix)
P. BOISSONNADE, Life and Work in Medieval Europe (Harper)
G. G. COULTON, Medieval Village, Manor, Monastery (Torch)
J. EVANS, Life in Mediaeval France (Oxford, 1925)
F. L. GANSHOF, Feudalism (Torch)
U. T. HOLMES, Daily Living in the Twelfth Century (Wisconsin, 1952)
C. W. OMAN, The Art of War in the Middle Ages (Cornell)
S. PAINTER, French Chivalry (Cornell)
H. PIRENNE, Medieval Cities (Anchor)
——, Mohammed and Charlemagne (Meridian)
E. POWER, Medieval People (Barnes & Noble)
R. W. SOUTHERN, The Making of the Middle Ages (Yale)
D. M. STENTON, English Society in the Early Middle Ages (Penguin)
S. THRUPP, Merchant Class of Medieval London (Ann Arbor)

Chapter 8

G. BARRACLOUGH, The Origins of Modern Germany (Oxford, 1947)
R. FAWTIER, The Capetian Kings of France (St. Martin)
F. HEER, The Medieval World (Mentor)
E. KANTOROWICZ, Frederick II (London, 1931)
A. KELLY, Eleanor of Aquitaine and the Four Kings (Vintage)
S. PAINTER, The Rise of Feudal Monarchies (Cornell)
A. L. POOLE, From Domesday to Magna Carta, 1087–1216 (Oxford, 1955)
S. RUNCIMAN, A History of the Crusades (3 vols., Cambridge, 1951–54)
A History of the Crusades, ed. K. M. Setton (2 vols., Philadelphia, 1955–62)
F. M. STENTON, The First Century of English Feudalism (Oxford, 1961)
W. THOMPSON, Feudal Germany (Chicago, 1928)
The Great Charter, eds. S. Thorne et alii (Mentor)
H. TREECE, The Crusades (Mentor)
VILLEHARDOUIN and DE JOINVILLE: Memoirs of the Crusades (Everyman)

Chapter 9

HENRY ADAMS, Mont-Saint-Michel and Chartres (Anchor, Mentor)
E. AUERBACH, Introduction to Romance Languages and Literature (Capricorn)
M. W. BALDWIN, The Mediaeval Church (Cornell)
G. K. CHESTERTON, St. Francis of Assisi (Image)
F. C. COPLESTON, Aquinas (Penguin)
A. C. CROMBIE, Medieval and Early Modern Science (2 vols., Anchor)
H. DANIEL-ROPS, Cathedral and Crusade: Studies of the Medieval Church, 1050–1350 (Image)
C. H. HASKINS, Renaissance of the Twelfth Century (Meridian)
——, Rise of Universities (Cornell)
H. JANTZEN, High Gothic (Minerva)
W. P. KER, The Dark Ages (Mentor)
D. KNOWLES, The Religious Orders in England (2 vols., Cambridge, 1950–55)
——, The Evolution of Medieval Thought (Vintage)
H. C. LEA, The Inquisition of the Middle Ages (Citadel)
G. LEFF, Medieval Thought from St. Augustine to Ockham (Penguin)
H. RASHDALL, The Universities of Europe in the Middle Ages (3 vols., Oxford, 1936)
H. O. TAYLOR, The Mediaeval Mind (Cambridge, Mass., 1949)
W. ULLMANN, The Growth of Papal Government in the Middle Ages (London, 1955)
H. WADDELL, Medieval Latin Lyrics (Penguin)

Chapter 10

C. R. BEAZLEY, The Dawn of Modern Geography (3 vols., New York, 1949)

J. BEEVERS, Saint Joan of Arc (Image)

C. BUTLER, Western Mysticism (Harper)

E. P. CHEYNEY, The Dawn of a New Era: 1250–1453 (Torch)

E. K. CHAMBERS, English Literature at the Close of the Middle Ages (Oxford, 1945)

J. M. CLARK, The Great German Mystics: Eckhart, Tauler, and Suso (Oxford, 1949)

Mission to Asia, ed. C. Dawson (Harper)

J. FROISSART, The Chronicles of England, France, and Spain (Everyman)

M. P. GILMORE, The World of Humanism (Torch)

J. HUIZINGA, Waning of the Middle Ages (Anchor)

T. KEMPIS, Imitation of Christ (Image)

E. PERROY, The Hundred Years War (London, 1951)

MARCO POLO, Travels (several editions)

M. PRAWDIN, The Mongol Empire (Macmillan)

H. F. M. PRESCOTT, Friar Felix at Large (Yale)

J. C. L. DE SISMONDI, A History of the Italian Republics (Anchor)

J. A. SYMONDS, The Age of Despots (Capricorn)

B. TIERNEY, Foundations of the Conciliar Theory (Cambridge, 1955)

Index